HARCOURT BRACE & COMPANY
1919–
1994
· SEVENTY-FIVE YEARS ·

THE MAN WHO WASN'T MAIGRET

THE MAN WHO WASN'T
Maigret

A Portrait of Georges Simenon

PATRICK

MARNHAM

A Harvest Book
Harcourt Brace & Company
San Diego   New York   London

Requests for permission to make copies of any part of the work
should be mailed to: Permissions Department,
Harcourt Brace & Company,
6277 Sea Harbor Drive, Orlando, Florida 32887-6777.

First published in Great Britain in 1992 by Bloomsbury and first
published in the United States in 1993 by Farrar, Straus & Giroux.
This Harvest edition published by arrangement
with Farrar, Straus & Giroux.

Library of Congress Cataloging-in-Publication Data
Marnham, Patrick.
The man who wasn't Maigret: a portrait of Georges Simenon /
Patrick Marnham.
p.   cm.
Includes bibliographical references and index.
1. Simenon, Georges: 1903–89 — Biography.   2. Novelists.
Belgian — 20th century — Biography.   3. Maigret, Jules (Fictitious
character)   I. Title.
PQ2637.I53Z638   1992
843'.912 — dc20   92-16351

ISBN 0-15-600059-8

Printed in the United States of America

First Harvest edition 1994

A B C D E

CONTENTS

ILLUSTRATIONS

Photo acknowledgements
My thanks are due to the owners of the photographs produced. The
Centre d'Etudes Georges Simenon at the Université de Liège supplied
all the illustrations except Nos. 6, 19, 22, 23, 24, 26 and 28 (Marc
Simenon), No. 32 (Denyse Simenon), No. 11 (the author), No. 13
(Photo Planchar, Liège), No. 35 (*Look* magazine, New York), No. 36
(*Le Soir Illustré*, Brussels), and No. 43 (*Elle*, Paris).

AUTHOR'S NOTE

Novelists sometimes try to outwit biographers by arranging for their papers to be destroyed. Georges Simenon used a more subtle method. He endowed a foundation at the University of Liège, his native city, with an extensive collection of professional papers. At the same time he published an autobiography of 1048 pages and followed this with a 21-volume series of memoirs. He had previously published two autobiographical novels, a diary, and two earlier volumes of memoirs. This adds up to twenty-seven volumes, of which only four have been translated into English. In this collection of writings about the events of his life he contradicted himself merrily, and frequently warned readers about the unreliability of the earlier accounts. I believe the key to his life lies in the pattern formed by these contradictions. I have also been influenced by his comment that 'a man absorbs material until the age of about 18. What he has not taken in by then, he never will.'

One of the themes of the book is the tracing of links between the events of Simenon's real life and those in his fiction. If this account encourages readers to return to the work of the writer whom André Gide described as 'the greatest French novelist of our times', so much the better. Simenon's genius brought him high praise from his peers, and enormous sales, but despite this he remained a modest man. At the height of his fame he once said, 'The artist is above all else a sick person, in any case an unstable one – if the doctors are to be believed . . . Why see in that some form of superiority? I would do better to ask people's forgiveness.'

I acknowledge the help of Mme Christine Swings, the administrator of the Centre d'Etudes Georges Simenon at the University of Liège. Her practical advice and encouragement have been an inspiration. I also acknowledge with gratitude the help and hospitality of the members of Georges Simenon's family circle, Mme Denyse Simenon, Marc Simenon and his wife Mylène Demongeot, John Simenon, Mme Henriette Liberge and Mme Teresa Sburelin. Bernard de Fallois, formerly president of the Presses de la Cité, who was for many years Simenon's closest friend, gave me invaluable guidance and information. Mme Joyce Pache-Aitken, administrator of the Simenon estate in Lausanne, his literary executrix and for over thirty years his secretary, answered many questions and supplied me with documents unobtainable elsewhere.

I also acknowledge the help of (among many others) Professor Paul Delbouille, President of the Centre d'Etudes Georges Simenon, Jean-Christophe Camus, Willy Rutten, Pierre Zink and Paul Giesberg in Liège; Bernard Alavoine in Amiens; Jean-Pierre Sanguy, Directeur de la Police Judiciaire, Patrick Riou, Chef de la Brigade Criminelle, Mme Françoise Verdier of the Préfecture de Police, Commissaire Thierry Boulouque of 36 Quai des Orfèvres, the Librarian of the BILIPO, Pierre Assouline, Claude Gauteur, Robert Doisneau and Robin Smythe in Paris; the Curator of the Museum at the Ecole Nationale Supérieure de la Police in Saint-Cyr au Mont d'Or; Paul Mercier in Besançon; Paul Martinon in Nice; Julian Symons, Eric Norris and the late Caroline Hobhouse in London.

I would like to thank the Estate of Georges Simenon for permission to quote from the following published works in copyright: *Je me souviens, Un homme comme un autre, Vent du nord, vent du sud, De la cave au grenier, Je suis resté un enfant de choeur, On dit que j'ai 75 ans, Quand vient le froid, La femme endormie, Jour et nuit* and *Destinées*. I am also grateful to the Estate of Georges Simenon and to Hamish Hamilton Ltd for permission to quote from *The Night Club, Monsieur Monde Vanishes, The Fate of the Malous, The Son, Pedigree, Letter to my Mother* and *Intimate Memoirs*, all of which are published works in copyright which have been translated into English. I have used my own translations throughout this book except in the case of *The Fate of the Malous* where I have used the translation by Denis George published by Hamish Hamilton Ltd.

Finally my wife, Chantal, helped me enormously, in the first place by her criticism and encouragement and subsequently by the many hours of research spent in the French Bibliothèque Nationale and the Bibliothèque des Littératures Policières in the rue Mouffetard, Paris 6ème, as well as by tracking down many editions of out of print books.

I assume responsibility for any errors that remain.

Paris, February 1992

CHRONOLOGY

1903
12 February   Birth of Georges Simenon at 26 rue Léopold, Liège

1904
April   Family settle on island of Outremeuse in centre of
                     city, 1 rue Pasteur

1906
21 September   Birth of younger brother, Christian; Georges starts
                     infant school in parish of St Nicolas

1908
September   Georges moves up to Christian Brothers' primary
                     school, Institut St André

1911
February   Family move to 53 rue de la Loi

1914
August   Outbreak of war; German army occupies Liège
October   Georges enters the Jesuit College of St Louis

1915
July   Summer holiday in Embourg; Georges meets 'Renée'
September   Renounces vocation to priesthood. Moves to the
                     College of St Servais

1918
July   Father, Désiré Simenon, suffers heart attack; Georges
                     leaves school
November   German army surrenders; liberation of Liège

1919

January	Georges joins *Gazette de Liège* as a reporter
June	Joins group of artists and anarchists, 'La Caque'

1920

31 December	Meets art student, Régine Renchon

1921

February	Publication of first novel, *Au Pont des Arches*
Spring	Becomes engaged to Régine, now known as 'Tigy'
28 November	Death of Désiré Simenon

1922

March	Suicide of his friend, Kleine
10 December	Takes night train to Paris

1923

24 March	Returns to Liège for two days to marry Tigy
September	Colette finally accepts one of his short stories for *Le Matin*. He uses the name 'Georges Sim'

1924

March	Leaves employ of Marquis de Tracy to live by his writing
Summer	Finishes first novel written in Paris, *Le roman d'une dactylo*

1925

Summer	Holiday near port of Etretat, Normandy; Henriette Liberge, the 18-year-old daughter of a local fisherman, becomes Tigy's maid; Sim rechristens her 'Boule'

1926

April	Tigy sells her first pictures; they spend summer on Mediterranean island of Porquerolles

1927

January	Sim signs contract with entrepreneur Eugène Merle to write a novel while locked inside a glass cage
Summer	Retreats to Ile d'Aix to break off attachment to Josephine Baker

1928

March   Sets off with Tigy and Boule on tour of France by river and canal

October   Contributes stories to new magazine, *Détective*

1929

March   Sets off on one-year trip around waterways of northern Europe

September   At Delfzijl, Holland, he concentrates on development of new fictional character, Commissaire Maigret

1930

Spring   Voyage to Lapland with Tigy

April   Returns to Paris. Signs contract with Fayard for a series of Maigret books, the first to be published under Simenon's own name

1931

February   Throws '*bal anthropométrique*' to launch the first two 'Maigrets'

1932

April   Becomes tenant of small country estate, La Richardière, near La Rochelle

June   Sets off on tour of tropical Africa

1933

January   Writes first 'dark' or 'psychological' novel, *La maison du canal*

June   Writes ninth and 'last' 'Maigret'. Sets off on tour of Eastern Europe. Interviews Trotsky

October   Signs contract with Gallimard to write six novels a year

1934

January   Investigates the 'Stavisky' scandal

April   Forced to leave La Richardière; spends summer cruising the Mediterranean

September   Moves to hunting lodge in forest of Orléans, La Cour-Dieu

1935

January	Sets off on world tour to Tahiti and back
October	Takes luxurious apartment in Neuilly
August	Retires to Porquerolles to write major work, *Le testament Donadieu*

1937

December	Announces he will win Nobel Prize 'in ten years'

1938

June	Buys house at Nieul-sur-Mer, near La Rochelle
July	Tigy becomes pregnant
August	Munich crisis. Simenon called up in general mobilisation of Belgian army

1939

19 April	Birth of son, Marc Simenon
3 September	France and Great Britain declare war. Belgium remains neutral

1940

10 May	Germany invades Holland and Belgium
11 May	On his way to join his unit, Simenon is turned back at Paris and appointed commissioner for Belgian refugees at La Rochelle
22 June	French army surrenders; Simenon, Tigy, Marc and Boule caught in German occupied zone
August	Moves house away from the coast to Forest of Vouvant
September	Moves house again to Fontenay-le-Comte; misdiagnosed as case of incurable heart disease, believes he has only a short time to live
9 December	Starts to write a family memoir for Marc called *Je me souviens*

1941

June	Encouraged by André Gide to start work on autobiographical novel, *Pedigree*

1942

June	Accused by Vichy authorities of being Jewish and threatened with deportation to concentration camp

July	Moves house again to remote hamlet of St Mesmin-le-Vieux
November	Attempts to cross illegally into Vichy Zone; thwarted by German occupation of whole of France

1943

January	Finishes *Pedigree*; auctions manuscripts for war charities

1944

Summer	After fifteen years Tigy discovers liaison between her husband and Boule
July	Simenon flees Resistance purge

1945

May	Released from house arrest; returns to Paris
August	Simenon, Tigy and Marc leave France, without Boule
September	Family settles at St Luc Masson, Canada
November	Simenon hires French-Canadian Denyse (rechristened Denise) Ouimet as resident secretary. She becomes his mistress

1946

January	Writes *Trois chambres à Manhattan*
September	Sets off for tour of United States with Denise
November	Settles in Bradenton Beach, Florida. Writes *Lettre à mon juge*

1947

January	To Havana, Cuba, with Denise
June	Settles in Snob Hollow, Tucson, Arizona, with Denise, Tigy and Marc

1948

March	Writes a masterpiece, *La neige était sale*
June	Moves to Stud Barn, Tumacacori, Arizona; the arrival of Boule turns his *ménage à trois* into a *ménage à quatre*

1949

January	Denise announces that she is pregnant and Simenon tells Tigy that they must divorce; Tigy, Boule and Marc move to California

| 29 September | Birth of John Simenon |
| October | Simenon, Denise and John move to Carmel, California, to be near Marc |

1950

| June | At Reno, Nevada, Simenon divorces Tigy and marries Denise on successive days and in the same courthouse |
| September | Simenon and Denise settle at Shadow Rock Farm, Lakeville, Connecticut |

1951 World sales reach 3 million a year

1952

| March | Huge crowds welcome Simenon's train at the Gare St Lazare on his triumphant visit to Paris; elected member of Belgian Académie Royale |

1953

| 23 February | Birth of the writer's only daughter, Marie-Jo Simenon |

1954 Simenon starts to take out US citizenship

1955

March	Acting on impulse Simenon packs up and leaves for Europe
April	Settles at La Gatounière, Cannes
June	Denise suffers miscarriage
October	Family move to luxurious villa, Golden Gates, Cannes

1957

| July | Takes up permanent residence in Swiss canton of Vaud; takes lease of Château d'Echandens, a castle outside Lausanne |

1959

| 26 May | Birth of son, Pierre Simenon |

1960

| May | President of jury at Cannes Film Festival |

1961

| December | Denise hires a new maid, Teresa Sburelin, a native of Venice; shortly afterwards she becomes Simenon's mistress |

1962

March	Simenon becomes a grandfather
June	Denise agrees to enter a psychiatric clinic at Nyon for treatment
October	Writes *Les anneaux de Bicêtre*

1963

| December | Simenon and Denise move to vast new house built to their design at Epalinges on opposite side of Lausanne |

1964

| April | Denise leaves Epalinges for ever; returns to psychiatric clinic |
| November | Boule leaves Epalinges |

1966

May	Marie-Jo, aged 13, undergoes first psychiatric treatment
September	Simenon returns to Delfzijl for major celebrations of the creation of Commissaire Maigret attended by his publishers from all over the world
December	Falls and breaks several ribs; Teresa becomes his nurse and official companion

1967

| February | Publication of *Le chat*, a pitiless description of his mother's second marriage |

1970

July	Marie-Jo suffers nervous breakdown
October	Simenon writes *La disparition d'Odile*, about a young girl who suffers nervous breakdown and attempts suicide
8 December	Death of Henriette Simenon

1971

| October | Simenon finishes what is to be his last *roman dur*, *Les innocents* |

1972

February	Finishes the last 'Maigret', *Maigret et M. Charles*
September	Puts Epalinges on the market
October	Moves with Teresa to eighth-floor apartment in avenue de Cour, Lausanne

1973

7 February
Announces retirement as a writer; six days later buys tape-recorder and starts to dictate twenty-one volumes of memoirs

1974

February
Moves with Teresa and Pierre, now aged 14, to small house in the avenue des Figuiers

April
Dictates *Lettre à ma mère*, a description of his relationship with his mother

1977

February
During interview with Fellini, intended to publicise latter's new film *Casanova*, makes world headlines by announcing that he has enjoyed sexual relations with 10,000 women

November
The Fonds Simenon opens at Liège University

1978

April
Denise (now 'Denyse') Simenon publishes *Un oiseau pour le chat*, an uninhibited account of her marriage

20 May
Marie-Jo commits suicide in her Paris apartment

1980

November
Finishes *Mémoires intimes*, an autobiography addressed to Marie-Jo

1981

September
Denyse publishes *Le phallus d'or*, a *roman à clef* based on her marriage to Simenon

October
Simenon publishes *Mémoires intimes*, in which he blames Denyse for the suicide of their daughter

November
Denyse wins a court order suppressing several passages in *Mémoires intimes*

1985

18 June
Death of Tigy, aged 84, in her son Marc's house in Porquerolles

1989

4 September
Death of Georges Simenon, aged 86, at his house in Lausanne; his children hear the news of his death on the radio, after the cremation

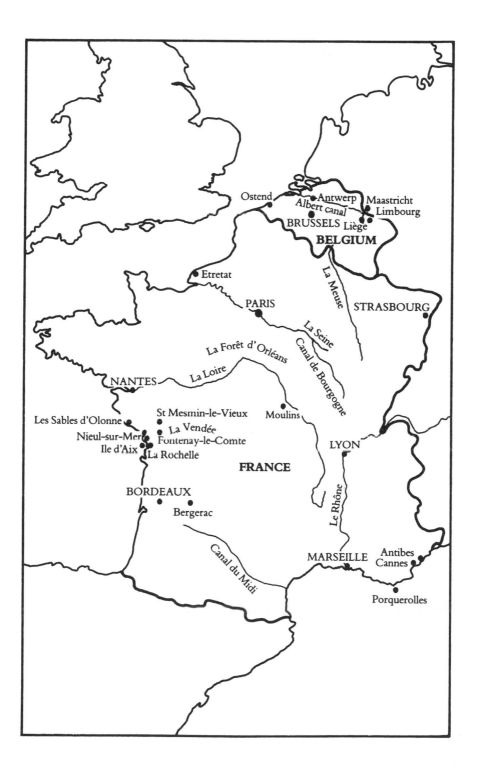

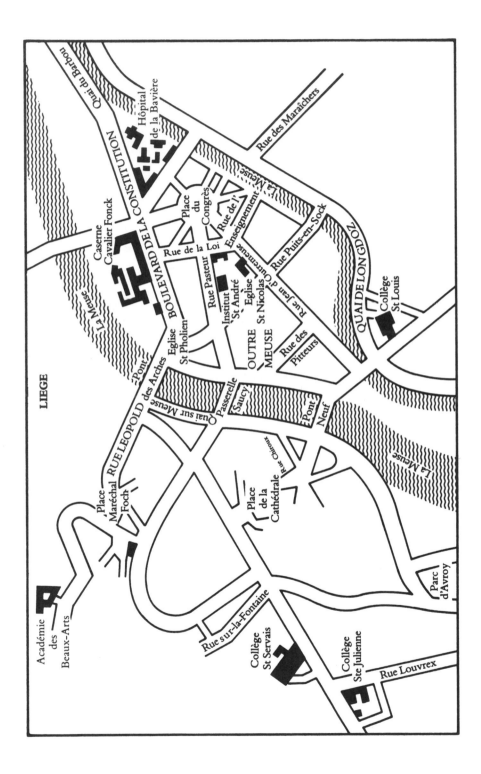

LIEGE

Quai du Barbou

Hôpital de la Bavière

Rue des Maraîchers

LA MEUSE

QUAI DE LON GDOZ

Caserne Cavalier Fonck

La Meuse

BOULEVARD DE LA CONSTITUTION

Place du Congrès

Rue de l'Enseignement

Rue de la Loi

Rue de l'

Rue Pasteur

Institut St André

Eglise St Nicolas

Rue Puits-en-Sock

Collège St Louis

Rue Jean d'Outremeuse

Eglise St Pholien

OUTRE MEUSE

Rue des Pitteurs

Pont

RUE LEOPOLD des Arches

Quai sur Meuse

Passerelle

Saucy

Pont Neuf

La Meuse

Place Maréchal Foch

Place de la Cathédrale

Rue Chiroux

Académie des Beaux-Arts

Rue sur-la-Fontaine

Collège St Servais

Collège Ste Julienne

Parc d'Avroy

Rue Louvrex

PRELUDE

Lausanne 1989:
Death of a man with no profession

I don't want to travel any more, I'm happy at Lausanne. In Switzerland I have discovered a country where people have respect for human beings. I have never had anyone ringing my doorbell without an invitation. Nobody has ever asked me about my political, religious or philosophical ideas.

Simenon, interview (1973)

On the morning of 6 September 1989, a woman in late middle-age stepped into the garden of her house in Lausanne and walked towards a tall cedar tree which dominated the house and was said to be the oldest tree in the town. She was carrying a small stone pot which contained the ashes of Georges Simenon, the man with whom she had lived for the previous twenty-five years and who had died two days earlier. Having scattered the ashes under the cedar tree she returned to the house and authorised the announcement of Simenon's death. The news made headlines across the world and drew a tribute from the President of France, but by the time the reporters reached the door of the little house in the avenue des Figuiers there was nothing to see. The cremation had taken place without any form of ceremony. Teresa, Simenon's companion, had asked not to be disturbed. Of Simenon there was nothing left at all. It was a press conference called by a ghost, which was just as he had wanted it to be. Simenon had a lifelong mastery of publicity as he had a lifelong horror of the ceremonies surrounding death.

The following day's papers devoted hundreds of column inches to the life and work of Georges Simenon. In Moscow TASS issued a special release. In Brussels *Le Soir* made the story the front-page lead and carried three full pages inside. In Paris *Le Monde* also carried the news on the front page and in the course of the week devoted nine further articles to the novelist. The popular paper *France-Soir*, in letters 3.5 centimetres high, announced '*Le père de Maigret est mort*', and the Simenon display cases in the Paris chain store FNAC emptied within hours. The French-language tributes to Simenon told a fabulous story.

He had written 193 novels under his own name and over 200 under eighteen pseudonyms. His world sales were said to be over 500 million copies in fifty-five languages, exceeded among writers of fiction only by Jules Verne and William Shakespeare, which made him the world's best-selling novelist. At the same time his work had been compared to that of Balzac, Dostoevsky and Dickens and had been praised by Céline, Max Jacob, Robert Brasillach, Colette, Anouilh, Cocteau, Pagnol, Mauriac, T.S. Eliot, Henry Miller, Thornton Wilder, Somerset Maugham, John Cowper Powys, George Steiner, John le Carré, Charlie Chaplin, Fellini, Jean Renoir and Sacha Guitry, among others. André Gide had described him as 'the greatest of all, the most genuine novelist we have had in literature'. Simenon's press cuttings went back over sixty years and filled two large cupboards at his publisher's office in Paris. The story of his life was a publicist's dream. Coming from a poor family in Liège, Belgium, he had made himself a multi-millionaire. He had taken less than two weeks to write most of his books and in the forty-four years up to 1972, when he retired from writing fiction, he had produced an average of between four and five titles each year. He had moved house thirty-three times. Fifty-five cinema films had been based on his books and 279 television films. A doctor had advised him to restrict himself to two bottles of red Bordeaux a day while writing, the wine being neither too young nor too old. He had employed a vocabulary of 2000 words, while admitting that he knew more for his personal use. At the height of his fame he had built a house of thirty rooms overlooking Lake Geneva where he had employed eleven servants and kept a garage of five cars. He had been married twice and had twice conducted lengthy affairs with his wives' maids. He had been a devoted father of four children and had once sent his son 133 letters during a separation of three weeks. And, as almost everyone knows, he once claimed to have made love to 10,000 women.

But although the obituaries of Simenon were full of detail and well researched they were also highly inaccurate. They were bound to be inaccurate, because their authors had relied on the numerous accounts which the writer himself had given of his life. Simenon wrote two autobiographical novels and four autobiographies, and after his retirement as a novelist dictated twenty-one volumes of memoirs. But his autobiographical writings formed a complex web of fact and fantasy which he ended by partly believing himself. He once said that he found it difficult to tell the story of his early years 'because we make up the memories of our childhood for the rest of our life, and we change them as we go along'. Certainly in his own case this was true.

In his numerous accounts of his upbringing and family background Simenon frequently claimed to be descended from a Breton soldier who had settled in Belgium on returning from Napoleon's campaign in Russia and had married the daughter of a Walloon farmer. The Simenons, he said, were settled people and reasonably prosperous, small traders and craftsmen. 'Everything that moved was to a Simenon suspect.' His mother's family, the Brülls, were on the other hand constantly on the move. They had known ruin and despair. They were Flemish and therefore, to the Walloon Simenons, they were 'foreigners'. Henriette, his mother, had lost her father at the age of 5 and had been sent out to do the family shopping in the streets of Liège even though she could not speak French. She never learnt the language properly and to the end of her life the mistakes she made would cause people to smile. The early years of Henriette's marriage to Désiré Simenon were dominated by fear of her Walloon mother-in-law, Marie Catherine Simenon, a woman 'who entered the room like an icy draught', who never kissed Georges and who never smiled because she was in permanent mourning for a child of her own who had died young. Both Désiré and Henriette came from families of thirteen children. When the Simenon clan were seated for Sunday lunch there were twenty-five around the table. Georges's maternal great-grandfather, 'Vieux-Papa', lived to be over 90.

During Georges's childhood his mother took in Russian students as lodgers and they taught him to read Gogol and Dostoevsky. When he was 15 his father became seriously ill and Georges was instructed by the family doctor to leave school immediately in order to support his family. He never benefited from family influence or connections. He became a newspaper reporter purely by chance after wandering into a newspaper office one day, driven mainly by curiosity. Later he arrived in Paris, penniless and without a friend, and was forced to tramp the streets looking for lodgings, to live off croissants and Camembert cheese, and to take work as an office-boy. He never studied scientific police methods. He invented the character of Maigret one grey morning on the quayside of a Dutch canal after drinking one or three gin and bitters and gradually perceiving 'the powerful and impassive bulk' of a feasible *commissaire de police* looming through the mist. During the Second World War, while living in occupied France, a radiologist made a serious misdiagnosis and convinced Simenon that within two years he would be dead of heart disease. These were among the legendary milestones in Simenon's life which were reproduced in his obituaries but which were largely fictional. There was usually a basis in fact, but the facts were embroidered.

Simenon's life spanned the most destructive national conflicts that Europe has so far experienced, but as a Belgian citizen of partly Dutch and German descent he himself was inoculated against all national sentiment. He loved Liège and '*le plat pays*' beyond it, but as for Belgium he once said that his country was 'always occupied'. Yet Simenon, a man with no country, invented a country of his own which became familiar to over 500 million readers. They recognised his land as part of their world and his vision as a truthful and sometimes dreadful version of life in their century. Simenon's country town, Simenon's hotel rooms, could be frightening places where ordinary people were overpowered by superficially banal events, where every refuge proved illusory, where love was misdirected and turned to hate, where elderly couples attempted to poison each other, where family ties were founded on the inheritance of property, where one brother would deliver another up to his killers; where passion was divorced from affection, and where affection was often fatal.

Georges Simenon, after a certain age, also started to conceal his tracks in other ways. A convivial man, known for his wealth, his large house, his obsessive interest in '*l'homme nu*' and his pressing need for the company of women, he actually started to become a recluse twenty-three years before his death, and spent his last sixteen years living in a cottage with one companion, giving very few interviews and seeing very few of his friends. He had made his fortune from his gift for evoking the colours and smells and urgency of life in bars and markets and streets in France, Flanders and North America, and yet, when he could have lived anywhere in the world, he chose the clinical surroundings of a country where 'no one ever rang his doorbell without an invitation'. All his life he had surrounded himself with books and pictures and been proud of his craftsmanship as a writer. Yet at the end he moved his library into an apartment on the opposite side of town which he never visited, stored his pictures in a bank and said that he, was 'almost ashamed' of all the books he had written and no longer wished to see them. He went to the Belgian consulate and changed the description in his passport from 'Novelist' to 'No profession'. The rooms he lived in were bare, lit by strip-lighting like a cheap hotel. There were no pictures on the walls, few ornaments on the shelves, no bookcases, no carpets on the floor. The furniture he chose was made from metal and plastic – he was convinced that wooden furniture harboured insects – and he rarely went into the garden unless it was to please a press photographer. His previous home had enjoyed a magnificent view of Lake Geneva, and this too he gave up without regrets. The new house was 500 metres from Lake Geneva but had no view at all. Simenon had been born into a large family and had always wanted a large family of his own, but when his children came to visit him in his final years they generally stayed in a hotel and he told them that they would learn of his death from the radio. He had acquired the habits of a man pursued.

Georges Simenon's life was a series of flights and exiles. He left his native city at the age of 19 and when he left he promised himself that nothing in his future would resemble the world he had been surrounded by as a child. He kept that promise. But in almost everything he wrote the shadow of that childhood can be seen.

PART I

THE SCENE OF THE CRIME

I was born in the dark and in the rain, and I got away. The crimes I write about are the crimes I would have committed if I had not got away. I am one of the lucky ones. What is there to say about the lucky ones except that they got away?
Simenon interviewed in *The New Yorker* (1953)

ONE

Liège 1903:
Preliminaries to the death of a man
with no profession

*My father took life as a perfectly straight line . . . my mother
came from a tormented race.*

Simenon, *Je me souviens* (1945)

In 1903 in the rue Léopold in Liège a man was standing in the rain
on a February night looking up at the second-floor window of
one of the terraced houses on the opposite side of the street. The
man stood there for five hours. Despite the fact that it was
raining, and the fashion of the period, and although he was the
son of a hatter and was standing opposite a hat shop, the man in
the rain was not wearing a hat. He had left his rooms in such a
hurry that he had forgotten to take his hat with him. Anyone
looking down at him from the window opposite would have seen
his unusually high brow running with water and gleaming in the
gaslight which was shining from the nearby street-lamp. The man
had no companions. When he began his vigil the last shoppers and
office-workers were making their way home along the rue
Léopold towards the district of Outremeuse. Later there was only
the occasional tram clanking along the street towards the Pont des
Arches, from where the tramlines led out to the city's eastern
suburbs. Once a policeman spoke to him. That afternoon there
had been a bomb attack on the Grand Bazaar, one of the city's

main department stores, which stood on the corner at the end of the street. In 1903 Liège was full of foreign students and anarchists and Marxist groups, preparing for the Revolution. The policeman was satisfied with his answers and left him alone again with the closed steel shutters and empty pavements. The man was called Désiré Simenon and he worked as an accountant in an insurance office. The window he was watching was in the front room of his own two-room apartment. Twice he crossed the road and climbed the stairs leading up past the hat shop to his own front door. On each occasion he returned without entering, discouraged by the noises coming from within. At last, around midnight, a lamp moved in the window, the signal for which he had been waiting. When Désiré reached his rooms he burst into tears. His wife had given birth to a son. The names they had already chosen for this contingency were Georges Joseph Christian.

The birth of Georges Simenon took place on Thursday, 12 February at 11.30 p.m. Or it took place on Friday, 13 February at ten minutes past midnight. The birth certificate gives the first date but family tradition insists that when Henriette Simenon, herself the youngest of thirteen children, heard that her son had been born on Friday the 13th, by ten minutes, she burst into tears, swore the midwife to secrecy and instructed her husband – who was to go to the town hall to make the declaration of birth at 2 o'clock that afternoon – to fill in a false date on the certificate. It is not therefore possible to start a biography of George Simenon in the time-honoured way, 'He was born on . . .', even if one wanted to. Shortly after making his false, or accurate, declaration at the town hall, Désiré Simenon brought his mother to see her grandson.* 'My God, Henriette,' said Grandmother Simenon, 'what an ugly baby.' This was a remark Henriette was unlikely to forget. For good measure her mother-in-law added, 'He's green.' It was true. The little fellow had been born with bronchitis. He was baptised within two days of his birth and the doctor eventually put him on a diet of *'laits de poule'*: raw eggs and sugar whipped up in milk and taken from a glass. The child quickly

---

* Simenon later claimed that it was his father who had told him he was actually born on Friday the 13th. Some have doubted the truth of the story since Désiré Simenon does not seem to have been the kind of man who would have falsified a birth certificate on a whim of his wife's.

developed an allergy to milk so the prescription was changed to *'laits de poule à la bière'*, raw eggs and sugar whipped up in beer, and he drank a glass of this for 'elevenses' throughout his childhood.

Liège in 1903 was like London, a city which counted for more than it does today. By its main river, the Meuse, and the Albert Canal it was linked to Antwerp and the sea. The kingdom of Belgium possessed the largest colony in Africa, the Congo, a region so vast that its area had never been calculated and its borders never defined. Many Liégeois were old colonials. Simenon grew up in a street where one of the neighbours was dying from sleeping-sickness; on sunny days this man was put out on the pavement in his chair, to doze his life away in public. Liège did a significant trade with Africa and was an important manufacturing centre in its own right, notably for small arms in which its armouries led the world. To the south-east of the city lay the coalfields of the Ardennes. To the south-west blast furnaces lined the railway tracks providing a night-time vision of hell. In *Stamboul Train* Graham Greene described 'the great blast furnaces of Liège' rising along the railway line 'like ancient castles burning in a border raid'. Liège was a place that counted not only in Belgium but in Europe and therefore throughout the world. Fifty years later passing through Birmingham, Simenon was to say that the second city in the United Kingdom reminded him of the Liège of his youth.

In the city the streets were full of farm animals and novel, frequently dangerous, machinery, such as trams or steam lorries. Liège had its private language, a patois formed from a mixture of Flemish, German and French. The sound of this dialect being shouted by the tradespeople hawking goods in the street outside the house was one of the earliest of Georges Simenon's memories. Mussels, shrimps, cherries, nuts and sweets were sold in the streets in this way, each from a different barrow or tray, each specialist having a different cry. There was a mustard and vinegar seller who balanced two covered wooden tubs from a yoke which he carried over his shoulders, crying *'Mostade! Vinegue!'* He turned a tap at the bottom of the tub to fill up the glasses which his customers supplied. And there was the goat's-milk seller who drove his flock beneath the chestnut trees down the wide boulevard de la Constitution and milked the goats directly into the jugs provided. Years later Simenon could remember the note of the little trumpet blown by the vegetable merchant and the cry of the potato seller, '*Crompires à cinq cens li kilos . . .*' The potato seller came with an ox-drawn cart rather than a hand-barrow. One of Georges's Flemish cousins sometimes journeyed in from his farm in the Limbourg, his horse and cart loaded with barrels of home-made *eau de vie.*

Then there was the newspaper seller whose cart was drawn by a dog and who on the evening of Simenon's birth had been shouting about the discovery of an underground passage between the royal palace in Brussels and the house of the King's mistress, the Baroness Vaughan. And there was the mousetrap seller, and the seller of cooked peas and garlic, and the man who sold only shoelaces, and the pedlar of sacred and profane plaster statues, who was Italian, and the miracle cleaning-powder merchant who sold an abrasive product from Paris, which worked. Even the cobblers came to the door and in place of shoeshine boys there were '*décrotteurs-brosseurs*' who merely cleaned the mud off your boots without shining them. That the streets were muddy is confirmed by the fact that until 1909 Mathieu Schroyen was successfully hawking his ingenious suspenders made from elastic and metal hooks, which enabled women to keep their long skirts dry in the wet streets. He advertised his wares by dangling the suspenders from the brim of his hat. He was known by his cry of '*Facile aheye*' – 'Easy to attach'. We know that Georges's mother, Henriette, was one of his customers from a passage in the auto-biographical novel *Pedigree*, where 'Elise' (Henriette) has to hitch up her skirts when using a narrow passage as a short cut.

The rag-and-bone merchants who called – frequently women – were highly specialised, collecting only broken scews or only broken glass. But perhaps the most specialised trader of all was the collector of urine. He had a barrel on his cart into which he emptied jugs of urine, purchased by prior arrangement, which had been allowed to stand for a few days. He sold it on to dyers, and the barrel was regularly scraped for phosphorus, which was sold to match makers. We can take it that no one in the Simenon family dealt with him. Had they done so Simenon would have been unable to resist the temptation to refer to it sooner or later.

Georges and his mother made daily excursions on foot to the markets of Outremeuse or over one of the bridges to the centre of the city. It was on these outings that the little boy would have seen a man running at full tilt with a small wicker basket clenched between his teeth. Inside the basket was a racing pigeon. The man held the basket between his teeth to enable him to run as fast as he could while minimising the movement experienced by the valuable bird within. The point was to carry the pigeon as rapidly as possible from the loft where it had landed to the city's central registration bureau. Pigeon racing was a popular pastime. A successful breeder and trainer could expect fame and fortune. There was a pharmacy at the bottom of the rue Léopold, visible from the Pont des Arches, which advertised as a speciality 'laxatives for pigeons'. The years passed and the runners continued, but eventually without the basket, since they carried only the ring which had been removed from the pigeon's leg. Then the time punch was invented and there were no more furious runners through the streets.

But there was still plenty to see. On a good day the noise of a band might be heard in the distance and a crowd would gather to greet the arrival of the tooth-puller, the *'arracheur de dents'*. Operating from a large wagon, this invaluable man would offer to pull teeth 'without charge, without pain and for nothing'. His band, dressed in elaborate uniform and seated on the roof of the wagon, above the operating table, would play soothingly until a victim, responding to the growing eagerness of the crowd and his own chronic pain, would be urged forward and strapped down. The band would then begin to play much louder to drown the victim's cries. Any last-minute struggles would be useless; the tooth-puller, armed with a large pair of pliers, would have his way. Eventually the blood would spurt and the tooth would emerge to be held aloft in triumph. The patient would be released to heal himself elsewhere and the tooth-puller would start a roaring trade in bogus potions.

The Simenons had been settled in Outremeuse for many years; the Brülls had arrived in Liège more recently after living and working in various other parts of Belgium. The two families were of rather different origins though both had lived in the Limbourg. The Limbourg is the irrigated flatland – *'le plat pays'* – to the north of Liège, a fertile but sometimes forlorn landscape which formed a united duchy until in 1288 it became a battleground and remained one for more than 500 years. Today the Limbourg is divided between Belgium and Holland. Its people are either Flemish or Walloon. But in the nineteenth century there were many German residents, referred to as 'Prussian' because the German borders of the Limbourg did for many years form part of Greater Prussia. In official Belgian documents the Flemish people are sometimes called 'Hollanders'. The Walloon population is sometimes described as 'French', and under Napoleon much of the Limbourg was annexed by France. The long struggle between the rulers of the Netherlands, Prussia, France, Austria and even England for domination of this area meant that the national identity of its population frequently changed and the communal divisions within and around the city of Liège at the turn of the century were sometimes obscure. But the various populations were proud of their different identities and mutually contemptuous.

The Simenons who came to Liège from the Limbourg were originally French-speaking Walloons but they were absorbed into the Limbourg in the seventeenth century and for five generations they became, to all appearances, Flemish: they inhabited Vlijtingen, a village with a Flemish name; the men married girls with Flemish names; and for five generations the Simenons gave Flemish Christian names to their children. For over 200 years their first language was Flemish. The family regained its Walloon identity with the marriage of Georges's grandfather, who had been baptised 'Christiaan', to Marie Catherine Moors.

The Moors, like the Simenons, were a family of Walloon origin who had been living in Vlijtingen since the seventeenth century, but Marie's father had married a girl called Marie Louise Leblanc, from the Walloon village of Alleur just north of Liège. Marie Louise Leblanc christened her daughter 'Marie Catherine' and brought her up to speak French. When Marie Catherine Moors married Christiaan Simenon he was an illiterate workman, as his father had been before him. The young couple settled in Alleur, not Vlijtingen, and Christiaan abandoned his work as a casual labourer and became an apprentice straw-hat maker. When their first child was born in 1870, a year after their wedding, Christiaan was still illiterate; he could not sign the birth certificate. But one year later, with the birth of their second child, he was able to sign his name, and in 1874 Christiaan (now calling himself 'Chrétien' and describing himself as a qualified straw hatter) and Marie

Catherine moved to Liège. Two years later Chrétien was running his own business as a master-hatter. By then the couple were settled in Outremeuse, sometimes called 'the free republic of Outremeuse', a district on an island in the Meuse which had a strong sense of independence and was a centre for craftsmen and small traders. In this transformation of an illiterate Flemish village labourer into an urban Walloon master-craftsman in seven years, Grandmother Marie Catherine Simenon seems to have played the decisive part.

Life in Liège in the nineteenth century, even for small trades-men doing reasonably well, could be precarious, and the sur-vivors were hardened by the experience. Marie Catherine Moors had married at the age of 19. Over the following seventeen years she had eleven confinements, but only seven of her children survived infancy. Of these seven, one became a nun and six married. Of the six who married only four had children, and although Marie Catherine was eventually to have thirteen grand-children only two were born in her lifetime.

Simenon frequently claimed in *Je me souviens* that thirteen children sat round his grandmother's table, whereas there were by the time of his birth only five. Uncle Lucien, like Désiré, con-tinued the daily visit after his marriage, and Uncle Arthur – later to become a *casquettier* (a hatter specialising in caps) – was still living at home. But Marie-Jean Louise had become Sister Marie-Madeleine, an Ursuline nun (she died in 1965 at the age of 91), and Uncle Guillaume, the eldest son, although remaining reasonably faithful to the family's traditional preoccupation with the head by becoming an umbrella maker, lived in Brussels and was banished from the house with his second wife. When Marie Catherine died at the age of 54 her eldest daughter had produced only one grandchild in eleven years of marriage. A woman who survived eleven confinements in the nineteenth century might reasonably expect to found a dynasty which would be a comfort to her in her old age, but Marie Catherine Simenon never enjoyed this reward.

Years later Georges Simenon recalled that one of the character-istics of large families was family mourning – somebody was always dying. He said that his grandmother had spent the rest of her life in mourning after the loss of one child. What in fact happened was that in 1884, when Marie Catherine was aged 34, she suffered a stillbirth in May and lost her 4–year-old daughter in

June, from smallpox. This was only the worst example of a repeated experience. Her total number of children went from one to four, to three, to four, to three, to eight, to seven, to six, to seven. Désiré, the writer's father, who grew up as the fourth child of the family, was the third child to occupy this position. His birth ended his mother's first run of bad luck, which may have helped to make him her favourite. That the dead children remained a constant presence in Marie Catherine Simenon's family is shown by the way in which their names were repeated. Marie Catherine gave birth to six girls who bore between them seventeen names but only eight different names. And the names of each of the dead daughters were repeated in the naming of the next girl to be born. So Marie-Josephine, who died at the age of one month, was commemorated in the naming of Marie-Josephine Céline, who was born three years later. And when Marie-Josephine Céline died at the age of 4 she was commemorated two years later in the naming of Marie-Anne Céline. In this way a christening became a ritual invocation of the family dead.

In 1893, when Désiré was 16, Chrétien Simenon found a permanent home for his business at no. 58 rue Puits-en-Sock. The hatter's shop was established in the front room of the terrace house, but Simenon family life revolved around the kitchen. The rue Puits-en-Sock was, and is, a narrow street. The houses are not big, and life was an intimate affair in which in order to discover what the neighbours had had for lunch it was only necessary to glance at the foot of the communal drainpipe. There was a communal lavatory in the courtyard and the house sometimes smelt of chamber-pots. Once a week Georges would eventually be placed in a wash-tub in the kitchen and given a clean shirt and socks. Into this closed community Désiré had one day introduced Henriette Brüll, a shop assistant at the Innovation department store in the centre of Liège, but a foreigner to the Walloons of Outremeuse. The Brülls were not even Flemish, but were Flemish and German, and when Désiré and Henriette announced their engagement the news was greeted without enthusiasm by Marie Catherine Simenon. 'Marry if you must,' she said to Désiré. 'But wait and see what you'll be given to eat.' It had not taken the Simenons long to forget their own 200 years of Flemish identity.

Désiré and Henriette were married on 22 April 1902. They lived in a succession of rented apartments in the centre of the city until two years after the birth of Georges when they too settled on Outremeuse, in the rue Pasteur – now the rue Georges Simenon – the district where Georges was to live until he left the city for good. In *Je me souviens* and in *Pedigree* Simenon claimed that his mother had been dominated and intimidated by Marie Catherine Simenon, a grandmother who was 'as cold as stone' and who had never kissed him as a little child. What he omitted to mention was that his grandmother died when he was 2, one week before Georges and his parents crossed the river to the rue Pasteur. Henriette therefore lived under her mother-in-law's domination for a period of only three years (to the day, the death taking place quite suddenly on Henriette's third wedding anniversary). The picture which Simenon later gave of life revolving around Marie Catherine and the rue Puits-en-Sock is to that extent misleading, but it is otherwise not entirely unreliable. Its central character was '*Vieux-Papa*', who had been born in 1823 and who could remember the political uprising in 1831 when Belgium gained its independence from Holland. '*Vieux-Papa*', '*une carcasse monstrueuse*' with the peppered-blue skin of the coal-face worker, hairy arms seeming to reach down to the ground, above his shoulders the great head with its enormous mouth and ears, spent most of the day in an armchair. Sometimes he munched his favourite snack, a raw onion, as lesser men would munch an apple. Every two months one of his sons would shave him in the kitchen. Once, after complaining of toothache, '*Vieux-Papa*' put on a show that was as good as anything Georges had seen in the street. He instructed one of his grandsons, Georges's Uncle Arthur, to remove the tooth. '*Vieux-Papa*' had never had a tooth removed before, and Arthur, thinking he was joking, fetched the big pliers normally used for pulling nails. But the old man was perfectly serious, and Arthur was made to go through with the business. '*Vieux-Papa*' was equally unperturbed when he woke up one morning to find that he had gone blind. He never complained, but learnt to recognise his family by their steps. He lived till the age of 85, outliving his daughter by four years, and Georges, aged 5, seeing a glimmer of light pass through his own bedroom on the night of his great-grandfather's death, apparently said, 'Look, it's *Vieux-Papa*.'

'*Vieux-Papa*'s' son-in-law Chrétien had, according to Simenon, served a long apprenticeship before setting up as a hatter. He had travelled as far as London, Italy and Vienna to learn the craft of straw plaiting so that he might add boaters and Panamas to his stock-in-trade. This claim, also made by Simenon in *Je me souviens*, has since been doubted, since such a journey did not conform to local practice at the time. On the mornings when Georges called in to visit his grandfather, the younger old man of the two old men in his life would give him a little coin and kiss him, and his lips 'smelt of the glass'. The shop next door to no. 58 was a dolls' hospital run by an elderly 'native of Nuremburg called Herr Krantz' (he was actually called Creutz, and was a Belgian native of the nearby German-speaking Belgian frontier village of Raeren-sous-Eupen). Each morning, before opening their shops, Herr Creutz and Monsieur Simenon would take a glass of schnapps together. Recalling this in *Je me souviens* Simenon added that it was the only alcohol either man touched throughout the day.

Until the day of her death Marie Catherine was generally to be found in the kitchen keeping an eye on her bear-like father in case he attempted a second raw onion, with potentially disastrous consequences. After his marriage Désiré continued to visit his mother every day on his way to work, even though it was not on the way at all. Marie Catherine would have put the day's soup on before the rest of the family were even awake, and by 8.30 in the morning she would be simmering something more substantial, perhaps a *'boeuf à la mode'*. The Simenon family battle-cry had always been *'J'ai faim'*, and they confirmed their Flemish origins in this use of food as a solace for the rigours of life. It did not matter at what time any of Marie Catherine's children came home, there was always something to eat. When Désiré called in, full of his Flemish breakfast of duck's eggs and dripping, and not calling *'J'ai faim'* out of loyalty to Henriette, his mother always said, 'Do you want a bowl of soup?' 'No, Mother.' 'That means Yes . . .' And so Désiré ate his soup, and then had a slice of cake that had been set aside for him the day before, and his mother was confirmed in her view that her son was not being looked after. *'J'ai faim'* was not only a battle-cry, it was a call for love. It gave Marie Catherine Simenon a lifetime's work and a lifetime's power, and may have compensated her for her lack of grandchildren.

Simenon once summed up the contrast between his parents by

saying that whereas Désiré took life as 'a perfectly straight line', Henriette came from 'a tormented race'. The reason for the Brülls' torment was not made clear to Simenon until the end of his life. All he knew was that in the official records of Liège Henriette's family were always listed as 'foreigners' because her father, Wilhelm Brüll, had been born in Prussia and her mother, Maria Loijens, in Holland. Mathieu Rutten, after studying the seven generations of the Brüll family that preceded Henriette, wrote that 'the story of the Brülls from the professional, social and psychological points of view is an uninterrupted succession of problems – temporary lodgings, transient occupations, false starts – a destiny that was hazardous and even dark'. And Henriette's generation was 'a family without attachments, cut off from their native region, with no fixed address, "foreigners" in the official records wherever they went'.

Part of the problem was alcoholism, but in the case of Henriette's father it is not certain whether or not this led to his downfall. Wilhelm Brüll was born the son of a butcher in Herzogenrath, Germany, in 1828, and in due course did his military service with the Prussian army. According to family tradition he was treated so harshly – his best friend was drowned and his own health ruined when recruits were made to swim an icy river in winter – that he took against all things Prussian and emigrated to the Dutch Limburg. When Wilhelm was recalled to the Prussian colours for the Franco-Prussian War of 1870 he is said to have remained in Belgium and refused to serve, thereby falling out with his four brothers and four sisters who had remained in Germany. In the Dutch Limburg, Wilhelm Brüll married in 1854 Maria Loijens, the daughter of one of the richest families in the Limburg. He was described on the marriage certificate as a 'steward'. The young couple immediately moved from the Dutch to the Belgian Limbourg, and with his father-in-law's backing Wilhelm became 'dyke-master' on an important irrigation. Their imposing farmhouse by the side of the Zuid-Willemsvart Canal, was the scene of Wilhelm's legendary prosperity. In 'le plat pays' Wilhelm and Maria started their family, six children being born by 1865. 'The whole country,' Simenon was to write in Je me souviens, 'as far as one could see, was below sea-level . . .' The land was below sea-level and the banks of the canal were raised high above the land. The barges passed at eye-level if one was on the first floor of the house. It was one hour's walk in any direction to the next dwelling. 'From the water in the canal, from the way in which the water was shared out, from the way in which it was allowed to run along the feeder canals and then released over the land at appropriate seasons, depended the prosperity or ruin of everyone for leagues and leagues around. And Brüll was the master of the water, the maker of riches.'

But in 1866 Wilhelm Brüll was ruined. He owned five canal boats which were used to transport timber from his land down to Liège, and which brought night-soil back up to the Limbourg where it was sold as fertiliser. In 1866 there was an outbreak of cholera in the city and the Dutch authorities in Maastricht closed the Albert Canal to barges carrying night-soil from Liège. The two sewage contractors whom Brüll dealt with in Liège needed a loan to buy the necessary wagons to fulfil their contract by the overland route, and the Liège city authorities were pressing them as the night-soil was accumulating on the Quai Barbou on Outremeuse. Wilhelm Brüll agreed to sign a promissory note for 3000 francs, but he wrote it carelessly and his partners altered the figure to 30,000 francs and then left him to pay it. It was after this misadventure that Wilhelm abandoned the influential position of dyke-master in the Limbourg and the family moved first to the province of Anvers and later to Brabant, where Wilhelm was described variously as a 'surveyor' or 'butcher'. In 1880 the Brülls moved to Liège and Wilhelm was describing himself as a 'wholesale grocer'. It was in July of that year that Henriette, their thirteenth and last child, was born. One year after Henriette's birth the 'wholesale grocer' had become a 'domestic servant' in Germany at the Fontaine d'Elise restaurant in Aix-la-Chapelle. A year later he was back in Liège, this time listed as a 'timber merchant', with a wife and seven children. It was as a timber and coal merchant that he died in 1885. Simenon was always told that if his grandfather had taken to drink it was in despair at his ruin, but he eventually decided that Wilhelm had been ruined because he drank too much, and it was that which accounted for his carelessness over the promissory note. This conclusion has been hotly disputed by another of Wilhelm's grandchildren, Sylvie Wilsens-Brüll.

With Wilhelm's death his wife Maria was left to struggle on alone. Her life was even harder than that of Marie Catherine

Simenon. Married at the age of 18, coming from a prosperous family, with her husband ruined twelve years later, Maria Brüll had thirteen confinements over a period of twenty-six years. Three of the children died before her husband. In March 1885, in what must have been the worst year of her life, her husband died. Then, on 10 May, two of her children died, a son aged 22 and her 7-year-old daughter. The family funeral which followed was remembered by the people of the *quartier* for many years. But whereas Marie Catherine Simenon after the double blow of 1884 could take shelter behind a façade of grief for the remaining twenty-one years of her life, Maria Brüll, without a husband after her triple blow of 1885, had to make the best of things. She had three children still at home and Henriette was only 4. And although the family had Belgian residency, '*la petite naturalisation*', they remained foreigners in Belgium. Maria decided that the only thing to be done was to try to continue running her husband's timber and coal business, which was already failing. It was during this period that Henriette remembered their being so poor that her mother used to put a saucepan of water to steam on the stove so that the neighbours would think that she was preparing a hot meal.

In the nine years between 1892 and 1901, when she died at the age of 64, Maria Brüll moved house in Liège seven times. For seven months in 1896 she was living at 12 rue Puits-en-Sock. Henriette's registered address by then was in a suburb to the north of the city. She was 16 years old and had just left her mother's house for the first time to start work at L'Innovation; she no doubt came to the rue Puits-en-Sock to visit her mother regularly. Désiré Simenon was at that time aged 18 and had been living in the rue Puits-en-Sock since 1893. He had just started his daily journey to and from the insurance office and passed the door of no. 12 twice a day. Simenon never knew that his Brüll grandmother had lived for a time in the rue Puits-en-Sock, and it was always a mystery to him how Désiré and Henriette first met. But it seems likely that the first time Désiré saw Henriette was during this seven-month period when the Brülls and the Simenons would have been attending the same parish church, St Nicolas, every Sunday.

The memory of childhood poverty dominated the rest of Henriette's life, and marked the lives of her children in their turn.

But the experience had a more spectacular effect on several of her brothers and sisters. In 1881, at the lowest point in his fortunes, Wilhelm had left his wife and family and spent a mysterious year in Germany working in a restaurant as a servant. Alcoholism was, and still is, a frequent problem for waiters in bars and cafés. Four years later, Wilhelm died an alcoholic. Of the nine of his children who reached adulthood, three are known to have worked in the same trade and three are known to have been alcoholics. Henriette's sister Louisa, whom Simenon called 'Tante Marthe' in *Je me souviens*, would creep furtively into bargees' bars on the quays of the Meuse, ostensibly to do *'pipi'*. Uncle Léopold, who had qualified to enter Liège University according to Simenon, became a house-painter until he was no longer capable of remaining upright on a ladder, at which point he took to drinking in the street and doing *'pipi'* against the wall. And Georges's pretty and impulsive Aunt Félicie, who as a teenager had been put on a diet of stout because she was anaemic, unfortunately married a café-owner. Perched behind her till at the corner of the bar, she was invariably drinking when Georges and his mother started the day's shopping at 7 a.m. *'Mon dieu, Félicie . . .'* Henriette would exclaim, to no avail.

As a child Georges sometimes witnessed the more dramatic effects of alcohol on his mother's family. After Aunt Louisa married a wealthy shop-owner and bank director, Jean-Mathieu Schrooten, she sometimes became unmanageable, threatened to shoot herself or her husband and had to be locked up. Sometimes she would lock herself up, and when this happened Henriette might be called in to help. Georges would be left sitting with Uncle Jean and they listened together to the screaming and the sound of heavy objects striking the inside of the bedroom door. After some time the screaming stopped, and later Henriette returned to take Georges home. These attacks always occurred after Louisa had managed to get round one of the shop assistants who worked for her husband and who were strictly forbidden to let her have any money from the till. The family name for her condition after a raid on the till was *'brindezingue'*.

Georges's favourite uncle was Léopold, the family *clochard*. Léopold had been 10 when his family left the Limbourg. Georges could remember him sitting in the kitchen in the rue Pasteur while Henriette peeled vegetables, describing the days of family glory in the house by the canal. The downfall of the Brüll family had taken place forty years before Georges's birth, and when he came to write about it for the first time forty years after his birth, in *Je me souviens*, he seems to have somewhat romanticised Uncle Léopold. He wrote that Léopold had been brought up to hunt with the nobility and had a brilliant future ahead of him until the day when he decided to wear the skin-tight uniform of the Lancers. He had fallen in love and married one of his regiment's camp-followers, Eugénie, a beauty with Spanish blood in her veins. This impetuous decision meant that he had been shunned by the Brüll family (with the exception of Henriette) to the end of his days. Léopold 'had chosen to see everything . . . live every-thing . . . and eventually he reached the point where he was no longer ashamed to be seen peeing in the street'. Léopold would disappear for months on end, so that not even Eugénie knew where he was, and in any case none of the family would acknowl-edge Eugénie when they met her. Then one day a message reached Henriette that Léopold was dying of cancer in the Bavière hospital, 400 metres from their house. A few weeks after his death another message arrived. Eugénie had been found in a garret, dead of starvation, unable to face life without Léopold. Henriette, on returning from identifying the corpse, had said, 'She weighed no more than a child of ten. She was just a skeleton.' By the time Simenon ended his account of the story of Léopold and Eugénie in *Je me souviens* he had convinced himself that theirs had been the greatest love affair he had ever encountered. Perhaps it was, but he nonetheless altered many of the details.

It seems unlikely that Léopold ever had hopes of associating with the nobility, since his father had been ruined when he was only 10. He had never worn the skin-tight pants of the Lancers, since he had enlisted in a foot regiment, the 2nd *chasseurs à pied*. Although Eugénie was indeed the name of his wife, it seems unlikely that she was ever a camp-follower, since at the time of her marriage she had a fixed address in Mons, where she worked as cook. The possibility of 'Spanish blood' remains open. But Eugénie was born in the village of Wiheries, just south of Mons, and her maiden name was Dubuisson. It seems that Henriette was indeed called to Léopold's death-bed, since it was she who signed his death certificate, but Eugénie was not found dead in a garret a

few weeks after the death of Léopold. She died three years later in
the Valdor hospital.

The most dramatic view of family alcoholism was eventually
provided for Georges by the shapely Aunt Félicie. Her husband,
the bar-owner, was known to Georges as Uncle Coucou. He had
the Café des Cultivateurs on the Quai-sur-Meuse, opposite
Outremeuse, by the Pont des Arches. After her mother's death in
January 1901, and before her own marriage to Désiré in 1902,
Henriette had lived with Coucou and Félicie above the Café des
Cultivateurs. But in 1908, at the age of 34, after eight years of
marriage, Félicie was bundled into a straitjacket by two male
nurses and carried off to an asylum. She died three days later, in
the Sainte-Agathe sanatorium, of *delirium tremens*. Georges, aged
5, watched Aunt Félicie being forced, screaming, out of the house
while Uncle Coucou sobbed and beat his head against the corridor
wall. The Brüll family demanded a police investigation, and
Uncle Coucou got two years in the St-Léonard prison for causing
grievous bodily harm to his wife. He had been savagely jealous of
Félicie. The more he had beaten her, the more she had drunk. The
more she had drunk, the more he had beaten her. After Félicie's
death Georges was told to stop referring to Coucou as 'Uncle'.

'*Mon dieu, Françoise!*' '*Mon dieu, Henriette!*' '*Jésus, Marie!*' 'In this
Vale of Tears!' These were the conversational interjections of the
ladies of the Brüll family and, according to *Je me souviens* and,
later, *Destinées*, they were usually in Flemish. Simenon remembered that Henriette and her sisters invariably spoke Flemish
when they were together, and that Léopold and Henriette spoke
Flemish. The Brülls' use of Flemish was one of the reasons why
Marie Catherine Simenon had so distrusted Henriette. But in 1975
Simenon's implacable first cousin, Mme Sylvie Wilsens-Brüll,
dismissed the Flemish context of Simenon's childhood out-of-
hand. In a letter to Mathieu Rutten she wrote that her grandfather, Wilhelm, Henriette's father, 'raised his children with a
horror of everything Prussian and always spoke French to them'.
Referring to *Lettre à ma mère* (*Letter to My Mother*), which Simenon
had then just published, she added:

The mixture of Flemish and German presumably refers to the
patois of the Meuse country but only the old people spoke it

occasionally. Aunt Henriette could do no more than jabber a few words of it, in a strong Walloon accent. The little girl doing the family shopping at the age of 5 without being able to speak French is just fiction.

Her account is supported by Denyse Simenon, who remembers that Henriette spoke fluent French, 'but as a Walloon, with one or two vernacular words'. So if Denyse and Mme Wilsens-Brüll are correct (and Mme Wilsens-Brüll was eight years older than Simenon, and so knew their Brüll ancestors personally), it would seem that in his first published autobiography Georges Simenon deliberately misrepresented his mother's character.

If so, it was not for want of accurate material. Even as a small child Georges seems to have observed his mother with a pitiless attention to detail. This is how Simenon described his mother in *Je me souviens* twenty years after he had left her house and at a time when he had just acquired a small son of his own whom he wished to instruct about their family background. Henriette was a very small woman whose head seemed too big for her body, rather like a certain kind of doll's. She was always worried about being thought vulgar, having been bullied about her supposed vulgarity in her first job as a 16-year-old shop assistant in a large department store. She was always excusing herself, even when she was not in the wrong. She pretended that embarrassing events had never happened. She counted her pennies and brooded for years over the loss of a valuable ornament. She blackmailed her son into good behaviour when he was small by telling him that if he did not stop teasing his little brother 'they' would take her away and operate on her at the hospital. She humiliated herself ingratiatingly in front of wealthy neighbours.

One of Simenon's most uncompromising descriptions of his mother's behaviour concerned a large unmuzzled dog that lived in the rue Pasteur. Henriette had to pass this frightening animal as it lay in the middle of the road beneath its owners' balcony. She would smile up at her betters as they sat on their balcony, and then she would bend down to pat the brute:

The proof that I am not ungrateful, the proof that I am better educated than our neighbours, is that I stroke your large dog, even though I am frightened of it and even though one day it might go for one of my children. Thank you so much! Believe me I appreciate this opportunity.

In the street, appearances had to be kept up at all times, and Simenon's subconscious register also noted how easily his mother passed from arguing with his father to smiling politely and falsely at some passing acquaintance. The little Simenon made a note of his mother's inconsistency to her own standards when she lied about his age in the tram in order to get him a reduced fare. Henriette, he wrote, was always obsessed with '*le strict nécessaire*' – the bare minimum – on which she made sure they all had to live. This, as she constantly pointed out, had been imposed on them all by Désiré's stubborn refusal to take out a life-insurance policy, and by his lack of foresight in choosing to specialise in fire insurance rather than the more lucrative life insurance. Henriette 'found unhappiness where no one else had suspected its existence'. Her life was a search for security, which meant having your own house to live and die in. Henriette was certainly not an alcoholic: there are no references to her ever touching alcohol. But it seems that her reaction to her childhood experience was just as profound as Léopold's or Félicie's, and – as described by her eldest son – it may even have been more destructive.

Henriette's husband could hardly have provided a more contrasting personality. Désiré was a calm, strong presence, confident and untroubled even in his choice of Henriette. In his son's idealised picture of him he walked with his long regular steps, crossing the river to work, returning home for a late lunch, retracing his steps in the afternoon, finding all his happiness in the little life of the *quartier* and the family: the second return home in the evening, '*J'ai faim*', the food being prepared on the stove, putting his children to bed, using his affectionate name for Georges ('*fiston*'), then reading the newspaper seated in his wicker chair by the fire while his wife sewed. Simenon found heroism in his father's simplicity, in his patience at work, his contentment at home, his lack of complaint about his lack of success. As senior clerk at the local office of the Agences Générales et la Winterthur he had been offered a choice between running the traditional business of fire insurance or switching to the newly popular life insurance. Selling life insurance meant tramping the streets. Fire insurance was managed from the office. Désiré preferred the

orderliness and comfort of the office and so never earned more
than 150 francs a month. The monthly commission alone of his
ambitious deputy far exceeded that, much to Henriette's irritation. But it was Désiré who was entrusted with the keys to the
office safe. He was happiest each day when the rooms in the rue
Sohet emptied at midday and he could continue his work alone,
seated at the desk at which he would eventually die. The office in
which he worked has now disappeared, but just nearby, in the rue
des Guillemins, there is a replica still in use: a small private bank
with a tiled floor and a wooden counter. The counter is divided
by a partition which is pierced by 'guichets'; behind each hatch
there sits a clerk. The silence, discretion and formality of the outer
room contrasts with the gossip and camaraderie which flow out
over the counter every time a hatch is opened to reveal a glimpse
of the world inside. Désiré formed part of that contented group
who never ask more from life than they can get. 'My father lacked
nothing, my mother lacked everything, that was the difference
between them,' Simenon wrote in Je me souviens.

Both Henriette and Désiré were Catholic, and Henriette at least
was devout. The Simenons had a family pew in the parish church
of St Nicolas; it was the pew dedicated to the confraternity of St
Roch, and from this pew every Sunday Grandfather Chrétien
would set out to take the collection at Mass. On Sunday morning
Georges accompanied his father to St Nicolas. He noticed that
Désiré was too tall to kneel in the family's narrow pew and that he
did not genuflect, even during the most solemn moment of the
Mass, the Elevation, but merely bowed his head.

In Liège before the Great War it was not difficult for a mother
like Henriette to ensure that her son was devout. Soon after his
birth Georges was vowed to the protection of the Virgin Mary,
which meant that on special occasions he had to be dressed in blue
and white. This caused problems when his generous Uncle
Guillaume, on a flying visit from the umbrella shop in Brussels
and wearing a fashionable coat that was cut so short that it was
known as 'a fart in the air', took him out for the day and bought
him a smart red suit. The red suit had to be returned to the shop,
which was not easy since Georges had already peed in it. At the
annual Corpus Christi Day procession, Georges, dressed in blue
and white, was among the children who scattered rose petals
along the path taken by the priest bearing the Host. And on Easter

Monday Georges would be taken on the traditional pilgrimage to
the shrine of Our Lady of Chèvremont. The little boy watched
the more devout pilgrims mounting the stony hill on their knees
and the women genuflecting in front of the statues. Years later he
recalled that there always seemed to be a cloudburst on the long
road home. In due course Georges decided that he had a vocation
for the priesthood. There were already several family connections
with the Church. Apart from Aunt Marie-Jean Louise, now Sister
Marie-Madeleine, there was Aunt Françoise, who was married to
the sacristan of the nearby parish church of St Louis, and according to Simenon there was a distant cousin who was also called
'Georges' and who had once been bishop of Liège. This cousin did
not exist. But another distant cousin, Monsignor Willem
Simenon, who did exist, became vicar-general of the diocese,
dying in 1951 laden with the honours of the Church. Simenon's
claim of a relationship with an ecclesiastical dignitary who did not
exist but who would shortly do so was an early example of his
ability to invent the future as well as the past.

One of Désiré's church duties was his work as a charity inspector, which meant that every month he had to visit the poorest
parts of Liège, where families slept ten or twelve to a room,
usually on the floor. These visits did not turn Désiré into a
socialist. Instead they confirmed his existing views. Désiré was
one of '*les petites gens*', and '*les petites gens*' were people who
'loathed the rich but did not exactly like the poor'. Désiré was also
a member of another voluntary organisation, the *garde civique*,
whose chief function was to put down civil disorder. In the years
before the First World War, when several European countries
were at various times on the verge of revolution, Liège was one of
the industrial cities repeatedly threatened by a general strike, and
the *garde civique* was frequently in action. Summoned by a drum-
mer marching through the streets, Désiré would don the elaborate
blue and red uniform and 'double-bowler' cap with plume, and
take down his long-barrelled Mauser rifle which was normally
kept on top of the bedroom wardrobe. Then, watched by his
admiring son, he would set out to join his section. The *petit-
bourgeois*, or '*petites gens*' as Simenon preferred to call them, were
entirely on the side of the authorities if there was any question of
civil disturbance. They regarded the industrial workers as feck-
less, unwashed, disorderly and overpaid. The workers, it was

said, earned almost as much as office workers, but they spent it all on drink. They saved nothing for medical care or education, since both were provided for them free. They neglected their children and dressed them in rags. The workers on strike were a serious threat to everything the *'petites gens'* held dear. At one demonstration, in favour of trades-union rights, two strikers were shot dead by the *garde civique*. Désiré was on duty, but the clash took place in another part of the city and when he returned that evening it was only to report that the day's highlight for his section had occurred when, blocked by a line of mounted *gendarmes*, they had been forced to pee through the grating beneath the shutters of an elegant jeweller's shop. Désiré's platoon seem to have had more in common with Dogberry's than with Rembrandt's 'Night Watch'. And in his son's memory, Désiré, the man in a uniform upholding authority, became one with Léopold, the drunken *clochard* who defied public order – united by the simple act of unbuttoning their trousers and letting fly.

Simenon endowed his father with a quasi-saintly stature and later claimed that he had modelled some of the character of Maigret – the good detective, dependable, just and brave – on Désiré. His attitude to his father was consistent. It started with a small boy's love for the physical presence: the long measured strides of his walk – Georges had to take three steps to each of his father's; the strength of his hands – 'impossible to say whether son or father reached for the other's hand first'; and the way in which Désiré brushed his hair to emphasise his 'poet's brow'. Later there was his father's exhausted tolerance of Georges's own adolescent misdeeds. Simenon was finally rewarded with confirmation of Désiré's goodness after the latter's death. As a young man working in an insurance agency Désiré had applied to take out life cover. He had submitted to the customary examination by the company doctor and been told that cover would have to be refused because he had an enlarged heart. In order not to worry Henriette he said nothing about this, so that throughout their marriage his wife continually nagged him about his failure to provide for her in case of disaster. He died at the age of 44, of *angina pectoris*, and spent his last three years following the first acute attack as a semi-invalid. The truth about his original application and his heroic silence under provocation only came out after his death and it gave Simenon a lifelong contempt for the power of bureaucrats. But the sympathy which Simenon could so easily extend towards his father was withheld from his mother. Her chronic anxiety and self-indulgent panics disturbed Georges, and in his memories of her he portrayed a woman who eventually turned into a shrew.

Relations between Georges and his mother began to deteriorate after the birth of his brother Christian in 1906, when Georges was 3. While Georges had demanded constant attention – even before he could walk he had been fenced into an upturned chair to keep him in order – Christian was a rather quiet, rather fat, rather placid baby, who sat in his seat in the kitchen 'plump and smug like a canon at Vespers'. The idea gradually dawned on Georges that his mother preferred Christian. Perhaps the mistake had been to send Georges to infant school the week before the new baby was born, or perhaps there was always some truth in Georges's conviction. In any event this was an idea that Henriette was never able to correct, even if she had wished to, and in due course the differences between Désiré and Henriette were reflected in the relationship between Georges and his little brother. Henriette began to call Christian 'my son' whereas Georges was '*le fils de Désiré*'. Henriette would, when referring to Georges, say 'your son' to Désiré, and Désiré would use the same term to refer to Christian. This practice seems to have had more of an effect on Georges than on Christian. Christian, according to Georges and other witnesses, always looked up to his brother and turned to him in time of trouble. Georges's feelings were less generous. Like many eldest children he resented the arrival of his younger brother. In book after book he slighted or ignored Christian. In his first autobiographical work, *Les trois crimes de mes amis*, he twice referred to his brother. Once he recalled Christian, aged 12, looking at him in horror because Georges had been carried home drunk at 6 in the morning. Later he recalled that during the famine months of the occupation Christian alone was capable of hoarding his bread ration for two or three days so that he could save it for when he was really hungry, and that the rest of the family looked away when he finally consumed it. In 1932 Simenon visited Christian and his wife in the Belgian Congo, where Christian was the harbour-master at Matadi, and described them in a magazine article as selfish and absurd colonials. Then, in 1940, writing supposedly to provide his own son with family information, Simenon in *Je me souviens* presented the infant Christian as a passive consumer of food and mother love, a child who did no wrong. In fact the differences between the brothers as children were not immediately obvious. At the Institut St André, and then for one year at the Collège St Louis, Georges was certainly an outstanding pupil, but so in his turn was Christian. In 1913, Christian, aged 6, won first place in the *Prix d'Honneur* and the *Prix en Réunion.** In 1916, aged 10, Christian came third in the annual marks, and in 1918, the year when Georges left school abruptly, Christian achieved '*la plus grande distinction*' in the Christian Brothers' national exam '*le Concours Général*'. This was exactly the same mark as Georges had received in 1914.

In *Je me souviens* Georges admits teasing Christian, but only in order to mention that Henriette's reaction was to say to him that if he did not leave Christian alone 'they' would take her away and operate on her. Later, in *Pedigree*, he recounted the story of how, at the age of 11, he saved Christian from death by drowning, but instead of naming the child who falls into the river as his brother he referred only to '*un gamin*' (a kid), thereby avoiding the need to mention that he had a brother at all. As late as 1981, writing in his final *Dictée, Destinées*, Simenon was still avoiding the subject. 'My brother died at the age of 40 or 45,' he wrote, suggesting that he was not sure whether his brother died in 1946 or 1951. In fact, Christian Simenon, by then a sergeant in the French Foreign Legion, died in action at That-Khe in the Khu-Tu-Tri region, to the east of Tonkin and the Red River near the Chinese frontier, on 31 October 1947, and the family were immediately informed of the details. The final step of the eclipse of one brother by the other followed Christian's death. His place of birth, 3 rue Pasteur, no longer exists. In 1978 it was renamed 25 rue Georges Simenon.

The feeling that he had been rejected by his mother and re-placed by Christian was to become one of the dominant forces of Simenon's life. Faced with this problem, Georges, at the age of 4, took the initiative, and so made himself even more difficult and less appealing. He was capable when small of injuring himself quite badly without crying, a feat which caused his mother to

---

* The boy who invariably beat Georges and came top was called van Ham, a name which Simenon was sometimes to give to unsympathetic characters in his books.

look at him as though he were unnatural. He offered another reaction which was almost worthy of Henriette: he took to sleep-walking constantly, but particularly when there was a full moon, a habit which continued into his adult life. In childhood it confirmed Henriette's suspicion that there was 'something strange about that boy' rather than winning him a reassuring sympathy. A doctor later said of Georges Simenon that his psychological profile was that of 'a small boy holding the hand of a mother who would always withhold her approval'. And at the age of 78, after Henriette's death, Simenon was to write in *Mémoires intimes* (*Intimate Memoirs*), 'You never believed in me, Mother. You were always worried about me, as though I was bound to turn out a failure.'

But these problems lay in the future and did not overshadow the happiness of Simenon's infancy. More important were the elements of his ideal world, the world which inspired the domestic contentment of Commissaire Maigret. They included the orderliness and comfort of Grandmother Simenon's household, the casserole simmering on the stove, '*Vieux-Papa*'s massive and unthreatening bulk, the smell of the markets and the life of the streets, the certainty of the calendar of saints and the strength of Désiré. Added to this was the pleasure the little boy took in his early success at school. In September 1906, when Henriette gave birth to Christian and Georges was sent to the nearby Ecole Gardienne run by the Sisters of Notre Dame, he was taught by a nun whom he remembered in later life as having been 'so sweet and mushy that she made one think of something good to eat'. Against all the rules 'Sister Adonie' taught Georges to read by the time he was 5. At that age he was sent to the primary school, the Institut St André, run by the Christian Brothers, which was also just around the corner from the house in the rue Pasteur. Here, since the Christian Brothers followed all the rules, he was taught to read all over again and Georges found that he could take one of the top three places in the class without effort. Later they moved house, to no. 53 rue de la Loi, directly opposite the school gates. When he looked out of his front window Georges could see the courtyard and the door and bell-tower of the school.

Once a week, before school started, Georges would go to the public baths in the rue de Pitteurs with Chrétien, and the old hatter and his grandson would bathe in water from the River Meuse that swilled through the pool. In summer a policeman would knock at all the doors on Outremeuse and instruct the inhabitants to weed their street, and everyone would spend an hour or more on their hands and knees scraping the grass and moss out from between the cobbles. For this task Georges used a kitchen knife that set his teeth on edge as it scratched the stones. He lived in a world where he could count on his father to trace a cross on his forehead before he too went to bed, where he could count on his Uncle Léon to turn up to the 11 o'clock Mass at St Nicolas every Sunday still wearing an apparatus for shaping his moustache. He only took it off on the church steps. The *quartier* of little streets was dominated, as it is today, by the spire of the church and the church was to dominate the first twelve years of his life. For Henriette, and therefore for Georges, everything important in life was connected to St Nicolas. The priests and nuns of the parish bestowed education, and the saint himself bestowed the almonds and nuts and toys which were distributed before Christmas; the children of the rue de la Loi and the rue Pasteur and rue Puits-en-Sock were especially blessed since they were living in the parish of Santa Claus.

If there was a recurring anxiety it came at 5.45 every morning when Georges would be turned out of the front door of the terrace house in the rue de la Loi and would set off towards the chapel of the nearby Bavière hospital, where he was to serve the 6 o'clock Mass. In order to reach the chapel he had to walk down the rue Pasteur, cross the Place du Congrès and then make his way to the boulevard de la Constitution. In the winter it was still dark and he sometimes became frightened. He would hear a noise behind him and would start to walk in the middle of the road to avoid the shadows in front of the houses. He would start to talk to himself, and then he would start to run. By the time he reached the doors of the hospital he would be running as hard as he could. In front of him was the knocker on the door. When he grasped that he had reached sanctuary. Mass was heard by those hospital patients who were well enough. Some came on crutches, some were carried in chairs; since it was a public hospital, many of the patients wore a uniform of striped pyjamas. In the eyes of a child they formed a grim, even spectral, congregation. The little altar boy knew that a number of them would shortly be dead. After Mass he had to accompany the priest who took the last sacrament to the bedsides of those who were too ill to attend the service. His task was to walk in front of the priest carrying a cross and ringing the Sanctus bell. He was the herald of their approaching death. Frequently when one of the patients died a Requiem Mass was held in the hospital chapel, and this too he served. He was paid extra for each Requiem Mass and so his prayers by the beds of the dying patients, though respectful, may not always have been fervent. Years later his recollection of the panicky run through the dark streets around his home became one of the clearest memories of his childhood.

What might have been a major upheaval in family life occurred in 1911, when Georges was 8, and proved in fact to be an amusing addition. That year Outremeuse was filled with foreign students coming from Eastern and Central Europe to study at a French-language university. Many of them were political refugees, Jews fleeing from persecution, or anarchists or revolutionaries fleeing from the Tsar's secret police. Liège was a popular university because of its low fees and cost of living, and the city was renowned among East European students for the strength of its trade union movement, based on the coal-mining industry, and for having been the scene of general strikes in 1891 and 1902. Outremeuse was popular with these *immigrés* because it was a newly-built *quartier* where there was an abundance of cheap lodging. So chance placed Georges Simenon, at the age of 8, in the centre of a society that took him far beyond the boundaries of his city or his country.

   Henriette, always on the lookout for a chance to improve the family fortunes, immediately saw the point of moving from their family's second-floor apartment in the rue Pasteur to the gloomier rue de la Loi, where they could rent an entire house directly opposite Georges's school. To this house, no. 53, came a succession of figures, mostly young women, who were to make a deep impression on Georges. Two in particular, who arrived in 1910, were to appear in several of his subsequent books. There was, first, 'Mademoiselle Frida', as Henriette termed her respectfully – Frida Stavitskaïa, from Odessa, a medical student and a revolutionary nihilist. Then there was 'Mademoiselle Pauline' – Pauline Feinstein from Warsaw – reading natural sciences and mathematics. There was also Monsieur Saft from the same general direction, and Monsieur Bogdanowski. Mlle Frida's father was a political exile in Siberia and she herself would one day be a Soviet commissar. Georges, sensing something of this, noted that in preference to playing with the children and their toys Mlle Frida would invariably be on her way to the mortuary to cut up a corpse. Simenon later claimed that casual visitors included both Trotsky and Lenin, although this seems unlikely. On the other hand it was true that Mlle Pauline, whose father had a garment stall in the Warsaw ghetto, would in due course become a professor of mathematics at Warsaw University. And 'Mademoiselle Lola' was also a reality: Lola Resnick, 'the fat Caucasian', who had one of the best rooms in the house, the pink room on the first floor overlooking the street. Lola came to symbolise a certain kind of woman for Simenon. In more than one of his early romantic novels there is a character called 'Lola' or 'Lolita', smiling and languid, sometimes to be found on the staircase in a dressing-gown, 'pulpy as an exotic fruit', her eyes betraying her sensual Slavonic inner life.

As the lodgers advanced the family retreated. Henriette had at last found a means of overcoming the régime of '*le strict nécessaire*', and no superfluous comforts were going to stand in her way. Désiré was turned out of his wicker armchair by the fire, his supper was moved to an hour which suited the lodgers' timetable, and he was moved from his bedroom into the little spare room and then out of the little spare room into a cot off the kitchen. Henriette's health underwent a remarkable improvement. Her bouts of tearfulness became less frequent, her backache disappeared, the cleaner was dismissed, as 53 rue de la Loi was transformed into a *machine à sous*. For a few *sous* more Henriette found that she was able to carry buckets of coal up to the lodgers' rooms. It mattered little to her that Désiré no longer had anywhere to sit in the evening to read his newspaper in comfort, or that he could no longer preside over the family dinner table, or that there were no hooks left in the hall for the family's coats, or that Georges and Christian frequently had to be turned out to play in the cold street to give the new arrivals peace and quiet for their studies. What mattered was the growing size of Henriette's *petites économies*. The lodgers' rooms had been furnished by some preliminary savings which she had been able to make despite her endless complaints about the régime of *le strict nécessaire*, but Désiré knew better than to reproach her with this. The inevitable reaction would have been a return to the tears and the litany of complaints: '*Mon dieu, Désiré* . . .' Georges later recalled that it was about this time that his father added a new stock phrase to his vocabulary: 'Do as you please.'

In Simenon's account of his childhood, the Russian and Polish and Jewish lodgers of the rue de la Loi played a colourful part. The children found the amusement they provided more than compensated for the discomfort they caused. Simenon was to claim later that they had allowed him to examine their medical textbooks, which contained numerous interesting illustrations, and that they had introduced him to the great writers of Russian literature, Pushkin, Chekhov and above all Gogol. But the foreign students left Liège in 1914, when Georges was 11, and it seems unlikely that they persuaded him to read all these authors before their departure. His real source of books was the branch of the municipal library run by an eccentric Walloon poet called Joseph Vriendts, which he did not begin to visit until 1915. If he turned first to the Russian authors, it was perhaps out of nostalgia for the vanished lodgers.

On 30 July 1914 Georges left the Institut St André covered with glory. Having come within the top three of his year for five years running he was one of only three pupils in the school to score nine points out of ten in the Christian Brothers' national examinations, so being placed in the top category, '*la plus grande distinction*'. In addition he was presented with a medal for heroism after saving his brother from drowning. Years later he recalled that the headmaster who gave him the medal told a lie in his speech about how the accident had occurred as he did not want to admit that boys from his school sometimes fell into the river because they had nothing better to do. But at the time Georges much enjoyed being the centre of attention, and most of the mothers present gave him a kiss. July 1914 was, after all, a good time for an 11-year-old to win a medal. Three days later Georges wrote a postcard to his aunt, Sister Marie-Madeleine, in the Ursuline convent at Ans, just outside the city. The postcard was a photograph of Georges in his costume as a drum-major, the part he had taken in a school play earlier that year. It bore a suitably martial message:

> *Chère petite tante,* War is declared! That is the cry that runs through the streets of Outremeuse. Father has been told to

report for duty. Uncle Arthur has been called up, Mother is stocking up and I am condemned to sit down with a stiff leg as I have water on the knee following a fall. We place our trust in God who brought our fathers out of the land of Egypt and who will once again blind the eyes of our enemies with his power. We hope to have some news of you soon. Your loving nephew Georges.

In the last two days of peace the trains passing through Liège on their way to Cologne were packed with young German men returning from Paris to rejoin their units. During those two days Georges could limp along to the end of the rue de la Loi, which was directly opposite the biggest cavalry barracks in the city, and from there watch the preparations. Among those who rode out from those barracks was Trooper Fonck, who was to become famous as the first soldier to be killed. On 4 August war really was declared. The troops rode out, pennants flying, bands playing, the clatter of hundreds of horses' hooves filling the length of the boulevard de la Constitution, a sight to stir the heart of any boy. Twelve days later, on 16 August, the line broke and the first scattered survivors came galloping back into Liège, followed by the Uhlans, the leading German unit, who brought with them defeat, humiliation and fear. It was the end of the innocent certainties of childhood.

TWO

The death of a childhood

At the end of the school yard a pitiless wall – like the wall of a prison.

Simenon, *Pedigree* (1948)

The First World War had a lamentable effect on Henriette Simenon's little boy. At the outbreak of hostilities he was a devout child who sometimes experienced mystical interludes; he was an altar boy, a star pupil at school, a conformist and vowed to the priesthood. At the beginning of the new school year, in September 1914, Georges was due to start with the Jesuits at the Collège St Louis where he had been accepted at half-price thanks to his precocious vocation. By the time the war ended four years later Georges was still only 15, but he had lost his faith, abandoned all thoughts of the priesthood, left school, started work, lost his first two jobs, and was certain that although he was not yet an adult he was a failure. He had also begun to make contact with that criminal world which was to fascinate him for the rest of his life. It was the war-time occupation of Liège which worked this transformation.

The first days of the occupation were the most frightening. Liège, protected by a system of forts, had offered determined resistance to much stronger German forces and was made to pay for it. Désiré's platoon was sent to guard the municipal abattoir, but before the line broke the men were ordered home and instructed to throw their rifles and cartridges into the river. One of the lodgers in the rue de la Loi who had enlisted was not so lucky and was killed before the Germans even reached the city when two Belgian battalions mistook each other for the enemy in the thick woods to the south of Liège and fought each other to a standstill. The first atrocity occurred at Visé, a little town only twenty kilometres north of Liège which had been a favourite spot for Sunday excursions. Visé guarded one of the bridges over the Meuse and its inhabitants put up a fight. When it fell, the Germans massacred the population and burnt the town. Some time later Georges and his mother came on the ruins of Visé when they were walking through the countryside in search of food. On Outremeuse itself, on the day of defeat, the Germans burnt the municipal library a quarter of a mile away in the rue de Pitteurs, the street where Georges and his grandfather used to bathe. They then lined up 200 inhabitants of the street and shot them. That evening the Simenon family retreated to the cellar in the rue de la Loi and slept on mattresses. They were joined by some neighbours whose house did not offer this refuge. In the wall of the cellar a barred shaft let in light from the garden and Georges's adult memories were always 'dark, an oppressive weight . . . the burning paper [from the library books] floating through the air like infernal snow . . . after the bombardment the Uhlans, the first to enter the city, we watched them pass in anguish, [from the cellar window] we could only see their boots'.

Once the Belgian army had fallen back towards the coast and the city had been abandoned, life gradually assumed a form that soon passed for normality. From the German point of view Liège was an important rail junction for supplies on their way from Cologne and the Ruhr to Lille and the Western Front. Fit Belgian men could be forced to work on the railway line; saboteurs were shot or, if they were not caught, hostages were taken and shot in their place; attacks on German personnel were followed by reprisals. But as the months became years, relations between *occupants* and *occupés* steadily improved. The German military governor in Brussels, General von Bissing, controlled the national and local press, and any newspaper that did not turn itself into a German propaganda sheet had to suspend publication. There was also a serious food shortage, but this affected both German soldiers and Belgian civilians, and eventually drew the two sides closer together. In contrast to the situation in northern France the German authorities in Liège did not have to requisition all the

billets they needed. Officers were authorised to pay for lodgings if
people would take them in, and among those who agreed to do so
was Henriette. They were, after all, soldiers in the army her father
had served in, and she had an entire family of German first
cousins. Against Désiré's strong objections she replaced some of
her missing students with the people whose arrival had cut off her
normal source of income. The Germans enjoyed easier relations
with the Flemish population of Belgium than with the Walloons,
which meant that the first *filles à boches*, as they were known in
northern France and among Walloon patriots, were generally
Flemish. But as time passed the whole city became more open to
the Germans. First the brothels, then the front rooms, and then
the bedrooms even of French-speaking Outremeuse welcomed
their quota of vigorous and hungry Bavarians or Rhinelanders.
These young men replaced in some cases the Belgian youths who,
having retreated with their units in 1914, escaped capture and
were carried off to France or England for the duration, among
them two of Georges's Brüll cousins. Occupation was a slow
process of corruption, of abandoned standards and compromises,
and this did not escape the attention of an intelligent boy.

Many years later Simenon was asked by Roger Stephane about
those war-time years and replied that they had provided some of
the happiest days of his life. He remembered 'the perfect happiness' of the afternoons spent reading and smoking and eating,
sometimes all at the same time. True the food had been a sort of
home-made cake, which he made himself out of his bread ration,
and ersatz honey, and the pipe had been packed with 'war-
tobacco' made from a mixture of acorns and oak leaves, but the
books at least had been of the highest quality. His interviewer
asked him if that was all he could say about the occupation of
Belgium, whether he had not felt humiliated by the presence of
German soldiers in Liège, and Simenon, visibly impatient with
this conventional piety, replied truculently that Belgium was
generally occupied by one army or another, that occupation was
the whole of Belgian history. He added that for a child the
occupation had been memorable because, 'In the first place everyone cheated . . . my father cheated, my mother cheated, everyone
cheated.'

Sometimes the deceits were minor and amusing. There was the
example of his mother teaching him how to smuggle vegetables.

Henriette and Georges would walk out into the countryside to buy the beans and carrots which were unobtainable in the local markets. Rationing had been imposed, it was strictly forbidden to bring black market supplies into the city, so Henriette would conceal the vegetables under her skirts. To pass back into Liège it was necessary to cross a bridge guarded by a German sentry who had been posted to stop vegetable smuggling. If she judged it necessary, and just before they reached the bridge, Henriette would mount a diversion. Georges would have to start causing difficulties as though he did not want to return to Liège. Henriette would smack him. Georges would burst into tears. Henriette would smack him again. The disturbance would increase and the scene would reach a point where the sentry would simply want this troublesome child off his bridge as quickly as possible. Later such farces became superfluous. In 1916 the Americano-Hispanic Commission for Relief to Belgium organised regular supplies of essential items of food, and it was not long before the housewives and sentries of Liège were both taking part in an effective black-market operation that ensured for a period at least adequate nourishment for all concerned. Before that, however, Georges had caught his father red-handed, breaking a strict family rule and taking an extra hardboiled egg on his way out of the front door. When asked if this had not lowered his father in his estimation Simenon said, on the contrary, he had been comforted by it, since it confirmed that 'there was no such thing in life as strict rules which applied in all circumstances'.

Such resistance as there was to the German occupation of Liège in the First World War was largely confined to smuggling information to the allies across the minefields on the Dutch border or smuggling letters back from Belgian soldiers on the other side of the front line, again through Holland. Much of this was organised by the Christian Brothers of the Institut St André, who risked their lives in the process. Their involvement was known to the Simenon family, who did not however become part of the conspiracy, playing the more typical role of occupied civilian populations and being chiefly concerned with surviving in the best conditions possible. Most of the time one did not have a choice. It was not a situation in which the inhabitants of the city were divided into 'us and them'. Civilians in Liège were not required to salute German soldiers as they were in northern France. Von

Bissing's strategy was to play on potential Flemish sympathies and encourage friendly relations with the people who were, he assumed, shortly to be absorbed, as the people of Alsace and Lorraine had been absorbed forty-five years earlier, into the Reich. Although Liégeois had to step aside for German soldiers on the pavement, and if they failed to do this they were immediately required to report to the *Kommandantur*, it is hard to imagine this rule being applied in the rue de la Loi, where the German soldiers in question were quite likely to be residents, on excellent terms with their host families. Simenon subsequently wrote little about this new group of lodgers although their power to impress a small boy must have at least equalled the attractions of Mlle Frida or Mlle Pauline. The only comment he later made about the German occupiers of 1914, which must have been based on domestic intimacy, was that it was surprising how many of the officers wore corsets.

Nonetheless the experience of living through defeat and occupation scarred Georges Simenon. Nearly twenty years later, in *Les trois crimes de mes amis*, he wrote:

> I think that the occupation of Liège marked a generation of young people as deeply as the post-war inflation marked a generation of Germans a few years later . . . Occupation is not a chain of events. It's an atmosphere, a state of things, it's a smell of barracks in the street, a moving stain of unfamiliar uniforms, it's marks in your pocket instead of francs, and an overriding concern – that dominates all others – about what you are going to eat. It's new words, unfamiliar music and mobile canteens along the pavements; it's the eye's subconscious habit of checking the walls for a new notice which tells you at what time the curfew begins, or what time men 18 years old and over should report to military headquarters – unless the notice is in red ink when it gives you the list of the latest civilians to have been shot . . . The anxieties of a 13-year-old boy under occupation are the same as they were before it began, but with additional anxieties superimposed.

Among such anxieties, some must have been based on the connection between the men who wrote the lists printed in red ink and the men who sat down to supper at the family table every evening in the rue de la Loi.

The fact that Henriette accepted three German officers as lodgers was also a matter of anguish for Désiré. As described in *Pedigree*:

> Désiré alone snubbed his guests, pretending not to notice them, while 'Elise' [Henriette] was busy from morning to night talking to them in a curious, voluble German which had returned to her from her childhood . . . 'I can assure you, Désiré, that they are just the same as any other people. It's only because you don't understand what they say . . .'

Once, on returning from the office, Désiré found a notice written in German in the window of his house, offering wine for sale. It was the only time throughout their marriage that Henriette thought that her husband was going to hit her. She told him that her brother-in-law Jean-Mathieu Schrooten, the wealthy grocer married to her sister Louisa, had written out the notice and supplied her with the wine. Désiré destroyed the notice and the name of Schrooten could not be mentioned in the house for some considerable time. Shortly after that incident the Simenons left the rue de la Loi and moved into a disused post office in the rue des Maraîchers. The move made Désiré's walk to the office longer, at a time when he was already beginning to feel ill, but at least there would be no more question of German officers as lodgers.

The immediate effect of the German occupation on Georges's life was to prolong the summer holiday. School, which normally restarted in September, was put back in 1914, and it was not until 5 October that Georges was registered at the Collège St Louis. He had a longer walk to school now – he had to leave Outremeuse and cross the river. Halfway along his route he would have passed his grandfather's hat shop in the rue Puits-en-Sock. In later years Simenon was to say that everything important that he had learnt at school had been taught to him by the Jesuits. The Collège St Louis was the high point of his academic career, but it lasted only one year. Georges ended that year with the catechism prize and an oratory prize. His French was rated 'very good'. This was not quite as high a place as he had obtained at the Institut St André, and he had yet again been beaten into second place by Joseph van Ham, as had happened every year since 1911, but it was nonetheless very satisfactory. His ability in French was well known in the school. According to one of his schoolfellows, Nicolas Thioux, it was '*époustouflant*' (staggering): 'Simenon would write pages and pages with ridiculous ease, and the other pupils used to ask him to do their essays for them, which he was happy to do.' The Jesuits eventually let Simenon choose his own essay titles. It was during his first year at St Louis that Georges also began to read widely. Because the municipal library in the rue de Pitteurs had been destroyed he now had to cross the river to inscribe himself at the library in the rue des Chiroux. This was directed by the eccentric poet Joseph Vriendts, who was generally dressed as a poet should be dressed, in a wide-brimmed black hat and voluminous cravat, and who was in the habit of walking absentmindedly along the river quays. Years later Vriendts remembered his youngest and keenest customer and 'how one could read the intelligence in his narrowed eyes'. There were strict rules about how many books anyone could borrow from the library and which books could be lent to children, but Vriendts, who liked to encourage children to read, soon arranged that Georges could take up to two books a day using his own library card as well as the cards belonging to his parents, his brother and, if necessary, the lodgers. The library records show that Georges borrowed up to ten books a week. Having devoured the Russians, he read Balzac, Dumas, Stendhal, Flaubert and Chateaubriand, then Fenimore Cooper, Walter Scott, Dickens, Shakespeare, R.L. Stevenson and Joseph Conrad. He claimed that he had been capable of reading three books a day when he was not in school, despite the discouragement of Henriette who was not convinced that library books were hygienic.

In July 1915, poised at this high point in his life, Georges set out for a summer holiday at the house of a friend of his mother's, who lived on the main road outside the nearby village of Embourg. There he found a 15-year-old girl staying in the same house. In *Pedigree* he called this girl 'Renée'. One very hot afternoon the two of them went into the woods overlooking the River Ourthe and found a secret spring. Then Georges climbed a holly tree to present Renée with a branch of berries. He scratched himself quite badly but got the berries. On his return to the ground Renée decided that he would need to be nursed back to health, which took some time. It was the end of Georges's sexual innocence, and it was also the end of his interest in religion.

On his last night in Embourg, Georges clambered round to Renée's room by the zinc canopy surrounding the first floor of the house and entered by the window. That night she set him a further task, which was going to need more ingenuity than picking holly berries. She suggested that they could continue to see each other if he changed schools. The Jesuit college of St Servais, which served the left bank of the River Meuse, was in a neighbouring street to her convent school. If he were to become a pupil there they could walk home together on the dark winter nights across the park in the boulevard d'Avroy. Georges had fallen in love. He was 12 years old and he had two weeks to make the arrangements while Renée ended the summer holidays in Ostend with her parents. What he needed to find was a plausible reason. Georges discovered that the only difference between the two colleges was that at St Servais the Jesuits offered a science course which was not available at St Louis. But as a prospective priest he would not be studying science. Very well then, he would abandon the idea of the priesthood and tell his mother that he wanted to become an army officer. He was certain his mother would approve of that alternative if the priesthood were no longer a possibility. Army officers had titles. And they did not have to attend university, which was too expensive for Georges's parents anyway. The problem was money; once he said he no longer wanted to become a priest his parents would have to pay the full school fees and they could not afford to do so. Then Georges discovered that the Jesuits did sometimes allow half-price for other pupils as well. Furthermore his father had been to St Servais and had passed out with sufficiently high marks to be taken on immediately as an accountant in an insurance bureau.

When Henriette was persuaded that Georges no longer had a vocation, and once she heard that it might be possible to get reduced fees at St Servais as well, she adopted her son's cause and her persistence carried the day. On 14 September 1915 Georges was struck off the school register at St Louis and entered on the register at St Servais. He had gathered his second branch of holly berries, the miracle had come to pass. Both his parents and two headmasters had been persuaded that he had lost his vocation and that he had developed a serious interest in a military career. The Jesuits were allowing Désiré a one-third rebate instead of 50 per cent. It remained only for Georges to wait outside the front gates of the Ecoles des Filles de la Croix after his first day at school until the moment when Renée came out, eager to be once more in his arms. Georges did this. He managed to get to the gates at the right time, even though both schools came out at 4 p.m. Renée arrived at the gate as arranged. His heart leapt. He stepped forward, she stepped forward, and someone else stepped forward, a young man, rather older than Georges, perhaps someone she had met during her two weeks in Ostend. Renée and the young man disappeared down a side-street arm in arm, and Georges had to return to his new interest in scientific studies. The way to disaster lay straight ahead.

In later years Simenon wrote of his mother's family 'plotting' to make him a priest. He also claimed that he had considered the priesthood as he had considered the army, because they were the only two professions which would have offered him the income and the leisure necessary to write. Perhaps the 11- and 12-year-old Simenon was already planning a writing career in terms of the necessary leisure and income, a wise head on' young shoulders, but the alternative explanations for his interest in both professions are more plausible. At least the idea of Simenon as a priest is a diverting one. Even if the priesthood had provided him with the opportunity to write, and so proved a satisfactory career from his point of view, the Church must be counted as having had a lucky escape. Had he become a priest, the type of priest he might have become was depicted in one of his earliest novels, *Jehan Pinaguet*, where we meet the Abbé Chaumont, a learned voluptuary who had been retired from active parish duties more or less in disgrace. As it was, the Church was spared another spent priest, and the novels written by the Abbé Simenon could hardly have been more strange or powerful than those written by Georges. He was not to admit an interest in religion again until he was an old man; religion became merely one childish interest that was in due course replaced by others.

In his three years at St Servais, Georges received no prizes. His marks fell lower and lower although he continued to excel at French and his teachers continued to allow him to choose his own essay titles. He started to sign his essays 'Georges Sim'.

Otherwise he spent more and more of his time in the town, among the pleasures of the streets. In less than a year the star pupil of 12 became a 13-year-old truant and a petty criminal. The impulse which had been strong enough to make him break his links with his religion, his original schoolfriends and his mapped-out future did not allow his imagination to remain confined within the school walls. The school was a prison to him now. In one of his novels, *La neige était sale* (*The Stain on the Snow*) he was to compare a prison to a school and to describe the prison in terms that closely resembled the Collège St Servais. He hated the look of the place, describing it as '*vulgaire*', and it is much the same today. On summer evenings the boys and girls play football together in the vast, echoing courtyard caught up in the same intense, roman-tic emotions of adolescence which overthrew Georges's school career. His relations with the teachers, with the exception of the French teacher, Père Renchon, were not good. Georges started a satirical magazine, a roneoed sheet, the second and final issue of which carried a cartoon of the director of studies. For this Georges was summoned by the priest in charge of discipline, reminded that he had only been accepted in the school on special terms and threatened with expulsion. The interview with Père Van Bambeke made a lasting impression: '"Have you a sincere inten-tion of amendment?" "Yes, Father . . ." What a resounding No would have rung round the room if his real answer had been audible.' Faced with expulsion, and his father's sadness, Georges was still prepared to play the game of the adult world with a diplomatic lie. But he took a strong dislike to Père Van Bambeke, a former cavalry officer and the most formidable figure in the college. Simenon considered that he was a snob and noticed that he treated the richer pupils, one of whom came to school on a horse attended by a groom, better than social nonentities such as himself. Simenon eventually settled his accounts with Père Van Bambeke twice – first in a satirical newspaper, *Nanesse*, to which he contributed two years after leaving school, and later in his autobiographical novel *Pedigree*. Both Père 'Van Bambeck' (*Nanesse*) and Père 'Van Bambeek' (*Pedigree*) are former cavalry officers, and both have an ingratiating manner with the richer pupils and show an inflexible meanness towards the poor ones. The money which some of his fellow pupils had access to, even during months of semi-famine, also caused Georges to burn with resentment. He felt an outsider. He had to eat in the municipal soup kitchen where people queued up for a bowl of liquid which tasted of grease and washing-up powder. In this situation Georges started to steal money so that he could buy food which tasted better, but it was to be three years before he was able to steal enough to afford the expensive *pâtisserie* outside the school gates.

Georges first stole from the till in his grandfather's shop. Once he had started to take money he found that playing truant became more amusing. During school hours, in a school where he made no friends, he began to scrape through his classes, reading Dumas or another favourite author under the desk in German or maths classes, and then escaping whenever he could to watch the matinée at a music hall. Crossing the town twice a day, and outside the boundaries controlled by the Jesuits, he found a world full of distractions. He recalled these in *Mémoires intimes*:

> I wandered often early in the morning or late at night in the crowded streets or on the green hills nearby . . . I was hungry, hungry for everything, the sun's reflections on houses, trees and faces, hungry for the women I came across the sight of whose swaying hips was enough to give me almost painful erections . . . Above all I was hungry for life.

If the influence of school was diminishing it was not being compensated for by any influence in the home. Georges's loss of his religious vocation also marked an important step away from his mother. In the rue des Maraîchers, Henriette, not Désiré, was the figure of authority, a situation which her older son did not appreciate at all. Georges tried to defend his father against a wife who complained all day about everything. He could not understand why his father refused to become indignant on his own behalf. The war between Georges and his mother became almost incessant. He began to see his mother as a domestic tyrant who was victimising both his father and himself with her emotional blackmail, dowsing any moment of family happiness with her unquenchable fountain of private sorrows.

As the occupation became better established in November 1914 and the front line was stabilised over 160 kilometres to the south-west, it became possible for the people of Liège to leave the city and travel in the immediate countryside. There was no problem about spending the summer at Embourg, or even going to the coast at Ostend, although travel into France was restricted and it was dangerous to approach the Dutch border, which was heavily mined. It was, however, possible for Georges to visit the Brüll family's former home on the Zuid-Willemsvaart Canal, even though it was only a few hundred metres from Holland. Here at last was the farm on the banks of the canal which had been the home of Wilhelm and Maria Brüll for the twelve years immediately following their marriage. Henriette had never lived there but when her father went bankrupt and departed her mother's sister took over the house, and the irrigated lands that went with it, and the duties of dyke-master that made the property such a valuable holding. In 1971 Simenon claimed, in a curious lapse of memory, to have visited the house when he was 6, that is in 1909, and to have found his grandfather 'Henry' living there. His grandfather, who was called Wilhelm or Guillaume, had left the house in 1867 and had died in 1885, so this story will not do. Rutten has narrowed the date of the visit which Simenon made with his mother to Christmas 1915 or Christmas 1916. The object was straightforward enough, to obtain supplies of food, but the atmosphere in the house by the canal was oppressive and it made a lifelong impression on the little cousin from the big city who was then either 12 or 13 years old. This was the darkest Limbourg, the misty, sinister, enclosed land with its private rites and needs, from which his mother's family had emerged, to generally disastrous effect. Here were the Peeters, cousins of the Brülls, in the natural habitat of this 'tormented race'. Here were the people to whom he might so easily have belonged himself.

Georges's only visit to the *maison du canal* was followed in the autumn of 1917 by a return visit paid by one of the boys from the *wateringen* to Liège. The two cousins, Georges Simenon and Alfred Peeters, started to make black-market liquor, a practice strictly forbidden by the German military administration. It was Georges's introduction to drunkenness. The product which they made was a mixture of genuine liqueurs with water and raw alcohol, and since the only way to invent it was to taste it the results were disastrous. There was a brothel in the rue des Casquettes near the school gates, but this was staffed by young girls from the country and reserved for German army officers.

Instead Cousin Alfred and Georges, their pockets full of money
from the sale of poisonous 'chartreuse' or recycled car batteries,
would pick up half-starved girls who in normal times would still
have been at school, and take them anywhere dark and undis-
turbed. Alternately there were the women sitting in the windows
of their front rooms, knitting placidly and waiting for a knock at
the door. The image of one of these women stayed with Georges
for many years:

> She was in her thirties, very beautiful, a brunette with a sallow
> complexion, her hair was always tumbling down. I only ever
> saw her half-dressed, her pale blue silk dressing-gown parted
> carelessly so that one could glimpse her breasts and thighs.

Once the cousins ended up drinking in a café with some friendly
German soldiers, and Georges imagined his father's anger if he
had known where his son was. The girls he spent his time with
sometimes mentioned another of their customers, a sinister figure, '*un vicieux*' with original tastes, who carried a German *laissez-
passer* and who claimed to have the authority to carry out medical
examinations on behalf of the military authorities. They said that
he ran a bookshop, and Georges recognised the description of
Hyacinthe Danse, the bookseller to whom he had started to sell
his school textbooks and who kept a 'flagellation shelf' at the back
of the shop. Danse was one day to employ Georges and was to
become the second of his acquaintances to be convicted of
murder.

It was by now obvious to both Désiré and Henriette that
Georges was out of control. On most evenings he would return
late from some sordid adventure. Once he came home to find an
elderly and venomous female lodger sitting up to greet him.
Famously drunk, and in front of his mother, Georges proceeded
to tell the old lady what he thought of her, ending with the
words, 'If there was any justice it would be old dregs like you
who would be sent to the battlefields to die in place of the
soldiers.' Désiré, lying ill upstairs, was too tired to intervene. The
days were long gone when he would come striding through the
door of his house after a day's work and, still full of vitality and
optimism, say, 'Have you been crying, Henriette?' When there
was no one in the house to intervene between Georges and his

mother the scenes could reach hysterical levels and be accompanied by physical violence. Henriette would scream at her son
that she wished she were dead, then roll on the floor in her rage
and frustration. On one occasion she threw Georges down and
stamped on him.

Désiré, unaware of all this, could still be found in the evening
'sitting in his shirt sleeves by the hearth, in his wickerwork
armchair which creaked, surrounded by a cloud of cigarette
smoke, reading his newspaper'. If he was no longer the heroic
figure of strength he had once been he still tried to protect his son.
If Georges spent the night out Désiré would get up early and
disturb the sheets on his bed, and tell Henriette that he had heard
him going out early, perhaps to study, perhaps to Mass. Since
Georges could no longer cast his father in an actively heroic role
he developed a different sort of admiration for the parent he
adored, a secret complicity. 'No one ever understood what passed
between father and son,' he wrote later. 'There had only ever been
the two of them.'

By the summer term of 1918 Georges had serious problems at
home and was certain that he was about to be expelled by the
Jesuits. Then, on the morning of 20 June, he received a message at
school asking him to call in at the house of Dr Léon Fischer, the
family doctor, on his way home. When he did so it was to be told
that his father had suffered a heart attack, that it was *angina
pectoris*, then an incurable condition, and that Désiré could not be
expected to live for more than a few years at the most. Simenon
subsequently said that the doctor told him that he would have to
leave school at once and start work, as he would shortly become
the sole support of his family, and this is the version which has
passed into the Simenon legend. But it seems unlikely that a
family doctor would have been able to instruct a 15-year-old boy
to leave school, particularly as Georges was due to take his end-
of-year examinations in a month's time. Any attempt to find a job
could only have been helped by the fact that he had completed
that year's schooling. There was no reason stemming from
Désiré's illness that required Georges to leave on the day of the
diagnosis. Apart from anything else, the fees would have been
paid to the end of term. It seems more likely that he himself,
backed up by a panicking or distracted Henriette, decided to leave
the Collège St Servais that very day. For Georges it was freedom

at last, the end of a miserable way of life. His father's death
sentence had liberated him, and by forcing him to solve the
family's predicament had turned him into a man.

Unfortunately Georges's exhilaration did not last. It was not
very long before Henriette found a position for him as a pastry
cook in the *quartier* of Longdoz, where his last successful schooling, at the Collège St Louis, had taken place. The first consequence of this appointment was, of course, a weekly pay packet
which, however small, would have been riches after the pocket-
money and stolen small change of his schooldays. But despite
Henriette's encouragement – 'Have you ever heard of a poor
pâtissier?' she would say – the prospect of a lifetime of *pets de nonne*
was no more attractive than the priesthood. In *Je me souviens*
Georges was not kind about his mother's insistence on the
pâtisserie:

> A neat little shop with a bell attached to the door. You can hear
> it from the kitchen where you are busy about your daily tasks.
> Wonderful music! You wipe your hands. You make sure there
> is no stain on your apron, you pat your *chignon* subconsciously
> and you smile as you approach the counter. 'Good day
> Madame Plezer . . . Fine weather isn't it? What will it be
> today?'

He must have seen his life closing in on him with frightening
speed, and he left after two weeks. He said in old age that he could
still remember how to make a St Honoré cake.

After some weeks of idleness Georges obtained a second job, in
a bookshop, the Librairie Georges in the rue de la Cathédrale,
which was run by an elderly man, L. George-Renkin. The work
was at first sight more interesting, but there was a disadvantage.
Unlike the *pâtisserie* the bookshop was visited regularly by people
Georges knew. Apart from his wealthy cousins Sylvie and
Berthe-Marie, a constant stream of former school fellows came to
borrow books, as the shop also ran a library service. Georges felt
humiliated but was determined to keep the job. However, his best
intentions were thwarted after one month by L. George-Renkin
in person. Georges had the misfortune to contradict his employer
in front of a customer about the correct authorship of a book by
Alexandre Dumas. Although, as with Père Van Bambeke, he was

perfectly prepared to swear that he had been wrong, he found himself being shown the door. 'Goodbye, Monsieur Simenon. I wish you luck and a little more respect for your elders.' M. Renkin recovered his dignity but Georges took a multiple revenge by recounting the incident on numerous occasions, recalling the old man whose hands, 'with bulging veins', counted out his pay-off. He had, however, learned one lesson from his experience with L. George-Renkin. There was no need to continue apologising when he was not in the wrong. It did not work.

Georges was now at the low-point of his life so far. He was 15 years old. He had lost two jobs. His father was seriously ill. He had no qualifications and no money. He had a deteriorating relationship with his mother. There was a world war going on, and it was drawing closer. The Hindenburg line had been broken by British and French troops on 30 September and the fighting was now only eighty kilometres from Liège. In the city hints of defeat and chaos were everywhere. On the boulevard de la Constitution German troops were confined to barracks. Their place was taken in the streets by liberated Russian POWs, and two of these found lodgings with Henriette. Georges, wearing a jaunty hat, a wing-collar and a watch chain, and with a cigarette at the Jean Gabin angle years before Jean Gabin, had his photograph taken with a group of these Russians. He is dressed like a dandy and shows all the jaunty confidence of youth, but behind the façade he must have felt less sure of himself.

One day in November 1918 Georges went to the Palace music hall with the Russian lodgers. It was to an afternoon matinée, typical of the aimless life he was leading. It was here, from the stage of the Palace, that he heard the first news of the Armistice. There followed one of the most dramatic evenings of his life. Still a boy, he found himself in the centre of a city that had gone wild with joy and hatred, and that gave itself over to every excess. In *Pedigree* he described the scene:

> Despite the rain the streets filled with a crowd that grew wilder and wilder . . . suddenly, like a signal, there was the noise of breaking glass. It was the window of a charcuterie whose owner had worked for the Germans. Men surged into the shop and started throwing out hams and sausages. Then they started

to throw the furniture from the first- and second-floor windows, wardrobes, beds, a dressing table, a piano. The police
did not know what to do as the streets filled with looters
carrying their booty away. 'Smash what you like but don't take
anything,' one sergeant shouted out.

Earlier, in *Les trois crimes de mes amis*, he had written about the
same events:

In the quiet street people suddenly started running and shouting
and I can once again see a dishevelled woman vainly trying to
escape from her pursuers as they literally threw themselves on
to her. For several minutes there were indistinct movements, a
swirling, gestures which one could not make out from a distance, then there was an almost respectful silence as there is at
an execution, broken only by the weeping of the woman who
no longer had the strength to resist. And then, among all the
people in clothes, the woman's naked body appeared, seeming
even more naked in the street's cold light and on the hard grey
of the pavements . . . Another woman, from the market,
armed with scissors, stepped forward and cropped her hair to
the scalp, and she was forced to walk between the houses while
a hundred people followed. Nobody asked at the time whether
it was more comic or tragic, and nobody wondered what the
reactions of the soldier would be when he returned from the
front in a day or two and found his wife's head shaved and so
discovered that she had given herself to the Germans. Every
week there were parades and patriotic ceremonies, and on
every farm the pigs were rechristened Wilhelm after the Kaiser.

'Wilhelm' had been Georges's grandfather's name. He was still
15.

THREE

The boy columnist

Forget about Georges . . . He's a suicide case.
Published comment on Simenon (1921)

With the Armistice came the end of controls on the Belgian press. Liège once again had six newspapers, but very few journalists. The papers which had reopened at the end of November still lacked the staff who had died in the war or who had not yet been demobilised; there had effectively been a five-year freeze on recruiting. Among the newspapers which were once more free to publish was the *Gazette de Liège*. The paper had been edited since 1910 by a barrister, Joseph Demarteau III, who had succeeded his father, Joseph Demarteau II. On the surrender of Liège the *Gazette* had refused to continue publication under German military direction, since this would have meant, in the language of the Belgian criminal code, 'working for the occupying forces'.

There are several versions of how Georges Simenon started the job that was to launch his career and settle the course of the rest of his life. According to the authorised version one day in January 1919, just before his 16th birthday, having nothing in particular to do, he was crossing the place Verte when his eye fell on a sign on the corner of the rue Official, 'GAZETTE DE LIEGE'. Without knowing why, or what he was really doing, he went into the newspaper office and asked for a job. A few weeks earlier he had been reading the adventures of 'Rouletabille', detective stories by Gaston Leroux about a young crime reporter which were then at the height of their popularity. Simenon later said that he had even taken to dressing like Rouletabille, in a snap-brimmed hat, a mackintosh and a pipe. At other times Simenon said that when he entered the newspaper office asking for a job as a reporter he did not even know what a reporter did. Once inside, Simenon was interviewed either by the editor, Joseph Demarteau III, or by one of his veteran assistants, Désiré Drion, Demarteau being away that day. There is authority for both versions. Either he was invited to enter the editor's office or he pushed his way in uninvited. Once inside he was either told to write a short essay in which he misspelled the word 'Bazaar' as 'Bazard' but which was nonetheless so good that he was hired on the spot, or he was told to go away and report something he found happening on the following day as if it were for the newspaper. He frequently claimed that to the *Gazette* he was an unknown youth who had walked in off the street; in fact his uncle, Jean-Mathieu Schrooten, and M. Demarteau were on the board of the same bank, the Crédit Populaire Liégeois, and knew each other well. Whatever the truth about his approach to the *Gazette*, Georges reported the first horse-fair held in the city since the Armistice, which took place on 6 January, and his work was duly published. At the age of 15, he had found the perfect job.

Simenon was extremely fortunate in his editor, Joseph Demarteau, who noticed his talent and encouraged him to make the most of it. There was nothing grudging or envious about Demarteau's treatment of Simenon; he put up with behaviour which would frequently have justified the dismissal of his undisciplined junior reporter, but which only seemed to amuse Demarteau, who could be strict but who remained fair and generous. Simenon was to spend four years working for him. It was the chance of a lifetime and he made the most of it. Suddenly he was presented with all the life of the city, behind the scenes as well as on the streets. He was able to discover a great deal about human behaviour and for this education he was paid a reasonable wage. Above all he was encouraged to exercise his main talent, writing. In an interview in 1960 he explained what the chance had meant to him:

A traffic accident which alters the course of numerous lives, some violent drama which overturns a family; the prowler, the hooligan, the drug addict who runs out of supplies, the politician fishing for votes, a decent man looking for a medal or an appointment or any form of recognition which will enable him to drag himself out of the rut . . . Isn't it something for a kid to be plunged into all that? Suddenly all the doors are open . . . one can read the secrets of life. One runs up, notebook in hand, to the corpse which is still warm, one chases police cars, one brushes shoulders with the handcuffed murderer in the corridors outside the court, one mingles with strikers and the unemployed . . . One minute I was just a schoolboy. I crossed a threshold, I introduced myself in a trembling voice to a bearded gentleman with dirty fingernails, a man who was a sort of oracle for the local population, and suddenly the world belonged to me.

At first Georges worked as an office-boy while learning how to compose news reports, but he learnt fast. The first signed piece, by 'Georges Sim', the pseudonym he had used for his school essays and which he was to keep for the next twelve years, appeared on 24 January; a book review followed two days later. The *Gazette* was right-wing and Catholic, although Simenon later claimed that had it been anti-clerical and liberal he would not have noticed the difference. The place of the *Gazette* in national politics never interested him. At home as a child his father had read only a rival newspaper, *La Meuse*.

The junior reporter started with the jobs which the other two reporters did not want. These included coverage of the endless series of patriotic memorial services which ran the course of 1919, the surfeit of which may have helped Simenon to form his disenchanted views about the official celebration of patriotism. His routine duties were to telephone the police stations twice a day to find out what was going on. He went to work most days on a bicycle, setting out from the family home which was now back on Outremeuse after the two years in the rue des Maraîchers. The latest address was in the rue de l'Enseignement, an extension of the rue de la Loi, scene of most of Simenon's childhood, and to get to work each morning he passed the gates of the Institut St André, crossed the bottom of the boulevard de la Constitution, down which he had once run to serve daily Mass, crossed the River Meuse at the Pont des Arches, and then cycled down the rue Léopold where he had been born. At the *Gazette* he was soon directed to take over the crime reporting, which meant that, in place of the twice-daily telephone call, he attended each morning at the Commissariat Central behind the town hall, joining his colleagues from other newspapers at the daily press call. By April, Demarteau was sufficiently pleased with his work to give him his own daily column, and in November this was named '*Hors du Poulailler*' (From outside the Hen Coop), which Simenon signed 'M. le Coq'. The title was supposed to alert the readers to the fact that this was a column of unorthodox comment and personal opinion.

Simenon had to be at work by 10 a.m. and by 11 he had to be at the police station. So he had less than one hour in which to write his column of 300 words, but at least he had the choice of subjects. It was a significant timetable because it liberated him from the journalist's addiction to the last-minute deadline and accustomed him to finishing the most important part of his day's work early. These two habits were to be of use to him throughout his life. At first he wrote with pen and ink, the typewriter still being reserved for specialists, and he took notes in longhand; later he developed a private system of shorthand. Then, as now, Belgian and French reporters rarely took shorthand notes (which explains the rich variety of quoted sources in the continental press, even in the court reports). And he quickly found a professional model for his work. The *Gazette de Liège* received copies of newspapers from Holland, England and Paris – which city alone had more than forty daily newspapers at this period. It was the post-war heyday of France's Third Republic and no serious politician in Paris could expect to prosper without the support of his own newspaper. Among the Paris papers was *Le Journal*, and its star columnist, Clément Vautel, was Liégeois. 'His fame impressed me,' Simenon wrote later, '. . . perhaps the more so because I passed his brother's hairdressing shop every day. Because of Clément Vautel dozens of young Liégeois set out for Paris in search of a daily newspaper column and fame and fortune. And that was pretty well my case . . .' The choice was clear. Fame or the corner shop.

As a crime reporter Simenon quickly made the acquaintance of the city's examining magistrates and so inherited one of the great patrimonies of European journalism, the breach of the '*secret de l'instruction*', that is, the opening up of the prosecution's files for the use of newspaper reporters before the trial. This illegal but widespread practice in France, Italy and Belgium is justified by the examining magistrates on the grounds that it encourages the collection of new evidence and improves the chances of a conviction by softening up public opinion (including the opinions of the members of the jury). Whatever its consequences for the prospects of a fair trial it is manna from heaven for the newspapers, which are provided with authentic and fascinating material which they can publish without fear of any legal comebacks. It has led to a style of reporting which has no British or American equivalent; dramatic, taut and fruity, it frequently provides the best daily reading in even the up-market press. One of Simenon's first cases was a double infanticide known as 'the affair of the house on the Quai de Maestricht'. Simenon interviewed the neighbours, described the scene in the bedroom of the woman who had murdered two of her own children, and mingled with the crowd of women outside the prison shouting, 'Put her to death! Death!'

Simenon's debt to the various examining magistrates in charge of the cases he was reporting was usually discharged in the form of some complimentary references in his copy. One of them was called Coméliau, the name Simenon was to give to the pompous and fussy examining magistrate in the Maigret stories. Eventually he wrote a story about an examining magistrate who had himself been burgled. Having reported this grave matter on the front page under the byline 'Georges Sim', the paper printed on the usual inside page the less responsible thoughts of 'M. le Coq'. Le Coq mocked the victim of this burglary and added that it was a lamentable sign of the times when the city's magistrates, who were in charge of fighting crime, became the targets of it. He added that the next thing one knew a policeman's house would be broken into. Sure enough, four days later, 'Georges Sim' reported that a policeman's house had been burgled, a coincidence that may have provoked the interest of a suspicious policeman.

In later life Simenon denied that he had ever done any serious research into police methods before writing his Maigret books, apart from spending the odd afternoon with some friends in the Paris CID. In fact in 1920–21 the young reporter enrolled as an extra-mural student and attended a series of lectures at the University of Liège on the new science of forensics. Big cities throughout Europe had been criminalised by the experience of the Great War and by the arrival of the new army of unemployed and morally damaged survivors. The authorities awaited an explosion of crime. Modern means of transport and communication were being put to use by criminals, casual violence was commonplace and against all this the police had had little new to offer.

In Lyons Dr Edmond Locard, one of the fathers of forensic science, had founded the first police laboratory, and his ideas were being taken up in other countries. The fame of the 'Laboratoire de la Police Scientifique' had reached Liège, and Locard's system of fingerprinting had replaced the earlier charts of the ninety different shapes of the human ear which had been drawn up by his predecessor, Professor Lacassagne. In Liège the forensics lectures were given by a police surgeon called Dr Stockiste whose first subject was '*dactyloscopie*', or fingerprinting, with its three astonishing facts – that fingerprints could be traced, that they were different for every individual, and that they remained the same from birth until the putrefaction of the flesh. The systematic collection of fingerprints had just started in Belgium, where police held 50,000 sets of prints. In Paris there was already a collection of 4 million prints. Among those who routinely ignored the new technique were criminals, who were unaccustomed to working with gloves, and police, who were still not used to taking care that they did not destroy the fingerprints. Simenon mentioned this last problem in one of two articles he subsequently wrote for the *Gazette* about '*la police scientifique*'.

For Simenon, these lectures must have been a poignant experience. They are the only evidence that he ever entered the buildings of the University of Liège, the institution to which he could certainly have gone if his parents had been able to afford the fees and if his father had not fallen ill. It was also the university attended by several of his Brüll first cousins – for them the gateway to professional fame and fortune, for him the symbol of everything he had lost since the outbreak of war. Maigret too failed to attend university (where he would have studied medicine), and, like Simenon, he missed the opportunity because of the premature death of his father. Simenon's attendance at the series of lectures on forensic science would have made him, for a brief period, better informed than many policemen. That he never subsequently admitted that any of his knowledge of police matters came from academic study suggests a mixture of resentment, exclusion, and a pride in his own achievement that may have counted for much in his subsequent success.

When he started on the *Gazette de Liège* Simenon was paid 45 francs a month. This figure was steadily increased to match his growing responsibilities. Not surprisingly Simenon could not remember the exact figures when he was asked about them years later. He remembered the total in his first pay packet; he also remembered that after about a year he was earning 180 francs a month, the same as his father. But elsewhere he claimed to have been earning 250 francs a month by the end of his third month. At other times he claimed that the journalists on the *Gazette de Liège* were always the worst paid in the city. It depended on which point he wanted to make to which interviewer. The money enabled him to buy his own clothes for the first time in his life, but it did not enable him always to buy clothes that were a perfect fit. They tended to look better on the dummies in the shop windows than they did on him. And his new wages did not make him rich. Despite the fact that he had more money than ever before, he was usually overspent and would have to go to the accountant to ask for an advance on his monthly salary. If this means was exhausted, he could always go to his father's office, fifteen minutes' walk away in the rue Sohet, to ask for a small loan, which he invariably got. It is some measure of the extent to which Simenon was enjoying himself that, while Désiré on the same salary and seriously ill managed to run a household, pay for Christian's schooling and lend money to Georges, the latter could not even make his wages last out the month.

The first of his amusements was alcohol, and Simenon's first regular drink was English beer. With one of the clerks from the *Gazette* he would leave the building at about 5 o'clock. They went to a nearby café, where they would order three small bottles of beer – one pale ale, one light ale and one Guinness. They shared this out, mixing it according to taste and talking about nothing in particular for about an hour. 'He was not terribly intelligent but he was good company,' Simenon said later of his first drinking companion. The evening would then continue with other friends in a cabaret or a nightclub, and Georges soon got into the habit of not bothering to go home for dinner on the grounds that he was still working for the newspaper – which he sometimes was. On one occasion, deputed to report a lecture by a Jesuit priest, Père Rénus, a lecture which he had heard many times before, Simenon wrote his report from memory and spent the evening with a girl. Unfortunately the lecture was cancelled and he was appalled to see Père Rénus outside the editor's office when he arrived for work next morning. One of Simenon's favourite clubs was called 'L'Ane-Rouge', a place which he remembered for its friendly girls 'with bare shoulders, who pulled their skirts up to straighten their stockings'. The boy who had always found so much to interest and amuse him in the streets was now continuing to seek adventures in the same streets, but at a later hour. He had still not learned the rules of drinking. He was several times sick, either over his clothes or in the bed after returning home. Sometimes, to vary the pattern, he would be sick on the hall floor. In all of this his mother reacted predictably, while his father continued to cover up for him. Frequently, on arriving home late, he would find a note on the kitchen table: 'There's some ham in the larder and a slice of apple tart in the cupboard. Goodnight. Father.' That was all the reproach he got from his adored father. On one occasion, which he later bitterly regretted, Georges, passing as usual a brothel in the boulevard de la Constitution on his way to work, saw a magnificent Negress in the parlour window in place of the usual person. Seized with an urgent desire to couple with the Negress, and having no money on him, he paid instead with a watch which his father had given him a short time before. It was perhaps the only time that he regretted having paid for a *passe*. It was a silver watch, engraved with the Belgian arms, which his father had won in a sharpshooting competition. Simenon never forgave himself for giving it away.

On another occasion his drinking nearly cost him his job. Sent to cover an official banquet by the *Gazette*, he found himself at the press table with older colleagues from *La Meuse* and *Le Journal de Liège*. They, bored with the speeches, encouraged their young companion to drink. When he had reached the right degree of confusion one of them, Ferdinand Deblauwe, whispered in his ear, 'This is really boring, don't you think? What a bunch of old fools . . . Why don't you tell them so?' Immediately Simenon was on his feet, shouting, 'God this is boring; you are a bunch of old fools.' A few moments later he found himself out in the street with his helpful colleague Deblauwe at his side. They went to the theatre where there was a show on. Entering by the stage door Simenon started backstage by tickling the dancing girls. Then, shouting, 'That's the one I want,' he followed one of the girls on to the stage in the middle of a number. Having been thrown out of the theatre as well he somehow found his way back to the offices of the *Gazette* where, inevitably, he started to be sick in the hall just as M. Demarteau arrived. The solicitous editor offered him a black coffee, whereupon Simenon turned on him and, as recounted in *Les trois crimes de mes amis*, first called the editor a '*cochon*', and then threw the coffee on to the floor and called him 'a whited sepulchre with a nose like a strawberry'. He then lay down and fell fast asleep.

Next day, with no memory of what had happened but a distinct feeling that there was going to be trouble, Simenon reported to the office. 'Well, my little Sim,' said Demarteau, 'you understand what this means, your behaviour yesterday?' Simenon replied that he imagined he was going to be sacked. Then, deciding to make the experience as enjoyable as possible, he said that since he could remember nothing about the evening except pursuing a dancing girl across the stage during a performance, he would be glad if M. Demarteau could remind him. 'You little hypocrite,' shouted Demarteau, 'what about this revolting strawberry in the middle of my face! I demand your resignation.' But when Simenon had given it Demarteau relented. 'All right,' he said, 'we'll give it one more try. But no more banquets. You're still a bit young for that.'

'M. le Coq' was now an accepted member of a colourful group of reporters whose behaviour in court at a big criminal trial in June 1921 he described as follows:

The journalists here are just as they are everywhere else, that is to say very much at home. Their arrival, one by one, causes a considerable disruption. They always choose to come in by the barristers' entrance, greet the policeman in a friendly way, run their eyes over the public benches, shake leading counsel warmly by the hand and finally reach the press bench. There, turning their backs on the judge, they greet their colleagues and exchange the latest news before finally removing their hats in the courtroom . . . They form a small, closed circle which lives very much at its ease. There they sit, sharpening their pencils,

munching chocolate, swapping jokes, until suddenly the trial
takes an interesting direction and they start to scribble furiously
. . . Seized with a constant thirst and less respectful of the court
than the jurors, they frequently break off between sentences to
swig from bottles which they have brought into court, right
under the judge's nose . . .

But Simenon's life as a reporter was not entirely frivolous. He
also made a certain contribution to the *Gazette de Liège*. He
interviewed the Crown Prince of Japan, Hirohito, later to become
the Emperor Hirohito, and then came his proudest moment as an
interviewer, the only time in Liège he himself claimed to have
secured a scoop. Early one morning in March 1920, just a year
after he had started on the paper, M. Demarteau telephoned
Simenon, the only reporter available, to tell him that Marshal
Foch was in Brussels and might be on his way to Liège. 'Go to
Brussels at once and interview him,' said the editor. At that time,
Simenon recalled, Marshal Foch was a bronze statue on a horse as
far as he was concerned. 'But what questions should I ask?' he
said. 'Ask him if he will be going to Warsaw,' said Demarteau.
Unknown to Simenon, the point of this question was to discover
whether or not France was about to offer aid to the Polish
government, which had already lost territory to the newly
formed Soviet army and which faced the active threat of a Russian
invasion. In fact a Franco-Polish treaty was to be signed three
months later. As Jean-Christophe Camus has pointed out, there
are two entirely different accounts of the subsequent interview
with Marshal Foch, both by Simenon.
    In the first, which was published in the *Gazette de Liège* on 9
March 1920, the intrepid 17-year-old reporter told how he had
broken through the line of dignitaries on the platform just as the
official train arrived, and how, ignoring the furious gestures of the
station master, he had shaken 'the Victor of the Marne' by the
hand and accompanied him to his car, asking him whether he
would be going to Warsaw and receiving a very lengthy answer.
'I have indeed decided to go to Warsaw,' Foch told Simenon. 'Do
I not have a duty to greet the Polish army, the only Allied army to
which I have not yet rendered homage? I am not yet quite certain
of the date of my journey . . .' etc. etc.
    But in *La main dans la main*, written in 1978, Simenon recalled

that he had been unable to get near the Marshal at the station so had waited until the train began to leave again and had then sprinted along the platform and jumped on to the running board of the Marshal's private carriage. An aide-de-camp had seen him through the window and, since the train was gathering speed, had taken pity on him and let him in. He had then been given 'two minutes' with the Marshal:

> He looked me up and down from head to foot. His face was as impassive as in his photographs or on one of his statues. 'What do you want?' . . . I stammered out the editor's question. *'Monsieur le Maréchal*, will you be going to Warsaw?' And after a moment's hesitation he replied with a monosyllable, 'Yes.' When I returned to Liège I did not feel particularly proud of myself . . . I was surprised by the enthusiasm of M. Demarteau who said, 'It's a sensation' . . . I did not realise it then but it was the first sign of France's unconditional support for Poland, the origins of the phrase 'To die for Danzig!' and the beginning of the 1939 war.

Asked to choose which of these versions is the correct one, the biographer might well reply 'Neither'. The problem with the first is that the quote is clearly invented. No one would produce such a rotund answer to an unexpected question from a strange reporter on a railway platform. It is the answer for a formal occasion like a press conference, but had there been any such occasion then clearly the *Gazette* would not have had the story to itself. Presumably the quote was invented back in the office by M. Demarteau. But if the quote does not ring true, the means of obtaining it is considerably less unlikely than in the second version. Leaping on to running trains to get personal interviews with great men is the stuff of fiction, and if *'le petit Sim'* had indeed survived such an experience and returned with his monosyllable why did he not say so in his subsequent account? It would have been far more impressive than defying a station master's instructions. There is of course a third possibility, that Marshal Foch was never asked the question because Simenon was unable to get near him, and that the young reporter, having a shrewd idea which was the more interesting answer, duly provided it. Would the young man have been capable of inventing an interview with

Marshal Foch? The answer must be 'yes'. It may be unjust to
suggest that there is something unsatisfactory about the scoop
with Marshal Foch, but speculation is invited by the contradictory
accounts.

The following month, as Jean–Christophe Camus has revealed,
Simenon took the opportunity to mock his own 'scoop'. In his
column '*Hors du Poulailler*' he wrote:

> The only current ambition of many journalists seems to be to
> obtain an interview with any old personality. What the so-
> called personality says is of relatively little importance. The
> essential thing is that he say something . . . even one sentence
> will do . . . Still personalities and interviewers have to find
> something to do with themselves.

A few months earlier, in November 1919, 'Sim', who had been
working for the paper for ten months and was still only 16, was
chosen to carry out a delicate task. The first post-war legislative
elections were about to be held and it was necessary to introduce
the *Gazette*'s chosen candidate to the readers. He was called Jules
de Géradon, and was a member of the clerical party as well as
being one of the *Gazette*'s major shareholders. However, he had
no political experience and no gift for public speaking. Clearly if
he was going to be elected he would need a hand. Simenon later
claimed to have been put in charge of the *Gazette*'s campaign, but
there is only one published article in which Sim purported to have
interviewed de Géradon on the banks of a canal where the candidate was fishing. Simenon had discovered by asking questions at
the town hall, one of his favourite methods of investigation, that
the city's largest private association was the Anglers' Club. His
'interview', which was wholly imaginary, was simply an attempt
– possibly successful – to win the anglers' vote. Simenon presented both the candidate and himself as fervent anglers and
painted a picture of a man who was so engrossed in the movements of his float that he could be persuaded to repeat only the
major points of his programme. It was in fact an early but
sophisticated form of image-building. Shortly after this Simenon
received an offer from a rival newspaper, *La Wallonie Socialiste*, to
join the staff, with the promise that when he was 21 he could
become a socialist candidate in the local and then the national

elections. He was never seriously tempted but he later admitted that he had thought about it for a while before saying 'no'. Certainly his efforts on behalf of M. de Géradon were effective. The clerical candidate was duly elected, possibly fêted by thousands of grateful anglers, and in 1922 Jules de Géradon became chairman of the *Gazette de Liège*.

In July 1919 Simenon looked on as a mob tried to kill a hotelier. The incident started when a waiter, a demobilised soldier, was fired from his job in the Hôtel Schiller for cheating the customers. Later that day he returned to the hotel to have it out with the *patron*. The proprietor's son, defending his father, beat the waiter up badly and a number of soldiers drinking in the bar got it into their heads that an ex-soldier, wounded in the war, was being attacked. They started to wreck the hotel. A riot ensued, the father and son opened fire on the crowd, the *gendarmerie* were called and a gun battle broke out between the forces of law and order and the besieged hoteliers. One of Simenon's fellow reporters, Ferdinand Deblauwe, was shot, the hotel was looted and set on fire, the fire brigade was called and then the army. The father was eventually overcome and arrested but the son, who had disappeared into the building, was hunted by the mob. The riot which had broken out in the early afternoon continued into the evening. Eventually the crowd spotted the hunted man on the roof of a neighbouring building trying to find a refuge through an attic window. While the crowd bayed, 'Kill him, kill him!' a *gendarme* clambered over the sloping roof and tried to persuade the hotelier's son to give himself up and be taken to safety. In 1963 Simenon said to Roger Stephane that this incident demonstrated one of the unpleasant facts about war, that all defeated countries need an excuse, which is why they hunt for traitors when they are liberated.

However, his views as a young man were less detached. In April 1921 the main trial of Liège's war-time collaborators started at the assize courts and Simenon reported it for the *Gazette*. The accused was called Douhard and his offence lay in the fact that he had assisted the German forces to hunt down and round up members of the Belgian Resistance. He had been given police powers by the Germans and had gone so far as to carry out summary executions of captured resisters. The extent to which he was joined in this work by hundreds of other Belgians, men who had changed sides and placed themselves at the disposal of the victors before the victory was confirmed, was glossed over during the trial, and Douhard was made to seem a uniquely horrible example of treachery, instead of an extreme example of a general tendency to acquiesce in the fact of the occupation. For Belgium in 1921 Douhard was one of the supreme villains, denounced most loudly by some of those who hastened to camouflage their former opinions in the new orthodoxy.

This aspect of the matter escaped the normally acute Simenon, whose mother had of course taken in German lodgers. In any event, his reporting of the trial shows no sign of an intention to do anything but please the popular taste. Perhaps he found the overwhelming atmosphere of the lynch mob too strong to withstand. On the day of the death sentence 'M. le Coq' amused himself at the expense of the doomed man, suggesting a national competition for the makers of insecticide:

> Each of them should experiment with his product on the Douhard in question. Clearly the powder which succeeds in exterminating him would be an exceptional insecticide . . . This competition would at least ensure that Douhard could still be of some use.

It was to be some years before Simenon adopted the motto '*Comprendre et ne pas juger*'.

Five days after the ending of the Douhard trial the first of a series of seventeen articles on another patriotic theme appeared. It was headed '*Le péril juif*'. As Jean-Christophe Camus has pointed out, this was, by some way, the longest series of articles Simenon wrote on any subject during his four years with the *Gazette de Liège*. The articles were a classic statement of the intellectual anti-Semitism of the period, the '*anti-Sémitisme de l'esprit*' as it was known in France, as opposed to the vulgar '*anti-Sémitisme de peau*'. Quoting the authorities of the period, including the forged 'Protocols of the Elders of Zion', Simenon identified Judaism with various materialistic developments in contemporary civilisation and with Bolshevism, referring in support of the last point to the large number of Soviet commissars and German revolutionaries who were Jewish. He made a distinction between Germans and German Jews on the grounds that the patriotism of the latter was based on economic interests. He added that 'the slow political reaction which is running through the German empire today is accompanied by a strong current of anti-Semitism'.

In 1985 Camus wrote to Simenon asking him to explain his views as expressed in '*Le péril juif*' and received a reply which stated:

> Those articles in no sense reflected my opinions either now or then. I was instructed to write them and I had no choice. At that time, among the Russian and Polish tenants at my mother's, more than half were Jewish and I got on with them perfectly well. All my life I have had Jewish friends, including the closest friend of all, Pierre Lazareff. Therefore I am not in the slightest bit anti-Semitic, contrary to what these commissioned articles might lead a reader to believe.

As a politically committed, right-wing and ultra-Catholic newspaper, the *Gazette* referred to the Jewish people as '*déicides*' and regarded anti-Semitism as a respectable intellectual position. It was not long before Simenon showed abundant evidence in his writing of a broad and quick sympathy for the plight of European Jews, and not just for well-established French or Belgian Jews, but for Jewish refugees, people whose plight led to their being expelled or interned. At the time when he wrote '*Le péril juif*' he was a politically inexperienced and intellectually naïve young man, uncritical of the anti-Semitic views of his employers and capable of regurgitating pre-Nazi theories with spirit and conviction.

The foundation of 'Sim's' reputation in Liège was his column '*Hors du Poulailler*'. But beneath his jauntiness Simenon sometimes worried about his ability to write a column and secretly measured his own work against the column written by an older friend, Georges Rémy:

> He was six or eight years older than me and he had taken his classical 'bac' and then a university degree in philosophy. We each wrote a daily article. His was undoubtedly better written than mine, enriched by intellectual subtleties and studded with Latin and Greek quotations and references to historical charac-

ters whom I had never heard of and whom it took me a very long time to learn about.

Simenon allowed none of his diffidence to show in public, from the start adopting an unusually sophisticated style. One month after the column had been launched he felt confident enough to write, 'It is of course well-understood, is it not dear readers, that in this little corner we can talk discreetly?' The column showed a sturdily reactionary tendency. It attacked the American influence on the cinema – 'From Charlie Chaplin to Douglas Fairbanks these types are teaching us to think and live like citizens of the New World' – and it mocked the introduction of the telephone, complaining about the frequency of wrong numbers and the fact that creditors would now find it much easier to chase debtors. But quite early on Simenon was also showing signs of boredom with his duties. By November 1920, less than two years into his career, he was comparing the work of a daily columnist to that of 'a poor devil who has been condemned to hard labour for life', and it is true that in 1920 he contributed 314 columns, one for every day of the year on which the paper appeared. Later, he was to mock the influence of his articles: 'a few lines lost in the corner of a newspaper, stuck between an advertisement for skin care and a three-line news-story'. He soon found a way of compensating for this boredom.

Encouraged by his success with '*Hors du Poulailler*', Simenon developed ambitions to become a humorous writer. His first fictional works were short stories, which were published by the *Gazette* in May 1920. Three of these related incidents between a husband and his dominating, nagging wife. They were his first published fiction and the first evidence of his tendency to use autobiographical material in his fiction. The story which he published on 24 June 1920 was headed 'A Husband Who Killed His Wife'. Nearly fifty years later, in one of his last novels, he was to return to the same theme. Another story was about an imaginary friend who had made a fortune by recycling chewing gum which he scraped up off the pavements.

It was also in May 1920 that Simenon started work for the first time on a novel, which he finished by September. This too was a humorous work, called *Au Pont des Arches*, and it was illustrated by four of his friends who were artists: Luc Lafnet, Jef Lambert,

Joseph Coulon and Ernest Forguer. It was this book which was partly set in the chemist's shop which specialised in laxatives for pigeons. Simenon passed this shop, the Pharmacie Germain, every day on his way to work. For about six months he searched for a publisher for his book. Eventually he found a printer who agreed to undertake the job if the 17-year-old author could assemble a list of 300 subscribers. *Au Pont des Arches* was sold by publicity on billboards and M. Demarteau, who was among the subscribers, noted with his usual forbearance that the book contained a satirical attack on himself.

Following this successful start Simenon wrote a second novel, *Jehan Pinaguet*, heavily under the influence, as he later said, of Rabelais. But this time he managed to overstep the mark. While he was once again looking for a publisher he showed the book to Demarteau, who may have heard rumours about one of its characters. The search for a publisher was successful, but Demarteau decided that the portrait it contained of an epicurean priest who had been put out to grass for suspected heresy and alcoholism could not be published by the star writer of Liège's leading Catholic newspaper, and the book was never printed. In *On dit que j'ai soixante-quinze ans* Simenon recounted the conversation: "'*Mon petit Sim*, you can choose. Either you publish your book and you leave us, or you abandon the project and you stay with us." As I knew no trade apart from the reporter's, I abandoned it.' One of the scenes which therefore never entered literature was a description of an incident which Simenon had occasionally witnessed in the streets of the poorer quarters of Liège during his childhood, a violent dispute between two women:

> Pinaguet drank in the show. What magnificent muscles and flesh this marketwoman possessed. Through an open slit in her dress she momentarily revealed her armpits, which were pouring sweat. He was filled with admiration at the sight of her heavy breasts swelling up through her blouse and her white teeth which gleamed in the sunlight.

In the novel the arrival of the police prevented the scene from developing in the way Simenon had observed in real life, when the two participants, urged on by an interested crowd, proceeded to strip each other and wrestle together, half-naked. The spectacle of a half-naked marketwoman was bound to fascinate the young Simenon, combining, as it did, two of his main interests in life – food and sex.

Jehan Pinaguet was followed by another unpublished, and unfinished, work, *Bouton de col*, which was written in collaboration with his friend H.J. (Henri) Moers and was a parody of the Sherlock Holmes style of detective story. Simenon's detective, an Englishman, was called 'Gom Gutt'. The method of composition chosen by the two authors was to pass the manuscript back and forth, each taking turns to type or write as much as he wished. While this chaotic procedure meant that they both enjoyed themselves greatly, it did not lead to the production of a book. Re-reading it many years later, Simenon considered it so bad that if he had received such a manuscript through the post he would have advised its author to take up another profession. Although *Bouton de col* was never finished it confirmed Simenon's taste for satire. And it marked another departure. For the first time the hero of the book was not a young man living in Liège but was a personage, drawn, however fantastically, from an entirely imaginary world.

In November 1920, shortly after completing *Au Pont des Arches*, 'Georges Sim' started submitting signed articles to a new periodical called *Noss' Perron*. The motto of this paper was 'Belgians first, Walloons for ever', and Simenon's contributions appeared from the first issue. In one of his early articles Sim rebuked an imaginary mother of Liège for smacking one of her children who was speaking the Walloon dialect rather than good French. He urged her instead to let the child learn both languages. *Noss' Perron* was a paper dedicated to the Walloon cause, and to the glory of Liège, and 'Sim' firmly established his own Walloon identity in writing for it. But within a year he had fallen out with his collaborators and their friendship had been replaced by a bitter quarrel. In July 1921 the Belgian government passed a law which established Flemish as an official Belgian language and which made the country effectively bilingual. The francophone community did not welcome this development, and Walloon activists soon dubbed it the 'Von Bissing Law', in reference to the former German military administration which had also favoured Flemish. The quarrel was to some extent another consequence of the war–time occupation. *Noss' Perron* was in the forefront of the campaign against the establishment of Flemish, but in the *Gazette de Liège* Sim wrote several articles in favour of the new linguistic régime. The result was his expulsion from the pages of *Noss' Perron*. 'We counted you as one of us. But your contribution was only temporary. From now on, whether you want it or not, the pages of this paper will be closed to you,' wrote one of his former friends. There was a further attack, this time in Walloon. 'Forget about Georges Sim. He's a suicide case,' the magazine concluded about its most talented contributor. Simenon never mentioned this rejection in his later writing, but it is likely to have marked him. He had defended his Flemish heritage and been made to suffer for it.

FOUR

The death of a journalist

We were a little group of geniuses thrown together by chance.
Simenon, *Le pendu de St Pholien* (1931)

To his family and employers Simenon, in 1920, was a young
newspaper columnist who had begun to publish fiction. But there
was another side to his life which he was less anxious to publicise.
The man who introduced him to it was one of those he met at the
morning meetings at the Commissariat, Henri Moers, a reporter
on *La Meuse*. Simenon recalled the event in an article written in
1953,

> That Sunday [in June 1919] was probably one of the most
> important days of my adolescence . . . I still see myself, with
> my hands in the pockets of my overcoat, crossing the foot-
> bridge over the Meuse then turning left at the corner of the rue
> de la Régence and the rue de la Cathédrale . . . If Moers had not
> been waiting for me at the corner of the rue Louvreux I doubt
> whether I would have had the courage to ring the bell at the
> door of the enormous mansion where Luc Lafnet lived with his
> parents . . . Lafnet was the centre of attraction for every aes-
> thete, writer and dilettante in Liège . . . From that day on I
> became part of his group which called itself 'La Caque'.

'La Caque', originally 'Le Cénacle', later 'L'Aspic' – and there is
an accurate picture of the development of the group in its changing names – was originally formed by two smaller groups who

met in the bar called 'L'Ane-Rouge' in the rue sur-la-Fontaine. It
was not far from the Beaux-Arts, not far from the newspaper
quarter and not far from the university. 'L'Ane-Rouge' was the
nearest thing to Montmartre for the bohemians and students and
young artists of the city, and Luc Lafnet became their leader by
force of achievement and personality. When others were still
beginning their work Lafnet had a large house full of canvases. He
was already giving shows that were sell-outs and he talked as
impressively as he painted, being unusually well read. Following
Lafnet's influence the two groups known as 'Les Rapins' (the
daubers) and 'the Bohemians' began to meet regularly. At first
they went to a loft in the rue Basse-Sauvenière, which was
directly between 'L'Ane-Rouge' and the Académie de Beaux-
Arts. This was in 1917. Their proceedings were informal but
followed a pattern. According to Léon Koenig in *L'histoire de la
peinture au pays de Liège*:

> In about 1917 among young people a sort of romantic despair
> towards events seemed to take hold and become the fashion.
> That was when this brotherhood of painters and writers sprang
> up, distinguishable by its uniform of floppy hats and long
> cravats. They attempted to treat their 'overwhelming stupor'
> with endless debates about aesthetics or walks through the
> woods on the heights of Sart-Tilmann (to the south of the city)
> and psychic experiments. They were trapped in the atmosphere
> of dread and rejection which characterised that unhappy period.

In *Au-delà de ma porte-fenêtre* Simenon wrote in 1978:

> What did we talk about, all through the night, so passionately,
> as though the fate of the world depended on it? Philosophy. We
> devoured the philosophers. I remember one whole night was
> spent discussing the most famous phrase from Socrates, 'Know
> thyself' . . . On other occasions everyone would bring a text or
> sketch and pass them round. We would compare our work to
> Villon, Baudelaire or Verlaine, or Goya or Delacroix.

As 'Le Cénacle' degenerated into 'La Caque', so-called after the
herring barrel into which the herrings were stuffed so tightly that
there was no room left to move, the proceedings also degener-

ated. Their meetings moved over the river to Outremeuse, to
another loft, over a carpenter's shop which was reached via a
passageway and a dark sinister staircase:

> There was no electricity, an oil-lamp lit the scene, the only
> furniture was an old mattress, one or two broken-down chairs
> and a rickety table. Everyone brought a bottle, of either wine
> or spirits, and someone would bring some dry cake. For hours
> on end we would discuss the essential questions, God, philoso-
> phy, art . . . life and death and Michelangelo, heaven and hell.
> Our views were necessarily either gloomy or desperate . . .

Later still:

> We turned to *chiaroscuro*, motley and death's-heads, to make the
> atmosphere more menacing, and we would drink more to
> make it wilder. We addressed God and Satan in familiar terms
> while repressing a shudder, and we made love to 'Charlotte' to
> convince ourselves that making love was a repugnant act.

Lafnet, the young genius with a head drawn by Goya, was
capable in this atmosphere of producing the following lines:

> For you, these verses, Satan . . .
> Now show me your rump.
> Your sorcerer's haunches,
> The sorcerer's haunches which lie with Beelzebub.
> I want my erotic blasphemy
> To be sucked into the gluey swamp
> Of their aroused sex
> And I want to drink the blue-green sperm
> To their slippery rhythm.
> So, Satan, show me your rump.

That was in 1919.

To add to the excitement and debauchery it was only necessary
for drugs to be included in the programme, and this became
possible through the assistance of a man known to his acquaintances in 'L'Ane-Rouge' as the Fakir. 'One day,' Simenon wrote
in his *Dictées*, 'one of us met up with a sort of guru whom we

The Simenons of Outremeuse on 4 September 1900, just before the solemn profession of 'Aunt Louise' (Sister Marie-Madeleine) as an Ursuline nun. (Back row l. to r.) Jean Charles Coomans (sacristan), his wife Aunt Françoise Simenon, Uncle Lucien Simenon (cabinet maker), Désiré Simenon (accountant and father of Georges), Uncle Arthur Simenon (cap maker), Uncle Guillaume Simenon (umbrella maker, later barred from the house by his mother after his divorce and remarriage), Aunt Céline Simenon (aged 14½). Grandfather and Grandmother Simenon are seated on either side of Aunt Louise. At this stage Lucien, Désiré, Arthur and Céline were still living at home with their parents.

The Flemish side of the family, Grandfather Wilhelm (Guillaume) Brüll born in Prussia, and Grandmother Maria Brüll, born in the Dutch Limburg. 'The Simenons took life as a straight line . . . the
Brülls came from a tormented race.'

Désiré and Henriette Simenon, with Christian and Georges in 1910. Simenon worshipped his father. 'No one ever understood what passed between father and son.'

A pageant at the Institut St André in April 1914. Georges Simenon, aged 11, stands centre-front holding the staff.

Street scene in Liège at the turn of the century. A food and flower market in the place Cockerill. Henriette and Georges crossed the River Meuse by a footbridge to shop here every week.

Three altar boys from the chapel of the Bavière hospital. Georges (centre) would run through the streets on dark winter mornings to serve the 6 a.m. Mass.

At home in the rue de la Loi the house filled with student lodgers. Lola Resnick (left), 'the fat Caucasian . . . pulpy as an exotic fruit', and Frida Stavitskaïa from Odessa (right) a medical student specialising in morbid anatomy, later a Soviet commissar.

The house (left) in the rue de la Loi that stood directly opposite the school gates. Georges Simenon (below left), out of work in occupied Liège, November 1918, a 15-year-old black marketeer. And the man who gave him his chance, Joseph Demarteau III, barrister and editor of the *Gazette de Liège*.

We were 'a little group of geniuses, thrown together by chance.' Members of 'La Caque' in 1919. 'Le petit Kleine', who died in March 1922 hanging from the latch of a church door, is ringed.

The shabby district in which the bohemians of 'La Caque' held the sessions attended by Simenon at which Josef Kleine was drugged and hypnotised. Simenon wrote a newspaper report of Kleine's death, identifying it as suicide and not mentioning that he had spent the previous evening in Kleine's company.

In December 1922, wearing his poet's uniform of long hair and a loosely knotted cravat, Georges Simenon, aged 18, resigned from his newspaper, left Liège and took the night train for Paris. His first job was as an office boy.

1928. Within five years of his arrival 'Georges Sim' (left) had become one of the most prolific and popular writers in France, producing up to forty-four pulp novels a year. (Below) An evening at 'La Coupole' (l. to r.) 'Mrs Georges Sim' (Tigy), 'Georges Sim', the cabaret star Josephine Baker, Pepito Abatino (Miss Baker's manager), a fan. Simenon conducted a passionate affair with Josephine Baker, possessor of 'the only bottom that laughs'.

Henriette Liberge, known as 'Boule', the 18-year-old fisherman's daughter from Bénouville, Normandy, who became Tigy's maid and Simenon's mistress, here dressed as a cabin boy.

Portrait of her husband by Tigy, made in the summer of 1927 on the Ile d'Aix where he had gone to get away from Josephine Baker.

Simenon aboard the *Ostrogoth* before leaving Paris in March 1929 on the voyage north through the canals of Belgium and Holland during which he would develop the character of Commissaire Maigret.

La Richardière (above), near La Rochelle, the house which Simenon and Tigy lived in but could not buy. Christian Simenon (left) in the Belgian Congo in 1932 with his newborn son, 'Georget', named after Georges. Simenon later complained that this made it impossible for him to name any of his own children Georges.

Tigy and her Great Dane on a beach in the Vendée. 'In the region of La Rochelle I found exactly the light of Holland, the radiance you find in the skies of Vermeer.'

By 1935 Simenon had placed
Maigret in retirement and was
wealthy enough to set off with Tigy
on a world tour. They went to
Tahiti where he met 'Mamata', here
seen relaxing on the beach with a
friend's foot. The photographer,
Simenon, was wearing a sunhat.
Simenon enjoyed Tahiti.

called the Fakir and who came from I don't know which Asian country, and who was always up to his eyeballs in morphine.' According to Henri Moers this meeting took place in 1921. And according to Simenon in *Les trois crimes de mes amis* he himself had been introduced to the Fakir and to his young familiar, Joseph Kleine, by Ferdinand Deblauwe:

> The Fakir was capable of hypnotising most of us and he put one of the youngest and weakest of the painters in a state of catalepsy. There was no trickery involved. We laid out our friend Kleine with his head resting on the edge of one chair and his heels resting on the edge of another. His body stretched over the intervening gap was so stiff that one could sit on it.

The Fakir supplied Kleine with cocaine, and the little painter, forced by poverty to earn a living as a house decorator, became addicted to it.

Apart from poetry, drink and drugs 'La Caque' had two other amusements at its disposal. One was evidently sex. Apart from Charlotte there was a girl called Henriette who slept with most of the group. (Simenon later complained that he missed his chance with her because he was obliged to work late one evening at the *Gazette*.) There were also other girls associated with the group, but they were '*filles sérieuses*', and often of good family to boot, and there was no question for them of dalliance with more than one young man at once, however much they were committed to anarchism, the revolution and the death of the bourgeoisie. After Simenon's death one of them, Andrée Piéteur, who later married another member of 'La Caque', the painter Joseph Bonvoisin, remembered the writer as he had been at that time:

> We were both 17 [that is in 1920]. He was a big boy with blue eyes and wavy hair. He had a lot of charm . . . I was going out with Bonvoisin but serious girls did not interest Sim. He was looking for something else. He actually preferred whores. There was a district near 'La Caque' where they worked and he would come and tell us about his adventures with them. In the evenings we used to read aloud a lot, Anatole France and Nietzsche. We would talk about all that. Some of us were

broke. With their big hats, and their long pipes and their ideas, they were the last romantics.

Or as Simenon himself put it: 'We were an élite. A little group of geniuses thrown together by chance.'

'La Caque' had a symbol, the scorpion biting its own tail, which is sometimes taken as a symbol of eternity but could also be seen as a symbol of suicide. And the painters in the group had a theme which almost became an obsession: the hanged man, normally dangling not from a gallows but from the gargoyle of a church. The earliest surviving trace of this symbol is in an erotic and satanic painting by Luc Lafnet of 1918, called 'The Haunted Castle'. It is a watercolour done in the style of an illustration to a medieval fairy story – but not the sort of fairy story which Henriette Simenon would have read to her children. The central figure is of Innocence, a beautiful young girl, being led by a prince across a moat towards the gateway of a walled city. Ahead of this couple walks Death, attended by devils. A black cat stalks Innocence past the outstretched bones of what appears to be a living skeleton, who is surrounded by skulls. The Prince, against whom the girl is leaning so trustingly, has, protruding from the hem of his robe, a reptile's tail. Over the whole scene, suspended from a stone gargoyle, hangs the body of a young man.

The image of the hanged man remained sufficiently powerful for another painter associated with 'La Caque', Robert Crommelynck, to include it in a collection that was published in 1930. In this case only the feet of the body are visible, framed, with the end of a rope, in a gothic window which looks out over a river landscape. The picture is entitled 'Water's Edge'. In the following year the image appeared again, this time on the cover of the second Maigret novel, *Le pendu de St Pholien* (*Maigret and the Hundred Gibbets*). Again the body is suspended from a gargoyle. In a self-portrait made in 1919, Lafnet varied the theme by showing a cat swinging from a staff by a rope attached to its neck. A human skull, perhaps his own, is peering over the artist's shoulder. Simenon referred to the power of the image in *Le pendu de St Pholien*:

[Maigret] was haunted by the pictures . . . by the hanged men dangling everywhere, from the church cross, from trees in a wood, from a nail in a garret; they were grotesque or sinister, crimson or pale, decked out in clothes of every age.

Only one picture of Kleine's is known to have survived, and it does not show a hanged man but the face of a Bacchante who could well have found himself at home in Lafnet's haunted castle. The presence of 'M. le Coq' at these meeting shows that the chirpy columnist had begun to develop a second, less conventional, personality.

Among those who occasionally joined 'La Caque' was Ferdinand Deblauwe, the journalist on *La Meuse* who had urged Simenon to follow a dancing girl on to the stage and who had been wounded during the hotel riot. One day in October 1920 Deblauwe told Simenon that he had a proposition to make that would be worth a bit more than spending the evening locked up in a garret talking nonsense and drinking bad wine by candlelight. Deblauwe was going to start a satirical magazine. It would be backed by a wealthy Romanian and its motto would be 'A newspaper written by journalists, not by politicians or bankers'. 'Sim' could write what he wanted to write – in fact he could write the whole paper if he liked, because Deblauwe intended to write nothing. Simenon would be paid at twice the rate paid by the *Gazette* and his name did not have to appear on the masthead.

Simenon was delighted with the new arrangement and immediately took the opportunity to use the paper, which they called *Nanesse*, to settle scores which he was unable to settle in the *Gazette*. Among his first targets was the majority shareholder of the *Gazette*, the man he had done so much to assist in the elections to the Chambre des Représentants, Jules de Géradon. 'Until the elections,' the anonymous contributor to *Nanesse* wrote, 'M. de Géradon monopolised the pleasure to be had from his particle, his rents and his paunch. Then he decided to place two of these pleasures, the first and the last, at the disposition of his fellow citizens. As for the second he intended merely to increase it.' The article went on to mock M. de Géradon for his stance as the anglers' friend and concluded on a note of great friendliness: 'To sum it up, he is not at all a bad chap, and certainly has no more brains than a pickled herring.'

When Henriette was shown the first number of *Nanesse* she is supposed to have said, 'You should be ashamed to be writing in such a rag.' But the paper had an immediate success in a city which had forgotten what it was like to enjoy the benefits of a muck-raking newspaper. *Nanesse* was not above making friends as well as enemies. There were further signs of Sim's collaboration in a friendly profile of his first patron, the librarian and poet Joseph Vriendts, and in a defence – for once – of the *Gazette de Liège* against accusations that at the beginning of the occupation the paper's management had allowed the German authorities to use its presses to print a collaborationist newspaper. (In fact when the *Gazette* ceased publication for the duration its plant was commandeered by the Germans.) In defending the *Gazette* against this charge Sim was of course defending his friend Demarteau rather than the new chairman of the board, de Géradon. When he was asked in later life about his contributions to *Nanesse* Simenon twice professed to have 'vague memories' of the period. While he was writing for it and living in Liège this discretion was understandable; any later discretion was doubtless connected with the fact that *Nanesse* quite quickly deteriorated into a 'blackmail sheet'. And it had the unusual distinction among newspapers in Europe or North America or anywhere else of being edited by two men who were later to be convicted of murder.

Simenon's collaboration with *Nanesse* did not last very long. Once again it was Joseph Demarteau III who intervened. Concerned by the attacks on M. de Géradon and by the fact that his star columnist's association with *Nanesse* was becoming general knowledge, he instructed Simenon to sever his connections with the magazine in November 1921. By this time the Romanian had disappeared and his money had dried up. He had funded the paper to settle a couple of scores of his own. Having inserted some unsigned items about the private affairs of a rich Liégeois, and having been paid off, recouping his investment and making a handsome profit, the Romanian had left the country. With his departure, Deblauwe resigned as editor in favour of Hyacinthe Danse, the '*vicieux*' so well-known to the child prostitutes of the occupation. Danse then tried to pull the same trick as the Romanian. And the paper which had set out 'to clean the Augean stables' quickly gained a reputation for refilling them. Both editors were quite quickly forced to leave the country. Deblauwe abandoned journalism and turned to pimping. He left Belgium for Paris and then for Spain. In July 1931, when his girl turned to a

rival pimp, Deblauwe murdered this rival in Paris, then fled back
to Liège. Deblauwe had been a friend, not just a colleague, of
Simenon's, and the two of them, both coming from Outremeuse,
had often walked to work together, since Simenon's route lay past
the ironmonger's shop belonging to Deblauwe's parents. The
friendship was apparently broken when Simenon left Liège, but
when Deblauwe was eventually arrested and tried in Paris in 1933,
Simenon followed the story closely. Ferdinand Paul Joseph
Deblauwe was found guilty of the murder of the gigolo and pimp
Carlos de Tejada y Galban by the Seine Assizes on 10 October
1933 and condemned to twenty years' hard labour; 'extenuating
circumstances', that is, jealousy, saved him from the guillotine.

Nanesse eventually crashed in 1925 and in 1926 Danse was
sentenced to two years for blackmail and criminal libel. He was
on the run at the time of his trial, so avoided prison. By 1932 he
was living in Boullay-les-Trous, a little village to the south of
Paris, with his mistress and his mother, and styling himself the
'Sage of Boullay', an expert in black magic. Here on 10 May 1933
he murdered both his mother and his mistress. Then, realising
that this time he would certainly be caught and guillotined, he
took the train to Liège where on 12 May he tracked down his
childhood confessor at the Collège St Servais, the Jesuit Father
Hault, and murdered him as well. He hoped that this meant that
he would be tried in Belgium for murder, where there was no
death penalty. And so it happened. In due course he was condemned to death in Liège in December 1934 for murder and the
sentence was commuted to life imprisonment, which meant that
he could not be extradited to France until he was dead.

These two men, Deblauwe and Danse, very nearly played a
decisive role in Simenon's life. It had been Deblauwe who had
introduced Simenon to the brothel where the girl Deblauwe was
later to murder worked, and Deblauwe who had presided over
the disastrous evening when '*le petit Sim*' had pursued a chorus
girl across the stage. He had walked to work with Deblauwe and
enjoyed the company of girls in the same brothels. Deblauwe also
had a daily newspaper column and had once worked as a journalist in Paris. He was 30 years old, '*un beau garçon*', handsome,
'with delicate features, and a curled-up moustache and slightly
precious mannerisms'. If Simenon had fallen in love with a prostitute he could easily have gone the same way as Deblauwe and

Danse, both of whom came from 'respectable' families as he did; Deblauwe's family were also *'petites gens'* from Outremeuse; Danse had gone to the Collège St Servais. But what really bound them together, what gave them their fascination with crime, was the shared experience of occupation. They had lived through it and it had marked them. In *Les trois crimes de mes amis* Simenon recalled the shape of that scar. It had been a time when an entire school class had been arrested after the death of a little girl, a little girl who had been brought to school by her brother 'to be used as a test bench' by each of the boys in turn. It had been a time when fathers were ruined within a few days, when suicide was common, when boys whose fathers were away at the war watched their mothers taking a German lover in order to eat. Each family weighed out the bread allowance and each parent and child watched the others to make sure they did not cheat. 'We used to count out the potatoes on to each plate, and I forged a pass key to my parents' loft so that I could steal sugar lumps.' And after the liberation the whole city had seen that none of the real profiteers was arrested but that, on the contrary, they had consolidated their success and established themselves and their families comfortably for life:

> When I was 11 years old I was rushed down into the cellar because they were shelling the city, and suddenly we all heard cries and a hundred yards away they were rounding up 200 civilians, chosen at random, and shooting them up against the walls of our houses . . . We were taught to cheat and defraud and lie . . . we were taught how to live in the shadows and how to whisper . . . and they told us, the children, to carry letters around the town which had come from the other side of the front line, and which a grown-up would have been shot for carrying.

Simenon, on M. Demarteau's insistence, left *Nanesse* just before things got serious, while the other two stayed on and 'put their heads down and pushed on towards a life of crime'. But all his life he continued to enjoy one pleasure he had learnt in the company of Deblauwe, and that was a preference for the company of prostitutes.

But it was not only Joseph Demarteau III who saved Simenon. One evening in December 1920 he was drinking with some friends from 'La Caque' when they met a young architect who invited them to a New Year's Eve party at his parents' house. By the time Simenon reached the tall house in the rue Louvrex, the same long, bourgeois street in which Lafnet lived, he was so drunk that he could no longer stand. 'I entered matrimony on my hands and knees,' he wrote in *Un homme comme un autre*. That evening he had started celebrating the New Year early. By 9 o'clock he was drunk. He scaled the first two flights of the architect's staircase, but could only manage the last flight on all fours. At the top of the house he found the architect's sister, a young girl whose hair was drawn back under a headband and who, as he sobered up, talked to him about art and literature. She was still a student at the Beaux-Arts where she was studying painting and drawing. Her name was Régine, she was three years older than him, and this is how she remembered their meeting:

> We were both Liégeois and our meeting was pure chance. I remember it was at a party for friends in our house one New Year's Eve. I was twenty, he was seventeen and a half. He was a journalist on the *Gazette de Liège* and I was in the last year of my studies. I had nonetheless already had a first exhibition and people had talked about it a little. I was certainly his first love, judging by the ardour he showed at the time!

In their directness, simplicity and conviction these sentences are typical of Régine Renchon, a strong personality who was fundamentally honest and uncomplicated in a way that her husband was not. Contrast them with Simenon's memories of the occasion, written many years later:

> Was it first love? I don't think so. I don't think I was really in love with her. I am almost certain I wasn't. There was no sensation of falling in love, but I sought out her company. I was dreaming of two shadows silhouetted on a dimly lit blind and I thought it would be good to find myself with her in the evening behind such a blind, to be one of those two shadows.

But in another passage from *Mémoires intimes* Simenon appeared to confirm Régine's version of events. During the winter of 1921–2, when he was doing his first period of military service in the German border town of Aix-la-Chapelle, he remembered that every morning, with his fingers frozen by the cold, he would write a long letter to Régine: 'They were a sort of hymn to love, because my heart overflowed with it.'

Quite soon after meeting Régine, Simenon decided that he did not like her name and it would have to be changed. He rebaptised her 'Tigy'. The name caught on and became the one Régine was generally known by. Tigy was the first '*fille sérieuse*' to whom Simenon had been attracted, his experience of women being at that time limited to either prostitutes or '*filles légères*', girls of more or less his own age and sometimes of his own family who found sex as amusing a way of passing the time as he did. Tigy was altogether a different proposition. It was not long, two or three weeks he claimed later, before they were lovers, but he wanted more than that from her, and from early days they were making plans to share their lives.

In February 1921 Simenon celebrated his 18th birthday and started one of the happiest years of his life. He had fallen in love and was already making plans to leave Liège. Simenon, Tigy said later, 'did not want to get married before he had done his military service. So he brought that forward by one year and afterwards we planned to go to Paris. You know, when you are young and from the provinces or Belgium . . . Paris is a great draw . . . *Paris consacre*.' Tigy had far clearer ideas than Simenon; she was older, and she became the dominant member in their early partnership. He looked up to her. In their move to Paris it is clear that Simenon was going along with a plan of his wife's. Indeed in their plans to get married the escape to Paris played a determining role. Simenon once claimed that Tigy even made it a condition of their marriage that they should live there. But on another occasion he admitted that he too was happy with the plan. 'I would have flown in the face of all traditions if I had not shown a sovereign contempt for my little native town and if I had not decided that only Paris was fit to welcome me,' he wrote in *Le Romancier*. '*Manger de la vache enragée*' (to suffer hard times) in Paris, and preferably in Montmartre, was as indispensable to a future writer as the work on the school magazine and the first novel on his childhood and youth.

Simenon met Tigy on New Year's Eve and when soon afterwards they became lovers they regarded themselves as unofficially engaged. This engagement became less unofficial when Tigy's father, a prominent interior decorator called Jules Renchon, read some explicit letters Georges had written to Tigy and asked the young man what his intentions were towards his daughter. Simenon did not appreciate this hint. He wanted to marry Tigy anyway. She had to some extent replaced Désiré as a figure of gentle authority and a steadying influence, someone to save him from the bottle or worse; he had met her just in time. They both wanted to have their chance but they agreed that Tigy should have hers first. It was impossible for two geniuses to starve in a garret together, one had to buy the Camembert. Tigy was older, and she was ready. It was agreed between them that when they went she would be able to concentrate on her painting while Simenon found some means of keeping them alive.

He had already shown how he might do this by publishing *Au Pont des Arches*, also in February, and in June for Tigy's 21st birthday he presented her with a pamphlet which he had written and had printed on expensive paper by the presses of the *Gazette de Liège*. It was called *Les ridicules* and was a satire on four of his closest friends, all known to Tigy, and all members of 'La Caque'. In July he finished *Jehan Pinaguet* and overcame his disappointment at having this banned by launching his impudent attack on M. de Géradon in *Nanesse*. In September he declared his independence from *Noss' Perron*, then mocked the city's examining magistrates in the *Gazette* and predicted, correctly, that burglars would shortly strike at the house of a policeman. In October he committed a theft on his own behalf and made himself the most talked-about figure in town in the process.

At that time the *bourgmestre* of Liège and the deputy mayor, the '*échevin*', were socialists. Simenon chose to make these political opponents a major target for ridicule in a conservative paper. The story started when Simenon, in the course of his frequent visits to the town hall, noticed that three heavy metal boxes had been lying in the corridor for some time. On enquiry he discovered that they contained a collection of all the French newspapers which had been published during the war, and which had been donated to the city by a Liégeois living in Paris. Simenon's precocious talent for publicity was brought into play. Taking this essentially uninteresting fact he managed to construct a major scandal out of the event by personalising the story and laying the blame for this 'scandalous neglect of valuable documents' on the hapless *échevin*, Louis Fraigneux, a reasonably busy man who was doubtless occupied with a number of other duties of more immediate importance.

With the permission of M. Demarteau, but having been warned that if things went wrong he would be on his own, Simenon went back to the town hall accompanied by a muscular printer dressed in working clothes and pushing a trolley. Together they loaded one of the boxes on to the trolley and removed it. The act was all the more insolent because it was committed just outside the office of the city's transport police, run at that time by a certain Commissaire Arnold Maigret. The next day the *Gazette* announced that as a result of administrative negligence valuable documents had been stolen from the town hall. The front-page headline was, 'How to steal a strongbox from the town hall at midday'. 'For two years,' wrote Georges Sim, 'these boxes had been left lying in a corridor':

> They were addressed personally to M. l'Echevin Fraigneux. No doubt the generous donor thought that the surest means of making a gift to the city of Liège was to confide it to one of our representatives . . . Documents such as these are in heavy demand in the university library and are extremely difficult to obtain . . . Even today many issues of the most important reviews are still missing from the municipal collection. Are these missing numbers in the boxes entrusted to M. Fraigneux? We do not know. M. Fraigneux does not know. Nobody knows! The boxes have not even been opened, they have just been left in the corridor rusting away, gathering mildew, for two years. It is a case of the most flagrant negligence. Foreseeing the traditional objection that it is impossible to steal anything from our town hall we decided to carry out the theft of one of the boxes ourselves. Today the box is in a safe place, the premises of the Municipal Library.

M. Demarteau was so pleased with the success of the operation that he offered Sim a box of twenty-five cigars, but there was better to come. That afternoon Simenon was summoned to the

Commissariat to be questioned about a charge of theft which the *échevin* had brought against him. This was another mistake on the part of M. Fraigneux. The story grew and grew. First the stolen box was returned to the town hall by Simenon. Then M. Fraigneux wrote to a rival newspaper to defend himself, explaining that the collection had been donated to the city only because of his personal friendship with the donor. Then the donor wrote to the *Gazette de Liège* to express his disappointment with the neglect of his gift and to thank the paper for its role in exposing it. Then Simenon returned to the attack, this time anonymously, in (for the last time) *Nanesse*, mocking the *échevin*'s attempts to defend himself. Then Simenon discovered that M. Fraigneux had been stimulated into opening one of the boxes and was now to be found in his private office reading its contents. 'There is no need for him to monopolise the documents in this way, even if the sinecure promised him on his impending retirement is a job in the municipal library,' he wrote.

The charge of theft had to be withdrawn on the *bourgmestre*'s instructions and for two weeks or so 'Sim's' exploit was the talk of Liège. The future novelist had received an invaluable lesson in the art of self-publicity. And since the crime of the stolen documents was both committed and solved by Simenon, it provided him with the perfect means of running with the hare and hunting with the hounds. It satisfied two of the young reporter's deepest interests, breaking the law and upholding it. Perhaps it was, on a minor scale, Simenon's perfect news story. And it made him famous for a fortnight.

Demarteau, keen to capitalise on 'Sim's' fame, immediately asked him to cover another sensitive story, the post-war smuggling trade which had grown up between Belgium and Germany and which was the foundation of the Liège black market. Smuggled goods included eggs and butter as well as watches and leather goods, where the mark-up in Belgium was 50 per cent. Simenon himself had intimate childhood experience of smuggling and the black market both on his own account and from his expeditions with his mother. Although his readers probably would not have guessed it from what he wrote, there was one oblique reference to those days. On the train approaching the border, he noted, 'small packages are folded into a bundle of dirty washing . . . and the skirts of some women contain mysterious folds which recall the outline of the war-time smugglers of corn and potatoes.' He discovered that on a particular day in the week 965 passports for Germany had been issued at the town hall, showing that smuggling was a mass pursuit in the city at that time. 'Not only is legitimate commerce suffering as a result,' wrote Simenon, 'but such behaviour is doing nothing for Belgian prestige in the country of the vanquished . . . Let the state take up its responsibilities!' This conclusion was as public-spirited as his attack on the unfortunate *échevin*, but for many of his readers it would have been less amusing. It was one thing to expose the town hall, but in exposing a racket which was supported by nearly a thousand fellow citizens every day 'Sim' was attacking the man in the street and the woman behind the market stall. But he no longer cared. He was on top of the world. He was about to start one year's military service, and then he would be leaving for Paris.

To show his independence from everything to do with Liège Simenon decided to circulate *Les ridicules*. On 26 November he distributed one copy to each of his four friends; they were so angry with him that they all destroyed their copies. 'There was nothing malicious in the portrait I drew of my friends,' Simenon was to write later in *Jour et nuit*:

> I described them without harshness as I saw them, but probably not as they saw themselves. However for several months afterwards I reproached myself for having written this little volume and felt awkward and guilty each time I met one of my victims.

The pamphlet never mentioned the names of the author or victims but described their physical appearance and mannerisms so well that it was perfectly obvious who was referred to. One painter was mocked for having painted his wife in labour. Two friends, who were inseparable, were told that they formed a normal human personality only when they were together. And Simenon mocked Lafnet's use of a spiritual vocabulary, and his initial admiration for 'this artist who had read so much' was turned instead into a portrait of a man parroting from his latest book, incapable of thinking for himself. His victims were the painters of 'La Caque' who had been generous enough to illustrate *Au Pont des Arches* only the year before, and it was no consolation to any of them when their friend ended by suggesting that he himself was the most ridiculous of all. It did not carry the same sting. *Les ridicules* was a pitiless study of four of Simenon's friends whose talents were unequal to their ambitions; the only copy to survive was the one presented to Tigy.

'The most important day in a man's life is the day of his father's death,' Simenon wrote in *Le fils* (*The Son*) in 1956. For him that day came on 28 November 1921, a Monday. He had spent the day in Antwerp, where the *Gazette* had sent him on a story, although for much of the time he had been in a *hôtel de passe* with a distant cousin. On his return to Les Guillemins station at 7 o'clock that evening it was to find Tigy and her father waiting for him at the end of the platform – '*Mon petit Georges*, you must be brave.' Désiré had died suddenly in his office in the rue Sohet, just by the railway station. The body had been taken back to the house in the rue de l'Enseignement. By the time his son arrived Désiré 'was already laid out on his bed, surrounded by candles and all the equipment which they bring out for the dead and which fills me with horror'. His father was fully dressed, hands crossed piously on his chest, and Simenon 'had to make an effort to brush his cold forehead with my lips'. He had experienced hubris; this calamity was his punishment. The year had been one long triumph, from the day in the spring when he published his first novel to the moment two days before the death of his father when he danced on the grave of his friendship with 'La Caque'. He had mocked the chairman of his own newspaper with impunity in *Nanesse* and had scored a public victory over the city's deputy mayor. Although he was engaged to Tigy, he retained his sexual freedom and had indeed been celebrating it that morning. He must have felt that the whole world was his and that he was untouchable, instead of being in the miserable position he had occupied just three years earlier. And then he walked along a railway platform and found he had lost the person he loved most in his life. 'No one ever understood what passed between father and son. There were no words to describe it. There had only ever been the two of them.' Time did little to heal this wound, and at the end of his life Simenon could still write, 'Scarcely a day has gone by, since my father's death, when I have not thought of him.'

When Désiré died there were only 300 francs in his wallet and it was all the ready money the family had available. It was not enough to pay for the funeral. Simenon was forced in these circumstances to approach several of his wealthy uncles to ask for a loan. All refused. The uncles in question were Joseph Croissant, who had a colonial produce business on the Quai Coronmeuse and who was married to Simenon's Aunt Joséphine, and Jean-Mathieu Schrooten, the wholesale grocer married to Aunt Louisa who had arranged for Henriette to sell wine to the German soldiers. A third uncle, Henri Brüll, also declined to make a loan and instead removed valuable family furniture from Henriette's house after the funeral, taking it to his 'château' in the Limbourg and replacing it with cheap furniture. Faced with a triple refusal, Simenon went to M. Demarteau. 'If I had not been able to borrow some money from the *Gazette* to pay the undertaker, my father would have gone to a pauper's grave,' he wrote in *De la cave au grenier* in 1977, still settling scores with the Brülls in Liège from his refuge in Lausanne fifty-six years later. The funeral *cortège* which started from the rue de l'Enseignement included Charles Coomans, his first cousin on the Simenon side, who remembered that for the occasion Georges wore his army uniform. On 5 December he was due to report for military service.

His grief over his father's death did not blind Georges to the alarming prospect of his mother in her new role as legal head of the family. He lost no time and even before joining up went to a magistrate and applied for 'a declaration of majority' or '*émancipa-tion*'. He had been earning his living for over three years, he was engaged to be married and he had volunteered to bring forward his military service, all were factors in his favour. From now on Simenon had all the duties and freedoms of an adult, although for the time being his home address was still the rue de l'Enseignement.

Simenon's picture of his position in life as a member of the '*petites gens*' is not entirely supported by the story of his military service. Years later he recalled that he had joined the army on the morning after his father's funeral, but the Belgian National Defence Ministry records state that for the class of 1920 the '*appel sous les armes*' was for the Monday of the week following Désiré's death. Simenon, who had learnt to ride demonstration Harley-Davidson motor-cycles for the *Gazette de Liège*, applied for enlist-ment in the motorised infantry, not realising that if his request were granted he would be posted abroad. The fact that he had brought forward his service meant that his request was granted without difficulty but his love of motor-cycles did not grow into a love of occupied Germany. The winter was very cold, there was no food and not much fuel or money. He continued to send articles back to the *Gazette* in which he described the comforts of the Belgian army beside the miseries of the German population, but after one month in the 'Rote Kaserne' in Aix-la-Chapelle he had had enough and his application to be posted back to the 2nd Lancers in Liège as sole support of a fatherless family was granted.

The posting may not have been due to personal connections, but what followed undoubtedly was. Relieved to find that he was no longer a member of any occupying force, Simenon, now stationed at the cavalry barracks in the boulevard de la Constitution, a few minutes' walk from his mother's house, learning to break and ride horses, resumed his regular contributions as 'M. le Coq'. By February he was interviewing President Poincaré of France (whom he found wearing a dressing-gown in his suite in the Hôtel Suède, which was probably more interesting than breaking horses). Since much of M. le Coq's journalistic material came from life in the Caserne Cavalier Fonck his superiors eventually noticed that one of the 2nd Lancers in the barracks was writing in the newspapers about army life. His commanding officer summoned him and at first threatened him with military prison for this breach of regulations. Then, having discovered who 'Cavalier Simenon' was, the colonel – an old friend of Joseph Demarteau – responded to a request from the *Gazette* and allowed Simenon to abandon his military duties as long as he continued to sleep in the barracks at night and refrained from writing about life in the Caserne Cavalier Fonck. Personal connections had triumphed again. Since the house in the rue de l'Enseignement was only a few minutes' walk from the barracks, and since Simenon was now reporting daily to the *Gazette* rather than to the barracks, it was not long before he had abandoned his uniform, leaving instructions for the adjutant to telephone him if he were needed. The official reason for his absence was illness: he had spent a short time in the military hospital situated on a hill overlooking the Collège St Servais with a fever. By September he felt sufficiently confident of his special status to risk the colonel's wrath and write once again about military affairs, in this case a double murder in the Belgian army of occupation stationed in Germany. But before that happened there was the death of Kleine.

FIVE

The death of Kleine

In the last resort, wasn't it us who killed him?
Simenon, *Les trois crimes de mes amis* (1938)

Joseph Jean Kleine had been born on Christmas Day 1898 in a suburb of Liège to an unmarried sempstress called Marie-Josephe Ciset. His birth certificate was filled in by the midwife – in other words, the father was unknown. At the age of 5 the child was legitimised by the marriage of his mother to a Dutch confectioner Léonard Kleine who was four years her junior. So like Simenon's mother, Henriette, Kleine was half Dutch, an *'étranger'*. From the age of 7 Kleine lived with his parents in the rue de Gueldre, no. 4 *bis*, the same little street off the rue Léopold where the Simenons had lived for two years after the birth of Georges. But the Simenons moved out in April 1905, when Georges was 2, and the Kleines did not move in until May 1906, when *'le petit Kleine'* was 7. Léonard died in April 1910, aged 29, still in the rue de Gueldre. But some years earlier, between September 1907 and September 1910, Kleine attended the state primary school in the rue de l'Enseignement. For up to two years Simenon and Kleine were attending neighbouring schools on Outremeuse, one in the Catholic system of education, the *réseau libre*, and the other in the state system, the *réseau communal*, which meant that if they met at all it would have been as potential rivals. Kleine was probably living at this time in his aunt's house in the rue Curtius,* the only

---

* Curiously enough when I visited no. 5 rue Curtius in 1991 I noticed that no. 9, the house next door but one to the Kleine address, was marked 'Enterprise Luc Simenon

known address for the Kleine family on Outremeuse. It is entirely possible that '*le petit Kleine*' was a member of one of the gangs of older children who raided the Place du Congrès during Simenon's childhood, to little Georges's terror and delight. One can imagine their paths crossing earlier in the day, when Georges was running through the dark from the rue de la Loi along the boulevard de la Constitution to the Hôpital de la Bavière, passing close to the end of the rue Curtius before reaching the safety of the church's latch, while Joseph Jean Kleine was running perhaps from the rue Curtius towards the latch on the door of St Nicolas, also earning pocket-money by serving Mass; neither child suspecting that the life of one of them would end while dangling by his scarf from the latch of a third church in the same boulevard de la Constitution, and that the pocket-money of the other would be increased by writing about it three times. The patterns which time was to weave in the streets of Outremeuse from the lives of these children were still mercifully obscure.

After primary school Kleine went to the *école moyenne* in the boulevard Saucy, still on Outremeuse, and then to the Athénée Royale de Liège, just across the river. From there he went on to become a student at the Beaux-Arts where he would have found himself in the year above a girl called Régine Renchon. Kleine and Régine Renchon were both members of the Beaux-Arts's self-appointed *élite* known as 'les Rapins'. But only Kleine was a founder member of 'La Caque'.

The night of Kleine's death was a cold night in late winter, the first night of March, a Wednesday. Kleine was no longer living with his only surviving relative, his aunt, at 5 rue Curtius, but had moved some weeks before into the apartment of his closest friend, Jean Lebeau, a violinist as well as a painter and a fellow member of 'La Caque'. Lebeau's apartment was in the rue Chaussée-des-Près, no. 11, near the point where the street became the rue Puits-en-Sock. But that day and for some days before Kleine had not been seen at either Lebeau's apartment or by his aunt. He apparently had a third hole, all his own, in a dingy *quartier* nearby.

It was 1922. Kleine was a little chap, still only 23 years old. He had finished his studies and was already on the way down. He was

– Asphalt surfaces and See-Through Concrete'. I pulled the bell but there was no reply.

no longer an artist, he was a decorator. He was addicted to cocaine and he regularly took other stimulants, morphine and ether, as well as alcohol, to a point well beyond excess. His slight build matched his fine features. He had fair hair, slightly wavy, which he wore long. In two surviving photographs his face bears the same expression – absent. He does not smile. He looks mildly uneasy. He has become the victim of a stronger character, a drug dealer with links in the *milieu*. Kleine is used by this man, the Fakir, as a means of demonstrating his hypnotic powers. Kleine is an orphan. When he was small he frequently watched his mother being beaten by a drunkard, and the Fakir frequently taunts him about his mother while he is hypnotised. His friends, who might have protected Kleine from this fate, do nothing to intervene. They watch him deteriorate. He has already made an attempt to kill himself. He is the living example of what to his friends are just theories, about death, futility, self-destruction, abandonment. To those like Deblauwe, who say that they are dilettantes in such matters, the member of 'La Caque' can point in reply to Kleine. He at least is not a dilettante. He is real. He is practising on himself various interesting and original methods of dying. While the others sit around discussing Nietzsche and Plato and Epicurus, and drinking and keeping the guttering candles alight, Kleine is extinguishing a little bit more of himself quietly, or sometimes extremely noisily, in the corner. Kleine is available, he is at their disposal, that is the genial thing about him; he is no longer in possession of himself and this adds a certain amount of interest to their gatherings.

So, on the night in question, 'La Caque' met and started to drink. *Ils se mettent à boire.* It was a ritual, a sanctified moment. Kleine joined them. This meant it was going to be one of the more interesting nights. Excesses could be expected. They might be observed or, certainly in Kleine's case, committed. Excesses could even be practised on Kleine, if there was no one else around and one felt so disposed. At some point, not very early, not very late, perhaps around midnight, Kleine became incapable of walking:

> We had a friend whose origins were a mystery to all of us . . .
> He was 20 years old. He was very fair, almost white, very thin
> with feverish eyes . . . He was already drunk. We drank a few

glasses together and at a certain moment the young man with the very fair hair was incapable of walking. It was raining. I hoisted him up on my shoulders. I asked my friends where he lived . . . One of them had seen him coming out of a house due for demolition. We rang several doorbells. The boy was unconscious on my shoulder and very wet as he had spent the day and much of the night on the pavement. Eventually a woman showed us a dark corridor and we went down it. We pushed open the door of what could hardly be described as a room. It was a cubbyhole with a narrow window, an easel, some canvases and a straw mattress on the floor. No water tap on the landing, not even the most basic facilities. We left our friend on the mattress and I no longer remember how we spent the rest of the night. In the morning the unhappy painter was found hanging from the door of the church of St Pholien.

At 5.45 next morning the sacristan of St Pholien's, at the other end of the boulevard de la Constitution to the Bavière hospital, walked up the steps of the porch as usual to open the doors for the 6 o'clock Mass. He was accompanied by his son. It was a very dark morning and as he approached the door the sacristan, Joseph Geilenkirchen, sensed a solid shape in the gloom ahead of him. Thinking that a tramp was sheltering in the porch he leaned forward to shake the man awake saying, 'Come on now, you can't sleep here.' There was no reply, but the shape swung slowly towards him and Geilenkirchen was suddenly aware that he was shaking the body of a man who was hanging by a scarf from the church doorknocker. The man seemed to be dead but his body was still warm. Geilenkirchen undid the scarf and laid the body out in the porch. He placed candles round it partly as a mark of respect and partly in order to prevent arriving members of the congregation from tripping over it. One of the latter, a doctor, certified the death, and the police quickly established that the dead man was Joseph Jean Kleine.

Police suspicions were of suicide, or murder by strangulation made to look like suicide. If Kleine had killed himself, then despite the fact that he had been left unconscious and incapable of walking late at night he had apparently been capable of making his own way to the church and hanging himself before 5.30 the next morning with his own scarf from the handle on the church door.

No chair or drop was used. Kleine's scarf, which was made of wool, was apparently strong enough to support the weight of his body. Kleine, even in his befuddled state, was apparently able to manage the difficult business of knots and somehow able to hoist himself off his feet by the use of a knitted woollen scarf. Either that or he was able to hang himself with his feet still on the ground: a remarkable achievement. According to the sacristan and his 14-year-old son, who was beside his father, Kleine's body swung when his father touched it. This suggests that its weight was off the ground. Two other witnesses stated that his body was in contact with the ground. One or more people who had passed the church door during the night told the reporter from *La Meuse* that they had noticed Kleine in front of the door but had thought he had been sitting on the step in front of it. These people may actually have been looking at Kleine sitting on the step before he hanged himself, but another witness told the reporter from the *Gazette de Liège* that the body had been 'slumped half folded on the stone steps, the arms dangling and the face contorted'. And there is a further contradiction between the evidence of the sacristan and the newspaper accounts. The newspaper reported that the police surgeon said that Kleine had been dead for some hours. M. Geilenkirchen remembered that the body was still warm.

The problems with Kleine's 'suicide' were threefold. First, there were the physical difficulties involved. He could not walk; the scarf was not strong enough; he could not tie the knots. He lacked the height to hang himself. He had nothing to jump off. Secondly there were the contradictions in the witnesses' accounts. The body was warm, or the body had been dead for several hours. The body was suspended from the door knob, or the body was almost folded in two and resting on the stone step. The police officer said that the position in which the body was found supported the suspicion of suicide, whereas the contrary seems to be true. The night was so dark that the sacristan had to touch the body before he could see that it was hanging, whereas other witnesses stated that they had been able to see the body from the street as they passed the church. Thirdly, there was the suspicion that immediately grew among Kleine's friends that his death had actually been murder. The initial police enquiry did not rule out murder and considered the possibility that it was a murder which had been dressed up as suicide. Against the theory of murder there is the dangerously public method chosen. And hanging from a church door was clearly a reference to 'La Caque'. If Kleine had been murdered, why had it been done in this way?

The other curiosity in the story relates to the part played by Simenon. Although he was by his own admission the last person to see Kleine alive he never, in his numerous accounts of the event, made any reference to being questioned by the police or even to having told the police that he had been with the dead man on the previous evening. And how on the following morning could all the Liège papers have been so certain that it was a case of suicide? There was clearly a strong possibility that it was – Kleine was in a black mood made worse by his drug addiction – but nonetheless there was the Fakir who would seem to have been a prime target for questioning. And there is the question of the use of St Pholien's church. Were the police ever told about 'La Caque's' obsession with the symbolism of the hanged man? Did they question the members of the group at all? If Kleine had been murdered by a drug dealer, as some of his friends believed, the only drug dealer who might have bothered with the method used would have been the Fakir, who was on the fringes of 'La Caque' and might have been intending to warn other members of the group that this was what would happen to them if they too fell behind with their instalments. Because it seems unlikely that Kleine was the only member of 'La Caque' to use drugs.

The unsigned report in the following morning's *Gazette* was headlined, 'Man in despair hangs himself from church door – A victim of drugs'. And the accompanying story stated that the dead man had been 'reported missing from his home in the rue Curtius for several days'. But when this story was written the police enquiries were still under way and no death certificate had been issued. And the readers of the *Gazette* might have been interested to know that the unidentified reporter who had discovered that Kleine had been 'missing from his home for several days' was the same man who had carried Kleine home and put him to bed a few hours before he was found dangling from the church door knob, even if the police officer in charge of the case, Commissaire-Adjoint Pirard, did eventually reach the same conclusion as the *Gazette*'s headline writer.

Simenon was always fascinated by the story of the death of Kleine. But it was years before he admitted that he had been the author of the newspaper report which gave such a convenient explanation of the mystery well ahead of the result of police enquiries. As recently as 1989 Michel Lemoine in *Liège dans l'oeuvre de Simenon*, a publication sponsored by the Centre d'Etudes Simenon, noted Rutten's suggestion that Simenon may well have been the author of the *Gazette*'s report but emphasised that it was speculative. It was left to Jean-Christophe Camus to confirm Rutten's suspicion by revealing that he had received a letter from Simenon in 1984 in which the writer confirmed that he had personally visited the scene of the drama and that he had indeed been the author of the *Gazette*'s report.

The death of Kleine precipitated the dissolution of 'La Caque'. Luc Lafnet was on the point of leaving for Paris, and the Fakir started to avoid his former friends. 'I plead not guilty on our behalf,' Simenon wrote later. 'Or rather I plead lack of premeditation . . . We did not know the true state of "*le petit Kleine*". But in the last resort, wasn't it us who killed him?'

It is worth recalling that despite his having spent the night out drinking with Kleine, and despite his routine attendance, first at the office and then at the scene of the hanging, Simenon was actually supposed to be doing his military service in March 1922. Since his father's death he had established his premature majority, chosen his preferred unit in the army, changed his unit and arranged to have himself recalled from abroad and posted to the barracks just round the corner from his mother's house, breached army regulations about journalism with impunity, benefited from an effective leave of absence from his military service, abandoned his uniform and resumed his former civilian life. After some of the tricks he had pulled in the previous three months, overcoming the potential embarrassment of the death of Kleine must have seemed relatively straightforward. If the colonel commanding the 2nd Lancers could not resist him, what could Commissaire-Adjoint Pirard of the 6th Division do? The man who had exposed the scandals of the town-hall strongboxes and the food smugglers of the post-war period was able, apparently without difficulty, to suppress a much more embarrassing scandal involving himself.

The story of the death of Kleine was the time in Simenon's life when he came closest to the world of serious crime, but it was not the only occasion. Crime formed part of the essential background of his childhood. It started to do so in 1914 when he was 11 and had to watch the criminalisation of a respectable, rather conventional world under the stress of war and occupation. The real world of '*les petites gens*', of the hatters, the walk to work, the insurance office, came to an abrupt end in August 1914. From then on lawful authority was rendered powerless, an alien force having burnt the district library and shot the inhabitants of an entire street, a street just like the rue Puits-en-Sock, and imposed its rule. Parents became petty criminals and children turning into adolescents could run free. Their parents taught them 'to cheat and to defraud and to lie', and Deblauwe and Danse 'first together, and then separately, pushed on with their heads down towards degradation and a life of crime'. Church, home and state, the internal and external forces of law and order, were overthrown, and sex was another form of crime.

The effects on Simenon can be seen recurring throughout the rest of his life. On several occasions, confronted with a personal challenge, he threatened or hesitated on the edge of a criminal response: once when he sought out a man who was pirating editions of his books and stealing a small fortune from his estate; once, during a marital argument, when he removed his pistol from its case; once when a book was about to be published which breached his family privacy and he obtained stolen proof copies. On each of these occasions he undertook or prepared the way for direct action, for crime. In his earliest journalism there is the same fascination with the forbidden. Stealing a strongbox from the town hall was more than just a publicity stunt; it was going one step too far. Correctly predicting a burglary at the home of a police officer was also a risky joke, and one which might have led to unpleasant consequences. Later in life Simenon claimed that he had done everything possible to avoid bringing his own children up as 'respectable'.

Perhaps the most enduring mark left on Simenon by the occupation of Liège was an ambivalence towards conventional ideas of right and wrong. This became one of the major themes of the Maigret books; it might almost be called the 'message' of the Maigret saga. On the whole Commissaire Maigret finds criminality easy to understand and adopts a frankly sympathetic attitude towards many of his clients. His first question is not 'Who committed this crime?' but 'Why was it committed?', and in order to answer, he has to understand the person who committed it. The criminals, in Maigret's world, are often less guilty than their victims. This is true from the earliest of the Maigrets. In *Le chien jaune* (*A Face for a Clue*), the sixth Maigret to be written but the fourth to be published, a group of local notables are terrorised by a shadowy enemy who turns out to be a poor man they have all wronged. The same theme runs through another novel, not a Maigret, *Le destin des Malou* (*The Fate of the Malous*), where a boy discovers that his dead father was a criminal and, for that reason, a hero. This may be quite a common attitude among the children of the *milieu*, but in *Le destin des Malou* the hero, Alain, is a virtuous character who has never had any contact with the criminal world inhabited by his father. To make the paradox stronger, Simenon lets the boy's discovery of his father's real activities provide him with the inspiration to commit a generous act.

In the first chapter Alain's father is murdered in the street by a wealthy and prominent member of the community. Alain finds out that the man who shot his father claimed that he was being blackmailed by him. At the end of his quest Alain asks one of his father's friends, in fact accomplices, 'Was my father dishonest?' and receives the reply, 'Your father was a man. And that, believe me, as you will find out for yourself one day, is a rarer thing than being respectable.' Alain learns that his father came from an extremely poor background, that his grandmother had been insane and that his grandfather had lived in a shack on the outskirts of a village and eaten crows. His father had overcome all this to set himself up as a prosperous businessman. 'When you're down to a certain level,' says his father's former accomplice, 'there's nobody to hold out his hand to you. People go by, well-fed, well-dressed, their pockets full of money, and not one thinks of stopping.' Old Malou's method of persuading them to 'stop' had been to take up a career as a journalist. When he obtained confidential information showing that a company had been paying bribes to officials he did not write a story about it but used the information to obtain a job with the company. In certain circumstances, Alain was being told, even blackmail can be the mark of a man. Virtue is largely relative; there are usually extenuating circumstances, and real vice exists only where there are no extenuating circumstances, which is usually among the 'respectable' classes.

On 4 December 1922 Simenon's year of military service ended. Ten days later he took the train to Paris. He would return to Liège in three months' time to be married to Tigy; after that his visits would be few and brief. But if he was rarely in Liège the geography of Outremeuse and the characters he had met on the enchanted island of his childhood accompanied him for the rest of the journey. The pigeon sprinter and the tooth-puller, and the uncle who walked to church with his moustache in a special apparatus; his own terror as he ran through the dark streets towards the chapel door; the smells of the market, the muscles of the marketwomen, the hypnotising effect of sunlight on the wall of a quiet bedroom, the glory of Désiré's uniform; his father's long Mauser rifle abandoned in the Meuse, the magic world broken and burnt by the Uhlans, the years of fear and hunger and sexual trafficking that followed, these emblems returned to him again and again down all the years to come.

In Simenon's last six months on the *Gazette de Liège* he noted the future commercial appeal of detective stories and predicted that before too long they would be recognised as a respectable genre of literature. He added that 'with the aid of the cinema they might even begin to dominate it'. His farewell to Belgium was an article which appeared in the *Revue Sincère* of Brussels on 15 December 1922, on the morning after his departure, which described his final meal at home with his mother. He had tried to explain that he needed to start his own life and to have his own home, just as she had once done, but his mother, busy in the kitchen, polishing silver, making jam, did not understand. Mothers never did understand. Why start another life, when there was a perfectly good one established in this house and shared for nearly twenty years, they said. But the links were cut, his mother was crying and he was leaving anyway. Everything in the familiar room reproached him for making her unhappy. It was the last kind thing he wrote about Henriette until her death nearly fifty years later, by which time he himself was on the verge of old age.

On the night train to Paris he saw once again the blast furnaces around the city, with their servants, stripped and sweating, toiling in front of them, lit by the atrocious flames, and he must have thought of his father who had died just over a year before. Twenty-five years later he evoked the memory in *Le destin des Malou*, describing the young Alain Malou leaving his provincial

city and travelling to Paris to make his life, having solved the
mystery of his dead father's character:

> The rocking of the train lulled him, and little by little he slipped
> into a doze . . . Alain Malou was going to Paris to meet his
> destiny. He would work at anything, usher in a cinema, waiter
> in a café, anything they wanted. He would take his examin-
> ations . . . Why shouldn't he become a doctor? . . . Now he
> had time. He had the time to sleep . . . The train whistled as it
> sped through the countryside white with frost. One by one
> remote little stations were swallowed up in the past, the house
> in the little square with the fountain was swallowed up too, and
> so many things, so many people with it. There was only a
> sleeping Malou who would soon wake up to a new life and
> who, in his sleep, occasionally moved his lips. A Malou who
> would do his utmost, all a man can.

PART II

THE IDIOT GENIUS

God created you to write like he created my father to paint.
That is why you both do it so well.

Jean Renoir, letter to Simenon

SIX

'Manger et faire l'amour'

It is, without question, the most famous bottom in the world
. . . it is everywhere . . . plastered all over the city's walls,
because it is the only bottom that laughs!
Simenon, of Josephine Baker (1927)

The seventeen years from 1923 to 1939 when Simenon lived in France were generally happy ones. During that period he started his career, as a writer of pulp fiction, and within only five years he had made his name and a considerable sum of money. This was followed by the creation of Commissaire Maigret, his most famous character, who was to become the hero of seventy-six novels and bring Simenon world fame. In moving from Liège to Paris, Simenon was following the classic pattern of the ambitious provincial. He was escaping from the suffocating proximity of family life, the feeling that 'someone was always dying' and the constant sense of being watched and questioned. There were so many questions that no one would ask in Paris because no one was interested in the answers. If they were not asked in Liège it would be because the answers were already known, which was worse. Paris in the 1920s, after the Great War, was an ideal city, beautiful, sensuous and very rewarding for the little band of outsiders whose talent it was prepared to acknowledge.

Among the legends which have grown up around the arrival of Simenon in Paris is that of the penniless and solitary young man, without friends or lodging or contacts, forced to survive on *croissants* and camembert in a hotel garret, who spent his days tramping the streets looking for work and the evenings with his face pressed against the glass of *brasserie* windows, gazing at the food he could not afford to eat. In fact when his train drew into the Gare du Nord on a December morning in 1922 he had money in his pocket, an introduction to his new employer, and a friend, Luc Lafnet, at the station to meet him and guide him to the Hôtel Bertha off the boulevard des Batignolles. He was still wearing the large black hat and cravat that were the uniform of La Caque. In the Hôtel Bertha he quickly discovered that one of the chambermaids was the niece of a novelist who had won the Prix Goncourt, and, hoping to launch his literary career, he had her in the hotel corridor one morning while she was kneeling down cleaning the shoes.

The job was a disappointment. Expecting to be the private secretary to a writer, Binet-Valmer, he found himself reduced to the status of office-boy at the headquarters of a political group, the 'Ligue des Chefs de Sections et des Anciens Combattants', which Binet-Valmer directed. The only advantage was that his duties included acting as a messenger; this meant that he quickly got to know the forty-five newspaper offices which Paris contained in 1923 and which Binet-Valmer flooded with tracts and handouts from his extreme right-wing organisation.

Christmas 1922 was the low-point of Simenon's new adventure. His daily letters to Tigy at this time show him in tears, utterly reliant on her encouragement and completely in love with her. He sometimes wrote to her four times in a day. He felt miserable and vulnerable without her. In one letter he wrote, 'I now understand everything one has to do to win success in Paris. And I will do it. But I am appalled by what I will have to do.' However from the week of his arrival he had been sending articles to the *Revue Sincère* of Brussels, which had appointed him its Paris correspondent; among them were profiles of prominent Parisian figures such as Léon Daudet, Claude Farrère and Paul Fort. And it was not long before he was writing his first short stories. Within a few months he had begun to find a market for these at 100 francs a time in *Frou-Frou*, *Plaisir* and *Paris-Flirt*.

On 23 March 1923 Simenon returned to Liège to be married to Tigy. Both the civil and the religious ceremonies were to take place the following day. They had only agreed to a church service

to please Henriette – whose first comment on meeting Tigy had
been, 'My God, she's ugly,' the same remark her long dead
mother-in-law had made about baby Georges. Tigy, who had
been brought up an atheist, had undergone months of religious
instruction, and Simenon had been obliged to buy a second-hand
dinner jacket from a friend. He spent one night under his mother's
roof in the rue Villette. Henriette had at last been able to buy a
house in the rue de l'Enseignement but had not yet moved in. On
the way to church Simenon talked to his mother about the various
ways the Parisians had of frying chips, to distract her from the
tears which threatened to flow, despite Henriette's gratification at
her son's social promotion. A church wedding was not a
bohemian occasion, but the bride did what she could by wearing a
full-length black tulle dress, a black silk coat and a vast hat
covered in bird of paradise feathers. Dressed like this, she walked
to the Eglise Ste Véronique from her father's house which stood
in the adjoining rue Fabry. The ceremony at the town hall was
jollier. '*Le petit Sim*' was still a figure in Liège. All his journalist
friends were there, and the couple were married by the city's
deputy mayor; but it was not the unfortunate M. Fraigneux.
Liège now had its first communist *échevin*, who marked the
occasion with a long rambling speech in Walloon and who was
shortly afterwards taken away and confined to a lunatic asylum.
Simenon's new wife was exactly what he wanted. As he said years
later, 'I felt I was capable of any stupidity. I needed a ball and
chain.' That same evening they set off for Paris, to the apartment
in the rue St Honoré near the Parc Monceau, which Simenon had
exchanged for the neighbourhood of the boulevard des
Batignolles as a more suitable place to start married life. Next
morning they were awoken by the landlord, an elderly homosexual wearing a nightdress, who, with his boyfriend, was tiptoeing
through their bedroom to the only bathroom. (Tigy had wanted
to start married life in two apartments, to which each of them
could retire when they chose, an arrangement which Simenon
described as '*assez original*'.)

   With the arrival in Paris of Tigy, Simenon's hardest days were
over. Before there had only been the company of Lafnet and his
wife, who were living in the rue du Mont-Cenis, near
Sacré-Coeur. Now he had as much company as he wished, and he
had his short stories. While Tigy painted and tried to sell her

pictures he supported them both by writing stories for the newspapers and little magazines, then romantic novels for serialisation,
then novels for six different publishers under twenty-four registered pseudonyms, the best known of which were 'Georges Sim'
and 'Christian Brulls'. He called these books his *romans alimen-
taires* ('pot-boilers'). His hopes kept him going through the dreary
hours he had to put in at the headquarters of the 'Ligue', sorting
out foreign postage stamps, or filling envelopes. His colleagues in
the office had installed a 'swear-box' into which he had to put 10
centimes every time he uttered a Belgian phrase such as '*n'est-ce-
pas*'.

Henri Binet-Valmer's real name was Jean Binet, and he had
become notorious in 1910 for publishing a novel, *Lucien*, whose
hero was a homosexual. He was a prominent member of 'Action
Française' and the chief excitement in the office came when there
was news of an industrial strike. The *'anciens combattants'* of the
'Ligue' would then be summoned at short notice to break it. The
office was in a dull cul-de-sac, the avenue Beaucour, whose only
advantage was that it was five minutes' walk from the apartment.
Simenon must sometimes have wondered whether Georges Plu-
mier, the Liégeois friend of his father's who had introduced him
to Binet-Valmer, had really intended to do him a good turn.

At this time Simenon was earning 600 francs a month and
sending 250 francs home to his mother. Despite the occasional
sale to a literary editor he began to run short of money, and he
may have been tempted to take a number of unauthorised advances from the petty cash or from the stamp book; certainly that
is what one of his later fictional characters, also working at the
headquarters of a patriotic league, did in *Les noces de Poitiers* (*The
Couple from Poitiers*). In fact Binet-Valmer, who had read his
references from the *Gazette*, was teaching him a hard lesson. What
is a 20-year-old journalist with four years' experience behind him
and a high reputation in a Belgian provincial city worth in Paris?
He is worth an immediate appointment to the position of office-
boy. Simenon had the impudence to remind Binet-Valmer of his
original expectations by reviewing two of his employer's novels
in the *Revue Sincère*; but he had the good sense to review them
favourably.

One of the 'Ligue's' most important supporters was a wealthy
misogynist and aristocrat, the Marquis de Tracy. One day, visit-

ing Binet-Valmer, Raymond de Tracy noticed the frustrated young man in the corner of the room and enquired who he was. The Marquis wanted a private secretary and since Binet-Valmer, who was no longer a novelist anyway, did not know what to do with '*le petit Sim*' it was quickly arranged. Binet-Valmer asked Simenon how he would like to become private secretary to one of the richest men in France. He had been an office-boy for just six months. His new employer called him 'Sim' and that was the name he was to be best known by for the next ten years. His work consisted in travelling around France with his employer, who owned five châteaux and estates, his principal residence being at Paray-le-Frésil, near Moulins in the Allier. He also owned properties in Italy and Tunisia. Since the Marquis did not approve of a married secretary Sim had to leave Tigy behind. Tigy's plan had been realised: her husband was absent from Paris for nine months a year. But she found that she missed him, and started following him on his journeys, at first taking a hotel room in a neighbouring town. De Tracy soon found out, but was merely amused and suggested that in future his secretary's wife should take a room in the village. The new arrangement also meant that Tigy could keep an eye on Sim. He complained later that although she did not make love to him with much gusto she was ferociously jealous and she warned him that if he was ever unfaithful to her she would kill herself.

At this period Sim wore his fair hair long, because he considered himself to be an artist. One day the Marquis, passing behind his chair, lifted his golden locks and murmured, '*Mon petit Sim . . .*' meaning, 'Do you really need this?' '*Le petit Sim*' had his hair cut. He had found another of his father-figures, a man who treated him as a friend and who showed him behind the scenes of a world he would never otherwise have entered. The Marquis had a steward, Pierre Tardivon, who impressed Sim so much that he later made him the model for the father of Maigret. One great advantage of the job was that it allowed Sim plenty of time to write. He had by now begun to find a regular market for his *contes galants*, but he wanted to expand and he thought of the popular daily newspaper *Le Matin*. The system at *Le Matin* was that five known writers contributed one story each day, but Friday was open day. Sim was among the dozens of potential contributors who competed for the Friday slot. Modelling his work on the

stories that this newspaper published already, he sent it in to the
literary editor, Colette, who was also one of the regular contributors and who had won fame three years earlier with the publication of *Chéri*. After some weeks Sim received a message that she
wanted to see him. She told him that he was on the right track but
he should drop 'the literature'. '*Pas de littérature!*' she said. '*Suppri-
mez toute la littérature et ça ira!*' Sim was deeply impressed by
Colette, seated in her editorial armchair, but baffled by her advice. He took it to mean that he should simplify his descriptions,
use as few words as possible and make every word count. So he
did this, and once more his work was rejected by the tiny lady
behind the enormous desk with her frizzy hair and down-turned
smile and glinting eyes. But when he simplified his style even
more his stories were accepted and published. This was in
September 1923. In February the following year Colette pro-
moted him to the select group of regular contributors. He had
been in France for fifteen months, and he had arrived. He felt
confident enough to resign his position with the Marquis de Tracy
one month later. He had enjoyed the job and learnt a great deal
(about wine, among other things), but the Marquis spent far too
much time in the country and Sim wanted to get back to Paris.
They parted good friends.

When he left the service of the Marquis, Sim and Tigy moved
to the rue des Dames, back in the Batignolles near the hotel where
he had spent his first night in Paris. They had grown tired of the
cul-de-sac close to the offices of Binet-Valmer. But they spent
only three months in the rue des Dames because one day, while
wandering through the city, Sim saw a notice advertising an
apartment in the place des Vosges. There were only two rooms,
but he took it at once. It was on the ground floor of a courtyard at
the end of which Hoffman-Laroche had their laboratories. The
building had once been the *hôtel particulier* of Richelieu. The place
des Vosges is one of the most famous and historical squares of the
city, surrounded by the *Marais*, one of the oldest parts of the city,
which was in those days a jumble of shops, craftsmen's studios,
tumbledown palaces and dubious alleys. Free from office hours
Sim could now spend his time writing and wandering around,
Tigy would paint all day and in the evenings they would go out
together looking for fun. Tigy painted everything, still-lifes,
landscapes, interiors and portraits, but she was becoming inter-

ested in the nude, generally the female nude, and one of Sim's tasks was to find her amateur models, girls who needed the money enough to be paid very little. He generally found them in bars, frequently in Montparnasse. The procedure as he later remembered it was to spot a likely girl on the other side of the bar and ask if she was interested in posing for his wife. If she said 'yes' he would invite her to unbutton her dress. If all seemed in order, he would palpate her breast and the deal would then be clinched. Girls came to Paris from all over Europe hoping for fame and perhaps even fortune as artists' models. One of them was called Alice Prin, who came from a small town in Burgundy. She was 16 when she walked into La Rotonde for the first time, the day after she had been thrown out of her home by her mother. She was seen, not by Sim, although it was one of his favourite bars, but by the painter Moïse Kisling, later to become one of Sim's friends. She was fresh, pretty and composed and sitting in front of a *café au lait*. '*Tiens*,' said Kisling, 'who's the new tart?' Alice Prin was not amused and told him so in no uncertain terms. Kisling was delighted, and invited her to pose. Then Modigliani, Foujita and Picasso asked her to pose and very soon she was the best-known model in Paris. She became famous as 'Kiki of Montparnasse', and had a long and passionate affair with the American photographer Man Ray, who made her even more famous. She posed, among many other pictures, for his 'Violon d'Ingres' in 1924. Kiki later said that she had been '*un modèle triste*' and that Kisling, to make her laugh, had let out lunatic screams while he painted her. Kisling remembered that she had been a gay model and that in order to amuse him she used to imitate opera divas. This gave her the idea of singing in public, and she would frequently be found in Le Jockey singing songs about whores and their boyfriends in a voice that approached the baritone, passing round one of the customer's hats at the end of the performance. On numerous other occasions Kiki had the sympathetic idea of removing her clothes in public, generally while dancing. Her admirers said that 'her skirt went up and down like a theatre curtain'. Kisling was a sociable painter. He found that conversation stimulated his work, and his studio was frequently full of a crowd of friends, including Tigy and Sim – who was duly impressed by Kiki.

For Kiki these were the best days of her life. She stayed on in

Montparnasse after most of the painters departed in the early 1930s, but she was no longer its queen. Quite soon she stopped removing her clothes, then her voice went, and she ended as a drug-addicted alcoholic, reading palms amid the tables of La Coupole while the paintings and photographs which had immortalised her changed hands for ever-increasing millions. The photographer Brassaï wrote of her, 'Most of the victims of those mad days went away to die. Kiki stayed on the bridge and went down with the ship.' She died in her 50s, in 1953, and her funeral procession included delegations carrying banners from all the leading cafés and brasseries of Montparnasse – La Coupole, Le Dôme, Le Jockey and of course La Rotonde. But the only painter to follow her coffin to the cemetery was Foujita.

Another of Sim's favourite haunts was Le Sphinx, an unusual brothel on the boulevard Edgar-Quinet which resembled an elegant café, where many husbands would bring their wives and children and where Kisling would come in his ceaseless search for models. The sixty girls who worked at Le Sphinx did not have to prostitute themselves, but if they did so they were allowed to take their clients home with them if they wished, after paying a small fee. Many of the girls also danced at the Folies Bergère and were just looking for introductions or for the pocket-money which they could earn as hostesses. Because of its novel rules Le Sphinx had an enormous success. It became one of the fashionable sights of Paris. Journalists started using the bar as their office and worked from it by telephone. The interior decoration was elegant and funded by bank loans, and the owner, Marthe Lemestre, known as 'Martoune', was on excellent terms, and openly so, with the city's *préfet de police* and with the minister of the interior, Albert Sarraut.

Sim had plenty of time to devote to these amusements because of his phenomenal writing speed. The facility with which he had completed his newspaper column first thing each morning at the *Gazette de Liège* had been developed through the medium of the popular short stories, so that before long he found that he could type eighty pages a day, which equalled four to seven stories. None was commissioned, which introduced to him another valuable practice of never writing against an advance. All his life Sim considered this an extremely 'dangerous habit' which was likely to lead to debt. He was always prepared to sign contracts binding him to produce so many titles a year, but he took his money from the royalties and was able to negotiate a higher royalty rate as a result. However in 1924 Sim's royalties were a thing of the future. His pulp short stories were sold outright, most of them never being reprinted. Before long he felt he was ready to extend his range.

When Tigy and Sim first came to Paris they depended a great deal on Luc Lafnet. Lafnet had a sad end. His little daughter died, and he died shortly afterwards, of cirrhosis of the liver. Like other members of 'La Caque' he was a failure, but in 1922 he lived in Montmartre, in the rue du Mont-Cenis, and he introduced Tigy to the open-air show held every month in the place Constantin-Pecqueur. This was for young painters and was known as the 'Foire aux Croûtes'. One summer morning in 1924, after they had moved into the place des Vosges, Tigy and Sim set out for an exhibition. Tigy made the pictures, Sim made the frames, but on this day Tigy found his attendance an irritation. He was too restless and she told him he would frighten off the customers. So Sim went off to a café nearby, possibly in the rue Caulaincourt, and sat down and decided to write a longer than usual story, that is a novel. He almost finished it still sitting on the café terrace and before he had ordered a late lunch and called it *Le roman d'une dactylo* since it was about a typist and since that was the market he was aiming for. He took it to J. Ferenczi, publisher of a pulp series called 'Le Petit Livre', who accepted it at once, paying him the equivalent of what he would receive for three short stories. By the end of the year he had written and published two more short novels with J. Ferenczi under the pseudonyms of 'Jean du Perry' and 'Georges Simm' (sic).

From 1925 to 1927 Sim and Tigy enjoyed life to the full in the place des Vosges and Montparnasse. At first, to get from one to the other, they would cross the Ile de la Cité, walk up the boulevard St Michel and cross the Jardin du Luxembourg. Later they could afford taxis. Before too long Sim had purchased a car and hired a chauffeur whom he later claimed to have dressed in naval uniform in order to avoid problems with the police. From all this it can be seen that the character who eventually made Georges Sim's fame and fortune was not the work of an inspired morning, it was the fruit of six years' apprenticeship, a period during which Sim deliberately set out to learn his trade. But unlike many apprentice novelists he did not starve in a garret while constructing a first masterpiece. He did not attend a 'creative writing course' or read for a degree in literature. He had no chance of attending university and no private means either. He had to earn a living and he wanted to write, so, naturally enough, he tried to earn a living immediately from writing, and this meant not writing what he wanted to write but writing what people wanted to read and publishers were prepared to pay for.

Sim never admitted that he had a model for his career, but the coincidences between his life and that of Balzac are striking. Balzac wrote ninety-one novels, which together made up his *Comédie humaine*. Balzac started by producing popular or pulp books which he published under various pseudonyms until, at the age of 28, he wrote a novel, *Les Chouans*, which he judged good enough to publish under his own name. Immediately he started producing novels at a very fast rate, writing the *Comédie humaine* in nineteen years, while continuing for much of that time to work as a journalist in order to pay his debts. Unlike Sim, Balzac suffered precarious financial circumstances because he was addicted to gambling and speculation. Unlike Sim, Balzac produced work which recommended itself to critics because it was intended to form part of an artistic whole. The 2000 characters who appear and reappear illustrate a range of human weaknesses, and he imposed on this chaotic and lifelike world a sufficiently rigorous structure to enable him to claim that it amounted to one work. That was *'sérieux'*. Sim never achieved that, nor even consciously aimed at it, although he too used many similar characters and his novels might have been presented as parts of a saga had he chosen to do so. On the other hand, Sim produced his work with a wonderful economy and orderliness of effort, in contrast to the confusion which governed Balzac's life, and Sim had far more business sense.

From 1924 to 1928 Sim's annual total of published *romans populaires* rose from three to forty-four. At the same time he was serving his apprenticeship in other ways. Many French writers work for the publishing houses which publish them, in a part-time capacity, and Sim was unusual in never having worked for a publisher. But he nonetheless acquired a detailed knowledge of publishing contracts and of publishing finance. He never used an agent, preferring to conduct all negotiations himself, but he had a

precise knowledge of a publisher's expected profits on any particular title, and during his years as a pulp novelist he is known to
have dealt with six different publishers and with several dozen
magazine editors. From the start of his career Sim showed a rare
talent for marketing. As early as 1925 he managed to persuade a
senior reporter on *Paris-Soir* to write a front-page article about his
unusual writing methods. It appeared on 5 June and discussed the
facility and speed of this young man's writing methods.
According to *Paris-Soir* the 22-year-old Georges Sim would be at
his typist's elbow at 9 a.m. each morning and would before
midday dictate three short stories. That afternoon he would
deliver the stories to their publishers and that evening he would be
working on two longer stories of 10,000 words each which were
due for delivery within a week. Sim was already one of the most
popular short-story writers of *Le Matin*. He was producing sixty
stories of 1000 words each every month, as well as three longer
stories of 20,000 words in the same period. The article gave a
conventional picture of an ambitious young provincial in a hurry,
but it added, 'The day when he has earned the right to some
leisure, he will do great things.'

This was the first article written about Sim in the Paris press. It
came two years after his first stories were accepted by Colette for
Le Matin and one year after the publication of *Le roman d'une
dactylo*. The reference to the typist taking dictation is curious and
is the only indication that Sim ever used this method. The
implication is that he had to use a typist in order to maintain his
production rate. This young writer wrote so fast that a professional typist had to mark down the words on the paper for
him. Perhaps one can already see the Sim touch here, the exotic
detail which made the interview worth the front page. After all, it
would have cost little to hire a typist for a morning and to have
dictated to her three of his unpublished stories.

In the summer of 1924 Tigy and Sim had taken no holiday. They
were both too busy working, they had spent much of the previous twelve months travelling out of Paris with the Marquis de
Tracy and anyway they had no money. But in 1925 they had the
time and enough money to take a holiday in a house in Normandy
which had been lent them by a friend who was a picture restorer.
It was near Etretat, the seaside village famous for its cliffs and

shingle beach. The holiday was important because it was here that
they met Henriette Liberge, the 18-year-old daughter of a local
cod fisherman, one of a group of children who came to spy on
them through the window of their cottage while they made love.
Henriette had been born and brought up in the village of
Bénouville, the eldest in a family of eleven children. Her grandfather had been drowned at sea. Her father, Henri Liberge, had a
small boat which provided barely enough income to feed them
all. Her mother, Berthe Cornu, would send one or other of them
out most days to a neighbouring farm to ask for 'quarante sous de
crème' to put in the family soup, and they had to be careful not to
go to the same farm twice running. They had no relations who
worked on the land, fishermen's children, as Henriette remembers
now, did not marry paysans: 'compared to us they were practically
nobles, they had so many things, all we had was a little boat'.

Henriette's father was a good cook and it was fun growing up
in such a large family. The worst punishment they were given
was to be made to kneel in front of the grandfather clock while the
other children ate supper and then to be sent to bed hungry. When
this happened their mother usually smuggled up some food to the
room in which they all slept together. Henriette's father was eager
for his eldest daughter to start earning a living and there was no
hesitation when at the end of their holiday Tigy offered to take
Henriette back to Paris as her maid, to live with them in their two
rooms in the place des Vosges. Mlle Liberge had round eyes and a
creamy, fair Norman skin, and Sim (it was becoming a habit)
changed her name and rechristened her 'Boule', and so she was
known from then on. She became part of the family and later
remembered how she disapproved of Sim's frequent successes
with Tigy's models, and how she would jealously chase them out
with a broom. Sim liked Boule very much and would sometimes
read his novels aloud to her to get a non-intellectual reaction – 'en
tant de publique ordinaire' is how she puts it today. He knew that
her comments might be short but that they would be direct and
honest. Sim did not then know of the part Boule was going to
play in his and his family's life, but for Tigy her supposed role
was clear. As Sim's work had increased the amount of housework
that fell to Tigy had also increased. Now she could once again
find the time to paint as much as she wished. By the end of 1925
their first three years in Paris would be over and the time given to

Tigy in their original agreement would be up. At art school she had excelled at portraits and figures, and in the summer of 1926 she exhibited again at the 'Foire aux Croûtes' and this time sold a large nude. She had asked 1000 francs for the picture, sure that the customer would shake his head and walk away. But to her surprise and delight he paid for it and then purchased a smaller canvas for 800 francs. They were the first pictures Tigy had sold in over three years. They decided to blow the money on a summer holiday on a Mediterranean island, found the name 'Porquerolles' in *Larousse*, and set out on the train with Boule and their dog, a Great Dane called Olaf.

In those days Porquerolles was the unspoilt home of a small fishing community. There were only two hotels. When they reached the island, off Toulon, they hired a two-room hut with a bamboo verandah. The verandah became Sim's study. He wrote in the open air wearing only shorts, and when he had finished he learnt how to fish, 'gorged on sunshine and heat' and enchanted by the light and the clear water. It was a place to which they would return again and again.

After the weeks spent on Porquerolles Tigy and Sim threw themselves into a frenzy of parties and excursions which was to last ten months and was finally to exhaust their taste for Paris. It was the climax of the *années folles* which preceded Wall Street's Great Crash. Sim was writing up to eighty pages a day for six publishers, and it was during this period that he met an important new patron, Eugène Merle, a left-wing confidence-trickster and publisher born in Marseille who before the Great War had been a pacifist and anarchist and was imprisoned by the government. In 1919, Merle launched a satirical review, *Le Merle Blanc*, which advertised its 'revolting bias, its unfair abuse and its stench of bad faith' and proceeded to outsell the well-established satirical and political review *Le Canard Enchaîné*. Simenon later described Merle as 'a blackmailer', though his victims were not private individuals but banks. He would discover their irregularities and use the information to obtain generous credit. Merle seems to have been one of the models for Alain Malou's father in Simenon's *Le destin des Malou*. He built up a chain of publications which had a tendency to fail, and he was a specialist in rubber cheques, but he also had a talent for raising new money which he used to pay off his old creditors while bouncing more cheques on his new contributors. It was a remarkable system of what might be called 'debit control' and fortunately for Merle 'credit control' was yet to become a profession. Once a week Sim found himself in the queue of angry contributors outside the office of Merle's cashier. Also in the queue would be Pierre Lazareff, Marcel Achard, Robert Desnos, Pierre MacOrlan and Jean Cocteau, but it was Sim, writing under so many pseudonyms, who was generally owed the largest sums of money, who was, therefore, the most exasperated, and who one day left the queue and went in search of the proprietor. By the time he found Merle Sim was so nervous that he lost his temper and started to become abusive, whereupon Merle said, 'Oh, thank you. What a good idea. You leave all the others queueing up like a bunch of cretins while you come in here to start a row. And why are you so surprised about the cheques? I sign so many cheques each day some of them are bound to bounce!'

After that, and for some years, Sim and Eugène Merle became friends. On Sundays, Merle, in search of political gossip for his new evening paper, *Paris-Soir*, would entertain at his country house at Avrainville, near Paris. He himself would cook, and he invited politicians and journalists out for indiscreet lunch-time conversations. It was there that Sim discovered how men like Edouard Herriot, the prime minister, talked when they were off-stage, and noted the contrast between their conversation on Sundays and the press releases and speeches they made on Mondays. He was fascinated and disgusted at the same time. And it was from Merle that Sim learnt the importance of publicity. *Paris-Soir* quickly achieved the highest sales in France. It was Merle who sold out a novel by one of his contributors, Jef Kessel, with posters ten metres square, and Merle who made Henri Béraud the most feared drama critic in Paris with the slogan 'the only man who tells the truth about new plays'. And in 1927 Merle hit on the idea of using '*le petit Sim*' to launch his new daily paper, which was to be called *Paris-Matinal*. It was a publicity stunt which was such a success that it became famous, even though it never took place.

On 14 January 1927 M. Georges Sim, 'Homme de Lettres', signed a contract with Eugène Merle undertaking to be locked into a glass cage, where he would write a novel for serialisation in the new paper. The theme, the title and the characters of the novel would be chosen by referendum and communicated to Sim by a court official as he entered the enclosure where he was to spend the next seven days until he had finished his task. He was to receive 50,000 francs on signature of the contract and a further 50,000 francs on completion. He also received a generous cut of all subsidiary rights. In fact, although *Paris-Matinal* was launched shortly afterwards, it folded before Sim could be locked into his glass cage. However under the terms of the contract he kept the original 50,000 francs, and the advance publicity was such that for years afterwards people used to come up to him and tell him how they had been among the large crowds gathered round the cage watching him at work. Over the years the legend of the glass cage grew and grew. At various times between 1933 and 1958 the cage was said to have been erected in the place des Vosges, or in the entrance hall of the daily paper *L'Oeuvre*, or in the entrance hall of another newspaper. Sim said that the cage was actually constructed by leading glass-makers in the rue de Paradis but that it was never erected outside the Moulin Rouge where the exploit was billed to take place. In fact, if Sim had not insisted over many years that the exploit of the glass cage had never taken place, it would undoubtedly have remained an historical event, complete with eye-witnesses and detailed plans. The illusion was entirely created by the advance publicity. 'A sensational exploit,' said the pre-launch posters; 'one of the best of the young generation of novelists will write a record-breaking novel, a record for speed, for endurance and, let's face it, for talent, enclosed in a glass cage under the constant inspection of the public. The proprietor of *Paris-Matinal*, M. Eugène Merle, has outbid every other paper to sign a contract with Georges Sim for 300,000 francs.' For the purposes of publicity Merle, needless to say, had tripled Simenon's fee.

Throughout these months in 1927 Sim's social life was keeping pace with his new wealth and his professional success. He installed an American bar in the corner of the front room in the place des Vosges which he later claimed was the first private bar to have been built in Paris and where he and Tigy threw parties that became famous. Sim learnt how to make cocktails and encouraged his guests to drink in order to watch their behaviour. The results were what he described as 'semi-orgies'. The room would fill with recumbent but not inert bodies, some behind the long black curtains installed by the fashionable interior decorator Dim, some not behind the curtains, some on the landing outside, where their presence led to eruptions from the concierge in the morning. By then Sim would already be at work. At 4 a.m. Boule had instructions to wake him with a cup of coffee and he would sit down at his desk in the corner of the room and start to type; by the time his guests had departed or woken for breakfast his day's work was frequently finished. The photographs taken at one of these parties show Tigy sitting on a high bar-stool beside her friends while Sim, cocktail shaker in hand, stands behind the bar watching her. He would resemble the perfect, deferential, discreet barman except for the pipe in his mouth. Behind his shoulder, attached to the wall above the rack of whisky and *pastis*, is a picture of the singer, dancer and cabaret star Josephine Baker, with whom he had just fallen in love.

Josephine Baker was, from 1925 to 1928, just about the most famous woman in Paris. She had arrived from St Louis; she was 19 years old; and she lived in an apartment near the Parc Monceau. In 1925 she had been the star of 'La Revue Nègre' in the Théâtre des Champs-Elysées, a show which people either walked out of after the second number or returned to constantly. This is how one reviewer described her:

> Her lips were painted black, her skin was the colour of a banana, her short hair was stuck down on to her head and gleamed dully like caviare, her voice was shrill, her body moved in a perpetual trembling and twisting. She grimaced, she tied herself in knots, she limped, she did the splits, and finally she left the stage on all fours with her legs stiff and her bottom higher than her head, like a giraffe in old age. Was she horrible, delicious, black, white? She moved so quickly nobody could decide . . . Her finale was a barbaric dance . . . a triumph of lewdness, a return to prehistoric morality.

Another reviewer saw her in 1926 at the Folies Bergère wearing her famous belt of bananas:

> A gilded body with breasts thrust forward like a figurehead, moving in spasms of desire . . . Long legs, her bottom jerking in a frenzy, her fine long fingers tensed straight or caressing

herself and an extraordinarily expressive and mobile face . . .
Her act, which was partly a caricature, offered a powerful
challenge to civilisation in the name of primitive instinct . . .
She combined a little hatred, a hint of revenge and the justified
pride of pure animality. She was full of mockery, instinct and
sensual fury.

And everything moved. She was obscene and divine as she
excited her audience, mocked them and then rejected them. She
was accompanied by a Negro jazz band and she soon opened her
own nightclub in the rue Fontaine in Montmartre, where Sim
became a regular visitor. In private life Josephine Baker was rather
as she was on stage: she adored all the attention she was getting
and she adored making love, which she did with many people and
with great exuberance. Among her lovers was '*le petit Sim*' who,
unknown to Tigy, became one of her most fervent and regular
admirers. They made love with a violent energy that Sim found
overwhelming. He wrote in *Mémoires intimes*: 'I would have
married her if I had not been afraid, obscure figure that I was, of
becoming known as Monsieur Josephine Baker.' As it was he
became her part-time secretary, which was one way of explaining
to Tigy why he was spending so much of the day with her, and he
also edited 'Josephine Baker's Magazine'. At the same time he was
editing another magazine, for Merle, called *La Merle Rose*, which
was intended for lesbians. Sim's own description of Josephine
Baker, in *La Merle Rose* rather than in the fan magazine, was
certainly enthusiastic. A meditation on her body ended with the
words: 'It is, without question, the most famous bottom in the
world. It must be the only bottom which has become the centre of
a cult. And it is everywhere, on music sheets, on magazine
covers, plastered all over the city's walls, because it is the only
bottom that laughs!'
  1927 was the most frantic, the most exciting, the most dangerous year for Sim and Tigy, but it was not finally what he wanted,
and he retained enough lucidity to realise that. Distracted by
Josephine Baker, he wrote and published in 1927 only one collection of short stories and eleven *romans populaires*; in the previous
year the total of novels had been sixteen, and in 1928 it was to be
forty-four. In every crowd of pleasure-seekers and debauchees
there are the true believers and the frauds. Sim was a fraud. And

wherever there are talented people amusing themselves and
burying themselves in a life of pleasure there are one or two who
are secretly working hard. Tigy and Sim were members of a circle
in Paris which by now included Jean Renoir, Kisling and
Vlaminck, among others. All those of their friends whose names
were to become celebrated were frauds. They did not just have
talent, they worked. In the summer of 1927 Sim realised that he
too was a member of this secret society. He and Tigy left Paris for
a holiday on the Ile d'Aix near La Rochelle. Sim said later that he
had fled to get away from Josephine Baker because his affection
for her was disturbing his marriage, but it was as much a flight
from the kind of life they had been living, which had started
going too fast and which was threatening his work. He had just
started his career and nothing was going to stop him now. They
were away for most of the summer and they left suddenly without saying goodbye. They were to spend many years near La
Rochelle, in the Vendée and the Charentes Maritimes. It became
his favourite part of France. He was drawn to it partly by its
people, who lived from both the land and the sea. 'Between La
Rochelle and the Vendée,' he wrote, 'there lives a race of very
special people. One might say that they are land-peasants and sea-
peasants at the same time. They have land and cows as well as
mussel beds and oyster farms.' They returned to Paris in the
autumn and Josephine Baker and all their friends were still there.
For the others life resumed its previous pace, but for Sim the spell
was broken and he started a new life.

Tigy and Sim did not break with Paris immediately, but on their
return they entertained less and spent more time in Montparnasse,
particularly in La Coupole, the vast brasserie which served up to
1300 *couverts* each day, and where an extraordinary mixed crowd
of people came to gaze at itself. Until now Sim had frequently
gone out in the evenings with Tigy, Boule and a Bretonne, a
junior maid called 'Madeleine'. They would sit at a table in a *bal
musette*, Sim with his three women, dancing with each in turn.
But that winter he began to spend more time exploring Paris
alone and at night. The place des Vosges was close to some of the
most abandoned quarters of the city, the rue de Lappe, a dangerous little street off the place de la Bastille and near the Gare de
l'Arsenal, from where Simenon walked up the Canal St Martin,

which was solitary and unpoliced and where there were moored barges and vagabonds. He was looking for prostitutes and other sordid adventures, and he was searching for ideas for his novels. It was on these solitary expeditions that he gathered the material he was to use nine years later in *L'homme qui regardait passer les trains* (*The Man Who Watched the Trains Go By*). The matter-of-fact conversations of prostitutes at work, the furnishings of cheap hotel rooms near the Gare du Nord or in Pigalle, the routine police raids during which every bedroom would be turned out in the search for people without papers, all this became part of his first-hand experience. But there was also the more lighthearted company of women such as 'la Môme Crevette', an occasional singer and dancer, who wore no knickers, 'since' as she said, 'in the time it took to remove them I might lose an opportunity,' a remark which Sim would later attribute to characters such as Angèle and Nelly in *Le chat* (*The Cat*), girls who always made love in high spirits and who would sometimes exclaim, at the height of the action, 'Who invented that trick? They should put up his statue.'

Simenon was becoming tired of the *contes galants*, and the sort of love stories which 'appealed to domestic servants and concierges'. He had had a big success, but finally he had lost Josephine Baker because he felt he was a nobody. It was no longer enough for him to make a lot of money from journalism and pulp fiction and to have a lot of fun. '*Manger et faire l'amour*' was no longer his motto. He was learning a lot about the techniques of writing novels, but he needed something to write about. He was drawing on a deeper part of his nature, and he was immediately attracted to that side of life which he remembered as being testing and vivid, the criminal world.

At the same time Sim was drawn away from Paris altogether. He was on the verge of being bored by it and he did not want to be sucked back into the hectic round, fuelled by the money of Eugène Merle and limited by the circle of superficial friends. He found the solution in the spring of 1928 in the form of a boat, which he bought and (naturally) rechristened, as the *Ginette*, and in which he and Tigy and Boule and Olaf, the Great Dane, set off on a six-month voyage of discovery round France. He was looking 'for an unknown France, an unknown world and an unknown life'. He found all that, and described it as 'one of my most astonishing discoveries'. The boat, four metres long, had cost 2000 francs, and the equipment, including an outboard motor, twice as much again. They set out in April, and the route was Paris, Epernay, Chaumont, Chalon-sur-Saône, Lyon, Marseille, Sète, Carcassonne, Toulouse, Bordeaux, Montluçon, Orléans, Paris. They stayed on rivers and canals except for the short Mediterranean voyage between Marseille and Sète. They towed a smaller boat behind them which carried most of their equipment, including the tent. Tigy and Sim slept in the larger boat, under a canvas cover, while Boule and Olaf slept in the tent, which meant that every night had to be passed in the countryside. Boule woke first and made the coffee, then at 6 o'clock she woke Sim who set up his typewriter and started work. By 10 o'clock Sim had finished work and Boule had been to the nearest market and filled up the water cans. Then they struck camp and set off. They moved at ten kilometres an hour throughout the day, sometimes stopping briefly in a town or village. They set up tent at nightfall having dined on the riverbank. Sim kept in touch with his publishers by *poste restante*, sending off the manuscripts and receiving commissions and the vital cheques. During the sea passage Boule's tent was pitched on the beach and in the morning she was summoned by trumpet. Carrying the morning coffee she waded out into the sea through water that came up to her breasts. The two main hazards of the voyage were the descent of the Rhône from Lyon to Marseille, which a boat such as theirs was supposed to be too small to survive, and the tunnel beneath the plateau of Langres, which was nine kilometres long and had no lighting and which they had to navigate in pitch dark with the aid only of a red warning light:

> We spent nearly six months on the water, usually dressed in no more than a bathing costume. We passed through a thousand locks, most of which we worked ourselves. We ended with calloused hands, broken nails, a cooked skin and bleached hair, and one month after getting back to Paris we still looked in our town clothes like clumsy peasants dressed up in their Sunday best.

Sim had discovered a magical new world, the sights and smells and life of *la France profonde*; it was a knowledge which he was shortly to put to good use although he did not yet know how.

In the winter of 1928 Sim and Tigy were once more in the place des Vosges but it was clear that he at least had finally lost interest in their life in Paris. His steady work over the six months spent on board the *Ginette* had enabled him to bring his annual total of books published to forty-four, the highest he was ever to reach in his life, and he now had enough money to buy a larger boat, for he intended to spend most of the following three years on the water. The boat he commissioned was a Normandy fisherman's cutter. It was small enough to be useful on canals and shallow rivers, but strong enough for inshore maritime cruises. It was built at the little port of Fécamp, close to Etretat, Boule's home. By the time the boat was ready the following spring, and unknown to Tigy, Sim and Boule had become lovers. 'I fell in love with him at once,' she said in 1991. 'I was very impressed because he was a writer and I had no idea what being a writer meant. I thought they lived in châteaux and walked around all day in a silk dressing-gown. I didn't realise they had to work hard like other men.' Boule remains discreet about her relationship with Simenon, but a similar arrangement is perhaps to be seen in the relations between the unhappily married Emile and the easy-going Nelly, described in *Le chat*. Nelly was 'always ready to make love' and would do so standing behind the kitchen door, quickly and frequently, on the watch for interruptions. Then she would return to her work, preparing a '*plat peuple*', perhaps '*saucisses de Toulouse*, swollen and juicy, served with red cabbage and surrounded by an agreeable hint of garlic'. Boule was to remain with Sim longer than any other woman in his life.

SEVEN

A certain idea of France

Don't forget that the policeman was often born in the same street as the criminal, had the same sort of childhood, stole sweets from the same sweetshop . . . Deep down the policeman understands the criminal because he could so easily have become one. They inhabit the same underworld.

Simenon, interview (1963)

'Georges Sim has the honour to invite you to the christening of his boat, the *Ostrogoth*, which will be carried out by M. Le Curé of Notre-Dame next Tuesday at the place du Vert-Galant.'

It had not taken the boat-builders of Fécamp long to build the fishing cutter, even if, as became clear later, they had cut some corners. The *Ostrogoth* had survived the short sea passage to Le Havre and had ascended the Seine as far as the Ile de la Cité where it was moored in the spring of 1929. Sim and Tigy invited all their friends to the naming ceremony, although Josephine Baker was not there, having set off on a two-year world tour in August 1928, shortly before the return of the *Ginette*, noting sadly in her diary that 'Georges disappeared one day, as suddenly as he arrived. He is married.' But otherwise *le tout Paris* was present and the christening (the only form of religious ceremony Sim requested in his life, apart from his first wedding) was followed by a three-day party. The party was not just celebrating the arrival of the *Ostrogoth* but the departure of Tigy and Sim. The boat was to become their home for the next three years and they did not berth in Paris again for over twelve months.

In his life on the water Sim had discovered the perfect solution to several problems. There was a discipline and regularity to proceeding along a river or canal which was the perfect framework for his daily work, but which also assured him of constant change. Tigy could continue to paint, although she had to abandon her portraits. But her work had taken precedence for six years, instead of three, and she was now ready to place it second to his. Finally the distractions of Paris were banished, but life on the water remained full of new possibilities. Sim was in fact almost ready to start writing 'seriously'. All he needed was to find the appropriate form. He had called the *Ostrogoth* after his supposed ancestors, identifying himself in doing so as Flemish, and it was of some significance that in searching for the vital ingredient that remained to be found before he could begin his 'real' writing he turned the boat northwards, towards the mists and plains of Belgium and Holland and away from the sunshine and easy pleasant life of the south, the life of Porquerolles and the voyage of the *Ginette*. On their way north Tigy and Sim, once more with Boule and Olaf, passed by Liège but did not stay long. Sim wanted to show his old friends his new boat and he paid a brief visit to his mother. No doubt she would have gone through her current list of *misères* with him, among them the fate of her new friends Joseph André, a retired railway conductor, and his wife, also called Henriette, who was dying and whom Mme Simenon was helping to nurse. Mme André died in June and four months later – to the day – Henriette married Joseph André.

Before setting out Sim had contributed thirteen stories to a new magazine founded by Jef Kessel. The magazine was called *Détective*; it sold 350,000 copies with its first issue and the stories, billed as 'mystery' stories, were in fact classic 'whodunnits' in the English style, the sort of story in which Sim was quickly to lose interest. But they marked a new direction in his writing.

In 1929 Sim did not quite match his prodigious output of the previous year, but he still published thirty-four novels, many of them for Fayard, a leading house which had become his most important publisher. The seeds of what was to follow can be found in several of these last *romans populaires*, for three of them contained a police inspector called 'Maigret'.

Sim gave a precise account of the origins of Jules Amédée François Maigret, and it stood unchallenged for many years:

It happened that one morning on board my boat the *Ostrogoth*, anchored in the port of Delfzijl, I tried to write a detective novel. It was something of a step up the ladder towards 'literature', much as I detest that word. There is nothing easier in fact than to write a detective story. For a start there is at least one corpse, more in American detective stories. Then there is an inspector or a superintendent who conducts the enquiry and who has the right to probe into the past and present life of each of the characters. And finally there are the suspects, in varying numbers and different degrees of camouflage as the author decides will best lead to the final dénouement . . . When I wrote my first detective story at Delfzijl in the North of Holland I was completely unaware that it would be followed by many others containing many of the same characters. Even the outline of Maigret was sketched. He was a big man, who ate a lot, drank a lot, followed the suspects patiently and eventually uncovered the truth. Most of my popular novels had been published by Fayard so I sent the manuscript there . . . I waited at Delfzijl, where I had to break the ice around my boat each morning because it was mid–winter. I did not have to wait for long. I was summoned to Paris by telegram and when I arrived I saw that my publisher had my manuscript on his desk.

That was written in 1979, in *Je suis resté un enfant de choeur*. In 1966 he had written in 'La naissance de Maigret':

I see myself once more on a sunny morning in a café which was called I think Le Pavillon, where the *patron* spent several hours each morning polishing his wooden tables with linseed oil. I never again saw such shining tables in all my life. At that hour there was no one sitting at the big central table, so typical of Holland, a café where newspapers, carefully folded around brass rods, awaited the regular customers. Had I drunk one, two or even three little glasses of schnapps and bitters? In any case after an hour, feeling rather sleepy, I began to see the powerful and imposing bulk of a gentleman emerging, who it seemed to me would make an acceptable detective–inspector.

During the course of the day I gave this character a number of accessories: a pipe, a bowler hat, a heavy overcoat with a velvet collar. And, as my deserted barge was cold and damp, I furnished his office with an old cast-iron stove . . . By noon the following day the first chapter of *Pietr-le-Letton* had been written.

Until quite recently these two accounts were accepted as the definitive version of the genesis of Maigret: *Pietr-le-Letton* (*The Case of Peter the Lett*), written at Delfzijl and published in 1931 by Fayard, was not only 'the first Maigret' but was the first novel Simenon agreed to have published under his own name. In fact, *Pietr-le-Letton* was *not* the first 'Maigret' to be published; it was not the first book to be published under Simenon's own name; it was not written in Delfzijl; and it was not the first book in which Commissaire Maigret appeared. A learned controversy has been mounted on all these points for several years which has established to date that although *Pietr-le-Letton* was the first proper 'Maigret' to be written, probably in Paris in the summer of 1930, and the first to be accepted, a bulky detective with a pipe first appears in *L'amant sans nom* by 'Christian Brulls' written in 1929 and published by Arthème Fayard. The detective was called N.49. In the following year Fayard published *Train de nuit* (also written in 1929) in which a 'Commissaire Maigret' attached to the *brigade mobile* of Marseille appears, who is calm and shows understanding towards criminals. This was the book actually written in Delfzijl in September 1929, when the *Ostrogoth* (due to the haste of its builders) was laid up for recaulking. But it was not written during the depths of winter, and not even in the *Ostrogoth*, but in a neighbouring abandoned barge where Sim set up a big packing case for the typewriter, a smaller one for his seat and two even smaller ones for his feet. Maigret next appeared in *La femme rousse*, written just after *Train de nuit* by which time the *Ostrogoth* had reached Wilhelmshaven; but here Maigret had a minor role compared to his junior inspector, Torrence, who had also been in *Train de nuit*.* However *La femme rousse* 'by G. Sim' was turned down by Fayard, and was published only in 1933, by Tallandier.

* Torrence, together with Commissaire Lucas, had first appeared in *L'inconnue* by C. Brulls (Fayard, 1930).

Next came the first Maigret book, where the Commissaire was the central character and Torrence was his assistant. Maigret was enormous, had a pipe, a bowler hat, a heavy overcoat and a stove, worked with Juge Coméliau, was married, lived in the boulevard Richard-Lenoir and was sympathetic to a young girl caught up in crime. This book, called *La maison de l'inquiétude*, was also written in the bitter cold of a northern winter, but at Stavoren in Friesia, not Delfzijl, and was indeed sent to Fayard, who once again refused it. So Simenon sent it instead to the magazine *L'Oeuvre* which published it as a serial from 1 March 1930, before *Train de nuit* and *La femme rousse*.

All of these novels were at first refused. All were experimental and popular rather than genuine 'Maigrets' but in quality they were better than anything Sim had written before. After Stavoren, Tigy and Sim went to the north of Norway and Lapland by passenger boat, and then returned to Paris on the *Ostrogoth* in April 1930, one year after setting out. It was probably here, rather than in Stavoren, that Sim wrote *Pietr-le-Letton*, since it seems to contain material from Lapland. It was accepted by Fayard and published on 26 May 1930 in *Ric et Rac*, a *feuilleton*, from July to October 1930.

Pietr-le-Letton was the first 'Maigret' written in the full sense, not just with the character but in the style. In these circumstances it is hardly surprising that Simenon always claimed it was the first 'Maigret'. In fact in telling how he invented Maigret, he improved the story in his usual way, recalling some of the amusing circumstances of the maiden voyage of the *Ostrogoth* when he was writing 'pre-Maigrets', and attributing these incidents to a book which he wrote only on his return to Paris.

In April 1930, when the *Ostrogoth* returned to Paris, Sim was in a curious position. He was the author of 122 successful pulp novels, sold outright without royalties and published under pseudonyms, and was in the process of producing another twenty-five similar works in the course of the current year, but he had become convinced that he was ready to write under his own name and that he had discovered the form and above all the character to start the next stage of his career. His publishers, however, did not agree with him. They were dismayed and even dismissive of his conviction that this unlikely seeming *commissaire de police*, who did not follow clues or a process of deduction and did not seem to be committed to the war against crime, would ever reach a large public. Time and again Sim's prototype 'Maigrets' were turned down, Fayard, his chief hope, being the least enthusiastic. Arthème Fayard saw Sim as a highly satisfactory producer of large sums of money for publisher and author, and the last thing he wanted to do was to disturb the arrangement. It took Simenon nearly a year to persuade him otherwise. 'My God it was a battle to launch Maigret,' Simenon recalled in his interview with Roger Stephane. 'It was the only time in my life when I became deeply involved in the commercial side of publishing a novel . . . I knew this was my big chance and it had to work immediately or it might hang fire for ten years.'

Although Georges Simenon was a master of publicity very few people knew his real name, even in private life, and when Arthème Fayard finally decided that the 'Maigrets' should be published, but under a different name to the previous pulps, and that this time they would use the writer's real name, he had to ask what this was. Most people thought he was called Georges Sim; he was sometimes still called '*le petit Sim*', as by Colette; and in Italy, when early 'Maigrets' started appearing in translation, one reviewer pointed out that Simenon was the *nom de plume* of the much better known Georges Sim. So, unknown as he was, Simenon decided that what was needed was a massive publicity investment. The result was the ball given for the launching of the 'Maigret' series on 20 February 1931 at a Montparnasse nightclub, La Boule Blanche, in the rue Vavin. It was called a *bal anthropométrique*, the police term for the department where suspects were stripped naked, measured and photographed. The guests wore fancy dress, anything evoking the criminal or police world, and many were in *apache* dancing costumes. There were painted faces, funny hats, paper streamers, everyone had to be fingerprinted at the door, and the invitations were designed like a police record card. Much of the life had gone out of Montparnasse in October 1929, with the Wall Street Crash. Simenon's ball was to be an attempt to revive the spirit of the old days. The 400 guests, led by 'Kiki of Montparnasse', were joined by nearly twice as many gatecrashers, and more whisky and champagne had to be sent round from La Coupole. The cost exceeded the whole of Fayard's publicity budget and the author had to invest some of his unearned royalties. But the ball was a great success and made the newspapers all over France. Even the *préfet de police* was reported to have been there. Simenon and Maigret became well-known names, and Simenon signed copies of the first two titles to be published, *M. Gallet, décédé* (*The Death of Monsieur Gallet*) and *Le pendu de St Pholien*, the covers for the first time bearing his own name (though it was later, not here, that he signed books 'The first novel by Simenon for eight days' in reference to a publicity campaign for Jef Kessel boasting of 'The first novel by Kessel for three years').

The first reviews for Maigret were good. Many of the reviewers took the point that this was an attempt to raise the standard of the detective novel. These detective stories were better, it was immediately said, than the average. But other reviews did not omit to mention what was to be a recurring source of suspicion, the author's speed of production, and *Le Canard Enchaîné*, as acid then as now, wrote: 'Georges Simenon wants to be famous at any price. If he doesn't achieve fame with his *bal anthropométrique* he intends to walk around the pond in the Jardins des Tuileries on his hands – whilst writing a novel.' The ball, described in several newspapers as 'a night of madness', was the last of Simenon's famous parties. He and Tigy gave up their apartment in the place des Vosges shortly afterwards.

In the first nineteen 'Maigrets' Simenon relied heavily for his settings on his recent travels through France. Not one of them is set entirely in Paris and nine of them are set entirely outside it. Since they concern the work of a *commissaire* in the Paris police force it is clear that he was already taking liberties with reality. Simenon, although this is a fact which it is easy for a foreign reader to overlook, always saw France through the eyes of a foreigner. He had acquired a certain idea of France and he was to make it a universal idea of France, in so far as any one writer's view of a country can ever be universal. Maigret's France is a pungent, colourful country where life is largely lived in public, in bars, markets and streets. It is less a land of private interiors, or family discussions in peasant kitchens, or private discussions in cabinet meetings or board rooms, or banal rites of passage such as weddings or First Communion celebrations. The only interior life which is almost always described is that of '*la maison*', the headquarters of the *police judiciaire*, the criminal investigation department of the Paris police, on the Quai des Orfèvres, the tall grey building on the Ile de la Cité which looks south over the Seine towards the left bank and the Latin Quarter. The rest of France, as described in the first series of nineteen 'Maigrets', is very much the France visited by the man from out of town – in this case, the visiting *commissaire*, in the author's case, the writer in search of a real landscape for his imaginary world. Two of the books are set on French canals; three are set on the banks of French rivers; in another a suspect attempts to drown Maigret in the torrential River Marne, and in the last of the series Maigret retires to a little house on the banks of the Loire; three are set in Channel ports; two are set in Dutch or Flemish towns which Simenon had visited in the *Ostrogoth*; and Liège provides the setting for another two of the books, Simenon thereby making another departure from reality by sending a French police officer outside France for nearly a quarter of his first nineteen enquiries. It is not difficult to see why Arthème Fayard was disconcerted.

The other unusual point about the early 'Maigrets' is the extent to which they were worked out in the author's subconscious from the beginning. If one takes the first, *Pietr-le-Letton*, it is noticeable how many themes are introduced which are to reappear in the seventy-five novels and forty-nine short stories which were to follow. Apart from the immediate importance of topography and atmosphere there is the use of hotel settings, both cheap hotels and luxury hotels, the power of political influence over justice, the power of social snobbery, the casual introduction of sex and the strongly cinematic nature of the descriptions of town life in general and port scenes in particular:

It was in that direction that he began to run. Once past the trawler not a soul was in sight. The night was pierced by the green and red lights of the harbour entrance. Then the light-house on the rocks lit up a great slice of the sea, every fifteen seconds, throwing its beams, for the length of a flash over the cliff below, which reappeared and disappeared like a ghost.

In *Pietr-le-Letton* the examining magistrate is already named Coméliau, and he is already out of sympathy with Maigret. Mme Maigret is already waiting at home, ready to kiss her husband on his return and not ask questions; she is already stirring her sauce-pans preparing '*quelque ragoût odorant*'. We already know that she

is from Alsace and she already has her drily humorous reaction to
Maigret's silences. And Maigret himself, although not fully
developed, is nobody else but Maigret – watchful, grumpy, large,
imperturbable and armed with his terrible patience. Wanting to
arrest a man, but having no reason to do so, he decides to follow
his quarry all over France if necessary. This method of investigation is exhausting and dangerous. Abused by a sharp-tongued
woman in public, Maigret has to hold his tongue. In the lobby of
the Hôtel Majestic he has to wait for hours being made to feel
uncomfortable by both staff and guests. Maigret is a sensitive man
and he suffers when he is uncomfortable. But when he decides to
act he has the ruthlessness of a man who cares for nothing. He
orders a place to be laid for him in the dining room of the
Majestic, at the table of his quarry. The waiter's horrified objections are brushed aside, his adversary says nothing, they sit there
silently, eating. Then, without warning, Maigret speaks: 'Your
moustache is coming unglued.' And when the book finishes
hunter and hunted are together again, in a cheap seaside hotel.
Both men have fallen in the sea during the arrest. Now they are
sitting in the little bedroom, wrapped in the proprietor's dressing-
gowns. Pietr the Latvian is small and elegant and well wrapped
up. Maigret is wearing a garment that fails to cover his knees and
reveals his strong, hairy calves. Maigret orders two grogs and, in
the intimacy of the bedroom, settles down to hear his man's life
story.

So, from the start, Maigret refuses to judge the criminals he is
tracking, preferring in most cases to understand them. He im-
merses himself in the life of those he hunts. He uses unorthodox
methods of investigation and does not hesitate to break the laws
of trespass and criminal damage if necessary. He can feel personal
embarrassment, he is indeed sensitive to rebuffs, but he has a
natural insolence and a brutality of manner which he deploys
when least expected to disconcert a witness. The plot of a 'Maigret' is like life, studded with absurdities rather than heroism.
And the life is, from the start, partly the author's life. We meet
Maigret at the beginning of *Pietr-le-Letton* on a winter's evening
in his office: 'Lifting his head he had the impression that the
murmuring from the cast-iron stove, which stood in the middle
of the room and which was attached to the ceiling by a thick black
pipe, was dying down.' And when, some minutes later, he sets

out for the first time down the Quai des Orfèvres, his brown hair already flecked with grey, he is going to the Gare du Nord, to meet a train arriving from Belgium. He is starting his enquiries on the same railway platform from which Simenon had set out, seven years earlier, to start his.

When Fayard was finally persuaded to publish Maigret, after Simenon had finished *Pietr-le-Letton* in the spring of 1930, it was on condition that he would have several titles to launch at the same time. So Simenon found himself back in France on the *Ostrogoth*, moored at Morsang outside Paris, and writing the next three 'Maigrets'. In the first of these, *M. Gallet, décédé*, Simenon used Sancerre, the Ile-de-France and Paris as his settings, and the intrigue takes place among the French royalists whom he had met when he first arrived from Liège. Then, in *Le pendu de St Pholien*, Maigret finds himself involved in a case which takes him to Liège. The private circle of friends he has to penetrate there is based on 'La Caque', and the key to the crime he is investigating is the suicide of *'le petit Kleine'*.

In *Le pendu de St Pholien* Simenon fictionalises the real story by suggesting that Klein, as he is called in the novel, killed himself out of remorse for a murder he himself had committed some time before, during a meeting of 'Les Compagnons de l'Apocalypse', the fictional equivalent of 'La Caque', when 'the little group of geniuses, thrown together by chance', had become so bored that it had to find something interesting to do, no matter what, and murder seemed the next experience to try. The exact ambience of the real 'La Caque' is re-created although in real life, so far as is known, it did not lead to murder. But Simenon played with the suggestion that it had done, and he evoked the guilt felt by the participants in such a casual, thoughtless crime in convincing detail.

The book confirms Maigret's eccentricity. It starts with an incident in which the great detective, motivated by idle curiosity in a hotel in Bremen, provokes the suicide of a man who is merely acting in a suspicious manner. In the dénouement it turns out that the man Maigret had driven to suicide was the only witness of the murder committed by Klein, and that he could not get over it. He was haunted by it every day of his life. But his remorse had not driven him to suicide, as it had Klein; instead he had turned to blackmail. He had forced the other former members of 'Les

Compagnons', who had all become wealthy or successful figures, to give him large amounts of money, and when he received the money the haunted man always burnt it.

Le pendu de St Pholien is a curious book, the first of many novels in which Simenon explored his childhood and his life in Liège. It contains a lachrymose mother and a devoted father who was patient and generous with a delinquent son. And it turns on the fact that the crime committed in Liège during a meeting of 'Les Compagnons' was about to become null and void by reason of lapse of time, the ten-year period of 'prescription' after which no one could be prosecuted for it. Interestingly enough Simenon wrote this story just eight years after the death of the real Kleine, and it was published one year later. If there were any consciences Simenon wished to tweak in Liège, they would have had a difficult twelve months.

One of the most characteristic phrases in the Maigret series is '*il s'est mis à boire*' (he started to drink). The role of alcohol in Simenon's imaginary world can hardly be overemphasised. In *Les vacances de Maigret* (*A Summer Holiday*), Maigret on holiday with his wife in Les Sables d'Olonne finds himself alone for much of the time because Mme Maigret has had to undergo an emergency appendix operation. When he visits the convent nursing home he turns his head away when talking to the nuns because of the smell of the calvados which he drinks every day after his lunch. He takes his supper alone in the evenings in the hotel dining-room. When people ask for M. Léonard, the hotel proprietor, he usually 'bursts out of his wine cellar', although he is generally 'more or less sober'. Each morning the *patron* offers Maigret a glass of white wine, the first of the day, '*le coup de blanc du patron*'. Maigret patrols the town, not wanting to sit on the beach with the mothers and children. In the market he stops in front of the shellfish stall and, testing for freshness, he offers a lobster a matchstick which the animal grasps at once. Another white wine. Then on to a bar with a terrace overlooking the sea, the usual table, which has become *his* table, what will he have to drink? A white wine. And when he returns to lunch the waitress remembers that he had ordered a calvados after his first lunch and assumes he always takes a calvados and 'he dared not refuse'.

In the nineteenth book, called simply *Maigret* (*Maigret Returns*), the book that was supposed to be the *commissaire*'s farewell,

Maigret, by now a rather old man in retirement, is recalled to Paris to defend the family honour. His incompetent nephew, not cut out to be a policeman, is mishandling a case and Maigret has to take it over as a private detective. For twelve hours he sits in a bar in Pigalle in the rue Fontaine, drinking beer and then calvados, saying nothing, watching and being insulted by the gang he will eventually arrest. For much of the rest of the time he is sitting in the Chope du Pont Neuf, the police bar, opposite the Quai des Orfèvres, drinking more beer and watching the senior officers who have replaced him and who have arrested his incompetent nephew.* In *La nuit du carrefour* (*The Crossroad Murders*), Maigret and a colleague are searching a premises at night, their guns in their hands, and they enter a room where a meal has been abandoned. There is a decanter containing white wine on the table and Maigret empties it into his mouth: '*Il s'est mis à boire.*' It is a refrain, and so faithful was the 1960s BBC TV series to this aspect of the Maigret books that a temperance pressure group started to count the amount of alcohol Maigret drank in each episode and an Anglican bishop implored the producers to reduce it. Wine, beer, *fine* or calvados, alcohol – as presented by Simenon – is a consolation, a medicine, a fuel, a celebration. For the crooks it is often *pastis*, the drink of Paris and the drink of real men. But for Maigret alcohol, an essential fuel, is generally beer. Maigret of course was born near the Loire, a region of excellent '*petits blancs*', and he worked in Paris, a city where men drink *pastis* or Beaujolais. So why did he drink beer, the drink of the north of France, the drink of Belgium?

In an unpublished talk which he gave in 1953, in Connecticut, Simenon answered this question as follows:

> It's a mistake to think that an author deliberately decides that a character will be constructed in such or such a way and will have this or that preference. The creation of a character is a more or less mysterious process which takes place largely in the subconscious. To be completely frank I might say, 'Maigret

---

* Maigret's usual haunt was the Brasserie Dauphine, in real life the Trois Marchés on the corner of the rue de Harlay, which has since disappeared. This has created a vacuum, usually filled, so far as tourists are concerned, by the Restaurant Paul in the place Dauphine.

drinks beer because he cannot drink anything else.' Why do *you* have a long nose, and why do *you* eat chips with most meals?

He went on to recount how, on a recent trip to Belgium, he had revisited three of the places where, as a young man, he had drunk beer, and he explained the exact differences between the three bars, the sort of glasses one drank from, the sort of beer they served, how it tasted and the different behaviour of the men and women who served it. 'Why does Maigret drink beer?' he concluded. 'I think I have answered that question . . . for me the delicious smell of freshly drawn beer remains the smell of Belgium.' And, later, Simenon said that one of the reasons why Maigret drank so much was because when he was writing the early 'Maigrets' he was drinking quite a lot himself.

If Maigret's acquaintance with drink was part of Simenon's 'certain idea of France' this was even more the case with Maigret's relationship with food. When he first arrived in Paris, and was too poor to eat properly, Maigret would spend hours looking through the windows of charcuteries. Maigret, like Simenon, was attracted to markets. He spent recreational hours patrolling the stalls. His social life was virtually confined to twice-monthly dinners with his friends Dr Pardon and his wife Francine. The dinners were held alternately in their apartments and before they were held Maigret and Pardon would talk to each other on the telephone during office hours for some time, in considerable detail, about what was to be eaten. There was never a case, of crime or illness, that was so pressing that it made this regular discussion of the menu impossible. Mme Maigret was of course a notable cook and housekeeper. Since she never knew when her husband would be home, or if he would be home at all, she had to prepare dishes which could be put aside and reheated, in this respect being part of the peasant tradition of cookery, and specialising in what Simenon called '*les plats peuple*', simple home-cooking. Maigret 'adored *ragoût*'; '*fricandeau à l'oseille*' (veal stewed in sorrel sauce) was another of his favourites and was a dish which Simenon regarded as '*un plat de concierge*', the one which is simmering gently as you come home in the evening and pass the door of the concierge's *loge*, the dish which gives you the necessary courage to ignore the broken lift and press on up to your own door on the fourth floor to find out what Mme Maigret, in her turn, has found in the market that day.

In *Le fou de Bergerac* (*The Madman of Bergerac*; 1932) Maigret takes a bullet in the arm in the first chapter while on his way to investigate a case in a small town in south-west France and is from then on confined to bed in Bergerac's principal hotel. His bedroom is above the hotel dining-room, and he is able to discover the daily menu by using his nose. Mme Maigret arrives to nurse him and quickly gains visiting rights in the hotel kitchen. Soon afterwards she produces a '*crème au citron*' which is, quite simply, a masterpiece. But Maigret's pleasure in this dish is marred by the smell of truffles which is rising from below. At the end of the enquiry, solved partly by Mme Maigret's skilful and energetic legwork, Maigret has recovered his health and is at last able to enjoy the cooking of this gastronomic region. As he crosses the town square for the last time it seems to him to be 'simmering gently' in the sunlight. Then he orders a meal of truffles and the local *foie gras*. And then he leaves Bergerac and goes back to Paris where we know he will not starve. For in Paris there will still be the cooking of the provinces, a *jambon à la crème*, a *boeuf bourguignon, une omelette aux peaux de canard, cassoulet, andouillette, cochonnaille, coq au vin*. And in Paris there are markets where a large and hungry man can meditate on lunch and pass from stall to stall, gazing at the contents like a schoolboy gazing through the window of a toyshop; or a young man just arrived from Liège, counting his money carefully, can gaze for the first time into the window of Fouquet's on the Champs-Elysées.

Another hallmark of the Maigret books is the simple style and limited vocabulary in which the stories are told. Some words occur again and again, like the refrain in a litany. '*Machinalement*' (automatically), '*fatalement*' (inevitably), '*balbutier*' (to stammer), '*broncher*' (to flinch), '*pudeur*' (modesty), '*hallucinant*' (incredible), '*lancinant*' (insistent or stabbing or haunting), '*narquois*' (mocking), '*appétissante*' (of a woman, usually plump) and, of course, '*il s'est mis à boire*'. Robert's *Dictionnaire des synonymes* gives thirteen synonyms for '*machinal*' and up to fifteen for '*pudeur*'; even '*lancinant*' has six. The only time Simenon used two words when one would do was in reference to cooking. Usually a dish is '*mitonné*' (simmered), but sometimes it is '*mijoté*' (simmered). It is one or the other again and again. Simenon narrowed his vocabulary deliberately. He estimated that he restricted himself to a vocabulary of about 2000 words, and he did this partly out of the habits he had acquired when writing *romans populaires*, partly because he did not wish to lose the size of the readership he had gained with the *romans populaires*, partly because he wanted to distinguish his work from the self-consciously 'literary', and partly as a statement about himself: he remained one of the *'petites gens'* and he was writing for everybody. The last thing he would have wished to do to a reader would have been to send him or her to the dictionary. He would have considered that rebarbative. For all that the Maigret books were intended to be a step in the literary direction they were also designed to be widely read, which is one of the reasons why they were short. Simenon had very commercial ideas of most people's reading habits and he thought that a book should be read at a single sitting, say in one night or in half a day. 'A book,' he said, 'should be like a play. You do not return to a play every night for a week and you should not have to do so with a book.' He may also have been aware of another advantage of writing short books, one which the publishers of popular novels would have drawn to his attention. If a reader has enjoyed a short novel he is left feeling unsatisfied, wanting more, another novel. Whereas the reader who has on the whole enjoyed a novel but found it too long has paid all the money he will pay for some time before once again feeling the need to enter the author's imaginary world. In other words a good novel cannot be too short. And there may have been another reason for the simplicity of Simenon's vocabulary. We know from his published journal *Quand j'étais vieux* (*When I Was Old*) that he had a horror of rising from his desk when he was writing. He wrote so fast that he was intolerant of any form of physical interruption. By restricting himself to his 2000 words he had absolutely no need at any stage to consult a dictionary, or a thesaurus, or any grammatical reference work.

The question of whether or not there was an original model for Commissaire Maigret has received several answers. Even the origin of the name is uncertain. Tigy remembered quite clearly that the name had been chosen by Simenon from the list of fellow tenants written up on the notice outside the concierge's *loge* in the place des Vosges. If so, this was a coincidence, bearing in mind the police officer called Maigret serving in Liège at the time

Simenon was a reporter on the *Gazette*, particularly as he was stationed in the town hall, which Simenon visited almost every day of the week.* Among the real-life policemen Simenon had known was a friend of his grandfather, a retired police inspector who used to drop into the house in the rue Puits-en-Sock for a pipe and a glass of schnapps. There were also numerous senior officers of the Liège police who were not called Maigret but whom Simenon certainly knew. But the policemen who were generally given the credit for a resemblance were Parisian, in particular there was Commissaire Guillaume, head of the *brigade spéciale* of the Parisian *police judiciaire*. Although the character of Maigret came from Simenon's imagination, and from his past, many of Maigret's methods seem to have been based on the techniques of Commissaire Guillaume.

The early 'Maigrets' were apparently such a success that they were read by the head of the Paris CID, Xavier Guichard. He later summoned Simenon and told him that a writer who was going to such lengths to make his books realistic should be told how to avoid so many fundamental errors. Simenon was then introduced to M. Guillaume and was allowed to roam behind the scenes at the Quai des Orfèvres and even to be present during the questioning of witnesses. He watched witnesses being broken down over a period of twenty-four or forty-eight hours during a questioning marathon conducted by a team of six or seven policemen, and he said that in his belief a man like Guillaume would never have used violence during an interrogation simply because he had no need to. He also watched while a witness was stripped naked and questioned in front of a room packed with fully clothed police officers. 'I assure you that nothing disconcerts a man like being stripped naked, without pockets, without anything at all. It's very difficult to tell lies for long in that costume,' he said.

In *Pietr-le-Letton*, as we have seen, Maigret already had the cast-iron stove in his office, an authentic interior detail of the Quai des Orfèvres. In *Le pendu de St Pholien* it is clear that Simenon was already familiar with police procedure at both the Paris and Bremen city mortuaries. The first book contains references to such police methods as the Interpol standard card index and Dr

---

* The real Commissaire Maigret was eventually deported from Liège during the Second World War and died in a concentration camp.

Locard's ear-identification chart, and the second to the detailed forensic examination of a dead man's suit. The opening words of *La nuit du carrefour* refer to an interrogation '*à la chansonnette*' which had lasted seventeen hours, and that was written in April 1931, only two months after the *bal anthropométrique*. It seems clear that before Xavier Guichard summoned Simenon to the Quai des Orfèvres the author, like an experienced reporter, had arranged to do some research, in order to update and bring to life the knowledge he had already acquired by attending the series of lectures at the University of Liège in 1920 and 1921. Yet Simenon consistently denied that he had made serious efforts to research police methods before creating Commissaire Maigret. 'When I wrote the first six or seven "Maigrets",' he said in 1963, 'I had never set foot in the Quai des Orfèvres. I had walked past it because I used to love walking beside the Seine, but I knew absolutely nothing about police organisation.'

Simenon's sensitivity may have come in part because he was anxious to emphasise the imaginative aspects of his most popular creation as opposed to the realistic nature of the books. In either case the real origins of Maigret lay far away from the Quai des Orfèvres and from the divisional inspectors of the 1st Division of Liège – men such as Oscar Neujean, Joseph Mignon and Alphonse Manaerts. For his real origins we must look to the imposing bulk of '*Vieux-Papa*' pouring over the edges of his armchair in the enclosing warmth of the family hearth in the rue Puits-en-Sock; to the authority of Chrétien Simenon with his pipe and his schnapps; and to the supportive interest and refusal to condemn of his own father Désiré. The real origins of Maigret are to be found in the disturbed child's ultimate resource, the father who did not reject a boy in trouble but who tried to put things right, the first person in Simenon's life who showed him how 'to understand and not to judge'. Maigret as the good policeman was an echo of the good father, the man who corrects you but who understands. In *Quand j'étais vieux* Simenon even declared that: 'For thirty years I have tried to make it understood that there are no criminals.' Maigret was the *redresseur des destins*, the 'mender of destinies', fulfilling this role even in the pre-Maigret books, as for instance in *Train de nuit* by 'Christian Brulls', when a police inspector based in Marseille called Maigret shows so much understanding for the sister of a murderer that he puts her on the train to Paris with her share of the stolen loot. In many of the subsequent stories Maigret frequently did what he could in order not to press charges, or at least to reduce their seriousness. He was of course, throughout his career, operating under the shadow of the guillotine. The crime of murder was still in legal terms an offence that attracted a uniquely severe punishment, and this gave Maigret's detections and his acts of merciful understanding an exceptional importance, for among the powers he disposed of was the power of life and death.

As to whether or not there was anything of Simenon in Maigret, there is directly conflicting authority. Simenon, like Maigret, had always wanted to be a *redresseur des destins*, and the profession of novelist was one of the few that allowed him to fulfil this ambition, since the Church was not in his line and since he, like Maigret, had been prevented by circumstances from becoming a doctor. In 1963 he told Roger Stephane, 'It's just another legend to say that I identify myself with Maigret. I have never imagined that I resembled Maigret.' But in 1976 he told Francis Lacassin, his Swiss publisher, that Maigret was 'one of the rare characters I created with whom I had a certain number of points in common'. What the two had most in common was an understanding of the criminal and therefore of the crime. Like Maigret, Simenon had been born in the same streets as the criminals, and had plundered the same shop tills. Like Maigret, Simenon could very easily have become a criminal. Like Maigret, Simenon – if he had become a criminal – would have been a formidable man to catch. He once said that if he had been born in an urban ghetto he might have become a killer. Could he ever have become a criminal, was he a criminal *manqué*? His second wife Denyse thinks not, 'because he lacked the courage to be a criminal'. But had he become one there is perhaps a model of his criminal character in one of the first series of 'Maigrets', *La tête d'un homme (A Battle of Nerves)*. In this book Maigret is up against a criminal who understands human frailty and motives as well as he himself does. Radek is a Czech and a failed medical student who haunts La Coupole in Montparnasse. Radek murders a rich old lady and sets up a burglar to make it look as though the latter has committed the crime. Radek's motive is hatred of a society which has failed to recognise his talent. He turns to crime to show society what a mistake it had made. Maigret finally proves a match for him and

sends him to the guillotine. *La tête d'un homme* was the fifth
'Maigret' but the first in which the murderer is executed. There
were no 'extenuating circumstances' for a killer like Radek, a
Maigret 'gone bad', as Simenon acknowledged in disposing of
him so ruthlessly.

Clearly there was something in Maigret which Simenon aspired
to be, whether or not he attained it. But this is not to say that
Maigret was not at the same time an authentically fictional character, one of his least autobiographical heroes. Simenon after all was
not a policeman, he was a novelist. But then so, perhaps, was
Maigret.

With the discovery of Commissaire Maigret, Simenon entered an
imaginative world that was to make his fortune. This character,
emerging as he later claimed through a haze of winter mist and
schnapps, was to lead to sales of 500 million and to make him the
most widely read living author in the world. But the invention of
Maigret was also of decisive importance for Simenon because it
liberated him from the weight of production which had been
forced on him by the writing of pulp fiction. What happened was
that he continued to write his novels at the same speed, but now
had to produce only four to six instead of twenty-five to forty
each year. Each 'Maigret' was soon earning as much money as
any five 'pulps'. The extra time gave him the interval necessary to
build up to the tremendous effort he had to make to create these
new, 'real', characters. His inability to sustain the effort for more
than a short period ensured that the production *speed* was kept up,
but the ensuing imaginative exhaustion meant that the production
rate dropped.

To get some idea of the effort it took for Simenon to switch
from pulp fiction to 'Maigrets' and the straight novels which
followed it is sufficient to study the change in his production rate
between 1924 and 1939. As we have seen, his first three pulp
novels were published in 1924. His annual total of pulp novels
published between then and 1928 went to fourteen, then sixteen,
then eleven, then forty-four. 'It sounds silly but I used to count
automatically, pulp novels eighty pages a day, detective stories
forty pages a day, in two sessions,' he wrote later. 'And I used to
tell myself then that when I had no need to write more than
twenty pages a day I would be a king, a landlord living off his

rents. And in fact after the first "Maigrets" I reached the point where I typed no more than twenty pages a day and for no more than sixty days a year.' In 1930 Simenon wrote four more 'Maigrets' and signed a contract to produce a further five so that in the following year the character could be launched with ten books. In 1931 he wrote eight 'Maigrets' and his first straight novel, and in these three transitional years his production of pulp novels dropped from thirty-four a year in 1929 to thirteen in 1931. He wrote the last of the 188 'pulps' in 1933.

Although the 'Maigrets' were an immediate success Simenon originally saw the *commissaire* as a transitional figure, a stepping-stone to fully fledged literary novels. 'I still needed a safety net. I was still not able to write a novel where all the characters could roam free . . . I thought of the "Maigrets" as semi-literary novels,' he recalled later. He wrote four 'Maigrets' in 1932, two in 1933 and then none for five years. This first series of nineteen culminated in *Maigret*, with which Simenon intended to say good-bye to his character, and in which he put the *commissaire* into retirement. He wrote *Maigret* in June 1933, only two years after the series had been launched, and four months later he signed a contract with Gallimard, the most prestigious publishing house in France. He had by then written fourteen novels which he called *romans littéraires* or *romans durs*. Although he had published only six of them he felt ready to embark on the main phase of his career.

In his new persona as a serious novelist Simenon remained as productive as with the 'Maigrets'. Seven novels were written in 1932, six in 1933, four in 1934, three in 1935, four in 1936, eight in 1937, four in 1938 and six in 1939. During the following six war years Simenon produced twelve more *romans durs*. So long as his major imaginative efforts were dedicated to the 'Maigrets' there were few problems. Maigret, a good man, was a good influence on Simenon's subconscious. It is significant that the *commissaire* was never overwhelmed by sexual desire. On at least one occasion, in *Maigret*, he did climb into bed with a young prostitute, but it was only to engage her in conversation.

EIGHT

Death of a playboy

I have written 349 novels, but all that amounts to nothing. I have not yet started the work I really want to do . . . When I am 40 I will publish my first real novel, and by the time I am 45 I will have won the Nobel Prize . . . Everything else I have predicted so far has come to pass. So, I will win the Nobel Prize in 1947.
                                    Simenon, aged 34 (December 1937)

The fact that Simenon first admitted to drinking heavily when he was writing the early 'Maigrets' was not coincidental. Maigret was first visualised under the influence of schnapps. Nine of the first twelve 'Maigrets' were written while Simenon was living on the *Ostrogoth*, and boats are notoriously conducive to increased drinking, either because the boat is under way, which is thirsty work, or because the boat is stationary and one is bored. But most of all Simenon was drinking because of the strain involved in his new method of writing. The fact that he drank while writing was quite well known, and was the subject of a satirical attack in the magazine *Père Ubu*. He had begun to immerse himself in his principal character; the way to literary achievement involved possession, the possession of the character by Simenon and, gradually, the possession of Simenon by the character. Simenon created Maigret by living him; he created the detective in the same way he described the detective undertaking an enquiry in the very first book, *Pietr-le-Letton*. Maigret attaches himself to his suspects, 'he casts about, he waits, he watches out for, *"la fissure"* [the crack] – the first sign of the man behind the adversary'. This process of immersion and of casting about was exhausting for Simenon. Between the spring of 1930 and the end of 1931 he wrote thirteen Maigret books, an average of one every seven weeks, and the process drained his energy far more than the mass-production of 147 pulp fictions in seven years, an average of one every two and a half weeks. By the end of 1931 Simenon was worn out. He decided that it was time for a complete change. He had already abandoned Paris in favour of life on board the *Ostrogoth*. Now, with some sadness, he sold the *Ostrogoth* and looked around for a home in the country. He had made a lot of money and he wanted a break. He was to write only four 'Maigrets' in 1932, an average of one every thirteen weeks, half his previous rate. He felt ready to start writing something else but he needed something to write about. Provincial France and the north European canal system had given him Maigret; now he needed something less familiar.

By April 1932, Simenon's search for a house was over and he and Tigy had moved into La Richardière, a sixteenth-century *gentilhommière* or country mansion near La Rochelle on the Atlantic coast in the Charente–Maritime. This part of the country was to be their base in war and peace for most of the next thirteen years, virtually all the remaining time that Simenon was to spend in France. In 1966 (when he was very unhappy) Simenon wrote in the visitors' book of the Café de la Paix of La Rochelle, 'In memory of the happiest days of my life'.

Having sold the *Ostrogoth*, Simenon and Tigy had gone first, in December 1931, to a villa in Cap d'Antibes, but they had not settled there and Simenon decided that if he could not live in both the north and the south he should have something of each. What he said he wanted most when he was in Antibes was 'fog', according to Boule, Simenon, making the same point rather differently, said that what attracted him to La Rochelle above all else was the light: 'In the region of La Rochelle I found exactly the light of Holland, the radiance you find in the skies of Vermeer.' The house they found was for rent, not for sale, although it was probably the house he would most have liked to own of all the houses he lived in. La Richardière had a tower, and stables and a farmyard, and its own land running down to the sea, and there

was a small lake which took in sea water at spring tides. There
was a walled vegetable garden and a wood. Simenon and Tigy
had adjoining rooms on the first floor where he could write and
she could paint. At this stage in his career Simenon relied considerably on Tigy's support and criticism. When he was planning
a book they would go on long walks together, and at the end of a
day's writing he would hand her the typescript. Many years later
he would say that the best books he wrote were those written
during the years when he had Tigy to criticise them. When he was
writing he would get up at 6 a.m. and the house had to be
absolutely silent. He wrote as though he were in a trance, according to Tigy. Tigy painted a lot at La Richardière. She signed her
pictures 'Régine Sim', in loyalty to the *nom de plume* that her
husband had already abandoned. In the stables there were five
horses, in the lake 400 ducks, and there were rabbits, turkeys,
geese and chickens, as well as pheasants in the woods. After a
while there were also two wolves, from Turkey, which were kept
in their own enclosure. There was also a mongoose which was
tame enough to wander round the estate until it wandered into the
wood and was inevitably, since it moved, shot by a passing
hunter.

    Simenon was by now a very well-known man. In La Rochelle
he became something of a celebrity. He would ride into the
walled city on his pure blood Arab stallion to visit the fishmarket
or to play bridge at the Café de la Paix. While he was at the card
table he paid a boy to hold the horse's head, and after a while the
mayor of La Rochelle arranged for a ring to be put into the
pavement outside the café and the boy was no longer required. At
the fishmarket Simenon would buy dozens of fresh sardines
which he liked to eat raw. This meant that Boule had to fillet them
while they were still alive, then place them in the fridge for several
hours. Boule did not find filleting live sardines easy and there
were noisy scenes when Simenon returned on his horse, which he
rode bareback, carrying a basket full of sardines. Simenon
enjoyed cooking and specialised in Belgian dishes, especially
soups. One of their Parisian friends who frequently visited them
at La Rochelle was the painter Vlaminck. He enjoyed his visits but
he saw Simenon with candid eyes. 'I've been to have lunch with
Georges Simenon,' he wrote later:

Simenon likes luxuriousness and comfort; beautiful cars, beautiful fabrics, expensive things. He has a marked taste for everything that distinguishes the rich man from the *premier venu*. When he travels he stays in sumptuous palaces and dines in the most celebrated restaurants. But when he writes he sets his stories in seedy hotels jumping with fleas, in shady bars and in low dives. His heroes are the poor and starving, men who are dragged down by misery and become murderers or suicides.

It was not in La Rochelle that Simenon was going to find the originals of these heroes.

In June 1932, two months after moving into the new house, Simenon and Tigy left La Richardière in Boule's charge and set out on a journey across Africa. Simenon had by now made so much money from Maigret that he could afford to travel to remote parts of the world in comfort.* But he did not intend to spend his own money. The trip would be paid for by journalism.

Simenon and Tigy sailed from Marseille to Alexandria and then flew from Cairo by Imperial Airways via Wadi Halfa to the southern Sudan and the border of the Belgian Congo. It was the first time Simenon had left Europe. In the Sudan they bought an old Fiat and drove on uncertain roads to Stanleyville. Then began the long descent of the Congo river to the port of Matadi, where Georges's brother Christian occupied a senior position in the port administration. Christian was by this time married to a girl from Liège, Blanche Binet. They had married in 1928, had left shortly afterwards for the Congo, and Blanche had given birth to a son, 'Georget', named after Georges, in February 1932, seven months before the arrival in Matadi of Tigy and Simenon. The West African climate was so unhealthy that it was not long before

---

* Following the *bal anthropométrique* in February 1931, Fayard had published a total of eleven 'Maigrets' by the end of the year. Before setting out Simenon supplied them with six more unpublished titles. The 'Maigrets' had been such an enormous success that they were already being filmed. Jean Renoir had pursued Simenon across France to sign the first film contract for *La nuit du carrefour*, and had eventually caught up with him where the *Ostrogoth* was moored in the port of Ouistreham in October 1931. Simenon himself tried to film *La tête d'un homme* in the basement of the Hôtel Carlton on the Champs-Elysées, but abandoned the project abruptly just before leaving for Africa.

Christian and Blanche sent little Georget back to Liège, where he was brought up by his doting grandmother.

At the time Citroën cars had organised an African rally and publicised it with a film called *L'Afrique vous parle* – 'Africa is talking to you!' When Simenon returned he subtitled his series of articles for the magazine *Voilà! 'l'Afrique vous parle: elle vous dit merde'*. In years to come he was to recount many times how he had always seen through colonialism, and even before his journey through Africa had been a resolute opponent of it. In fact what he wrote at the time in *Voilà!* and in the several novels which were based on his experience was both more complicated and more original. He calculated the cost of a colonial railway as 'one dead black man every sleeper and one dead white man every kilo-metre'. He came across one of these black men himself, a man who was still alive but who was about to die. He had been working in a construction gang on the Sudanese–Congo border and earlier in the day an enormous boulder had crushed his leg. The nearest doctor was 150 miles away and there was no means of reaching help. The black man was doomed to die of tetanus before anything could be done for him and so his friends were going to finish him off and eat him that night.

Simenon took these horrors in his stride. He was chiefly irri-tated by the prevailing 'exotic' approach to Africa and decided that it was a place where people were, essentially, much the same as anywhere else in the world. He was unreceptive to any sugges-tion that a different history, a different language, a different culture or climate, might make people different. He was more interested in noting the similarities between peoples. It was an essential part of his personal philosophy that *'l'homme nu'* was always the same. In Africa his conclusion was that colonialism was a fraud and that it would have been better to leave the people of Africa in peace than to make any attempt to introduce edu-cation or medical care or democratic government. Civilisation was for Africa a mistake. Describing the tragi-comedy of the building of the colonial railway whose eventual purpose was a mystery, Simenon concluded:

> The cotton crop had failed, coffee was being sold at a loss, nobody wanted to buy rubber, the tourists would find nothing to see, and the Africans could not afford the price of a railway

ticket. That left just Africa itself, laughing as it watched the human insects running round in circles until they died . . .

When he returned from Africa Simenon wrote that he hated it:

When you are there you sweat, you groan, you drag yourself around and you end by hating everyone including yourself. You swear you'll never go back, and then as soon as you reach France you find nostalgia creeping in.

As for colonialism, Simenon's chief objection to it, at the time, was for the effect it had on the white colonials. He was contemptuous of the easy life they led and the airs they gave themselves. He did not spare his brother Christian, noting that his African nickname – 'the white man with the loud voice' – could be taken two ways. Georges was not impressed when Christian told him, proudly, that he was able to sell his empty tins of *petits pois* for the same price he had paid for them when they were full, because the Africans needed the metal to make into ornamental souvenirs. At times Simenon's African journalism and novels read like an attempt to put Christian in his place. His brother may have gone out to the Congo and done rather well for himself, he seems to be saying, but this was what his life was really like. That at least is how Henriette must have read them back in Liège

Simenon and Tigy's trip to Africa lasted three months. They returned by sea from Matadi along the West Coast. They took a French boat heading for Bordeaux and calling on the way at French colonial ports such as Port-Gentil and Libreville. It was in a hotel in Libreville that Simenon finally found the material for his first 'exotic' novel, *Le coup de lune* (*Tropic Moon*).

On his return to France Simenon installed a punchbag at La Richardière, finding, perhaps, as is suggested by the photographs taken at that time, that he had put on weight. The 1930s were the only time in his life when he did put on weight. He was eating well, staying in expensive hotels and surrounding himself with luxuries. It was a period when memories of his childhood and family battle-cry '*J'ai faim*' faded a little and were replaced by the motto 'I'm full', meaning 'I'm happy'. His other innovation on returning from Africa was to construct a reed-hut in the park of

La Richardière. He wanted it to be an authentic African hut so he indented, in the best colonial style, for a platoon of native troops from a colonial regiment and set them to work cutting reeds, chopping wood and binding the wood together with wire. The men had almost forgotten how to build a hut, and since Simenon did not feel at ease in the colonial role he soon asked Boule to serve the soldiers with drinks (it was a hot day), and then more drinks. Before too long the soldiers had become so drunk that they were incapable of continuing work. They passed out or became unmanageable and before the day was out a second detachment of colonial troops had to be summoned to overpower the first detachment and return it to barracks. The hut was never finished.

Simenon's impressions of Africa, set out in *Voilà!* and his subsequent books, were resented in official circles, and when he tried to revisit the French colonies in 1936 he was refused a visa. He gave a dramatised account of this refusal in 1976, saying that he had been sitting in the Café Maurice in Porquerolles with some friends one evening, discussing his imminent departure, when from behind him a voice had boomed out a prohibition, and turning he had seen a man in shirtsleeves who identified himself as Pierre Cot, the minister of the interior. Pierre Cot was actually the junior minister for air at that time, but the refusal of a visa was real enough.

Simenon went on one other long tour while living at La Richardière. In 1933 he and Tigy set off across Europe, again charging part of their costs to magazines. They first headed for Berlin, where they stayed at the Hotel Adlon and where Simenon found himself in the lift with Hitler. He then watched Hitler in friendly conversation with the Kaiserin Herminie, the second wife of the last Kaiser. Simenon noted that Hitler was an ordinary looking little man and a much less impressive sight than the cossetted Prussian army officers he had encountered in the streets of Liège. During this visit Simenon was contacted by the Communists, who told him that they had been able to bug Nazi headquarters and knew that the Nazis were about to commit a political outrage but did not know precisely what it would be. He wired a story to *Paris-Soir*'s foreign desk on the impending '*coup de force*', but the newspaper's foreign desk spiked it. Forty-eight hours later the Nazis set fire to the Reichstag building in Berlin and managed to throw the blame for this shocking event on to the Communists. Shortly after that Hitler came to power.

Simenon and Tigy continued their journey to Poland, Czechoslovakia, Hungary and Romania. In Vilnius he met one of his mother's former lodgers and found to his amusement that she had called her son 'Christian', apparently after his brother. He entitled his series of articles about Eastern Europe for *Le Jour* '*Peuples qui ont faim*'. After travelling through Czechoslovakia, Hungary and Romania, Simenon's conclusion, emphasised in his ominous title, was that there was trouble ahead for Europe. But the crowning journalistic achievement of the journey was an interview he managed to secure with a man who was a specialist on trouble in Europe and who was generally unavailable for interview. In June the Simenons reached Istanbul and the special correspondent of *Paris-Soir* applied for permission to meet Trotsky.

In 1933 it was extremely difficult to gain access to the former Soviet leader, who was in exile and in fear of his life. He was living on the island of Prinkipo, off Constantinople, when Simenon wrote to him and succeeded in getting permission to call. This was a genuine journalistic 'scoop'. Simenon took the boat out to Prinkipo one hot afternoon. Having crossed the police barricade and entered the walled enclosure surrounding Trotsky's villa he was greeted by Trotsky's secretary. 'The secretary was not Russian. He was a young man from the North, bounding with health, pink-cheeked and clear-eyed and he spoke French as though he had been born in Paris.' The young man in question, unnamed in Simenon's article for *Paris-Soir*, was called Rudolph Klément.

Klément had been born in Hamburg in 1910. He was a gifted linguist who had joined the Trotskyist movement in 1932 and been chosen as one of the exiled dictator's bodyguard and secretariat. He learnt Russian in six months, he already spoke fluent German and French, and he arrived on the island of Prinkipo in April 1933, four weeks before the arrival of Simenon's letter. The reason why Simenon was given the interview, where so many others had failed (although he did not realise it at the time), was partly because the arrival of Klément meant that Simenon's questions and Trotsky's answers could be typed up in French at once, and partly because Trotsky, having recently applied in great secrecy for a French visa, was anxious to gain a little favourable publicity in the French press. Prinkipo was too isolated and too close to the Soviet Union. The Turkish authorities were not able to give Trotsky all the assurances he needed about his safety, and his presence on the island was widely known. The time had come to move on and Trotsky's idea was to go into hiding in France. He knew that if the French government allowed him in they would make a serious effort to keep his presence a secret and to protect him.

Simenon took a photograph of the wandering revolutionary seated at his desk and noted that he had been reading Céline's *Voyage au bout de la nuit* which had profoundly troubled him. Simenon asked Trotsky only three questions, which had had to be submitted in writing in advance as the great man had been too frequently misquoted in the press to agree to any other method. The questions concerned the role of race in human evolution, the historical role of dictatorships and the necessity of violent change in the march of progress. Trotsky used these questions to restate his ideas on Hitler, National Socialism, the threat of war, the fate of Europe and the future of nation states – all pitched for a popular readership. When Simenon walked into Trotsky's study he was handed a typed copy of the answers to his three questions, in French, which he had to sign. He was allowed to remove a second copy, and was also allowed one or two supplementary questions.

Simenon's interview was published in *Paris-Soir* on 16 June 1933, and in July Trotsky received his French visa and Rudolph Klément accompanied him to Paris. They set up house in a villa called 'Ker Monique' in Barbizon, and for nearly a year Trotsky was able to live quietly in this village on the edge of the forest of Fontainebleau. Klément would drive into Paris to the central post office in the rue du Louvre to collect the letters which had been sent *poste restante*. One night in April 1934 he was stopped by the *gendarmes* because his lights were not working properly. His papers were not in order either. Klément was arrested, the presence of Trotsky was discovered, the press were informed and *L'Humanité*, the Communist Party newspaper, led a violent press campaign for his immediate expulsion. In June 1935 Trotsky was expelled. Klément remained, in fear and in hiding, knowing that from now on he was a target for the liquidators of the NKVD. In due course a headless body was pulled from the Seine which was almost certainly his. That was in August 1938. Klément had been working in two small rooms, one in the rue Notre Dame-des-Champs and the other in the passage de Vanves, where he was sheltered by a future detective-story writer, Léo Malet. The police never established who killed Rudolph Klément but it is known that a man called 'Jacques Mornard', a mysterious Trotskyist sympathiser, arrived in Paris early in July, disappeared, ostensibly to Belgium, in mid-July, and reappeared one month later to be present at the founding conference of the 4th International. Klément had been preparing this conference at the time of his disappearance on 14 July. Just before his disappearance his briefcase containing confidential papers about the conference was stolen on the Métro. 'Jacques Mornard' made many friends among the Trotskyists at the 4th International and won their confidence sufficiently to gain an introduction to Trotsky himself three years later, in Mexico City, by which time he was known as 'Raimond Mercader' and armed with an ice-pick.

Simenon never realised the part his 'scoop' may have played in the murder of Rudolph Klément and the assassination of Trotsky. The nearest he came to the political underworld was when he agreed to investigate the 'Stavisky affair' for *Paris-Soir*, *Marianne* and *L'Excelsior* from January to April 1934. This major financial scandal led to the downfall of Daladier's government, several members of which were suspected of having profited from it, and also led to serious political disorders in central Paris and to an attack on the Chambre des Députés by a royalist mob. Simenon's attempts to throw light on the affair were not very impressive as examples of investigative journalism (this did not stop him from describing them later as an 'essential' part of the enquiry), but they were more impressive as background research for an eventual political novel. He started his investigation in a way no reporter would, sitting in a café offering to pay for information. Later he claimed that a senior police officer stuck a gun in his ribs and warned him off, and that he responded by sticking his own gun into the policeman's ribs and refusing to be warned. He eventually wrote eleven articles in *Paris-Soir* which drew the readers' attention to a rich cast of characters but took the search for the facts no further.

On returning from his European tour Simenon told Fayard that in future he would be writing no more about his famous and extremely popular detective. He was becoming tired of the jokes in *Le Canard Enchaîné* ('M. Georges Simenon makes his living by killing someone every month and then discovering the murderer') and he wanted to win a reputation as a serious novelist. From now on he would write novels. He had in fact already published two titles with Fayard, *Le relais d'Alsace* (*The Man from Everywhere*) and *Le passager du 'Polarlys'* (*The Mystery of the 'Polarlys'*), but though neither contained Maigret both were essentially detective stories about theft and murder. Just as Maigret appeared in several books before the launching of the Maigret series, so Simenon continued to write detective stories while attempting to escape from the identity of being the man who wrote Maigret stories. But by June 1933 Simenon had also written three genuine *romans durs*, *La maison du canal* (*The House by the Canal*), *Les fiançailles de M. Hire* (*Mr Hire's Engagement*) and *Le coup de lune*.

When Simenon told Fayard that Maigret was in retirement the publisher could hardly believe his ears, and this time decided to exert himself. First this lucrative but tiresome author had abandoned the pulp novels which were so profitable; now he intended to abandon the 'Maigrets' which had replaced them. Fortunately Fayard had him under contract to deliver seven more 'pulps' and two 'Maigrets', and now he insisted that Simenon fulfil these contracts. It was a very expensive mistake. Fayard had never drawn up a contract with options on future *romans durs*, but was publishing them as they came along. Simenon was therefore free to take these elsewhere. He was so irritated by Fayard's insistence on enforcing the pulp contract that he decided to find another publisher, and it was at just that moment that Gaston Gallimard, owner of the most prestigious publishing house in France, decided to add Simenon to his list.

Gallimard invited Simenon to his office and the interview that followed, as recounted by Simenon to Fenton Bresler, however implausible, has become famous. Gallimard having secured Simenon's agreement in principle suggested that they discuss the terms of the contract over a good lunch on another occasion. Simenon replied:

'Listen, Monsieur Gallimard. In the first place we will never have lunch together. I detest these business lunches where one talks about everything except business, and eventually has to make another appointment for a second such lunch. We will discuss the contract in your office with your secretary taking notes, the door shut and the telephone off the hook, and we will reach an agreement in less than half an hour. And furthermore I will never call you "Gaston" as everyone else here seems to do, and please stop calling me "*cher ami*" because I also detest expressions of that sort. Tell me the time and the day, I will return to your office, the contract will last one year and when the time comes to renew it you will in future come to my house.'

The conditions of the contract which was eventually signed were exceptionally favourable to the author. Simenon would provide six books a year at regular intervals and author and publisher would split the gross profits 50:50, which Simenon would help to determine. Gallimard could take it or leave it. He took it. It was a bolder decision than has been generally recognised and a tribute to Gaston Gallimard's ability. Because although he was acquiring a best-selling author, Simenon was only a best-seller of 'pulps' and 'Maigrets'. In backing him as a major producer of quality general fiction, Gallimard was backing his own judgment.

The contract, signed in October 1933, did not take effect until 1934. When he signed, Simenon had a stock of six unpublished *romans* completed, of which only two were destined for Fayard. He therefore started his contract with four books in hand, which was just as well, because his life was about to enter a turbulent period, and from 1934 to 1936 he was going to write an average of fewer than four books a year, a situation which meant that in 1937 he was facing the possibility of an unprecedented situation, an inability to supply his publisher with the number of titles for which he was contracted. Since Gallimard was sending him regular advances of 40,000 francs, since (according to Pierre Assouline in *Simenon Biographie*) he was earning up to 750,000 francs a year, and since he was spending the money like water, something had to be done to redress the situation.

The trouble had started in March 1934 when Simenon and Tigy had to face the fact that the lease to La Richardière was up and the owner still refused to sell them the property. They had spent a lot of money on the house and had always hoped that they would eventually be able to buy it. Although they had only a two-year lease the owner had given them the impression that anything might be possible in due course. Instead they found that not only would he not sell them the property, he would not even renew the lease. Homeless, they went to Porquerolles, where Simenon chartered a large sailing boat for a year and they spent much of that summer cruising the Mediterranean. Then, in September, Simenon took the lease of a château in the forest of Orléans called the Château de la Cour-Dieu, near Ingrannes. It was a former Cistercian abbey and the property included 10,000 hectares of private hunting. At Cour-Dieu, Simenon only once organised a hunt during which he succeeded in wounding a stag, which he was subsequently obliged to finish off. He said later that it was the last time he picked up a shotgun. And Tigy did not like the forest. It depressed her. Their life together had lost much of its point with the departure from La Richardière. Simenon was no longer as emotionally dependent on her as he had been at first. He no longer needed a ball and chain in order to prevent himself from committing some serious *bêtise*.

Simenon never accepted that he was a *un obsédé sexuel*, a sexual maniac. He considered his sexual appetite entirely normal; what was unusual was the extent to which he was successful in gratifying it. When living in Paris he was frequently 'obliged' to lie with four different women in the same day. In *Un homme comme un autre* he explained his constant need for sexual congress by:

> my extreme curiosity and also the need I had for a form of contact which only sexual relations could satisfy . . . Women have always been exceptional people for me whom I have vainly tried to understand. It has been a lifelong, ceaseless quest. And how could I have created dozens, perhaps hundreds, of female characters in my novels if I had not experienced these adventures which lasted for two hours or ten minutes?

He made love for the same reason that he wrote: because he had an unsatisfied hunger for human contact. He described this as 'a devouring hunger for women' and said that when he was a young man it was so acute that he literally suffered physical pain at the thought that there would be so many women who would escape him. He did his best to ensure that this number should be as small as possible and during the course of his life had sex with far more women than he could subsequently remember. He finally estimated that the total was 10,000; his second wife said that it was 1200. But however many it was, it is possible to meet and to know something of many of his partners even today because he described them again and again in his novels.

The way in which Simenon relied on his casual acquaintances to provide characters for his fiction is shown by the story of Pilar, the Spanish nursemaid whom he met and seduced on New Year's Day 1923, when he was alone in Paris. The unadorned story was retold in *Les anneaux de Bicêtre* (*The Patient*), published in 1963; earlier a more elaborate and fictionalised version had been given in *Le passage de la ligne*, published in 1958. But Pilar is not alone. Scores of similar girls appear in his work. Twelve of his characters are called 'Lili', eight are called 'Lola', twelve are called 'Léa'. Léa, typically, is young, unmarried, sometimes a prostitute or hostess (*'entraîneuse'*) in a bar, sometimes the mistress of one of the principal characters, once a *'strip-teaseuse'*, once a 60-year-old *'clocharde'*. She was in origin probably a girl whom Simenon met one day when he was drinking at the bar of La Coupole and whom he subsequently slept with, remembered and then brought back to life. No one, virtually no one, in Paris is called 'Zulma', but three characters in Simenon are called 'Zulma', two prostitutes and a typist. Zulma too, whoever she was, clearly left her impression. The names are repeated and so are the occupations; *'entraîneuse'*, *'femme de chambre'*, *'bonne'*, *'bonne d'enfants'*. *'Serveuse de café'* was the first occupation of fifteen girls called 'Julie'. 'Germaine' starts her journey through his fiction as a switchboard operator at *Le Petit Parisien*, the newspaper which brought the serialisation rights to several of his novels, and the name subsequently appears in twenty-seven books, 'Germaine' at one point achieving the position of *'patronne de maison close'*. Nursemaid, hat-check girl, seamstress, shop assistant, Céline, Irma, Sylvie, Jeanne. Whether they were 'Parisiennes of a certain age . . . their bodies creamier and more desirable . . . who had seen a lot, heard a lot, learnt a lot but who instead of losing their relish for life threw themselves into it with greater vigour'; or whether they were *'professionnelles de passage'*, who switched to using *'tu'* when they began to undress, a fine point of etiquette, who knew the best gossip about their customers, the town's prominent citizens, and how precisely to establish correct relations with the local police *commissaire*, they served their creator's purposes equally well.

In the Maigret books these girls are sometimes treated tragically; the policeman notes the swift progression of the newly arrived country girl from hotel maid, to dancer in a cheap cabaret, to street-walker, a process that, with the assistance of a plausible enough young man, could be effected in a few weeks. But 'Maigret' was not Simenon. Maigret was a compassionate observer of society; Simenon was an observant participant. Maigret expressed only part of his creator's personality.

John Simenon considers that his father's sexual vigour may have been a consequence of the family's acute sense of smell and wonders whether, since it is impossible to develop the capacity for sexual desire if one lacks a sense of smell, a heightened sense of smell leads to a heightened level of desire. Was Georges Simenon fated all his life to be led by the nose? Certainly his earliest descriptions of sexual interest were linked to a sense of smell, notably the marketwomen described in the early teenage novel *Jehan Pinaguet*. But Simenon's interest in sex started very young. He remembered his young aunts breast-feeding their children in the kitchen at the rue Puits-en-Sock and so made an association between sex and food which predated even his precocious interest in marketwomen. This fascination echoes through his fiction down the years. In *Le petit saint* (*The Little Saint*) the mother of the hero, when he is a little boy, is a sluttish, easygoing, marketwoman, a tender mother as well as being an occasional prostitute, who bends low and 'generously displays her breasts' every time she wants a male neighbour to help her carry a tub of hot water up the stairs. And the neighbour is glad to do so. The trick works. He never says no. In the same book Loulou, a plump *masseuse*, picks up a young artist outside a stationery shop near the Palais Royal, takes him home and refuses to let him pay. In *Dimanche* (*Sunday*) Emile, who is about to poison his wife, visits a prostitute in Cannes and is careless, and she complains because her bruises will show later in the day when she goes to the beach. In *Les volets verts* (*The Heart of a Man*) the drunken old actor, also called Emile, has the housemaid Camille, just after she has run his bath, while his wife is preoccupied with the child next door: '"Lie down." "Like this, right away?" "Like this, right away." ' These are among the hundreds of incidents and casual conversations remembered by a writer who celebrated his appointment as the Marquis de Tracy's secretary by visiting, for the first time, one of the elegant prostitutes working outside the Madeleine, and who celebrated his last night as a bachelor with 'deux Hollandaises plantureuses' (two ample Dutch ladies) whom he found himself trapped between on a bench at the Lapin Agile: 'the room was so crowded that I found I was able to slip my hands shamelessly beneath their dresses, which only made them laugh even more.'

Most people work every day and enjoy sex periodically. Simenon had sex every day and every few months indulged in a frenzied orgy of work. As time passed his outbreaks of work became slightly less frequent, but he maintained his sexual discipline unflinchingly, as though it were a hygienic necessity. For most people, as Bernard Pivot has observed, sex is a distraction from work, but Simenon 'baisait comme il respirait'. In his case, work was a distraction from sex. Several months would pass and one day he would withdraw into himself, and write a novel with the same sudden, violent energy with which he made love, his books frequently ending in a psychic explosion – a murder, a suicide or some other doom. When the book was finished he would return to the sexual attack. He was himself again.

Tigy never understood this side of her husband's nature. Although she herself was not particularly interested in sex she remained conventionally jealous, and Simenon felt obliged to conceal his activities. He later claimed that she repeatedly threatened to kill herself if he were ever unfaithful to her, but it seems that this was more a form of words than a serious threat and that Simenon later exaggerated its importance in order to justify his own position. In any event, since he was unfaithful to her several times a week, and sometimes several times a day, he was finding married life a bit of a strain, and matters were not helped by the fact that they had no children. The loss of La Richardière meant that they now had no home to raise a family in.

In order to distract himself from these problems Simenon resumed a way of life which interfered with his writing. In January 1935 he and Tigy set out on a world tour which lasted over eight months and during which Simenon produced only one novel, Ceux de la soif, during a two-month pause in Tahiti. He claimed, again to Fenton Bresler, that when passing through

Panama he called on a man who had flooded the Spanish market with pirated editions of his books. Having armed himself with a pistol he told the man how much he was owed and said he wanted the money within one hour. The pirate publisher said he needed more time. Simenon said he would be paid in one hour or he would shoot him. The man got busy on the telephone and 'within half an hour another man walked in with a bag containing the money'. The anecdote is the stuff of fantasy, but something like it may have occurred since Simenon did not generally invent the events in his life unless they had some basis in fact.

For Tigy the journey was an excitement and a distraction, and of course another opportunity to find subjects for her painting. But for Simenon it was more than a distraction; it was a flight. He had developed the habit of moving on whenever he felt trapped or perplexed. 'All my departures have been flights,' he was to write later. He fell in love with Tahiti and sometimes thought that he could happily have lived there, but it was an impracticable scheme since much of the attraction lay in the girls and, as it was, Tigy nearly caught him out one evening when he had given a farewell feast for the whole village and his companion had had to jump out of the bedroom window. On the voyage home from Australia there was another incident. Simenon fell completely in love with a young English girl who was travelling with her parents. He became so enamoured of her that he even tried to fight one of her younger admirers on the dance floor. This time even Tigy could not help noticing, and for the first time since leaving Liège she began to worry about her hold over him. The romance with the English girl remained platonic, the first time Simenon had experienced such a thing since those summers in Liège before he was a teenager. He took this to be confirmation of the seriousness of his intentions. They spent entire nights together talking in the girl's cabin, and after his return he continued to write to her in England for some months. But she was 16 and it eventually became clear to him that she had found some other novelty to occupy her attention. His dreams of another flight had come to nothing.

They had left Boule in charge of La Cour-Dieu but on their return in September 1935 the Simenons moved to a luxurious apartment on the boulevard Richard-Wallace in Neuilly, opposite the Bois de Boulogne, cancelling plans, which had been drawn up by an architect, to build a magnificent hunting lodge in the forest of Orléans. The rooms were expensively redecorated for Tigy's pleasure. Here, in October, Simenon wrote only his second novel of the year. The third came in December during a skiing holiday in the Haute-Savoie.

If 1935 turned out to be Simenon's worst year since 1924, when he had written his first three pulp novels, 1936 was a little better. There was no world tour, or any foreign travel at all, and four books followed. None was written in the boulevard Richard-Wallace. In the spring Simenon went down to Porquerolles to write *Le blanc à lunettes* (*Talatala*), then paid a final visit to the Château de la Cour-Dieu where he wrote *Chemin sans issue* (*Blind Path*). In the summer, again in Porquerolles, he wrote the untypically long *Le testament Donadieu* (*The Shadow Falls*), which was hailed as an early masterpiece, and finally, on another skiing holiday, this time in Igls in the Tyrol, he wrote *L'homme qui regardait passer les trains*, again acclaimed as a major work. Boule accompanied him to Igls and remembers that by then Simenon had become extremely jealous of her. If she ever said 'that one isn't bad-looking' about a passing stranger Simenon would become '*furibard*' (livid). In Igls the Austrian men were very '*galant*' and correct. Simenon would sit at a table with Tigy and Boule and the Austrians would ask his permission to invite them to dance. Simenon always gave permission, and the Austrians danced beautifully, but Boule could see that Simenon was becoming '*enragé*' and she eventually told the men to stop asking.

Back in Paris Simenon seemed to recover from the loss of La Richardière and from the restless attempts to escape the life he shared with Tigy. His drive to write had been restored, but his daily routine no longer satisfied him. He had returned to the hectic social habits of Montparnasse which he had fled in 1927, but now, against the background of Neuilly and the Champs-Elysées, conducted on a grander, less innocent, scale. He bought an expensive car, a Delage Cabriolet. He dressed in blue suits, or sometimes in plus-fours, and favoured pearly grey Homburg hats and kid gloves. He went to Rome for his ties and to London, where he stayed at the Savoy Hotel, for his shirts. Every afternoon at 5 o'clock he would draw up outside Fouquet's on the Champs-Elysées for the cocktail hour. His friends, no longer poor, were called Pagnol, Vlaminck, Foujita, Picasso and Rothschild. 'I became a snob,' he said later. He even had his own table at Maxim's, and he divided his time between social life in Paris and working somewhere else. Tigy was perfectly happy about the arrangement but a part of Simenon found it unbearable.

In 1937 the infernal round started again. Once the skiing holiday was over in the Tyrol it was back to Paris, where in January Simenon wrote only the second book he achieved in the boulevard Richard-Wallace. He called it a novel, presumably to satisfy his contract with Gallimard, but it was nothing of the sort, as he himself admitted in the first sentence. (That did not stop Gallimard describing it as a '*roman*' on the cover.) This was *Les trois crimes de mes amis*, and was based on recollections of the sordid poverty of Liège during the occupation.

On 19 February Simenon went down once more to Porquerolles to write *M. La Souris*. And then for five months he did nothing. He wrote no 'Maigrets', no short stories, no 'pulps' and no *romans durs*. Returning to the boulevard Richard-Wallace he found 'actors and film producers on every floor'. Into the Delage Cabriolet and over to the terrace of Fouquet's which he found packed with film producers and actors:

> What was I doing there? I have no idea . . . [sometimes] having spent the whole afternoon at Fouquet's I would drive to Le Bourget with Tigy, get on the first plane leaving and set off for Prague or Budapest, anywhere at all, without taking any baggage . . . I was about to go under and I don't know what saved me.

He returned to Porquerolles for long enough to write *Touriste de bananes* (*Banana Tourist*), a sequel to *Donadieu* but much shorter, which he finished on 8 June. That year saw a total of seven novels, apart from *Les trois crimes de mes amis*, a series which ended in December with one of his early sinister studies of an enclosed family, *Les soeurs Lacroix* (*Poisoned Relations*).* Then, in 1938, there was another block. To his deep dissatisfaction about living

---

* It was after writing this book that he announced that in ten years' time he would win the Nobel prize.

in Paris another distraction was added. He had become very worried about the possibility of war.

In January Simenon had taken an entirely uncharacteristic step, involving himself in a political movement called 'Sans Haine' (Without Hatred), a pacifist organisation, dedicated to the belief that there would be another European war. Its founder was Lucien Descaves, an influential literary critic who had been one of Simenon's first champions. The emblem of the movement was the dove of peace, and in associating himself with this pressure group Simenon was of course for the only time in his life making the classic commitment of the French intellectual. He was struck with the mocking slogan 'To die for Danzig' coined by the maverick leftist Marcel Déat, and he himself was in time to be *farouchement munichois.* ★

All through the successive European crises of 1938, the *Anschluss* in March, the Sudetenland in August and Munich in September, Simenon was haunted by his memories of war and its consequences. He went to Porquerolles and then to an inn in the Dordogne where he wrote a novel, *Le coup de vague*, which he set in Marsilly near La Richardière. Having buried himself in the countryside he set the book in his own ideal countryside. In May he returned to Paris, and it was there, one summer day, that his personal crisis came to a head. Whatever happened Simenon was determined not to be caught again in a large city during a war. He had been bombarded and half starved once, and knew that in time of defeat the place to be was in the country. He himself never admitted as much but it seems certain that in the impulsive decision he took one morning in the boulevard Richard-Wallace his memories of war must have played a decisive part. In *Mémoires intimes* he set the scene in 1937 but it actually took place one year later. 'Installed in my luxurious apartment in Neuilly I suddenly revolted against everything that surrounded me, against my role as a puppet in a world of puppets . . . I was sickened by the life I was leading . . . One morning I said to Tigy, "I want to work

---

★ There was nothing eccentric about being *munichois* in France in 1938. When *Paris-Soir* invited its readers to subscribe to a fund to buy a house for Neville Chamberlain, in gratitude for the Munich agreement, over one million Frenchmen responded.

somewhere else, in a little house which is my size, miles away from towns and tourists, with the sea close by." ' Tigy realised that he had had enough and agreed.

Again it was a return to the past. They started in the north of Holland in Delfzijl, driving there directly from Paris, then worked their way down the Channel coast. They passed through Holland, Belgium and northern France, then Normandy and Brittany. Eventually they reached the Vendée and the same thing happened as on the last occasion when they had been working their way northwards from Porquerolles in 1932, looking for mist: the light changed just before they got to La Rochelle. They were back by La Richardière and Simenon knew it was where he wanted to be. Very depressed, they invited themselves for lunch at the house of a friend, Dr de Béchevel, and asked him if there were any houses for sale in the neighbourhood. He said he thought he might know of one. An old man, father of a girl who had once worked for them as a maid, was rumoured to be considering selling up and moving in with one of his children. It proved to be true. The house was 500 metres from the sea, quite close to La Richardière, smaller and in every way ideal. The sale was completed one month later, in July. When they first saw it Simenon said to Tigy that it was 'the sort of house children come to, to spend their holidays with their grandmother'. His words, he claimed later, influenced Tigy and within a few weeks, while the builders were still at work on the house in Nieul-sur-Mer, after fourteen years of marriage, she was pregnant. She, on the contrary, said that the reason she had delayed for so long was for Simenon's sake, because he was not ready to settle down with a family.

Faced with the potential chaos of war Simenon had instinctively taken refuge in the only shelter he knew, family life. In August, just after they had bought the house in Nieul-sur-Mer, but before the builders were out of it, Simenon and Tigy were living in La Rochelle and had begun to re-establish themselves in the locality. In June their new dog, Loustic, won first prize in a local dog show. Then in July Simenon wrote a novel, Chez Krull (Chez Krull), which concerned the return to a French family of one of their German cousins, and the family tensions this relationship ignited, including memories of the First World War. In August, just at the time when Tigy discovered she was pregnant, the crisis broke in Sudetenland. This time war seemed certain, and on 29 September Simenon and Tigy set off for Brussels in their enormous chocolate-coloured Chrysler which he had bought in 1932. As a reservist he had been recalled to the colours, and the Belgian army was about to mobilise. As he told the story in *Mémoires intimes* he was just about to cross the frontier at 'La Panne' (actually De Panne) when the customs officer was called away and came back to say that the radio had announced the news of the Munich agreement and he could turn round, which, after spending one night in Belgium, he did. It was a reprieve, but Simenon remained shaken. In the exhilaration of July he had written, as well as *Chez Krull*, nineteen short stories mostly set in the area of La Rochelle. Now, after the scare of Munich, he found himself silent again and wrote only one more book that year, interestingly enough set in Belgium, *Le bourgmestre de Furnes* (*The Burgomaster of Furnes*).

Simenon was happy to be back in La Rochelle and happy to find a society into which he had already been accepted. 'The Rochelais are distrustful at first,' he recalled later. 'I am thinking of the bourgeoisie and the big families who own fishing fleets. They watch you for a bit and then one day they invite you to a tea party where everyone can examine you. And only then will they adopt you, and after that one can become very good friends.' The Simenons became close friends with the notable shipping clans of La Rochelle, the Delmas and the Vieljeux, although he and they sometimes observed each other with a sardonic eye. Simenon was astonished to learn that the children of one of these families were not allowed to drink in a café in La Rochelle or Nieul in case they found themselves side by side with one of their father's employees. Pierre Vieljeux, in his turn, recalled that Simenon came to see him one day and asked him how much he paid his domestic servants:

I gave him a figure and he told me that he paid twice that. I told him that was going to cost him a small fortune and he said, 'Oh no. I have a system of fines. A soup that is not just right means a retention of two francs, a broken wheelbarrow two francs and so on. The result is that at the end of the month I only have to pay about half of the total.'

Simenon hotly denied this story when it was repeated to him in 1985.

In 1928, when he bought the *Ginette*, Simenon had seen nothing of the world except Liège and Paris and a few weeks spent in the Limbourg, in Antwerp and Aix-la-Chapelle. By 1935 he had seen a large portion of the world. His travels had confirmed his theory that *'l'homme nu'* was the same the world over and he could now set his books either in exotic locations observed on his travels or in parts of France and Belgium which were already familiar to him. On the surface he was a worldly, cosmopolitan Parisian, but beneath this he retained his original preoccupations.

In Liège Simenon's grandfather, Chrétien, had died in 1927, aged 86, still living in the rue Puits-en-Sock, having survived his son Désiré by over five years. In 1928 his brother Christian had married and set out for the Congo. In 1929 Henriette had remarried. Her new husband, born in the same year as Désiré, was in many ways Henriette's ideal husband. He was a state pensioner who had worked for many years for Nord Belge as a railway guard, and she was now free from her lifelong nightmare of poverty. *'Le père André'*, as Henriette and later Simenon referred to him, although he had no children, had a little house on a hillside outside Liège, but he and Henriette lived at her house, the one she had been able to buy shortly after Désiré's death, 5 rue de l'Enseignement on Outremeuse.

'Where was I when I heard the news?' Simenon wrote in *Lettre à ma mère*. 'Was I in France, Africa or the United States when I received your letter saying that you had just remarried?' In fact Simenon was in none of those places. In October 1929, at the time of Henriette's remarriage, he was in Holland, on the *Ostrogoth*. That same spring he had taken the boat through Liège. In September he had written *Train de nuit* and sent the manuscript on a fruitless journey to Fayard. In October the *Ostrogoth* had just been recaulked at Delfzijl and he had set out for Wilhelmshaven, a military port from which he was to be expelled by the German police in November. 'I admit,' he wrote, 'that when I received the news I was shocked. I had such a worship of my father that I found it impossible to imagine you replacing him . . . You sent me your new husband's picture. He was a man of the Ardennes, thin and wizened, with jagged features and a blank look on his face. I only met him once . . .'

Henriette married Joseph André in 1929. André died in 1949. If Simenon met him only once in twenty years it was almost certainly during a visit he made to his mother in 1934, during which he made a brutal remark to Henriette about the human race being divided into '*fesseurs et fessés*' (the spankers and the spanked), adding that he preferred to be '*un fesseur*'. That was the extent of the relationship between mother and son after the remarriage of the mother. Simenon noted that although his mother had replaced his father with another man she still used his father's name. She now called herself Madame André Simenon. 'That hurt me,' he wrote in *Lettre à ma mère*. 'It was in my eyes a breach of trust. Another man had taken my father's place in your house, in your bed, but you continued to use your first husband's name. Was it because I was already famous? Did you look on my name as a lucky charm?' In 1931, when Simenon began to write his *romans durs*, the remarriage of Henriette, for which he was never to forgive her, was merely the most recent injury she had inflicted on him and a reminder of all the earlier ones. The lines of battle which were to dominate his subconscious and his fiction for the rest of his life were now drawn up. What was to follow was a detailed settling of accounts.

Henriette would not have appreciated the implication made in the highly autobiographical novel *L'Ane-Rouge* (*The Night Club*; 1933), that Désiré had not in fact died in his office but in a nearby brothel. But worse was to come with the book which Simenon always described as his first *roman*, *La maison du canal*, written in January 1933. The book drew a prompt letter of extravagant praise from the Cubist poet and Catholic convert Max Jacob. The house of the title is the old Brüll family house which Simenon had visited as a child during the First World War. It would have required only a short detour for the *Ostrogoth* to pass the original *maison du canal* on Simenon's voyage into darkest Flanders in 1929. So, while he was planning the Maigret series, the seeds of his later work were also being sown. The characters who inhabit the *maison du canal* are based on several members of the Brüll family, although they are not straightforward portraits. But it is the atmosphere of the house which is perhaps closest to actuality

and to the memories of the visiting cousin from Liège. Simenon
hardly altered the name of Neeroeteren, the nearest village.

The book opens in one of Simenon's most evocative settings,
the large railway station. In the first sentence his world springs
fully formed into life: 'Amid the crowd of travellers surging
through the barrier, she was the only person who was not in a
hurry.' 'She' is called Edmée Van Elst, her father was a doctor
who died suddenly, she is alone in the world, she is going to live
with her Flemish cousins who have agreed to take her in, she feels
embittered because her father's death means that she will never be
able to study medicine as she had planned. But she brings her
textbooks with her and uses them to avoid doing the washing-up
and to diagnose her cousins, her hosts, as hereditary syphilitics.
This is already a Simenon. It is certainly also an early Simenon –
there are several clumsy changes in the point of view, but sex is
already a potential source of shame and violence. It is the head of
the Van Elst (or Brüll) family, the dyke-master, who is syphilitic.
One of his sons, a monstrous figure, has hydrocephalus and
eventually rapes and strangles Edmée, the only woman he loves,
and his first cousin, who by then is also his sister-in-law. As the
tension in the family grows, Jef, the monster, kills and skins
squirrels, cats and mice, which he subsequently eats. The family's
use of Flemish in the sombre farmhouse darkens the atmosphere
still further in the eyes of Edmée. Sexual feelings are trapped
within the isolated family. Edmée's journey across Flanders, away
from the lights and life of Brussels to the dank farm, is accompanied by a sense of doom. All the demons which haunted the
childhood and adolescence of Simenon are present in this book,
transposed to the imaginary world of his Flemish fathers. There is
light and dark, city and Limbourg, Simenon and Brüll, and the
darkness enclosing a young person at the start of her life who
travels in the wrong direction, and who is lost as a consequence.
In *La maison du canal*, the canal itself is seen not as the giver of life
to the surrounding countryside but as a threatening mass of water
which can drown horses and ruin men following a moment's
inattention. The atmosphere of menace is so strong that when a
policeman asks Jef why he has raped and murdered the only
woman he ever loved he is able to reply, 'What would you have
done?'

Shortly after *La maison du canal* Simenon wrote another outstanding book, his fourth novel, *Les fiançailles de M. Hire*, which was made the basis for a cinema film as recently as 1989. This is a less autobiographical novel, but it nonetheless contains at least one scene taken straight from Simenon's life, that of an innocent man pursued by a vengeful mob on to the roof of a house where he is in danger of falling to his death. M. Hire is the son of a Jewish tailor. He lives alone, and the chief excitement in his life is watching a girl who works as an assistant in a *crèmerie*, who possesses '*une poitrine exubérante*' and who lives in the room opposite to his. The plot is simple. M. Hire's obsession allows the girl to frame him for a murder which was in fact committed by her boyfriend. While this plot unfolds several of Simenon's familiar themes are set out – the street life of Paris, the routine of daily life in a brothel, the near-prostitution and drudgery of domestic servants and shop assistants, the drama and hope offered by a railway station, the uncomfortable proximity of life in a jerry-built Paris apartment block and the methods of investigation used by the police. But this is the Paris police force seen from the suspect's point of view, and it is a police force without Maigret. These policemen drink heavily on duty, take the shop assistant into a doorway for 'a nice short time' and even go to sleep on M. Hire's bed while they are waiting to arrest him. The reader accustomed to Maigret has the impression that when in *Les fiançailles de M. Hire* a detective decides to suspect and investigate M. Hire, led on by the shop assistant and chiefly because the tailor's son is a convenient quarry, a more realistic picture of the police in action is being drawn. When M. Hire goes to talk to the police voluntarily he is questioned by a chief-inspector who lifts his head to look at him for the first time, 'his eyes still preoccupied with the previous case'. The police have a file on M. Hire, they know all about him, they interrupt him, they put the worst interpretation on everything, the best they can do for him is to tell him, 'We won't arrest you yet.'

It was during this period that Simenon's work began to attract the attention of a more discerning readership. The letter from Max Jacob, written before Simenon had even signed the contract with Gallimard, when he was still known only as a popular novelist, referred to Simenon as 'one of the greatest novelists in history'. Some time later François Mauriac wrote to him, 'I know nearly all your work . . . you have the humility of a great talent.

One only has to cast an eye over one of Robert Brasillach's novels to understand why he detests yours. You have everything which he hasn't got, the gift of being able to create living people in a living atmosphere . . .' And in 1938 Mauriac was joined by the doyen of the higher criticism, André Gide, whose first surviving letter to Simenon notes that 'a curious misunderstanding exists about you: you are regarded as a popular writer but your books are not intended for the general public but for . . . the discriminating'.

The direction in which Simenon's imagination was heading was already clear. His original interest in detective stories had grown while he was a police court reporter, and he based his literary novels on the same sort of material. In the age of mass communication Simenon is the supreme modern French novelist of the *fait divers*, the brief news item. He wanted, like Balzac, to portray the lives of the '*petites gens*' and, having started as a reporter in the great tradition of French newspaper crime writing, he knew to what extent the *fait divers* illuminated the unsuspected dramas in the lives of ordinary people. The world of his novels is the world of police stations, mortuaries, traffic accidents, suicides, criminal courts and lunatic asylums. Unlike so many reporters drawn to this sort of reporting by its vivid fictional possibilities, Simenon was the exception, the reporter who went on to make fictions out of it. In taking *faits divers* as his raw material Simenon was, of course, also following in the tradition of Stendhal, who had done the same in *Le rouge et le noir*, of Flaubert, in *Madame Bovary*, and of Gide in *Les caves du Vatican* or *Les faux-monnayeurs*. But one of his early novels was based a little too closely on real life and resulted in a libel action.

The case followed the publication of *Le coup de lune*, a novel written in 1933, directly after *M. Hire* and after his return from Africa, which Fayard had published in the same year. It is set in colonial Libreville and one of its principal characters is called Adèle Renaud, a Frenchwoman who keeps the only European hotel in town. Adèle, a widow, is '*généreuse de sa personne*', and one night a boy, an African servant, who has been blackmailing her, is found murdered. The public prosecutor delivers the telling line, 'We will soon find a guilty man,' meaning a black man. The hero, who has become one of Adèle's innumerable lovers, a young man newly arrived from Europe, denounces the plot by which a young black man is framed for the murder and, over-affected by West Africa like a character from Conrad's *Heart of Darkness*, is sent home suffering from dementia muttering, 'It doesn't exist. It doesn't exist.'

Unfortunately, Adèle was identified as a portrait by a real widow, Mme Mercier, a hotel keeper in Libreville whose hotel, like the hotel in the book, was called the Hôtel Central. She came back to France in May 1934 to give evidence in the libel case, but Simenon had chosen one of the most talented and sarcastic advocates in Paris, Maître Maurice Garçon (who was already a friend of his), and Maître Garçon destroyed Mme Mercier with his cross-examination. The weakness of her case was that she could claim the book was about her only by admitting to the accuracy of the portrait. Maître Garçon told the court that it was probably the first time they had witnessed a woman come halfway round the world to tell them that it was true that 'she had once been a whore in the place des Ternes'. Mme Mercier lost her case, and a lot of money, and what was left of her reputation, and Simenon's triumphant progress continued unhindered.

Simenon's brushes with the law of libel confirm the extent to which he depended for his plots on actuality. He was the opposite of a 'fantastic' novelist; his fiction was genuinely fictional, but nonetheless rooted in the world around him. Fiction and fact enjoyed an extremely close relationship in his imagination, and one which was eventually to cause him problems which were considerably more serious than a libel action. Throughout the series of forty-four *romans durs* which Simenon wrote between 1931 and September 1939 there is a consistent autobiographical strain. In *L'Ane-Rouge*, written in 1933, the hero is a young journalist on a local newspaper called the *Gazette de Nantes*. His mother is forever in tears, his father returns home in the evening to read his newspaper seated in a wicker armchair; his father's sudden death leaves the young man desolate. Much of the plot of *Le locataire* (*The Lodger*; 1932) is set in the kitchen of a house where the mother of the hero's girlfriend feeds her foreign student lodgers. The Universal Exhibition held in Liège in 1905 is mentioned in *L'évadé* (*The Disintegration of J.P.G*; 1932). A cargo steamer plying between Matadi and Bordeaux is the setting for *45° à l'ombre* (*Aboard the Aquitaine*; 1934). The hero of *L'assassin* (*The Murderer*; 1935), a married man, sleeps with his wife's maid.

In *Il pleut, bergère . . .* (*Black Rain*; 1939) a mob drives a hunted
man on to a roof (again). The hero of *Touriste de bananes* (1936) has
a passionate affair with a native girl while visiting Tahiti. And
alcoholism plays an essential part in the lives of numerous characters, including heroes, and particularly in *Quartier nègre* (1934),
Les inconnus dans la maison (*The Strangers in the House*; 1939) and
Bergelon (*The Country Doctor*; 1939). But if it is clear that autobiography was an essential part of Simenon's fictional apparatus, just
occasionally the apparatus which changed fact into fiction failed to
operate, notably in the case of *Les trois crimes de mes amis*, which he
wrote in Paris in January 1937.

The trial of Ferdinand Paul Joseph Deblauwe had taken place in
October 1933, that of Hyacinthe Danse in December 1934. Two
years later Simenon attempted to write a novel about these two
men, but succeeded only in writing his first volume of autobiography. Presumably the links with his own life were in this case
too numerous and too strong to fictionalise. Deblauwe,
Simenon's old friend, was arrested by Commissaire-
Divisionnaire Guillaume, Simenon's new friend. Deblauwe had
nearly got away with the murder of the gigolo Carlos de Tejada
by making the shooting look like a suicide. The forensic investi-
gator who failed to exclude this possibility was Dr Paul, a friend
of Simenon's and, of course, in his fictional persona, a friend of
Maigret's. Deblauwe killed the gigolo in the rue de Maubeuge
near the Gare du Nord in July 1931. Then he took the train to
Liège, and by the time the body was discovered four days later
Deblauwe was hiding with his parents on Outremeuse at 44 rue
des Recollets, the house where Simenon had so often called for
him on his way to work. He stayed there for some months while
the trail went cold but was eventually arrested and interrogated by
Guillaume in August 1932. (In *Le pendu de St Pholien* Simenon
had, of course, sent Maigret to Liège to investigate the criminal
background of his own childhood.) Simenon did not attend
Deblauwe's trial in Paris, though he followed it closely. But he
did not want to sit in the reporters' box while the man he had so
often sat beside in another reporters' box sat in the dock. And
besides, as he wrote in *Les trois crimes de mes amis*, 'It occurred to
me that Deblauwe risked losing his head and I had no right to go
to court and risk upsetting him or risk him losing the slightest
drop of his *sang-froid*.' When Simenon looked at the photographs

of Deblauwe in court, calmly denying his guilt, he thought that if he had only had his notebook in hand he could have been any court reporter at any trial.

In the first forty-four *romans durs*, the guillotine plays a role in one, alcoholism in two, lunacy in one, the seduction of domestic servants in three, the association of sex with death or paralysis in three, and suicide in twelve. Three of the suicides are by hanging. This was the world, as noted by his friend Vlaminck, of 'seedy hotels' and 'men dragged down by misery', and in each case Simenon entered it by the process of total immersion in the personality of his leading character. He had discovered a means of writing fiction whereby he did not imagine his fictions, he lived them. He subconsciously imitated the walks of his characters, he drank up to two litres of red wine a day while writing about them, he lost weight nonetheless, he *possessed* the world he was creating. He went into 'a sort of trance' which was too exhausting to keep up for more than a few days at a time. The trance could not be broken or the characters would die. He left the trance when the book was finished and his subsequent revisions of the text were perfunctory. He knew when it was time to start a novel because he felt uneasy, '*mal dans sa peau*', and he knew he would not feel better until he was rid of the phantoms beginning to form in his subconscious. The process of creation would usually start on a walk, and be 'triggered' by a colour or a smell. This would remind him of a previous time in another place, sometimes another country, when that colour or that smell had been associated with a view or a house, or a situation between two people, and he would begin to see the setting of his novel. The characters were at first less important; they were ordinary people, they might come from any walk of life, what was important was what was about to happen to them. The events which were about to overwhelm them were the expression of the anguish in his own mind which had led to his original sense of unease.

Simenon's methods of preparing for the 'Maigrets' and the *romans durs* were identical. In both cases he took a manila envelope (his famous '*enveloppe jaune*') and used it to sketch out the biographical details of his principal characters, and the geographical locations of the story. He needed to have that clear in his head before he started to write. But from then on the experience was completely different. There was less and less strain for him in writing the 'Maigrets'. They were not an expression of inner anguish, he did not need the 'trigger' or the 'immersion' and after a while he did not suffer the exhaustion which was associated with the writing of the *romans durs*. If anything the return to Maigret's world was an expression of an inner happiness.

There are further biographical references in two novels Simenon wrote concerning family life shortly before the outbreak of war. In December 1937 he finished *Les soeurs Lacroix*, his account of suffocating unhappiness in a family living in Bayeux. The epigram of the book is 'Every family has a skeleton in the cupboard', which was to become one of his favourite sayings and one which he regarded as 'typically English'. It is the story of a painter, Emmanuel Vernes, who lives with his wife, Mathilde, their sick daughter, Geneviève, and his wife's elder sister, the widow Léopoldine, or 'Poldine'. The household is dominated by Poldine, whose power rests on the fact that she too was seduced by Emmanuel and that her sister's husband is the real father of her own daughter, who also lives in the house. Emmanuel is reduced to helplessness when his wife discovers the truth, and eventually tries to poison both sisters with minute doses of arsenic, a move which Poldine discovers almost at once. Shortly afterwards Emmanuel hangs himself in the attic where for many years he has spent most of the time painting. After his death the sisters are able to look at his pictures. They discover that there are hundreds of them, all of the same scene, the roofscape visible from the attic window. Emmanuel's death leaves his beloved daughter, Geneviève, even more isolated than before, dying from an undiagnosed illness. *Les soeurs Lacroix* is a study of hatred enclosed within the walls of a family home, but also of a sexual secret within a family. There are references to Simenon's own domestic arrangements,* but it is also the story of a man whose life ends in suicide by hanging, and of a man who treats his private anguish, as Bernard de Fallois has pointed out, by locking himself up in a room at the top of the house where he obsessively repeats the same work of art throughout his working life. In that sense it is one of the earliest 'prophetic' novels of Simenon. It is also one of the very few Simenon novels to contain a character (Geneviève)

---

* In later life Simenon wrote that he had been secretly in love with Tita, Tigy's younger sister, when he married Tigy.

who prays devoutly. At the end of the book the sisters are left alone in occupation of only part of the house and the last words are, 'And their hatred became that much deeper, that much denser, that much heavier, that much better, as the space enclosing it was reduced.'

Simenon's other pre-war study of family life may have provided a more direct indication of one part of the anguish which he himself felt as he listened to the sounds of approaching war. In *Chez Krull* Hans Krull, the hero, is German. He has French cousins, also called Krull, and the town in which they live is not named but is quite clearly based on Liège, where in reality the Belgian-Dutch family of Brüll, his mother's family, lived, not far from their German cousins, also called Brüll. There are numerous references in the descriptions of the Krull family to the Brülls. Joseph Krull, the French cousin of Hans, is a medical student, as were two of Simenon's Brüll cousins. Joseph's father is a lock-keeper living in the district of Coronmeuse, where Simenon's lock-keeper uncle, Gilles, lived in real life. When a girl is found in the canal, raped and murdered, the suspicions of the inhabitants of the previously peaceful little town centre on Hans Krull, the stranger, the *boche*, and then on the whole Krull family. Joseph, the French cousin, is arrested, Hans is expelled from the Krull household and 'old Krull', the head of the family, hangs himself, again in the attic. It is a story of a family whom neighbours identify as being untrustworthy because they have divided loyalties, and who are consequently expelled from the heart of their own community, the fate of many Flemish families of Liège during and after the First World War.

In January 1939 Simenon wrote *Les inconnus dans la maison*, one of his masterpieces and possibly his greatest book about an alcoholic. Hector Loursat is a failure and something of a local figure of fun. He is a barrister who drinks all the waking hours God sends him and who lives a solitary life in the big family house in Moulins in central France. When his wife left him he lost the will to continue with his profession and took to the bottle, invariably a bottle of rather good Burgundy. Loursat lives surrounded by books and old wine. He chain-smokes. His grey moustache is yellowed with nicotine. His housekeeper cooks for him carefully enough but despises him for his untidiness and careless habits. When he is drunk, which he is every night, he goes to sleep in his armchair and turns in his sleep 'like a boar in its wallow'. When he goes to sleep he makes sure two things are to hand – a poker for the stove and a glass for his bottle. Loursat is a drunk but he remains mentally alert. He is apart from the world but he watches it. He prefers his 'good stove, some red wine – dark red – and some books, all the books in the world'. The house is full of books; he chooses them at random and starts reading in the middle and loses his place and fetches another. 'He knew everything! He'd read everything! He could stay in his corner, alone, and chuckle at the idiots in the world.' And then one night, slumbering over his bottle, he hears a pistol shot inside the house. Mounting the stairs to the vast, abandoned floors above he finds a fresh corpse in a bedroom that, to his knowledge, has not been used for years. And Loursat discovers numerous other things. That his daughter, who lives in the house, and with whom he is on extremely bad terms, and who may not – for all he knows – even be his daughter, entertains a band of friends there and that their activities verge on the criminal. One of them, his daughter's boyfriend, is charged with the murder on grounds that Loursat finds inadequate, by professional colleagues who are far more successful than he is but whom he despises. So Loursat dusts off his robe and defends the boy himself, triumphantly, and then returns to his dark red wine. 'As a young man Loursat had already been solitary, out of pride. He had thought that one could be solitary with someone else. Then one day he came home and found the house empty . . .' His success does not change his habits; Loursat remains outside the town's circle of successful figures, he carries the wound of his unhappiness with him still, he is still most content with his books and his bottles, but he is now slightly less solitary and can sometimes be found drinking in a bar in town rather than alone in his room.

Such was the world in which Simenon found himself taking refuge when he began to feel '*mal dans sa peau*'. Simenon was a sleepwalker as a child and he remained a sleepwalker all his life; he himself was convinced that he did not create his fictional world from his imagination, but that it came from his overdeveloped subsconscious. He would leave the real world for the unreal one, the sordid fate of his hopeless characters would dominate his own days, he would possess these people and bring them to life and accompany them to their fate. And then he would stop writing and emerge. The dénouement in a Simenon book is quite often abrupt: a suicide, as in *La porte* (*The Door*) or *Les complices* (*The Accomplices*), a confession – for inadequate reasons; a decision by a man who has started a new life to return to his family (*La fuite de M. Monde*; *Monsieur Monde Vanishes*). And one senses that it has been imposed by an author who could no longer stand the strain and who had to leave these phantoms and return to the real world – the Delage Cabriolet, the fishing boat in Porquerolles, the terrace at Fouquet's. But as time passed the phantoms began to notice the signs of an impending dénouement and they declined to be abandoned. They started coming into the real world too.

NINE

The commissioner for refugees

Cher Monsieur, I am staying here in Bourges for a while. The main bookshop has an announcement of a new novel from you early next month and I hope all is well with you. My parents are well and send you their best wishes. I would be delighted to get some news of you. Write to the concierge of my hotel, without mentioning my name either on the envelope or in the letter. Hoping to hear from you . . . Manfred Keyserling (Untersturmführer) (2nd Lieutenant)
                        Letter to Simenon, 30 October 1940

In August 1939 Simenon and Tigy were in Porquerolles entertaining a friend from Germany, the Graf Hermann von Keyserling, the philosopher and man of letters who had been a warm admirer of Simenon's work for some years and who had first written to him in 1936 and invited him in irresistible style to stay. ('I hope you are not anti-alcoholic. I need an atmosphere of excess in order to escape from my inhibitions although I am *normally* of temperate habits.') It was Keyserling who had dubbed Simenon 'an idiot genius', a label of which the still young writer was extremely proud. But on 23 August the local paper announced the Nazi-Soviet pact, and on 26 August France began a general mobilisation. Keyserling had to be packed off home quickly, before the trains were cancelled. He would probably have travelled via Nice and Italy rather than undertake the long journey across the length of France. A week later, on 1 September, with the news of

Hitler's invasion of Poland, Simenon and Tigy closed the house and, with Boule and their son Marc, who had been born in April, left Porquerolles for what was to be the last time as a family – although none of them could have known it then.

Marc's birth had been preceded by a trek first across France and then into Belgium. At a time when husbands are generally advised to make sure their wives are resting Simenon had decided that since Tigy was 39, and even though she was eight months pregnant, and even though war had been declared, she should have the best advice, and they would go to Strasbourg so that she could be *'suivie'* by Professor Lucien Pautrier, a distinguished gynaecologist who was also a family friend. (Simenon had dedicated his major work, *Le testament Donadieu*, to Pautrier in 1936.) Simenon was in fact obsessed with the possibility that the baby would not be healthy. Shortly after they had settled in the Château de Scarrachbergheim – where Simenon wrote *Malempin* (*The Family Lie*), a novel about a doctor's concern for his invalid son – there was a border alert and Alsace became a restricted area. Professor Pautrier advised the couple to head for Brussels where he had a trusted colleague. Belgium had the advantages of being both a neutral country and a native land. When Marc was born, on 19 April, Simenon was so worried that at the crucial moment he had to leave the hospital to be sick. He wrote later that he could not even remember whether or not his mother had come from Liège to see her splendid new grandchild, although he had a vivid memory of the arrival of Tigy's mother. Shortly after the birth they returned to Nieul where Marc was christened. There was a big party. The child's godfather was Professor Pautrier, who came all the way from Strasbourg. Vlaminck came down from Paris, but since both he and his wife were Protestants the godmother was their daughter Edwige, known as *'L'Amazone'*. Forty people sat down to lunch and Simenon ordered enough champagne to see him through the party and the next two years. He said later that he had arranged for all his children to be baptised so that if they grew up to marry Catholics none of them would have to undergo Tigy's ordeal of catechism, followed by baptism, confession and Communion all in one day. In Simenon's memory the day was dominated by Vlaminck, 'a sort of Gargantua in riding breeches and boots, with a red scarf wrapped round his neck, his ringing voice and categorical statements betraying his presence wherever he went in the garden'. It was to be the last party before the war. On 3 September at 10 a.m. Simenon, sitting in a café in La Rochelle with his new secretary, a striking-looking girl called Anne de Bretagne (Boule called her '*la Bretonne*'), heard the news of the French and British declaration of war over the café radio. That night he opened several more bottles of champagne 'to chase away dark thoughts'.

Simenon played virtually no part at all in the Second World War yet it had a profound effect on his life. When war broke out he and Tigy were well placed. The decision to abandon Paris for the second time had paid off. They were both happy with their life in the country near La Rochelle. His work was selling as well as ever and was attracting more and more serious critical attention. Marc was nearly six months old, they had enough money to live on the scale that amused them, and Boule was present to cook, run the house and play her still undiscovered role in brightening up her master's afternoons. But though very little that was really frightening or disagreeable occurred to Simenon during the war it nonetheless shattered his peace of mind. Afterwards, when it became possible for the Simenons to resume the life they had been leading in 1939, he decided instead to leave France, to leave Europe, and to start a new life in the United States.

In September 1939 Belgium remained neutral and there was, therefore, no general Belgian mobilisation. At first, during the eight months of the 'phoney war', life in the Vendée continued very much as before. It was only on 10 May 1940, when Germany attacked Holland, that the call for all Belgian reservists, including Simenon, came – needless to say far too late. At Nieul-sur-Mer it was another beautiful day. The radio reported that German tanks had passed through the Ardennes forest and entered southern Belgium. Then the massive artillery fort at Eben Emael, twenty miles north of Liège and a key point in Belgium's defences, was attacked by German commandos and captured almost at once. After lunch Simenon and Tigy searched the house for his military belt and jacket, which he had not worn since leaving Liège in 1922. As they did so refugees were beginning to pour across the Belgian frontier into France. That evening Simenon set his alarm clock and telephoned for a taxi to take him early next morning to the railway station in La Rochelle. In the morning while he shaved

Boule brought his usual enormous bowl of coffee in what she called his 'chamber-pot'. Then he dressed himself in a uniform of his own invention, which included riding breeches and a *képi*. It seemed to him that Tigy showed no particular emotion when he left; outwardly she remained as calm as ever. His own thoughts were chiefly for Marc.

There was nothing in Simenon that was attracted to the heroic. His experience as a child made him look on the martial simplicities as unconvincing. Perhaps it was as well, therefore, that his life as a soldier ended on the day it began. When his train reached the Gare Montparnasse he saw a notice instructing Belgian nationals returning for military duty to report first to their embassy, which was in the rue de Surène near the Madeleine. By the time Simenon arrived an enormous crowd of men – many, he noted, middle-aged and pot-bellied – had gathered outside. Some had been there since the previous day. Simenon had a friend at the embassy and managed to pass a note through the gates. He was sent away for lunch and told to return later. He telephoned a friend of Tigy's, Charley Delmas, wife of a La Rochelle *notable*, Franck Delmas, who would later die in a concentration camp, and she invited him to join her. He crossed the Seine and walked along the Quai d'Orsay to her apartment, feeling rather foolish in his tall Belgian *képi* with its tassel and pompom. 'He burst in,' remembered Charley Delmas, 'collapsed on the sofa, hid his face in his hands and sobbed, "Going to war isn't funny, but I'll have to do my duty with the rest. The worst thing is leaving my wife and son . . ."' After a delicious lunch, prepared by the maid, Simenon took what was to be his first and last military privilege and asked if he could stroke Mme Delmas's legs before leaving. He thought it might be his final opportunity. She smiled and beckoned him to her on the sofa:

If I were to say that my interest was chaste no one would believe me, but it was the truth. My hand stopped at the top of her long silk stocking, at the point where I could feel her bare skin . . . I got up, satisfied and probably blushing, and at the door we kissed each other goodbye on the cheeks. She was a tall young woman, a brunette, elegant and very beautiful . . . and I was very fond of her.

Then he turned, straightened his shoulders and strode off to war.

But when Simenon got back to the embassy he found that the authorities had other plans for him. The roads to Belgium were already blocked with convoys of people fleeing south, it was impossible to send reservists up to their units. Instead the embassy wanted Simenon to become Commissioner for Belgian refugees. The French government had designated the La Rochelle area as the reception centre for all Belgian refugees and Simenon had excellent connections in the region. He was given full powers to requisition Belgian property and he had a blank cheque from the Belgian government to pay for any goods or services provided by the French authorities. He was told to take the first train back to La Rochelle and to start work the following day, by which time the *préfet* and the mayor would have been informed. He took the night train and walked into his house early on the morning of 12 May, twenty-four hours after he had left it. Only Boule was awake. Tigy had already put a large framed photograph of him on her bedside table, 'as if I were already dead'. Shortly after his arrival the telephone rang. It was the local *préfet* telling him that four large Belgian fishing boats had broken through the boom into the port of La Rochelle; the crews spoke only Flemish, there were women and children on board, and they were refusing to leave. Simenon's work had begun.

In *Mémoires intimes* Simenon was to claim that over a period of five months he was responsible for 300,000 Belgian refugees, whereas the real total was probably 55,000 refugees in two months. In his '*Compte-rendu de Mission*', dated 17 August 1940, he estimated that the number of Belgian refugees in the department of the Charente-Inférieure was 18,000. But whatever the figure it was extremely hard work which by several accounts he accomplished effectively, doing everything possible until the job was finished and the refugees, following the armistice, had been sent back to their homes in Belgium. Simenon was a man of exceptional energy and considerable powers of organisation but some of his motivation for working with such devotion for the refugees may have come from a sense that he had benefited from an extraordinary stroke of luck. While thousands of his fellow Belgians were ordered into barracks outside Paris and thousands of others were killed or wounded or taken prisoner he, thanks to his official contacts, had been ordered home to his sanctuary in the

French countryside where he could expect to stay, feeding himself and his family and practising his profession for the duration of the war. He did not even have to experience the inconveniences and hazards of *'l'exode'*. For the remainder of May and up to the armistice of 22 June the refugee trains succeeded each other at La Rochelle. Some of them had been moving for three weeks before reaching the city. Some had been machine-gunned or bombed and were crowded with wounded or dying people.

Assisted by the Belgian vice-consul, a French official, fifty Belgian soldiers and the local 'Girl Guides', Simenon set up a reception centre outside the station and a camp nearby where people could be lodged and fed. The wounded and pregnant had to be dispersed through the local hospitals. Many local volunteers, including Charley Delmas, offered their help. Simenon got to know the Rochelais *notables* better than in time of peace. One woman asked him only to quarter refugees of breeding in her house, another spent days on end peeling vegetables and serving soup in the circus tent which served as a kitchen. Simenon operated with a desk and telephone from a green-painted hut outside the camp gates. Many of the refugees arrived locked into their carriages and the symbol of Simenon's authority was the pass key which enabled him to release them. Others arrived by car; one family used a hearse. One night a lorry arrived and without explanation dumped the bodies of five old men dressed in grey tunics. They were without papers, and since the autopsies showed that they had all died of natural causes he concluded that they were from a Belgian hospice and that the journey had simply proved too much for them. Simenon used his own car, a powerful model painted canary yellow and decorated with the *préfet*'s tricolour cockade, to move around the district. If the roof and bonnet were put to use he could carry up to twelve passengers. When there was nowhere else to place the refugees he would take them home to Nieul and they would sleep on the floor of the *salon* after Boule had fed them on bread and soup. Sometimes, if there was a refugee mother of young children, it was Boule who slept on the floor of the *salon*, much to her indignation. 'I was not very charitable,' she recalls today.

The refugees arrived in larger and larger numbers as the fighting drew closer to La Rochelle, and it was possible to follow the discouraging progress of the battle by asking where they had

come from. Among the first arrivals was a community of 1200
Jewish diamond cutters from Antwerp, who were sent on to the
port of Royan, at the mouth of the Gironde. La Rochelle was
continually bombed by the Germans. Sometimes Simenon had to
sleep on a bench at the station, sometimes he had to abandon the
car and jump into a ditch. Occasionally among the flood of
refugees he would recognise a friend from Liège, or Paris, for by
the end no distinction was made in nationalities. The population
of La Rochelle doubled from its original 50,000 as it was invaded
by a mass of people who choked every road. They were exhausted, frightened, sometimes wounded; they included defeated soldiers, families still trying to transport all their belongings in a
handcart and lone children separated from their parents; and they
were all heading for Simenon's camp because it was literally the
end of the road, there was nowhere else to go.

Simenon guessed the news of the armistice on 22 June from the
shouts and tears of joy that swept through the camp. The refugees
were pleased because they thought that they would at last be
allowed home. Eventually they were, but it meant that Simenon's
task started all over again. Working this time with Obersturmführer Hartmann of the Feld-Kommandantur, Simenon went to
Bordeaux to arrange for trains, provisions, medical supplies and
escorts to be made available, and it was not until 12 August that
the last train left and he could hand in the keys of the reception
centre and resign his commission.

By this time the house in Nieul-sur-Mer had become a dangerous place to live. Hardly had the German bombardment of La
Rochelle ceased than the British one started. A petrol refinery had
been erected between the house and the military harbour of La
Pallice 5 kilometres to the south. One night one of the petrol
tanks was hit by a bomb and Simenon had to drive through a
sheet of flame that had spread across the road, cutting him off
from home. Fortunately the storage tanks nearest the house did
not go up; they were only 100 metres from their boundary
stream. Simenon and Tigy decided that they must try and find
somewhere inland where they and Marc would be safe. There was
already a German officer quartered in Nieul, and he was sleeping
in Simenon's study.

They moved three times during the war, but never very far
from La Rochelle. In August they rented a farmhouse in the forest

of Vouvant. This was in the Vendée, fifty kilometres north-east of Nieul. Then, after a month, they were able to move to one wing of the Château de Terreneuve in the nearby town of Fontenay-le-Comte, where they were to remain for nearly two years. It was here, shortly after moving in, that Simenon received the discreet letter from Untersturmführer Manfred Keyserling. Manfred was at the time attached to the Armistice Commission, working as an interpreter. He cannot remember receiving any response to his letter. In July 1942 they moved north again, to a more remote part of the Vendée, the hamlet of St Mesmin-le-Vieux, where they stayed until the liberation. Their own house at Nieul was requisitioned for the duration by the German army.

As aliens Simenon and Tigy were at first in some danger of being interned, but in the event it merely became necessary for them to report weekly to the local police station, a chore which after a time they were allowed to overlook. In each of their temporary houses Simenon spent much of the time cultivating his garden, but what had started as a refreshing distraction after the stale pleasures of Paris was now, literally, a way of life. The main daily problem for most people in France during the occupation was hunger and lack of fuel. The Simenons were perfectly placed to overcome both. Much of the day was spent in the ancient pursuits of the peasant:

> I remembered the war of 1914, the successive years when I felt the continual pinch of hunger and the queues outside school buildings which had been converted into food distribution centres. In the playgrounds '*la soupe populaire*' was poured into whatever vessel the people in the crowd held forward.

As early as 1939 Simenon started to dig up the flower beds in the garden at Nieul in order to sow peas and beans and plant potatoes and turnips. Each time they moved the work had to be started again. At Vouvant a vegetable garden already existed and there were fruit trees, but they did not stay there long enough to harvest anything. At the Château Terreneuve there was a park and they could keep chickens, geese, guinea fowl, a donkey for Marc, a goat and even cows. Bread, milk, butter and clothes were all rationed, so with their own vegetable garden, orchard, bee-hives and dairy they were in a strong position to barter. Before setting out across country in search of petrol, Simenon would put a sackful of live chickens into the boot of the car. Later, when the car was converted to run off charcoal, the charcoal stove which drove it occupied most of the boot.

Sometimes Simenon's discoveries about country life were belated. He was surprised to learn, for instance, that a cow gives milk only for a certain number of months after calving. Then he was delighted to hear that one could get round this problem by keeping a second cow and putting it to the bull after an appropriate interval. He ended up with three cows and produced so much butter and milk, as well as meat, that he was able to supply friends in Paris with many of their needs. After a time he felt capable of raising a pig and ended by raising two pigs a year, weighing 200 kilograms each. He was by his own account a success as a peasant farmer and his greatest triumph occurred when the local corn merchant, a figure of some importance, called on him to ask if it was true that he had succeeded in raising aubergines despite the unsuitability of the local climate and soil. It was true, and the novelist was respectfully invited to inspect the corn merchant's garden and advise his gardener. Market days would be spent gossiping over several glasses of wine. He called the market-women by their names and the men by their christian names and became a member of the select group who knew which stream could produce 200 crayfish in a single night and where partridges might be trapped. The partridges, too, went to Paris when Boule started to complain that she no longer knew what to do with them in the kitchen.

Apart from the struggle to provide food Simenon's account of country life during the occupation is notably undramatic. In the bars of Fontenay in 1941 the customers, hunched over their *petits blancs* or *pastis*, were not apparently discussing the German army's advance on Moscow, or the significance of Pearl Harbor, but the revenge some village boys had taken on a prosperous farmer who was in the habit of inviting them to lower their trousers. They had attacked him *en masse*, stripped him, and tarred and feathered his bottom; the local doctor had had to be called in to set him to rights. The farmer made no complaint to the police. The older generation won less glory after carrying out a multiple assault on an elderly and drunken Polish woman. She normally kept open house and permitted a wide range of familiar gestures but the rule was one at a time. Simenon saw several of his drinking companions disappear to the district court and thence to prison after a night of excessive disorder. Apart from these excitements there were the usual highlights of the rural calendar, including a monthly horse fair to which Simenon would take Marc whenever he could.

His happiest memories of this period were all of Marc. If Simenon was away for the day it was Marc he looked for first on his return as he leaned out of the railway carriage window. On Sundays he and the little boy would walk into Fontenay, crossing the bridge over the river to buy the newspapers and a picture book. They would go on to the Café du Pont-Neuf where Marc would sit on the high bench swinging his legs beneath the marble-topped table, while his father sipped a *petit blanc* and he examined the world of waiters dressed in long white aprons that was reflected in the mirrors that lined the walls. On Friday, 2 May 1941, Simenon wrote an account of how he had spent the previous day, a public holiday, with his son. 'Yesterday we had such a day as one remembers for the rest of one's life.' It had been an idyll. 'On other mornings the sky was as beautiful, on other evenings the sunset was as splendid. But yesterday, from dawn onwards, was a day which exemplified spring, it was as though it was the spring of your childhood.' A few days earlier Tigy had cut Marc's hair and put a few locks into tissue paper:

> Together we two set out, just us two, your hand in mine, along the alley beneath the chestnut trees which were in flower. Magpies were nesting, the cows were in the meadow; the mare and the donkey watched our progress . . . You would not have been surprised if the donkey had lifted its head as we passed and said 'Good-morning, Marc!'

Throughout that day Simenon examined the world with the eyes of a 2-year-old child. When they reached the town a chattering band of boys and girls were setting out on bicycles for a day in the country. That morning Marshal Pétain had made a speech on the radio to the workers of France declaring that in future May Day would be a symbol of 'union and friendship' rather than 'division and hatred' and assuring his audience that all was right with the world. In the evening they saw the cyclists return decked with flowers, like good members of the republic of '*travail, famille, patrie.*' Earlier, in the afternoon, father and son had returned to the house and after lunch had fallen asleep with Tigy, all in the same sun-filled room, listening to the cries of the guinea fowl. There had been German soldiers in Fontenay, hundreds of them 'in their grey uniforms crowding the pavements'. They had even come into the park of the château and taken photographs of the house. German soldiers in Fontenay were a rarity. Their camp was on a plateau beyond the town and apart from sentries outside the military headquarters they were seldom seen. In his memory of the day's happiness Simenon suppressed the soldiers, overlooking them just as his son would. The intensity of his pleasure in the day partly stemmed from his own conviction that he would soon be dead.

One day some months earlier, while cutting wood with Marc in the grounds of the château, Simenon had received a painful stab in the chest from a branch which sprang back at him. He decided that it would be sensible to have an x-ray in case he had broken a rib. The radiologist he consulted in Fontenay told him that his ribs were fine but that his heart was in an advanced state of decay, 'enlarged and worn out', and that he had at most two years to live. Simenon limped home in a state of shock. He had been told to give up drink, sex, exercise, hard work and much of his food. If he followed these instructions he might last the full two years. He left the doctor's consulting room in despair. Simenon's reaction, in December 1940, was to sit down and write a volume of memoirs that was eventually published in 1945 under the title *Je me souviens*, but which he later suppressed for many years and which has never been translated into English.

The picture of Simenon's war as presented in *Je me souviens* and later expanded in *Mémoires intimes* is of a man who, while living in bucolic retirement and struggling to make ends meet, is first placed under sentence of death for two years by an incompetent or possibly malicious doctor, and then threatened with 'Night and Fog' (the concentration camp) by a malicious inspector from the Commissariat-Général aux Questions Juives; finally he is hunted by a Gestapo torturer in the last moments of the occupation. The facts were rather different.

When Simenon returned to his house after the consultation to give the news to Tigy and Boule, Tigy – as always – remained calm, apart from 'going rigid', which was her way of expressing her feelings. Boule burst into tears. Tigy in fact found the news almost incredible. Her husband after all was in visibly good health. He took exercise, he was physically vigorous, he lived for much of the time in the open air, war-time food restrictions were if anything to his advantage. She went to see the radiologist herself and he told her that there must have been a misunderstanding and that there was nothing very seriously wrong; her husband's health gave no particular cause for alarm. Simenon refused to be reassured and his own doctor, who was one of his regular bridge partners at the Café du Pont-Neuf, urged him to go to Paris to get a second opinion from a specialist. Simenon claimed that this was impossible because as an alien he would not be given a permit to travel to Paris. Tigy pointed out later that such permits were not needed unless one wanted to go to the coast. Eventually Simenon was persuaded to go to Paris to see the country's leading heart specialist. He dated the visit February 1944, but long before that he had resumed a normal, vigorous life. The visit to the radiologist had been in the autumn of 1940. He started *Je me souviens* that December and put it aside in June of the following year. In the twelve months that followed the x-ray and 'death sentence' he wrote an autobiography, seven novels and five short stories. Not only was he working at twice his usual rate throughout 1941, but he seems to have been smoking his pipe while he was writing *Je me souviens*, drinking moderately, and even starting an affair with a shopkeeper in Fontenay-le-Comte. And in May 1941 he was reported to have been present at a large banquet in Paris, which suggests that he was by then not only working but eating and travelling freely without any need for a permit. Simenon's fear of illness was genuine, but it does not seem to have lasted nearly as long as he later claimed, and it seems to have owed as much to his own hypochondria as to a misdiagnosis. The hypochondria was made worse by his memories of his father's death – at the same age and from the same condition – and by memories of war. The events had coincided once; now he convinced himself that they would do so again.

Je me souviens was, according to its author, written for Marc, so that on growing up as a fatherless child he would know something of his family history. But Simenon was writing under the stress of fear – fear of illness and of war – and the number of inaccuracies which the book contains about his family story suggests that a more accurate title would have been *Je ne me souviens pas*. It is in this book that the story first appears of the Simenons' Breton descent, a story the writer attributed to 'a family legend'. Before writing a word of the book Simenon drew a family tree. It is here, where his pen first touched the paper, that the fiction began.

'The Pedigree of Marc Simenon,' reads the caption 'by his father'. And on the facing page is a note: 'The Simenon family since the installation in Vlijtingen, Limbourg, of a Simenon who came from Nantes and who, wounded during the campaign in Russia, married the daughter of a Limbourg farmer.' The accompanying plan suggests that Simenon did not know the year of his father's birth, did not know the year of his grandfather's birth or the year in which he had died, and did not know either the name or the year of birth of his great-grandfather. Nor did he know the correct number of his grandmother's children; furthermore there are two question marks too many for the uncles or aunts who died in infancy, thus increasing the total to the apocryphal thirteen. The facts were that Simenon's grandfather, Chrétien, the hatter who had been christened Christiaan, had been born in Vlijtingen in 1841. Chrétien's father, Lambert, identified as 'Simenon of Vlijtingen' on the novelist's chart, had been born in Vlijtingen in 1809 (not 1830), and *his* father, also called Lambert – 'Simenon the First of Nantes' on the chart – had been born in Vlijtingen in 1774. This was the only Simenon in the direct line who, according to the family legend, could have been 'a Napoleonic soldier'. But since grandfather Chrétien was born in 1841 he would have known and remembered his grandmother, Ida Vanherft, who died in Vlijtingen in 1849, and he would have known that his grandfather was not a Napoleonic soldier but was Lambert Simenon of Vlijtingen, son of Lambert Simenon of Riemst and father of Lambert Simenon of Vlijtingen. So grandfather Christiaan, the son of an illiterate labourer from Vlijtingen, latterly Chrétien, the hatter of the rue Puits-en-Sock, Outremeuse, may have deliberately altered his ancestry and exercised an early family talent for fiction. Or his grandson Georges, a novelist, may have invented the whole story to amuse Marc, and to improve the plot of *Je me souviens.**

As for the life of bucolic retirement, there is evidence to suggest that although Simenon's main interests during the war, as before and after it, remained in his work, he was in constant touch with life in Paris, either making or receiving several visits. When he wrote about the war in *Je me souviens* it was in a curiously detached way. 'Will America come to Europe?' he wrote on 2 May 1941. 'There is talk of America entering the war. Yesterday the English were in Greece, today the Germans drove them out and took their place. The Japanese are in China and the Australians are in Egypt.' These distant events, viewed from the leafy sanctuaries of the Vendée, take on a dreamlike quality in Simenon's account. Whereas in his lengthy correspondence with friends such as André Gide, Simenon was his normal wide-awake self.

In May 1941 Gaston Gallimard's son Claude, who was living in Paris but who had been given a *laissez-passer* by the Germans to travel in the Vichy Zone, called on Simenon at Fontenay-le-Comte, just as he would have been obliged to do in peace-time under the terms of their contract. Gallimard was on his way to visit André Gide, who was living on the Côte d'Azur, and he offered to take a copy of the first eleven chapters of *Je me souviens* with him for Gide's inspection. Gide had become the most powerful advocate of the serious merits of Simenon's work, and the two had been in regular correspondence since December 1938. One year later Simenon wrote to Gide offering him his best wishes for 1940: 'I expect Belgium to call me up any day . . . but I feel no need to anticipate heroism.' He added that he had written three novels since the outbreak of war:

> In a world that seems to be on the point of collapse I attach myself to the likes of *Il pleut, bergère* . . . And I admit with

---

* In the conditions of 1940 Simenon, living on sufferance as a registered alien, may also have wished that he was of Breton descent. In *L'Ane-Rouge* he had already transferred whole portions of his Liège childhood to the Breton port of Nantes, and later he noted that there was a common Breton surname, 'Simonon'.

some shame that I am more concerned about your reactions to
these books than I am about the war news . . . To keep the
family pot on the boil I thought of writing some more 'Maigrets'. What do you think?

Gide chose to reply on 28 May, that is at the height of the Battle
of France, at which time he was staying in Vence at the Villa La
Conque. He noted that the battle was going so badly that it
seemed as though it would shortly be impossible for them to
continue their correspondence. However, a series of postcards
from Cannes, Grasse and Nice reached Fontenay-le-Comte after
the armistice. In 1941 Gide advised Simenon to abandon the first-
person narration of *Je me souviens*, to fictionalise the characters by
changing their names and to type out his work as usual, rather
than writing it in pen and ink. All this advice Simenon faithfully
followed, starting work on the new draft promptly. The letter to
Marc 'from a father under a death sentence' was put aside, and
Pedigree, as it was later to be called, was transformed into a full-
blown novel of childhood and development. In September 1941,
in the Grand Hôtel at Grasse, Gide was still criticising *Pedigree*.
Some of his comments read like a coaching course – '*En général:
très bon travail, à continuer sans défaillance*' (On the whole, very
good work. To be continued without fail). The last surviving
letter from Gide on the subject of *Pedigree* is dated 21 August
1942, and was posted from Tunis. 'Yes, I am in Tunis . . .' his
note of two months earlier had opened, on a slightly defiant note.
Referring to the fact that he would no longer be able to visit
Simenon, as he had half promised, Gide explained, 'I left Nice for
African soil in the hope of finding the peaceful rapture ['*une
tranquille exaltation*'] which is propitious for work.' In the event
Gide did little work in North Africa although soon after his
arrival, at the age of 73, he wrote in his *Journal* that he had enjoyed
'two nights of pleasure such as I had not expected to experience at
my age' with a young *indigène*. The typescript of *Pedigree* continued to arrive for his comments but he no longer considered that
it would be 'the major work' which he one day expected Simenon
to write.

Simenon came to look on Gide almost as a father, a role which
the senior novelist would not have appreciated. Simenon
addressed him in his letters as '*Mon cher maître*' and Gide's attitude

to the war would certainly have been taken as an example for his own. What passed for Gide, he must have reasoned, would pass for him. Gide was French, the most prominent of literary critics, a student of philosophy and one of the most committed intellectuals of the day. In 1939 Gide had had the courage to sign a public statement in favour of the imprisoned pacifist Jean Giono. In 1940 he was critical of the terms of the armistice while expressing his admiration for Pétain's speech announcing the decision to surrender.* One of the most dishonourable clauses in the armistice was Article 19, which stipulated that France should hand over all anti-Nazi German citizens who had taken refuge on French territory. Committed left-wing French intellectuals, such as Gide and André Malraux, were also considered by many to be at risk of punishment. But Gide nonetheless turned down the offer of a visa which was made by an American committee in 1940. At that time he was living with his daughter Catherine at Cabris and did not consider himself to be in danger. In 1942 Gide received a visit from Sartre who had been released from prisoner-of-war camp and who while undertaking a bicycling marathon of the Vichy Zone was considering the possibility of resistance. Sartre was not the obvious man to lead a resistance network and Gide, perhaps sensibly, turned him down too. Anyone wishing to follow the fine thread of Gide's war-time ideology would have to take into account the fact that in 1941 Gide remained on good terms with the *Nouvelle Revue Française* (*NRF*), the paper he had helped to found but which had become a collaborationist publication under the editorship of Drieu La Rochelle. The German ambassador, Otto Abetz, said, 'There are three things that count in France. Communism, "high finance" and the *NRF*.' It was to Drieu that Gide wrote in August 1942 when he wanted copies of Simenon's books that were unobtainable in Sidi Bou Said, and he continued to submit his articles at a time when André Malraux refused to do so and while François Mauriac not only did so but allowed his articles to be prefaced and altered under German guidance.

Then, in 1942, Gide gave a lecture in Nice on the Belgian prose-poet Henri Michaux. This was singled out for a noisy demonstration by the extreme-right 'Légion des Combattants' (suc-

---

* He did not know that Pétain's original speech had been so abject that he had been advised to alter it.

cessors of the organisation for which Simenon had once worked as an office-boy), whose views on prose-poetry proved to be fiercely critical. So in May of that year Gide left the Côte d'Azur for Tunis. In November Algeria was liberated by the Allies and southern France and Tunisia were occupied by the Germans. The 'Légion des Combattants' pursued Gide from Nice to German-occupied Tunisia. Gide went into hiding and claimed in a letter to Simenon dated 11 December 1944 that it was this interruption which had forced him to abandon his long-planned paper on Simenon's work. After a month in hiding Gide left Tunis and flew to Algiers, which was then under a provisional Gaullist government.

In his attitude to the war Gide displayed all the patrician detachment of the French intellectual faced with Nazism and the Fall of France. In Algiers Gide felt at home. He was once more able to obtain copies of the *NRF*. 'Extremely interesting piece by Drieu,' noted Gide in his *Journal* in 1943. 'Admittedly while I congratulate myself on resigning, I have to acknowledge the persuasiveness of many of Drieu's arguments.' He was never a warm supporter of General de Gaulle, but he was at least able to immerse himself in the literary squabbles of an ill-assorted Free French community that included Saint-Exupéry and Jef Kessel.

The timely persecution by the 'Légion des Combattants' helped Gide to establish his rather flimsy Free French credentials. Otherwise they would have rested on the hostility shown to him by Vichy propagandists. In Vichy legend there were three reasons for the defeat of 1940 – the film *Quai des Brumes* starring Jean Gabin (about a heroic deserter); paid holidays; and André Gide. This argument was supported by a series of articles in *Le Figaro Littéraire* in October 1940, arguing that intellectuals had betrayed their political responsibilities and that Gide, Cocteau and others had been directly responsible for the defeat.* Gide's final offence in Vichy's eyes was to have gone into exile. But had he stayed his homosexuality and left-wing views might have earned him the same fate at the hands of the *milice* as Federico García Lorca suffered at the hands of the *falange* outside Granada in 1936. Finally Gide's governing attitude to the war was marked by a

---

* One of the most famous cartoons of the period in reaction to this argument showed a French peasant being reproached for reading too much Gide and Proust.

lofty serenity. In his *Journal* he wrote of the Allied and enemy radio broadcasts, 'To fight brutes, one needs brutes, and so we are all brutalised.' If he needed an example of how to behave under occupation Simenon was offered a rich choice by André Gide.

In December 1939 when Simenon wrote to Gide to say he was thinking of returning to Maigret he started work on *Cécile est morte* (*Maigret and the Spinster*). His sales had fallen since he had stopped writing Maigrets. In 1940, after his visit to the radiologist, he wrote two *romans* and two more 'Maigrets', as well as *Je me souviens*. In 1941 he wrote three more *romans*, three 'Maigrets' and the first part of the final version of *Pedigree* (*Pedigree*). In 1942 he wrote only one novel and most of his time was spent on the second and final parts of *Pedigree*. During nearly six years of hostilities in Europe Simenon wrote twenty-two books and twenty-one short stories. None of them took the war as a theme or even mentioned its existence with the exception of the unpublished memoir, *Je me souviens*. But since Simenon was writing for immediate publication this is hardly surprising. French interest in literature during the war, like people's interest in the cinema, was primarily escapist, apart from which all books had to be passed by the German censors, the cunningly-named 'Comité de Publication et de la Censure de la Propagande', run by the friendly and intelligent Obersturmführer Heller. The paper supply available to publishers was reduced from 32,000 tonnes in 1938 to 3000 tonnes in 1943, so long print-runs were impossible. But the rate of library lending in Paris doubled and much of the shortage of paper was compensated for by the growing list of banned authors and subjects. One thousand titles were pulped, with the full co-operation of French publishers anxious to keep their businesses alive. The 'Liste Otto', as it was called, was composed of books hostile to Germany or books by English, American or Jewish authors. The Pétainist régime favoured, on the other hand, books exalting Napoleon and Joan of Arc, heroes of the eternal war against England, but also books about the family, rustic values and social harmony. Simenon did not qualify under any of these headings but he was not disqualified either and he remained a favourite among French readers throughout the war.

His least productive year was 1942. In July, Simenon, Tigy, Marc and Boule left Fontenay-le-Comte for the greater obscurity of a farmhouse in the little village of St Mesmin-le-Vieux. The

Château de Terreneuve was said to be too damp for Marc, which
provided a plausible reason for the move. But towards the end of
their time at Fontenay there had also been an unpleasant incident
with an inspector from the Commissariat-Général aux Questions
Juives. In May 1942 this agency was taken over by a brutish anti-
Semite known as 'Louis Darquier de Pellepoix', who succeeded
the foppish anti-Semite Xavier Vallat and whose brief was to
speed up the number of Jewish deportations. One of de
Pellepoix's inspectors visited Simenon and told him that his name
was obviously derived from Simon and that he must be Jewish.
He was given one month to produce the birth and baptism
certificates of himself, his parents and his four grandparents in
order to prove that he had three non-Jewish grandparents.
Simenon offered to show the inspector evidence that he had not
been circumcised, but this offer was declined on the grounds that
it was inconclusive. Instead he had to write to his mother in Liège
and ask for her assistance.

The inspector also accused Simenon of trading on the black
market, which may have been true. There seems to be some
possibility that the visit followed an anonymous denunciation.
Simenon had become a prominent and obviously wealthy member
of the community in Fontenay and he had aroused jealousy and
disapproval. In January of that year he had been visited by a
Parisian, 'la Môme Crevette' Spinelly, by now a celebrated variety
artist but still boasting that she 'wore no knickers in order not to
miss an opportunity'; and there had been local publicity along the
lines of 'a Parisian encounter at Fontenay-le-Comte'. Shortly afterwards Jean Tissier, the actor, had come to stay for the world
première of *La maison des sept jeunes filles*, a film based on one of
Simenon's least interesting novels, written in 1937. On this occasion Simenon had turned up for the première with his latest
mistress, a local shopkeeper, on his arm, a flaunting of convention
that may have caused resentment. Further suspicions were aroused
by his occasional visits to the Kommandantur, although these
were invariably made at the request of a neighbour or to obtain
a pass, because Simenon had a rudimentary grasp of German.
Whatever the reasons, in July, directly after Henriette had supplied
enough certificates to satisfy the inspector from the Commissariat-
Général, the Simenons left Fontenay. And in September Simenon
remained sufficiently rattled by the experience to dissociate himself
publicly from the Jewish community.

The actor Raimu, his friend and the star of the film of *Les inconnus dans la maison*, had been criticised for making too much money during the occupation. This was a criticism to which Simenon himself was sensitive, but the terms in which he chose to defend Raimu are surprising. In an article for the magazine *Vedette*, published on 5 September 1942, Simenon referred to the smugness ('*complaisance*') with which the newspapers frequently quoted the incomes of film-stars like Raimu, and then wrote:

Do the same newspapers publish their proprietor's salaries? Do they work out the price in francs and dollars of the telephone-calls made by this or that Rothschild or this or that shark speculating against the franc on the Stock Exchange? No, it's always the actor or the star. Watch out! Raimu is greedy . . . he has a bad character; in other words when he is offered contracts by Monsieur Ixovitch or some other Zetovief he does not sign them with his eyes shut. As a matter of fact, have the newspapers *ever* examined the salaries of these gentlemen? Never. It's always the actor who is hounded by the tax inspectors or the professional cadgers.

Apart from its insensitivity to current events, the suggestion that a film-actor had been exploited by Jewish producers was extraordinarily inept in France in 1942.★

By November Simenon was sufficiently depressed with life under the occupation to make a rather desperate move to escape from their new home in St Mesmin-le-Vieux. He obtained car number-plates and false papers from an acquaintance who had a permanent pass to take his car into the Vichy Zone, and he borrowed a large hearse to transport the family and some of their belongings. But on the morning of 11 November, as they were about to set off, they heard the news of the German occupation of the Vichy Zone. There was nowhere left to flee to.

★ Earlier, when he was commissioner for Belgian refugees, Simenon had apparently shown caution about offering aid to Jewish refugees. In his '*Compte-rendu du mission*', dated 17 August 1940, he emphasised that he had assisted Jewish refugees who were not Belgian citizens 'on the direct order' of Georges Mandel, the Minister of the Interior. Mandel had been arrested by the Vichy government seven days earlier, prior to his trial on charges of co-responsibility for France's military defeat. Simenon was evidently anxious to distance himself from Mandel's direct order.

TEN

Muddle, fear, treachery and deceit

'Which day did they lock you up?'
'They locked me up on the day of the liberation!'
1950s music-hall patter by Sacha Guitry

In deciding, so far as possible, to continue working normally throughout the occupation Simenon was taking the same decision as the great majority of writers and people in general. His war-time books were slightly less numerous than at other periods, but they included some of his best. The *romans* included *La fuite de M. Monde*, *La veuve Couderc* (*Ticket of Leave*) and *La vérité sur Bébé Donge* (*The Trial of Bébé Donge*), as well as *Pedigree*. The 'Maigrets' included *Les caves du Majestic* (*Maigret and the Hotel Majestic*) and *Signé Picpus* (*To Any Lengths*). But if Simenon's production rate fell slightly, Gallimard's publication rate did not. There was a backlog to draw on, and despite the war-time restrictions on paper Gallimard published two Simenons in 1940, six in 1941, five in 1942, two in 1943 and three in 1944. So Simenon's name remained before the public and his income remained high.

Many of his friends were among those who rather enjoyed the occupation, in a slightly guarded way. Certainly in the world of letters the *règle du jeu* was 'opportunism'. You did nothing 'against France' but you did as much as possible, with or without German assistance, to make the most of whatever opportunities came your way. A small number of writers declined this opportunity, Camus and 'Vercors' being among the leading examples. A few others went too far in the opposite direction. For this

Robert Brasillach was shot, Pierre Drieu La Rochelle avoided his treason trial by committing suicide and Bernard Grasset – who published a French edition of *Mein Kampf* – was disgraced. But the line between what was acceptable and what was not was not always clear. On 10 June 1944, four days after the Allied landings in Normandy, German and Alsatian soldiers serving with the SS 'Das Reich' division massacred 642 villagers in Oradour-sur-Glane, 160 kilometres to the south-east of St Mesmin-le-Vieux. It was also the day when Paris saw the première of a new play, *Huis clos*, by Jean-Paul Sartre. Sartre was heavily committed to the production and extremely worried that it might be wrecked by an electricity cut due to a bombing raid. It was a stiflingly hot night but all passed off well at the Théâtre du Vieux-Colombier, and fortunately the reviews, including the German reviews, were good. Meanwhile the deportation trains continued to roll through Paris carrying, among thousands of others, the poet and film scenarist Robert Desnos, who was being sent first to the concentration camp at Compiègne and then to Buchenwald, for being Jewish, while the streets of Paris still contained posters for his latest film.

A few days after the opening of *Huis clos*, with Allied forces still battling to break out of the beachhead, Sartre chaired a public debate in Paris 'on the state of the theatre'. With him on the platform were Camus and Cocteau. This was well judged of Cocteau, an old friend of Simenon's, who had enjoyed the occupation more than most. Both Sartre and Camus were members of the 'Comité National des Ecrivains' (CNE), a resistance organisation under Communist Party domination which was well ahead with its plans for the post-war purge or *épuration*. The CNE had already started to publish draft versions of its lethal black list, but Cocteau's name never appeared on that list. Early in March, Cocteau had received the following letter from Max Jacob:

Dear Jean,
I am writing to you from a railway wagon thanks to one of the *gendarmes* who are guarding us. We will shortly be arriving at Drancy. That is all I have to say. Sacha [Guitry] said when he was asked to intervene for my sister, 'If it had been him I could have done something'! Well, it is me. With love, Max.

Cocteau was able to attend Max Jacob's funeral later that month. Jacob, born Jewish, later a Catholic, one of Simenon's earliest and warmest admirers, died in Drancy of misery and exposure at the age of 68 before his influential friends could do anything to get him back.

If Gide sometimes seemed to suffer from a detachment that brought him surprisingly close to the borderline of the unacceptable, Cocteau danced along that line like a trapeze artist. Throughout the occupation he maintained close contact with the German authorities, men such as Karl Epting, who directed the Institut Allemand and who was the *de facto* organiser of the '*collaboration intellectuelle*'. For Cocteau the occupation was his '*belle époque*'. He had written to a friend at the beginning of the occupation that he found it 'a fascinating time except for the lack of opium'. When his play *L'éternel retour* opened in 1943 the Japanese ambassador was among those he invited. And when the Nazi régime's favourite sculptor, Arno Breker, came to Paris for an exhibition of his work in the Orangerie in May 1942, Cocteau published a front-page tribute to him in a weekly review. By the time Breker died in 1991 he had spent years pointing out that he had never held a Nazi Party card. This was true, but in 1943 Breker told a writer from the paper *Comoedia* that he always chose the models for his athletic statues from 'splendid physical specimens of a race renewed and purified'.

Cocteau's tribute to Breker was exuberant even by his own standards:

> I salute you, Breker. I salute you from the *haute patrie* [exalted homeland] of poets. The country where countries do not exist, except in so far as each of us contributes the fruits of our nation's work. I salute you because in that exalted homeland, where we are fellow citizens, you speak to me of France.

Non-residents of the '*haute patrie*' might be forgiven for wondering what exactly Breker's iron-muscled, pure Teutons had to say to Cocteau about France, apart from the fact that they were fashioned from bronze obtained by melting down French statues, including a fine statue of Victor Hugo taken in 1941 from the streets outside the Orangerie where Breker's work was displayed. But in stating that poets were untouched by politics – a view also held by Hitler – Cocteau was exaggerating the olympian detachment of Gide and shadowing the stance of the Communist Picasso, who sometimes frequented the German *beau monde* with Cocteau and who once told the German officer and diarist Ernst Junger, 'You and I, sitting down together as we are now, could sign a peace treaty this afternoon. Tonight the lights could go up all over Paris.'

Cocteau also cultivated Junger, and took care to invite him to a reading of his new play in February 1942. But eventually, as for Gide, his homosexuality came in useful and he managed to make himself unpopular enough with the extreme right to pick up some serviceable insults. The collaborationist critic Lucien Rebatet described one of Cocteau's plays as 'the prototype of the theatre of inverts', and subsequently a performance of *Les enfants terribles* was booed by a cabal from the PPF, the French Fascist Party. Cocteau remained in touch with Simenon during the occupation. When Simenon came to Paris they sometimes spent the evening together, and on 16 May 1944, three weeks before D-Day, Cocteau wrote to Simenon with characteristic enthusiasm:

Dear Georges,
    I will read your book [possibly an advance copy of *La fuite de M. Monde*] at once. It will be my very first relaxation after weeks of work and exhaustion. As you know, I could never refuse you anything and I will do the drawings whatever happens. I think of you ceaselessly,

                                                        With love . . .

Two other friends of Simenon's, Pierre Benoît and Vlaminck, were also among those who paid public tribute to Breker. His publisher, Gaston Gallimard, was not reported to be present, but he had different preoccupations. In 1939 Gallimard, a co-founder of the *Nouvelle Revue Française*, was temporarily acting as editor. He absented himself from Paris that autumn, awaiting developments, and did not return until October 1940, four months after the armistice. The German authorities regarded the *NRF* as highly suspect – '*judéo-bolsheviste*, high finance and communism' rolled into one. The magazine's offices were closed that November, but it suited the Germans far better to keep the paper going, and for that they needed the agreement of the editorial committee and a sympathetic editor. In becoming the editor Drieu La Rochelle signed his own death warrant, but Gallimard also remained a force behind the scenes throughout the occupation, being among those who selected the editorial committee. This participation may have helped Gallimard to obtain the paper necessary to continue publishing throughout the war. Among the books he published were *Les voyageurs de l'impériale* by Raymond Aron. This book, by a Jewish intellectual 'Bolshevik' working for de Gaulle in London, was violently attacked in *Je Suis Partout*, the collaborationist review, and had to be withdrawn. The editors of *Je Suis Partout* were particularly angry with Gallimard because he had simultaneously refused to publish an anti-Semitic work, *Les décombres*, by Lucien Rebatet, on the grounds that he lacked the paper.

Another friend of Simenon's, Marcel Pagnol, took a harder line. Pagnol was vulnerable to influence because he was running his own film studio in Marseille and wanted to keep it open. He agreed to develop some Vichy government propaganda films but he continued to employ the French Jewish actor Harry Baur, who merely had to supply a certificate stating that he was a Christian, a formality which is said to have cost Baur a lot of money. Pagnol also refused a valuable subsidy from Continental, the German production company run by Alfred Greven, which did everything it could to take over the French film industry. And it was in the matter of working with Continental that Simenon came closest to crossing the line.

German control of the French film industry was gradual but increasingly effective. German newsreels were shown, but, since these frequently provoked demonstrations, they could only be shown with the police present and the lights up. Three-quarters of French cinemas were in the Occupied Zone, and in these the Germans banned all pre-war American or British films with Jewish actors. The Vichy government's COIC (Comité d'Organisation Cinématographique) barred all Jews from working in the film industry on 3 October 1940. As the war progressed, the French film industry was starved of funds and Continental progressively took its place, making the huge number of 220 feature films in four years. And among the most popular films for French cinema audiences, desperate to escape from the miseries of the real world outside the hall, were detective thrillers.

Before the outbreak of war Simenon sold film rights in only three of his books, and none of them was much of a success. During the four years of the occupation nine of his books were filmed, more than any other French writer, including Balzac. The majority of these films, five of them, were produced by Continental. In May 1941 Simenon was invited to, and was reported to have attended, a lunch given at Ledoyen restaurant in the Champs-Elysées by Continental. Also present were Arletty, Harry Baur, Danielle Darrieux, Henri Decoin and Maurice Tourneur. Decoin and Tourneur were to direct two of the films for Continental which were based on books by Simenon, and Decoin was to adapt another, *Annette et la dame blonde*, the first to be made. Following the lunch Simenon signed a contract with Continental for *Annette et la dame blonde*, on which shooting started in September, and for *Les inconnus dans la maison*, on which shooting started in November. Henri Decoin adapted the first and directed the second. If Simenon had any doubts about what role Continental wished to play in the French cinema during the occupation they must have been dispelled when he saw the programme accompanying *Les inconnus dans la maison*.

In Simenon's book the murderer bears a foreign-sounding name, Justin Luska. The book is, if anything, pro-Semitic: Luska is said to have been a victim of anti-Semitism as a child. 'Because of his red hair, his name, his real first name which was Ephraim, and the Eastern origins of his father, Luska was the *bête noire* of his schoolfellows . . .' But Luska's Jewishness, which is marginal to the plot of the book, was emphasised in Decoin's film, which was then distributed with a work of crude anti-Semitic propaganda called *Les corrupteurs*. Anti-Jewish propaganda was frequently presented in this way, an overtly anti-Semitic propaganda film setting the context for a more interesting film in which the same message was consequently implied. In the context of the programme the film of *Les inconnus* became an anti-Semitic film, and took its place plainly enough in '*la chasse aux juifs*'. But when Continental came back to Simenon with proposals to buy the film rights of three of his new 'Maigrets', *Signé Picpus*, *Cécile est morte* and *Les caves du Majestic*, Simenon agreed. There is no doubt that the film rights were negotiated by Simenon himself. He confirmed in *Mémoires intimes* that he had always negotiated his own film and radio rights personally. *Picpus* was filmed in October

1942, only four months after the book was published; *Cécile est morte*, directed by Maurice Tourneur, was filmed in December 1943; and shooting started on *Les caves du Majestic* as late as February 1944. In this case shooting was delayed because the screenplay was written by Charles Spaak, whose brother was in the Resistance. In October 1943 the Gestapo arrested Spaak, hoping to flush out his brother, and imprisoned him in Fresnes. The fact that he was working for Continental did not get Charles Spaak out of Fresnes, but it did get him a pencil and paper so that he could finish his work in prison. By this time the Resistance underground newspapers such as *L'Ecran Français* were beginning to attack Continental and all who worked with it. The issue of March 1944 attacked the scenarist of one of Continental's most famous films, *Le corbeau*, and the June issue attacked *anyone* who had taken Continental's money: 'That money has a dirty smell and it will linger on.' The same issue singled out Nova Film, producers of *Les corrupteurs*, for special attack.

Simenon also sold numerous radio rights to Radio-Paris during the occupation. After the liberation Radio-Paris was denounced as an instrument of German propaganda, and its leading news announcer, Jean-Hérold Paquis, was shot. It was agreed however that actors and broadcasters who had merely continued to exercise their professions without deliberate political involvement were culpable of nothing. But on another occasion Simenon came closer to an involvement that might have caused him serious embarrassment later on.

On 19 August 1941, *Le Petit Parisien* reported that a new literary prize had been established in Paris to replace the Prix Goncourt, which had not been awarded in 1940. The new prize was called the Prix de la Nouvelle France, and the jury, which had reached its decision over lunch at the Tour d'Argent, was made up of twelve members: Pierre Benoît, Abel Hermant, Bernard Grasset, Paul Fort, Abel Bonnard, Sacha Guitry, Jean de La Varende, Pierre Mac Orlan, Henri Troyat, Drieu La Rochelle, Jean Luchaire and Georges Simenon. Of the twelve, Benoît, Paul Fort and Sacha Guitry were all friends of Simenon. And of the twelve members, nine got into serious trouble after the war. Bonnard was sentenced to death, Abel Hermant got life imprisonment, Paul Benoît was blacklisted and arrested, Jean Luchaire was shot, Sacha Guitry was imprisoned, Paul Fort was blacklisted, Jean de

La Varende was blacklisted, Bernard Grasset was blacklisted and sentenced to national disgrace, exile and confiscation of property, and Drieu La Rochelle only escaped the firing squad by taking an overdose, slashing his wrists and putting his head in a gas oven. Perhaps it was as well for Simenon that the Prix Goncourt was restored later in 1941 and that the Prix de la Nouvelle France became redundant.*

To savour to the full the pleasures of lunch at Ledoyen or Le Tour d'Argent during the occupation one has to recall the scarcity of food in the rest of the city. The whole of the area of St Germain was said to have smelt of cabbage and ersatz coffee. And when the mass murderer Dr Petiot absentmindedly allowed his domestic boiler to overheat while it was crammed with human remains one day in March 1944, and thick black smoke began to pour out of the chimney at 21 rue Le Sueur and a dreadful smell spread round the *quartier*, his neighbours did nothing at first because 'people were cooking such extraordinary things all the time'. After the record harvest of 1943 the daily bread ration was increased by 25 grammes. Butter and cheese were rationed at 200 grammes a month, meat at 300 grammes. In these circumstances tuberculosis became endemic and the infantile mortality rate rose sharply. To 'eat well and to eat a lot' – duck in the Tour d'Argent, *sole meunière* at Jimmy's, *bouillabaisse* at Drouant – 'gave one a feeling of power', as Ernst Jünger recorded in his *Journal*. When municipal restaurants were charging 4 francs for a meal, and when management dining-rooms were charging 25 francs, one dish in a good restaurant might cost 55 francs, lunch for four people 650 francs. Naturally restaurants able to serve food at these prices had ways of avoiding the draconian rationing regulations, which was why they were able to provide a memorable meal for the juror of the Prix de la Nouvelle France.

Shortly before the liberation an event occurred that was to have more important consequences for Simenon's life than the Second

---

* All three Goncourt prizes awarded under the occupation went to books published by Gallimard. At the end of the war four members of the Académie Goncourt were expelled and blacklisted, and Gallimard did not win another Prix Goncourt until 1949.

World War. While living at St Mesmin he had acquired the habit of taking a daily siesta in a small building near the farmhouse. At about 3 p.m. Boule would wake him with a cup of coffee and they would make love. It was a routine as settled as a marriage and had been carried on for fifteen years. One afternoon 'the door of the little room opened and there before us stood Tigy, pale and stiff, dressed in her usual beige dungarees . . . Neither of us dared to move.' Tigy beckoned Simenon outside 'with a gesture worthy of the *Comédie Française*' and told him to show '*cette fille là*' the door. Simenon was upset by this reference to Boule, 'whom we had considered a member of the family for twenty years', and he refused to dismiss her, but Tigy said, 'It's her or me.' In order to distract Tigy from Boule, Simenon told his wife that he had been unfaithful to her 'hundreds of times', and frequently with people she knew, including her friends. They went inside the house to give Marc his tea and then returned to the garden where they stayed talking till dusk. Simenon pointed out that neither Tigy nor he could bear to be separated from Marc. He reminded her of the red arrows which the Germans had recently painted on all the crossroads and which were rumoured to indicate the direction to be taken by all male civilians in the region when the Germans gave the order. If that happened, he argued, Tigy would be left with Marc, with only Boule to help her. And if they were both taken as aliens then Marc would be left with only Boule. It was not a time when people lightly separated small children from their familiar companions and Tigy had little choice. By the evening they had decided to stay together as friends, to keep their marriage going for the sake of Marc, but to give each other their freedom. Tigy would no longer threaten suicide if Simenon were to be unfaithful to her: And he would no longer be 'forced' to deceive her several times a week. He wrote in *Un homme comme un autre*, 'I had deceived her for twenty-two years. I had made love more frequently behind a door than in a bed . . . A man never forgives a woman who forces him to tell lies.' What has never been explained is why Tigy, after twenty years, should have taken it into her head to check up on her husband. If it was because she found an anonymous note on the kitchen table there is every chance it would have been written by Boule.

Just before this incident took place, in April 1944, Simenon wrote his finest book of the war period, *La fuite de M. Monde*, a story that reflected his state of mind after four years of German occupation and an unsatisfactory emotional life. M. Monde is a wealthy man married to a woman for whom he has no strong feelings. He looks on marriage as a means of having children; he had never wanted to be 'a tree without fruit'. One day he decides to walk out of his home, disappear and start a new life. He leaves Paris and takes the train to Marseille where he falls in with a girl who gets a job as a hostess in a casino. He is ready 'to go as far as he can', he reflects that some people doing this end up as '*clochards*'. But instead he finds himself working in a nightclub in Nice. His job is to sit behind a spyhole watching the staff at work, to make sure that they don't cheat the management. Everything about his new life amazes him. The colour of third–class rail tickets, the smell of his own sweat when he goes to bed in a cheap hotel without having a bath. One day his first wife comes into the nightclub. She has become a morphine addict. M. Monde leaves his spyhole and saves her from the hopeless life she is leading and takes her back to Paris where he puts her in the care of a doctor. He then returns home without giving a word of explanation to anyone.

La fuite de M. Monde is a story about a man trapped by a marriage and by a way of life. When M. Monde arrives in Marseille he makes his way to the Vieux Port: 'He saw the water and just beside him the little boats crowded together, rocking slightly to the breathing of the sea.' Simenon's description of the Mediterranean reflected his own war-time longing for Porquerolles, which he had not seen for five years: 'The light was typical of a Mediterranean inlet, the ever-present sunlight, but diluted, diffused, almost broken up as if through a prism, suddenly violet for example, or green . . .' M. Monde is also concerned about running out of time. He is 48 – 'a man who has already reached life's downhill slope'. Simenon was 41 when he wrote this. As a consolation M. Monde has his son. Simenon, since the birth of Marc, had felt much happier about describing parental relationships, something he had felt incapable of doing when he invented Maigret. There are also parts of Simenon's childhood in M. Monde: 'Once just after Lent he had experienced a period of acute mysticism, and had spent days and nights practising spiritual exercises in search of perfection.' And there are other aspects of his life which for his creator represented hope rather than experience. For M. Monde eventually finds salvation by way of flight. And when he returns to his house in Paris his friends notice that 'this man was no longer overshadowed, he had no more phantoms, and he looked you in the eyes with a cold serenity'.

After finishing M. Monde, Simenon did not write a book for a year, which in view of surrounding events was hardly surprising. If there was to be a second exodus in front of the Allied forces, in the reverse direction, then the Simenons this time would be at the head of the line rather than the end of it. In fact the Vendée lay on the route of one of the major running battles of the liberation, the line of march of the SS 'Das Reich' Division from the south of France towards Normandy. Resistance opposition to this was to be one of the organisation's main battle honours. In the spring of 1944 members of the *maquis* and parachuted saboteurs started to arrive in the region, and some of them came to the house in St Mesmin-le-Vieux for supplies. They also requisitioned the canary-yellow car which Simenon had kept hidden under some bales of straw since moving into the farmhouse. The car was repainted green and two heavy machine-guns were mounted in it, a development which must have worried Simenon since he knew that if his own involvement were to be revealed deportation would probably be the least unpleasant thing that would happen to him. Shortly afterwards systematic railway sabotage started in the area, and one night a German army car was machine-gunned three kilometres from St Mesmin and three German soldiers were killed, one of them a colonel. Reprisals were carried out at the neighbouring hamlet of La Chapelle. The villagers of St Mesmin watched the flames burning all night. 'It was the price of a German colonel,' Simenon wrote. In one of the houses destroyed a stock of pictures was hidden which had been saved from destruction in 1940; it included works by Renoir, Léger and Derain.

Simenon regarded war as a succession of muddle, fear, treachery and deceit, and because of his public success during the dark years of the occupation he lived through some of the worst moments of his war at the time of the liberation. He knew what followed liberation: *épuration*, the purge. He had lived through this once already; it was among the most vivid memories of his childhood. On 7 January 1943, two months after he had failed to make his escape to the Vichy Zone, Simenon finished writing

Pedigree. The last pages contain an appalled description of early scenes in the 1918 purge of Liège:

> The war was over . . . and suddenly like a signal the noise of a shop window being shattered. It was a charcuterie, whose owner had worked with the Germans . . . Ten, twenty, fifty charcuteries suffer the same fate . . . then in a dark corner the outline of a human form struggling against half-a-dozen furious men. Roger looked on without understanding. They were in the process of stripping a woman . . . the police stood by, inactive.

As the liberation of France approached, Continental Films were advertising their latest deal with Simenon all over France while the underground editions of *Les Lettres Françaises*, more and more widely diffused, published frequent attacks on 'the film company which was under the orders of its Nazi boss, Monsieur Greven'.

Simenon's true feelings about surrounding events were revealed one afternoon while he was working in his vegetable garden and Boule came to tell him that some members of the FFI had been asking for him. The FFI were the Resistance, but they were by that time a wild and unpredictable bunch, quite capable of taking the law into their own hands. Boule had said that Simenon was out and they had said they would come back in an hour or so. Simenon panicked and immediately concealed himself behind the tall hedge at the bottom of the garden. Boule brought out a haversack which Tigy had already prepared for such an occasion. It contained clothes, food, morphine and a hypodermic syringe. Simenon sent a message to a neighbour whom he trusted and the man came by on a motorbike and took him to a farm, where he spent two nights sleeping in a barn. Then, as the battle approached, Tigy, Marc and Boule joined him and the whole family went to a well-hidden field where various other villagers, including the local doctor, gathered. Here for two days they formed part of a small community of refugees who were in hiding in the open air, all of whom felt safer in the fields than they did in their own houses.

To explain his panic many years later Simenon claimed that the people calling at the house had not been resisters, but Germans. He even said that on their return one of them had been identified as a woman who strongly resembled a notorious female associate of the Gestapo known as 'Mademoiselle Docteur'. The picture he presented in *Mémoires intimes* was of a man who had been sheltering and supplying the Resistance, on the run from a last-minute round-up by the departing Gestapo. But Tigy and Boule were in no doubt (when asked about the incident by Fenton Bresler, in one of his invaluable interviews) that the callers had been people claiming to be in the Resistance. When Boule was asked in 1991 if the FFI were *'mauvais garçons'* she replied, *'Ils n'étaient pas toujours très intelligents.'* In fact there was no shame in fleeing from the self-appointed members of the FFI during the days of the liberation. The FFI numbered among them many brave men who were determined to fight for the honour of France, but also many chancers and violent criminals or Communist hatchet-men, out to settle obscure scores of their own or to line their pockets or simply to kill people for the fun of killing. They were particularly dangerous in remote areas like the Vendée where it was to be many weeks before they were brought under full military discipline. The question is, therefore, why did Simenon change the story? Did he do it because he had forgotten the facts? That seems unlikely. The answer must be that he deliberately changed the story to distract attention from the problems he eventually had when the FFI caught up with him in January 1945.

When the family were at last able to return to the house Simenon fell ill and was diagnosed as suffering from pleurisy. His illness was brought on as much by nervous exhaustion as by anything else. Earlier in the year the doctor who accompanied him to Paris for the definitive consultation about his heart said that Simenon appeared to be so ill when boarding the train in the morning that he had to be pushed on to it. A few hours later, having been told that there was nothing wrong with his heart, he felt fit enough for a night on the tiles with Cocteau and Pagnol. All his life Simenon had a tendency to hysterical illness, and in the late summer of 1944 took to his bed for four months suffering from pain and fevers and being nursed as though he were in danger of death. In November he was finally judged well enough to convalesce at the nearby resort of Les Sables d'Olonne, and he went to a hotel called Les Roches Noires. By this time the war had moved on, but in Paris the intellectual *épuration* was at its height. A move to Les Sables d'Olonne, fifty kilometres further away from Paris, was in itself a reassurance. Having been through two wars, two defeats, two occupations and two *épurations*, Simenon was, for the time being, a case of 'civilian shell-shock'.

Tigy went back to their house in Nieul, which was in poor condition after over four years of military occupation. Boule and Marc accompanied Simenon, and, for the first time in their sixteen-year relationship, Boule and Simenon shared a bedroom. Tigy was exhausted by the effort of nursing her imaginative husband, and exasperated with his behaviour in general. But Boule stood by him. In a house beside Les Roches Noires Simenon found another refugee from the *épuration*, a woman living alone, formerly a schoolteacher, whose head had been shaved by the 'Résistants de Septembre', as some of the FFI were mockingly called. 'What she had done was no concern of ours,' Simenon wrote at the time. 'Her hair was growing again, which would not have been the case with her breasts, which she only just managed to stop them from cutting off instead. She remained calm, nonetheless, and harboured no hatred for anyone.' And she agreed to teach Marc to read and write.

On 18 January 1945 Simenon wrote the last chapter of *Je me souviens*, which he had put aside in June 1941, when he started *Pedigree*. It was also at Les Sables d'Olonne that he wrote some of the stories that were later to be collected under the title *Le bateau d'Emile* and reread Balzac, Zola and Proust, as well as the Old and New Testaments. *Je me souviens* ends with a description of an incident which obviously marked him and which throws an interesting light on his morale at the end of the occupation. There was a woman staying at their hotel who dined at the table next to Simenon's and who had made a considerable fuss of him, giving the impression that she was excited to be living in the same house as 'a famous writer'. One day, after an acquaintance of several weeks, they started to talk about the post-war world and Simenon said he hoped the workers and the '*petites gens*' would do better this time than they had done before the war. At which point, without warning, the friendly woman replied, 'Well I hope Communism puts you back among the people, where you belong!' The woman's sudden malice hurt Simenon deeply but a more serious shock was to come. On 30 January 1945, as Pierre Assouline has revealed in *Simenon—Biographie*, the creator of Inspector Maigret, still suffering from pleurisy, was placed under house arrest in his seaside hotel by the police and FFI of Les Sables d'Olonne on unspecified charges of suspected collaboration. The subsequent investigation in the various districts Simenon had inhabited during the occupation cleared him of collaboration, but it was to be three months before he was free to travel again.

It was also at Les Sables d'Olonne that Simenon resumed contact with Gide. He had heard nothing from Gide since August 1942. In December 1944 Simenon received a letter dated 11 December. Gide wrote, '. . . I have been very worried about you, imagining you in a zone that was still unliberated and at the mercy of German tricks which are so frequently cruel.'

Gide, carrying on from where he had been so rudely interrupted, wrote that Simenon was a prisoner of his early success and suffered from a false reputation like Baudelaire or Chopin. The whole point of Gide's forthcoming paper on Simenon would be to show that he was 'much more important than was generally recognised'. Simenon's most serious limitation, in Gide's view, was that almost all of his characters were '*abouliques*', people suffering from a loss of will-power. He urged him to show that heroes, headstrong and wilful people, could also be 'driven'. It was because Simenon himself was the opposite of '*aboulique*' that Gide had hoped for so much from *Pedigree*, but he now thought it better to postpone publication.

In his reply, dated 18 December, Simenon wrote:

Mon cher maître, mon grand ami . . . We only have perhaps two, three or four chances of real friendship in life . . . two or three chances of real contact with another human being, which one should seize with both hands. What foolishness to refuse such a gift from the Gods. And the deeper I plunge into your work, the further I want to go . . .

Simenon was later to confess that he had never been able to read Gide's novels, so the first part of this letter seems to be polite rather than sincere. But having finished with the flattery he started to discuss his own work, and the tone of the letter changes:

Towards the end of March this year, having finished *La fuite de M. Monde*, which will be published in three weeks' time, I had the strong impression, which I still have, that a period of my

life had closed and that another was going to start . . . For a
very long time I have had the intuition that you would help me
to unravel this crisis of maturity which has been so painful . . .
God knows I await your advice more impatiently than ever.

Talking of his work Simenon said that he thought the long period
of introspection forced on him by the war had been beneficial and
that he now felt a great impatience to start writing again. As for
Pedigree, he agreed with Gide's opinion of it, wondered if it had
been a mistake to write it and said that he had no intention of
publishing it without further advice from Gide.* He ended the
letter by saying that his wife and son were with him at Les Sables
d'Olonne, and that his son, aged 5½, had been his real companion
during '*les années mornes*'. He signed the letter '*Votre Simenon*'.

In another letter, also written in December, but to François
Mauriac, Gide was more open than he had been to Simenon, to
whom he had simply said that he expected to return to Paris in the
spring. To Mauriac he wrote, 'I will not suffer too much by
prolonging my exile until the spring . . . waiting until the moral
and physical temperature has become a little more clement.' Gide
was in an unusual position. Driven out of Nice and then Tunisia
as a left-wing homosexual and anti-collaborator, he now hesitated
to return in case he was branded defeatist, an anti-Communist and
a Pétainist. In the chaos of the liberation the French Communist
Party was extremely powerful and well-organised. The word
'*épuration*' was one which came naturally to Communist lips. The
committed Communist intellectual Louis Aragon, an influential
member of the Party, had had it in for Gide since before the war,
when the latter had published *Retour de l'URSS*; a condemnation
of Stalinism. Now Aragon was asking hostile questions about
Gide's contributions to Drieu's *NRF* and to the collaborationist,
war-time *Figaro*.

Others among Simenon's friends and acquaintances were in
worse trouble. Pierre Benoît and Vlaminck were both in hiding

---

* In fact Simenon was to publish *Pedigree* three years later without taking account of
Gide's view, and he subsequently explained the delay in publication by saying that
he had for a long time wished to spare his mother's feelings. If that was indeed the
case he chose a strange time to publish it, since it came out shortly after the death of
his brother Christian.

from the Resistance. Benoît was eventually arrested in Dax. But while he was still in prison awaiting trial Louis Aragon arranged for him to be released and removed from the black list, apparently in exchange for serialisation rights for the Communist newspaper *Ce Soir* to Benoît's best-selling novel *L'Atlantide*. Another friend, the actor Michel Simon, found himself in the ridiculous position of being blacklisted (for having played *Tosca* in fascist Italy), on the run, and at the same time being pursued by a casting director who wanted him to play a Resistance hero in a new film. Simon agreed to play the part, but only on condition that he could keep his 'disguise', a thick beard and a tangled mop of hair. He still had the beard when he played the part of M. Hire in the film *Panique*, shot in 1946. Vlaminck stayed on the black list. His most serious offence had been to accept an invitation to tour Nazi Germany as one of an official delegation of artists from France. In later years Simenon was to claim that he and Pierre Benoît became close friends only after the war, although they 'had already met once or twice on the terrace of Fouquet's'. He did not mention the jury of the Prix de la Nouvelle France. Pierre Fresnay, star of *Le corbeau*, who had spoken the voice-over in *Les inconnus dans la maison*, was arrested and imprisoned for six weeks. *Les inconnus* was attacked in *Les Lettres Françaises* in March 1944 because it had been distributed by Continental in Germany under the new title *The Youth of France* and had thus presented the whole of French youth as gangsters.

In May 1945, Simenon was at last cleared by the police in Les Sables d'Olonne and allowed to go to Paris. But he had decided to abandon France as soon as possible. Sending Marc and Boule back to Tigy in Nieul he set off for Paris in the company of an attractive young secretary whom he subsequently called 'Odette' since he had forgotten her real name. The *épuration* had been going full swing for nearly a year and Simenon had not been listed by the Comité National des Ecrivains, nor had he been denounced in *L'Ecran Français* or *Les Lettres Françaises*.* Nonetheless, Simenon

---

* According to the late Maurice Richardson, as reported in *The Mystery of Georges Simenon* by Fenton Bresler, Louis Aragon 'was spreading it all over Paris that the creator of Maigret was a leading collaborator'. Richardson was a fine journalist and a magnificent gossip, and – thanks to its inclusion in Bresler's book – this remark has been widely republished in France and Belgium; but it would be rash to accept that

was determined to get out of the country. Even if Aragon could be faced down there was the possibility of a Communist election victory. Bernard de Fallois is in no doubt that Simenon left France in 1945 because 'he was frightened that the Russians were coming'. While waiting to leave Simenon found Paris as welcoming as it had been during the years of occupation; only the uniforms had changed. The problems of the black market were the same and the names of the 'good' restaurants which were doing whatever was necessary to bypass the restrictions were circulated by word of mouth.

The main trauma suffered in Paris during the summer of 1945 was no longer the hunt for collaborators but the return of the deportees from the prisons and concentration camps. Every day thousands arrived, many of them members of the legion of the living dead. From April to August the government had to welcome an average of 50,000 cases a week. Among them was Odette's father, a returning prisoner of war. Odette accompanied her father home, but without inconveniencing Simenon who, on the same day, met a former 'Girl Guide' who had been one of his helpers with the Belgian refugees in 1940 and whom he now found 'less *gamine*'. She filled the vacant position of secretary and moved into his room at the Claridge. Marc and Boule came up from Nieul and Simenon installed them in their old apartment in the place des Vosges, where he joined Boule in the double bed until Tigy arrived, at which point he returned to his room in the Claridge where his 'Girl Guide' was waiting. She spent the days in the queue outside the British consulate waiting to apply for British visas. All transatlantic sailings in the summer of 1945 went via Liverpool or Southampton, the French ports having been destroyed by German sabotage or Allied bombings. Once the British visa was secured it was necessary to get the far more

Simenon was accused of collaboration on the sole authority of an anecdote by Maurice Richardson. A reading of *L'Ecran Français*, *Les Lettres Françaises* and *Ce Soir*, the three publications immediately available to Aragon for denunciations, shows no trace of Simenon's name in any of the lists of suspected collaborators or in any of the hundreds of reports on the same subject. But Assouline has traced one hostile listing of Simenon in *Bir Hakheim* (an underground Resistance news-sheet published before the Liberation), and has established that in 1949, in its final hearing, the CNE proposed that Simenon's books be banned for two years because of his wartime deals with Continental Films. The proposed ban was never published and was quashed after objections from Maître Garçon, Simenon's lawyer.

elusive American visa. For a Belgian to get a United States visa, the armistice with Germany having been signed only on 8 May, was extremely difficult, but Simenon found a way round the problem when he heard that a former editor of *Le Journal* whom he had known well before the war was now a man of influence in the ministry of information. Simenon called on him in his office in the avenue Friedland and his friend suggested that the solution would be to send him on a government mission, in his case 'a mission to American and Canadian publishers'.

One day while Simenon happened to be in the apartment in the place des Vosges, visiting Marc and Tigy, a message was brought in saying that someone was waiting to see him in the gardens outside. He found his brother Christian sitting on a bench and refusing to come in because it was too dangerous. Simenon had last seen his brother in 1940 when Christian's boat, returning from Matadi on the outbreak of war, had put in briefly at La Rochelle. Christian was at that time in charge of a load of Belgian government gold which he later claimed to have returned to Brussels, in itself an unhelpful act just after the fall of Belgium. French gold was at the same time being shipped out of Bordeaux for safe-keeping in London. In fact it was never entirely clear whether or not Christian had accounted for the Congolese gold. During the occupation he had joined the Belgian fascist 'Rex' movement and, having driven a car while his fellow Rexists carried out machine-gun attacks on groups of Resisters, was now on the run and in fear of his life. He had managed to get into France and was appealing to Georges to help him. The solution Georges eventually proposed was that Christian should sign up with the French Foreign Legion under a false name. The Legion was prepared to accept wanted collaborators without asking questions (and was even prepared to recruit former members of the SS), so Christian was assured of a welcome. In later years Simenon said that it was André Gide who had suggested the Foreign Legion, although by the time he made this public Gide was dead so there is no confirmation that it was in fact his idea.

Once he had seen Christian safely out of Paris, and given him the money he would need until he had joined up, Simenon did not do the obvious thing and go to Liège to see his mother. Although he had not seen Henriette since April 1939, when Marc was born, and although he had never been to thank her for her help in supplying him with the necessary birth certificates in 1942, he was prepared to set out for the United States for an indefinite stay without saying goodbye. The breach between them may have been greater than he acknowledged, but it seems more likely that he was simply frightened that his own appearance in Liège would reactivate interest in Christian's or his own war-time activities.

One morning, while he was lying in bed with his 'Girl Guide' in the Claridge, the telephone rang; Gide was on the line. After their subsequent meeting Simenon wrote to apologise for talking only about himself. He offered to take Gide out to dinner at 'a good restaurant' and referred to his 'quasi-filial devotion'. Their relationship, at least as it appears in their correspondence, remained that of master and pupil – Gide friendly and intrigued, anxious to guide Simenon along the paths of literary righteousness; Simenon flattered, intimidated ('I am always so nervous because deep down I am unconvinced that I deserve your precious friendship') and, finally, rejecting. They spent two days together at Gide's sister-in-law's house in Normandy, and in July Gide introduced Simenon to another admirer, Raymond Mortimer, '*un garçon charmant*', who was staying with the British ambassador, Duff Cooper. It was in the letter containing the invitation to meet Mortimer, written on Bastille Day 1945, that Gide made his famous comparison between Simenon and Camus, saying of *La veuve Couderc* (written in April 1940) that it was 'remarkably analogous with *L'étranger* [published in 1942], about which everyone is talking, but that it goes much further, without appearing to do so, which as we know, is the height of art'.

The evening with Raymond Mortimer was judged a great success. 'After a delicious dinner at a black market restaurant (for which Simenon paid) Gide went home, and Simenon took me to a fair in Montmartre with roundabouts and shooting alleys . . .' Mortimer wrote later. Gide, who all this time was furiously devouring previously unread Simenons, next wanted to introduce Simenon to one of his oldest friends, the novelist, academician and Nobel Prize winner Roger Martin du Gard. This meeting, too, took place, Martin du Gard writing on 9 August to thank Simenon for the dinner, wishing him a pleasant journey, and calling him a '*fastueux vagabond*'. Simenon was still in Paris for the VJ-day procession, which took place after the bombing of Hiroshima and Nagasaki and followed the Japanese surrender on 15 August. He and Marc watched the parade from his balcony in the Claridge overlooking the Champs-Elysées. Simenon, who regarded war as an atrocity and victory as an imposter, must have viewed the VJ-day celebrations with particular distaste. For him France was a country, like Belgium and Germany, which had just lost a war, but which, unlike Belgium and Germany, was pretending to have won it. The French role in the atomic bombing of Japanese cities had been nil and the French decision to celebrate as another victory the use of the most terrible weapon yet invented, even though France had never used that weapon, crystallised his dislike for General de Gaulle, whom he regarded from then on as *'cocorico'*. In *Quand j'étais vieux* he would write of de Gaulle's 'conceit . . . his scorn of the opinions of others'.

But little of this mattered in August 1945. The American visas had come through, and they were on the point of departure. He was leaving France, the influence of Gide and even his publishers Gallimard. He was wiping the slate clean and starting his life again. His last surviving contribution to this part of his correspondence with Gide was written at the end of July and ends, 'I have the impression that I am beginning to know you better, and I like you more, though remaining all the time deeply "impressed".' No doubt Simenon's liking and admiration for Gide were entirely sincere, but he seems at the same time to have found it an unbalanced relationship, and an invitation to enter a world which – despite his self-confidence in 1937 when he had spoken of winning the Nobel Prize – he knew he could never call his own.

Just before leaving Simenon made the necessary arrangements to change his publishers. He increasingly resented the fact that Gallimard did not take his work sufficiently seriously and treated him as a merely popular novelist. While he had been convalescing at Les Sables d'Olonne he had received from an unknown Danish publisher, Sven Nielsen, the proofs of a novel by an unknown Norwegian author. This was *Traqué* by Arthur Omré, for which, most unusually, he agreed to write a preface. When Simenon came to Paris he met Nielsen and they became close friends. In defiance of all the advice he had received Simenon gave Nielsen the manuscript of the earlier, factual version of *Pedigree*. Nielsen published this under the title *Je me souviens* on 24 December 1945, in his infant publishing house Les Presses de la Cité, which is today, after several changes of ownership, the largest publishing group in France. The foundation of the house's success was undoubtedly Simenon and from 1947 onwards he gave all but four of his books to Nielsen, sending only one more novel to Gallimard.* His desertion came at a bad time for Gallimard, who was not fully forgiven for his activity during the occupation until 1949. This decision – to leave Gallimard for an unknown, thoroughly commercial, publisher – did Simenon's literary reputation in France no good at all. The silences of the great cathedral of French publishing are as eloquent as its sermons, and can be more devastating than the most savage criticism from less influential directions. For Simenon there was little chance from then on of a Prix Nobel. Gide never published his much-discussed paper on the 'importance' of Simenon; the manuscript remained unfinished at his death, and it seems clear that he too was disappointed by his protégé's rejection of his advice and patronage, confirmed by the decision to publish first *Je me souviens* and then *Pedigree*.

Also before leaving France, Simenon met Pierre Lazareff, his pre-war journalistic patron, who had spent the war running an agency for French actors in Hollywood. Lazareff had by now left *France-Soir* and had started a new paper, untainted by any form of collaboration and called *Libération*. Simenon agreed to write a short story for Lazareff and went to the village of St Fargeau-sur-Seine, upstream from Paris, for a few days to write it. They were to be the last days of his life spent on the banks of a river which had inspired so much of his work. Earlier, in the Hôtel Cambrai in the rue de Turenne, he had written *La pipe de Maigret* and the title story of *Le bateau d'Emile*. The only remaining formality to be completed before the departure for London was to buy the tickets, and here Simenon was surprised to learn from Tigy that he would need to buy only three, as Boule would not be coming with them.

The failure to take Boule to America in 1945 was one of the few

---

* Pierre Assouline has established that Simenon also criticised Gallimard for not doing enough to sell his books; apparently with justice, since the change of publishers resulted in average sales in France increasing by 350 per cent.

marital battles which Simenon fought and lost. The reason he lost it was because Tigy no longer had to take the initiative in ridding herself of Boule. All she had to do was refuse to go to America. She told Simenon that if Boule came she would refuse to take Marc out of France. Now it was no longer a case of 'her or me', but of 'her or us'. No French court would have given Simenon custody of Marc against his mother's wishes, and there was no question, in the conditions of 1945, of Simenon wanting to push matters that far with Tigy. With the greatest reluctance he had to agree to leave Boule behind, although he considered her a full member of the family. There is a sad picture taken at about this time of Simenon's family. It is the only picture of Boule and Marc together; it looks like a farewell photograph, and the saddest faces in it are those of Marc and Boule. Simenon's failure to defend Boule's position on this occasion had an important influence on his subsequent behaviour towards Tigy. His miscalculation had been to underestimate the depth of Tigy's resentment over his conduct with Boule. When he noted in the spring of 1945 that Tigy and Boule were 'getting on very well' he was deluding himself.

The Simenons flew from Le Bourget to Croydon to find a capital city which, though it had never been occupied, had suffered far more from the war than Paris had. For Simenon, London was the capital of the liberators, 'the English, the Americans, the Canadians, and a few French regiments as well', and he noted that some people in France would never forgive these foreigners for putting them in the position of owing them their freedom. London, for Tigy and Simenon, had always meant the Savoy Hotel, which they found open and undamaged. There were English royalties waiting for him at the bank, so – to the Savoy, with their thirty pieces of luggage. Simenon sent an article to *France-Soir* about life in post-war London; it was one way of saying goodbye to all the friends he had failed to see before his departure. He called on George Routledge & Sons to check his royalty statements, and he opened a Canadian bank account, since they had decided to start their North American adventure in French-speaking Quebec where they intended to learn English. In London, Marc was kept amused by repeated trips on the pleasure-steamers plying between Westminster Pier and Tower Bridge, which passed the lines of ocean-going boats moored in the Upper Pool. He also made friends with the porters outside the Savoy and learnt how to whistle for taxis. Simenon and Tigy had separate rooms, and in the evenings Simenon would set out across this new, strange city by himself, in search of adventure. 'I discovered,' he wrote later, 'that Englishwomen were not the cold, dull creatures of legend.'

They had to wait for a month before they could sail. The first move was to register with the committee which allocated berths on all transatlantic passages. There was such a demand for tickets that passenger vessel movements were regulated and the available number of berths were pooled and allocated at very short notice on stated priorities. It was the heyday of iron bureaucracy in a London which met any request for information, let alone any hint of a complaint, with the sneering response, 'Don't you know there's been a *war* on?' Once registered the Simenons were told to wait in their hotel since instructions to board the boat train to Liverpool or Southampton could come at any time and at one hour's notice. Boat tickets could not, however, be purchased before the order to embark was issued. So when the order eventually arrived, one day in September, Simenon, rushing to buy the tickets, found a long queue in front of a single booking office window. He reached the head of the queue with only minutes to spare to find that his arrival had coincided with that of the tea trolley. 'I offered the clerk my papers. He looked away. While I fumed he drank his tea, in greedy little sips, and nibbled his piece of cake.'

They were finally booked on to a small Swedish cargo vessel which had berths for twelve passengers and which, since it was carrying no cargo, gave them a rough passage through the equinoctial gales. Tigy and Marc shared a cabin. Simenon was lodged with '*un monsieur inconnu*'. During the voyage he became friendly with the only obvious criminal on board, a Frenchman who was smuggling two litres of 'essence of roses' into the United States as the basis of his future fortune, and whose mistress concealed her diamonds in a plain leather bracelet. And so they bucketed their way across the Atlantic, the perfume smuggler and the phoney government emissary, among the very first Europeans to enjoy the privilege of boarding the transatlantic boat, their presence a tribute to personal influence and bureaucratic ineptitude. In

New York they were met by 'Colonel' Justin O'Brien, whom
Simenon had first met in Paris some months before and who had
resumed teaching English literature at Columbia University in
New York. In order to get the Simenons through immigration
formalities as quickly as possible O'Brien had climbed back into
his colonel's uniform. Waving goodbye to the perfume smuggler,
the phoney *chef-de-mission* and the phoney colonel clambered into
a yellow cab and set off for the hotel. At least the skyscrapers were
real.

PART III

A SICKNESS
AND A CURSE

I would like to dedicate what follows to all those who write novels for pleasure or out of vanity or in the hopes of an easy living, to those who invite us to share their ideas and their little adventures, and also to [those] who imagine that the novelist's trade is a trade like any other . . . I would like to show them that it is, on the contrary, a vocation, a renunciation, or even a sickness and a curse.

Simenon, dedication to the unpublished text of
his broadcast on *Balzac* (1960)

ELEVEN

The trap shuts

She was the most complicated woman I ever met.
Georges Simenon, of Denyse (1980)
C'était un homme merveilleux, mais combien difficile!
Denyse Simenon, of Georges (1991)

Simenon and Tigy arrived in New York on 5 October 1945. Within a few weeks Simenon had met, and on the same day started an affair with, Denyse Ouimet, a 25-year-old French Canadian who was to become his second wife.

Observing the process of attraction to Denyse working in Simenon is like watching a man approaching a precipice and slowly leaning out, until he loses his balance and destroys himself. At the age of 19 he had left his home and his country for Paris; now, at the age of 42, he was leaving his adopted country, the household he had created in Nieul with Tigy and Boule, and seeking a new life in a country where he was relatively little known. His marriage was a dead letter, he had left the most prestigious publishing house in France for an unproved new-comer and he had apparently abandoned his attempts to win a literary reputation. He was adrift, and felt 'an immense void' within himself. And he had written only two novels, and one 'Maigret', in the previous two years.

Simenon spent about ten days in New York, seeing his pub-lishers, Harcourt Brace, and being fêted by the sizeable French community. He noted that whenever he was with the French they dined in French restaurants, and that these expatriate celebrities who had spent the entire war in the United States had made no concessions to the American way of life. After a while he began to avoid their company and to try not to let people overhear him speaking French in restaurants. In due course Simenon and Tigy and Marc took the Pullman to Montreal where Marc, now aged 6, met his first photo-electric cell, operating the glass doors of the railway station. It was October and the land was already covered in snow. In one afternoon Simenon interviewed 180 candidates for the post of bilingual secretary, an average of one candidate every ninety seconds if his figures are accurate, but hired none of them. At Ste Marguerite-du-Lac-Masson, twenty-five miles north of Montreal, they rented two bungalows on the edge of a frozen lake. One was to live in, the other was for Simenon to work in and was intended as the residence of his future secretary.

Simenon's plan, '*mon fameux plan*', once he was installed was to work at Ste Marguerite and to take the train down to New York when he wanted some diversion. Such journeys would be undertaken alone. He felt that he had a real friendship with Tigy now that he was no longer forced to lie. She seemed genuinely amused by his accounts of his adventures, she was leading her own life and she had started to paint soon after settling into their bungalow in Ste Marguerite. Marc, who had always loved animals and nature, was delighted with the bears and snowfields of the neighbourhood.

Almost as soon as he arrived in Montreal, Simenon set to work with his usual energy to rearrange his publishing contracts. The French-language rights sold in Quebec had been negotiated before the war separately from the Gallimard contract and Simenon was far from satisfied with the terms. One of the Montreal publishers, who knew that Simenon was looking for a secretary, said that he had just the person. She was French-Canadian, experienced and completely bilingual, but she was working in Philadelphia. Nevertheless she was said to be thinking of returning to Canada and a meeting could be arranged.

The picture which Simenon gives of his first meeting with Denyse Ouimet in *Mémoires intimes*, *Trois chambres à Manhattan* (*Three Beds in Manhattan*) and *Lettre à mon juge* (*Act of Passion*) hardly varies, whether it was written in love as in the two novels or in hate as in the memoir. The woman he fell so passionately in

love with was apparently an habitual liar, a flirt, a tease, provoca-
tive, not obviously attractive, possessing a smouldering sexual
charge, *une femme légère*, somebody with an extensive and harsh
experience of men, a spoilt child and a manipulative woman. The
exact circumstances of their meeting were seen by both of them as
crucial to their relationship. Simenon invited Denyse to lunch in
an expensive restaurant, the Brussels, on her next visit to
Manhattan. On the day in question he heard that his old friend
from Montparnasse, the painter Kisling, was ill, but well enough
to receive visitors, and he found him in fact so well and such good
company that he eventually arrived for his lunch appointment half
an hour late.

Denyse was furious. She already had a good job lined up in
Montreal which might eventually lead to a company directorship
and she had agreed to see Simenon, whose name meant nothing to
her, only to please her Montreal friend. She found herself sitting
alone in an expensive restaurant, feeling a fool and worrying
about paying for her drink because she had come without any
money. When Simenon eventually arrived she was on the point of
departure and she took an instant dislike to his manner, which she
found overconfident, and ingratiating. He walked across the
room towards her rubbing his hands together with the gesture of
a man who is covering them with soap and his first attempts to
mollify her were not a success. All in all it could hardly have been
a less auspicious start.

But beneath the surface an unpredictable event had occurred,
something which had never happened to Simenon before. He was
captivated by Denyse's husky contralto voice, what he described
in *Mémoires intimes* as 'her vaginal voice': 'For the first time I was
on the brink of what we call passion, a genuine fever which
psychologists and doctors compare to an illness.' His life was
empty; he had emptied it deliberately – he was like François
Combe, the hero of *Trois chambres à Manhattan*, 'he was a man
who had cut all his links . . . a man attached to nothing . . . no
profession, no country, not even an address; he was nothing but a
stranger sleeping in a room in a more or less dubious hotel'. He
was waiting for something important to happen, and by the end
of lunch it had happened and he was lost.

Later Simenon tried to analyse what it was about Denyse that
had proved overwhelmingly attractive. She had, in the first place,

the style of North America, a way of lighting a cigarette, of crossing her legs, of letting her coat fall off her shoulders, which he found intensely attractive, precisely because it was so American. 'She smoked like the American women smoked, with the same gestures, the same pout that one sees on magazine covers and in films.' In the second place Simenon was attracted to Denyse because she was *'une fille paumée'*, a lost soul, somebody who had played her chance many times without winning. She carried the marks of many adventures, she seemed as solitary and vulnerable as he felt himself. He had the sense that their adventure, which began that same night in a hotel room, might even be her last chance, a possibility that placed her in an unbearably pathetic position and made his own role appear even more romantic. But from Denyse's point of view, Simenon had a total misunderstanding of their relationship. Certainly she saw nothing 'pathetic' about her predicament in travelling to meet him.

Perhaps their mutual attraction was the result of one of those massive international misunderstandings in which both parties are convinced that the other possesses qualities that the other has never claimed – misunderstandings which do not exclude the possibility of strong, mutual affection over many years. Reading his subsequent account one gains the impression that in their early manoeuvres Simenon was up against an aggressive flirt, an *'allumeuse'*, who had him over a barrel from the first move. He, the sophisticated European, the more experienced player, the prospective employer, was outmanoeuvred instantly and never realised it. It was Denyse who called the shots – 'quite a pretty woman', thin, 'swarthy', small, whose physical deficiencies caused him to think wistfully of the red-headed model with the beautiful body and long silken legs with whom he had a date on the following day, a date which he already knew he was going to break. At the end of lunch Simenon had offered Denyse the job and she had told him that she had another interview to attend and that she would let him know by 4.30. He should return to his hotel and wait for her there. If she did not contact him it would be because she had accepted the other job. He waited, the deadline passed, but she turned up eventually and there followed several bars, dinner, several more bars and a hotel bed. Later there was talk of suicide, barrenness and her other lovers. He was already frightened of losing her as well as being furiously jealous, and angry with her for her relatively cool approach to him. In short, Denyse pulled the most stupendous number on him, and he, aged 42, bought it.

Simenon described Denyse, after their marriage was over, as the most complicated woman he had ever met. Part of him realised what she was doing but self-deception and mutual misunderstanding were to be the hallmark of their relationship for the next twenty years. During this time they made a family life together and had three children, and in their early years together, in North America, they seem to have been very happy. Simenon remained sexually transfixed by her almost until the day of their eventual separation. She was for him the only woman with whom 'sex and love were merged'. It was when she finally made him understand, after years of asserting it, that she was no longer interested in sexual relations with him that the scales fell from his eyes. Until then he remained under the spell she had cast on their first day together in Manhattan. What she saw in him is less clear, and one of those who knew them both doubts whether Denyse ever really loved Simenon at all.

The meeting between Simenon and Denyse took place on 4 November 1945, just one month after his arrival in New York, and one of its first effects was to lead him once again into deceiving Tigy. Although the new agreement he had with his wife allowed him complete sexual freedom it did not allow him to introduce a mistress into the house; Tigy had only just managed to rid herself of Boule and she had no intention of finding herself in the same situation again. Tigy was soon aware that he had a new girlfriend in New York but she had no idea how serious he was, finding the situation more amusing than anything else and teasing him about it as he himself said 'protectively'. In return he moved Denyse into the house on 4 January 1946, as his new secretary. By 26 January he had finished *Trois chambres à Manhattan*, the book which was an account of their meeting and which was to become one of the most popular titles he ever published, selling over half a million copies in France alone. The manuscript of *Trois chambres à Manhattan* is untypical of his work. Chapter VIII, in which the hero, 'François' (Simenon), discovers 'Kay's' (Denyse's) love letters from her previous admirers, is almost illegible. The handwriting, normally so neat, is scrawled, as though the writer is under the stress of great emotion. The handwriting only regains its usual appearance at the beginning of Chapter X, by which time the die is cast and François has nothing to do but wait for Kay's return. The contrast is all the stronger if one examines the neat, uncorrected script of most of his books. When passages are heavily worked-over they generally fail to appear in the published version. It was as though he could usually write to his satisfaction only when he was on automatic. This is contrary to the experience of most writers, who are condemned to rewrite. Simenon was equipped with an additional mechanism, which was why he called himself 'an instinctive' rather than an intellectual. When he was writing he might as well have been hypnotised by the Fakir. He 'cut all bridges with the outside world', as he told Henry Miller; he entered the inside world, started the mechanism and the music just ran on and on. That was why he was incapable of responding to the suggestion made by Gide and Robert Brasillach, among others, that he should introduce more than one principal character into his books. He dared not interfere with the mechanism. It was a gift which he had received and which he could only operate.

Tigy still believed that the real threat came from Boule and went through the incoming post to ensure that Boule was not writing to her husband. At one point, suspecting that Denyse might, after all, be the girl from New York she asked Denyse to pose for her, intending to find out more about her. She was reassured when she saw that Denyse was marked by a livid abdominal scar because she knew that Simenon found a scar a serious disfigurement. She knew this because she had once caught him making an assignment with one of her models in Paris in the 1920s and he had reassured her by explaining that the girl had a livid abdominal scar and that he could never make love to someone who was marked like that. (This was an unusual example of a lie coming in useful twice, rather than complicating life, as usually happens.) It was many weeks before Tigy discovered the true situation, and then only because Simenon fell ill.

When he fell ill Georges Simenon made the most of the occasion. This time he caught laryngitis after a violent bout of love-making in the snowfields with Denyse – the outside temperature at the time was minus 20 – and he could not bear the thought of Tigy looking after him. When he told her that it would be Denyse who would nurse him Tigy at last realised the truth. After recovering Simenon continued to sleep in Denyse's room, and so for the first time began a public *ménage à trois*. In March he set to work on the second book he wrote in America, *Maigret à New-York* (*Inspector Maigret in New York's Underworld*), and Denyse, unknown to him, began to reorganise his beloved filing system. He emerged from his novel to find that it was too late. She seemed so proud of her work that he could not ask her to change it back again. '*Tant pis pour le classement,*' he wrote in *Mémoires intimes,* '*tant pis pour moi!*'

Simenon was now embarked on an emotional roller-coaster that was to last until his old age. The passion was soon marked by violence. If Denyse's flirtatiousness was intended to make him jealous, it was highly effective, and she had many other ways of keeping the emotional temperature on the boil. She was never certain whether or not she had heard of him before they met and claimed that she could not even remember whether or not she had read any of his books. The first time he slapped her was when she told him that if she met her first boyfriend again she might go to bed with him. He wrote later that, when her provocation was followed by the blow, 'I swear that she was delighted, that in her eyes it was a victory.' In fact, she says, she was 'always terribly scared of being hit . . . although after he'd hit me I didn't want him to feel like a culprit.'

As time passed the violence between them became almost commonplace, especially after heavy drinking sessions. If he tore up a telephone directory she would do the same. If he did not respond to her taunts she would slap him. He sometimes took refuge with a call-girl but for the first time in his life found that '*les filles publiques*' offered little comfort. At least once, in Montreal, a brawl took place in the street. Simenon, who had given his heart for the first time, was incapable of dealing with an adversary who seemed to trifle with what he considered his most precious gift. 'There were moments when I could not decide whether I loved her or hated her while I looked at her, once more naked and fragile, with the livid scar which crossed her stomach.'

As so often in Simenon's life the beginning of an important new phase was marked by a change of name. Tigy and Boule both carried names invented by him. He now changed Denyse's name to 'Denise', regarding the original spelling as affected, and he

decided to change his own name as well. 'Sim' had been succeeded by Simenon; now Georges was to be succeeded, in family
life at least, by 'Jo'. One night Simenon discovered that Denise's
previous lover, an American naval officer based in Philadelphia,
had also been called George, and he did not want to think that
when Denise used his name during love-making she might be
referring to the sailor. Accordingly he told her never to call him
Georges again and to choose any other name she liked. She chose
'Jo', pronounced in her husky voice as 'Choe', and he acquiesced,
although he later claimed that he never liked the name and that it
had never occurred to anyone else to call him by it.* In changing
Denise's name Simenon was also hoping to change her personality. He found her too sophisticated, too superficial, too insincere,
and too thin. She complained that he was trying to make her as
plump as Mme Maigret, but he was not dissuaded and decided
that she should also change her hairstyle, and should stop wearing
make-up.

In May and June of 1946 Simenon took Marc, Tigy and Denise
for a summer holiday in a little fishing port, St Andrew's, on the
Canadian Atlantic coast. Here he wrote two novels set in La
Rochelle, one of them being the first of his three 'war' novels, *Le
clan des Ostendais* (*The Ostenders*), based on the story of the first
Belgian refugees with whom he had dealt in 1940. The *ménage à
trois* seemed to be going well, and Tigy even agreed to take
driving lessons from Denise. By the end of the summer Simenon
felt sufficiently confident of his English to set off across the
United States. He undertook to send a series of travel articles to
Pierre Lazareff describing his journey from Montreal to Florida.
Tigy travelled in one car with her English teacher, a young
woman who, according to Denise's recollection, appeared to be in
love with her, and Simenon, Marc and Denise travelled in a
second car. They did not meet on the journey but arranged a
rendezvous in Florida. Simenon was fascinated by the rootless,
wandering, automobile culture of the United States, a world
which he was to make the setting for several books. He was also
fascinated by motels, which he eventually decided were designed
for illicit encounters, the North American equivalent of a *maison*

---

* Though oddly enough Charley Delmas seems to have called Simenon 'Jo' in La
Rochelle before the war.

de passe. He was also amazed by business conventions but found them much less amusing, since time and again they made it impossible for him to find a hotel room for his little party. During his first five years in North America, Simenon was to live in Canada, Florida, Arizona and California, and in Connecticut for the second five years. It was in Florida and Arizona that his first marriage broke up.

On arriving in Florida Simenon found a house at Bradenton Beach where in December he wrote *Lettre à mon juge*, the second novel to have a heroine modelled on Denise. Charles Alavoine is a country doctor married to a cold woman with whom he has only occasional sexual relations. One day, while on a journey to Caen, he meets *'une fille paumée'*, Martine, who looks very much at home on a barstool. He spends the night with her in a hotel, and as they make love with a sudden ferocious violence he sees that she has a livid, pink scar across her stomach. Charles introduces Martine into his house as his secretary and eventually is driven by his obsession for her to leave the house and his wife and little daughter and to set up with Martine in a small practice in Paris. There his 'phantoms' drive him eventually to strangle Martine after a peaceful evening spent together during which they had made love. Charles, who is convicted of murder but saved from the guillotine by mitigating circumstances, then kills himself while in prison.

Simenon wrote *Lettre à mon juge* in the stifling heat of Florida in December, seated naked at his desk, his only garments the tennis-player's bands which he wore around his wrists to prevent the sweat from running on to the keys of the typewriter. Together with *Trois chambres à Manhattan* it is one of his greatest studies of sexual jealousy and obsession. In the first book the situation is resolved when François, in Kay's absence, takes another lover, confesses this to Kay and Kay forgives him. This event actually happened to Simenon when Denise left New York to spend several weeks in Philadelphia. François says to Kay that all he can offer in the way of explanation is that it happened, 'simply because I am a man – and it could happen again'. When Kay forgives him, understanding that his action had stemmed partly from his atrocious jealousy of her past, he knows that they will be able to start a new life together, leave Manhattan, return to France and resume his career, or go to Hollywood and start again from

scratch: 'Kay would decide.' But in *Lettre à mon juge* the phantoms
are too powerful for Charles. When he strangles Martine while
she is asleep he has the image in front of his eyes of 'the other
Martine', of the other hands which have caressed her. 'All the
phantoms were there, the other Martine was there, the one they
had sullied . . . the one who had defiled herself in a kind of
frenzy.' And as his fingers tightened on her throat she opened her
eyes: 'I cried, "Forgive me, Martine" . . . And I realised that she
was encouraging me, that it was what she wanted, that she had
always foreseen this moment, *that it was the only way out.*' *Lettre à
mon juge* is the story of an obsession taken one stage further than
Trois chambres à Manhattan, one without hope, which can end only
in death. It is the same two people in the same situation but going
to the limits ('*jusqu'au bout*') of possible experience, the theme
which had always fascinated Simenon and which was to recur in
an increasing number of his dark novels.

The most unusual biographical aspect of these two books is that
any writer in the grip of an overwhelming emotion should so
quickly have turned this emotion into material for his work. In
this way his account of the experience became part of the experience. There is no sign of the usual line between life and art, the
passage of time, the alteration of characters and feelings. No
matter how vivid or dramatic or all-encompassing an episode in
Simenon's life became, it could be refashioned and immediately
put to use. *Lettre à mon juge* is also of biographical interest because
it contains one of the rare examples of Simenon examining his
own behaviour from a moralistic point of view. Charles recalls
the fact that at his trial the prosecution was particularly critical of
him because he had used deceit to introduce his mistress into his
family home. It is a reproach which Charles raises three times and
which he defends himself against by arguing that the only alternative would have been to walk out of the house on the first day.
There seem to be echoes here of a reproach from Tigy, devastated
at finding the terms of their new agreement broken so quickly,
and herself betrayed once more.

Shortly after arriving in Florida a hitch occurred in Simenon's
plans. He wanted to exchange his bogus 'official' visa for a
permanent, private visa and was told that this could only be issued
outside the United States. He decided to fly to Cuba for a two-
day visit while the exchange was effected but on his arrival he

learned from the American consul in Havana that no new visa could be issued until official notification had been received that Simenon's government mission was terminated. The process of cabling from Havana to Paris and back took several weeks, chiefly because no one could be found in any of the Paris ministries who had any knowledge that Simenon's mission had ever taken place. There is of course something ridiculous in the spectacle of a man who has just jumped the queue, and used considerable ingenuity and influence in the service of his own convenience, finding that his best efforts have finally served to land him *dans la merde*. When the necessary authority from Paris finally came through Simenon had the grace to admit that he felt 'almost ashamed' by the length of the queue of people waiting on the pavement outside the consulate for nights on end, hoping one day to pass through the narrow gates to the promised land.

It was even hotter in Cuba than it had been in Florida. One vivid memory of their visit was the night when Denise, drunk, walked out of their beachside hotel outside Havana and set off into the sea. Simenon followed her at a distance. She swam straight out, he still following and calling her to come back. Finally he dragged her ashore, while she insisted that she wanted to die. Almost their sole amusement was a local brothel where Simenon went with Denise. Denise then selected two girls with whom they both retired to a bedroom for several hours. One of the girls, he later claimed, had been so grateful for all they had taught her that she presented them with a framed photograph of herself.

Simenon's openness about his sexual habits was made easier by his conception of sexual morality. This was founded on self-gratification, tempered to some extent by consideration for his opponents. Sometimes there were unfortunate consequences. Denise recalls that on one occasion at Bradenton Beach Simenon went to a nearby motel with a neighbour's wife. A few days later the husband was found dead from a snake-bite and suicide was suspected. Generally Simenon avoided possible complications by making his encounters as brief as possible. He had a horror of 'affairs' but found virtue in a brothel, a place which he considered as useful as a pharmacist's, to which men went to satisfy an urgent need and to which women went to earn some money. He recalled that in Paris in the smarter brothels one sometimes met bourgeois women, the wives of professional men, who would drop in on an irregular basis to supplement their dress allowance. In Arizona he noted with approval the frank, easy atmosphere of a favourite brothel, 'nothing furtive about it, or affected or secret. Since my youth,' he added in *Mémoires intimes*, 'I was accustomed to make love every day, frequently two or three times.' He was careful to let Denise understand this from early in their relationship as his worst memory of the years with Tigy was the continual strain of having to deceive her. He claimed later that if Denise had been jealous, 'I would no doubt have had the courage to break off my relations with her,' but it would have been more accurate to say that if Denise had been jealous there would scarcely have been a relationship in the first place. They frequently went to brothels together. Usually while Simenon retired upstairs he left Denise gossiping with the girls. If she was still enjoying herself when he returned she would say, 'Why not have another one, Jo?' And so he would go upstairs and have another one. In the course of time Denise's sexual interest in him waned. It was to be some years before her loss of interest became an evident problem, and until it did Simenon's passion and jealousy continued to envelop her, and to act as the motor of their relationship.

In the spring of 1947 Tigy returned from a visit to their house in Nieul to announce that she no longer objected to the presence of Boule. She gave no reasons, but it seems that she must have felt it was time to complicate her husband's domestic life a little. In a sense Boule had always complemented Tigy's role as Simenon's wife. Boule cooked, she made love with enthusiasm, she admired Simenon without reservation, she made the house comfortable and she was French. Furthermore, Marc adored her. It was clearly time to counteract the North American influence; from Tigy's point of view an amusing diversion was threatening to turn into a major nuisance. She had given Simenon twelve months' clear run with Denise and it was time to introduce a few trip wires.

In June Simenon decided to leave Florida and head west. He had no idea where he was going to settle next, but it turned out to be Arizona, first at a house called Snob Hollow in Tucson and then on a ranch called Stud Barn near the border settlement of Tumacacori. It was here that Boule rejoined them in 1948. Tigy returned to France to fetch her, and together they travelled by sea to Veracruz, then overland the length of Mexico to the frontier town of Nogales. When Boule arrived at the border she had to wait for several more weeks until her name reached the top of the list in her appropriate national quota. Simenon discovered to his horror that the money he had arranged for a friend to give to Boule in Paris had never been paid. She had been working as a seamstress and had spent some time with the retired concierge from the place des Vosges, the lady who had once complained so ferociously about the 'demi-orgies' of the 'années folles'. Before he left Simenon had helped Boule to buy a studio in Etretat, close to her family home.

Boule's arrival proved to be Tigy's last card. By this time Simenon had started to issue invitations from 'Mr and Mrs George [sic] Simenon and Miss Denise Ouimet'. But with Boule installed he had further responsibilities. Since Denise was not jealous Simenon would leave the bedroom which he shared with her late each evening and climb by the outside staircase to the balcony room which Boule inhabited. Then, after a passionate hour or so, he would return to his own bedroom where he would find Denise waiting for him. His wife followed the proceedings from the vantage point of her own room (the only bedroom he never entered) with a keen sense of anticipation, but the chances of Tigy winning her battle were always slight. The oldest and least demonstrative member of the *ménage*, the least adapted to a country whose language she never mastered, the least reconciled to leaving France, she now found herself in competition for the time and affection of both her husband and her son. She was determined not to repeat the mistake she had made initially when she had discovered Simenon in bed with Boule, so at first she made no objection to the presence of Denise, preferring instead to try to establish a distance between herself and Marc on the one hand, and Simenon and Denise on the other. For Marc this was an unhappy period of his life. He was troubled by the turmoil in the grown-up world surrounding him and he had started to sleepwalk even before the extended household left Canada. He was 7 at the time.

In Arizona Simenon adopted a relaxed but highly effective working routine. He would get up at about 6 a.m., while it was still cool, make coffee (Boule had, by then, been excused from this task) and retire to a room on the far side of the courtyard. By 9 a.m. he had finished his daily chapter, so he would take a shower and set off to do the shopping. The rest of the day was his own. *Un nouveau dans la ville* was written to this rhythm – 90,000 words written in twenty days at the rate of 4500 words a day, 1500 words an hour, one page typed every twenty minutes, no revision. Years later Denise described what was for so long a familiar background noise to her domestic life. 'The keys of the typewriter rattled down in bursts, at breathtaking speed . . . About every ten seconds the carriage return rang out. About every five or seven lines the noise of the "tab" marked a new paragraph.' It was as though a machine was operating the typewriter. The only person who was ever allowed to interrupt his work was Marc. Sometimes after starting in the early morning he would feel Marc's kiss on his cheek and, on looking up, find that his son had already left the room as silently as he had entered it.

Tigy expected Boule's arrival to strengthen her position but when it failed to have the desired effect she quickly lost patience. One night Marc fell ill and Tigy found herself looking after him alone. After a sleepless night and the prospect of another one she walked into Simenon's bedroom in the middle of the next night and said to Denise, 'Since you already have the husband you might as well come and get the son as well.' Naturally Denise took advantage of this tactical error without complaint. Denise's other trump card was her tolerance of the relationship between Boule and Simenon. She knew that Boule was no threat to her, and she had already learnt the advantages of sharing the burden of her lover's ferocious sexual appetite. It was at the end of 1948 that Denise won a decisive victory by becoming pregnant.

In November 1947, while still living outside Tucson and before moving to Stud Barn, Simenon had written *Les vacances de Maigret*, only the second 'Maigret' he had attempted since leaving France, and one which he set in Les Sables d'Olonne, the seaside resort to which he had gone to escape attention during the *épuration* in 1944 and 1945.★ *Les vacances de Maigret* turns on the situation of the town's doctor, who is ferociously jealous of his wife but who is suspected of having an affair with, and then of murdering, his wife's younger sister. There are similarities be-

★ All of the first four novels which Simenon wrote in America with French settings were set in the Vendée.

tween the feelings of Dr Bellamy and Dr Charles Alavoine in
Lettre à mon juge. Dr Alavoine of La Roche-sur-Yon, created in
December 1946 in Florida, had introduced his mistress into his
household. Dr Philippe Bellamy of Les Sables d'Olonne (thirty-
seven kilometres to the west, down Route Nationale 160), created
in November 1947, had apparently taken a mistress from among
the members of *his* household. In fact Maigret discovers that
matters are rather different. Dr Bellamy's beloved wife had been
having an affair with a young man in the town. The doctor had
murdered this young man and then the young man's sister. But he
had not murdered his own sister-in-law; her death was by suicide,
committed when she discovered that her venerated brother-in-
law, Dr Bellamy, with whom she was in love, had murdered her
sister's lover.

The thread that links the two books, apart from the settings and
the near-incestuous atmosphere of the two medical households, is
that of a sexual jealousy which is so strong that it can lead to
murder. Maigret understands this jealousy. He almost defends it.
Dr Bellamy explains to Maigret that he could have merely killed
the boy, that if he had arranged to do so at a moment when the
two were together 'any French jury would have acquitted me'.
Instead he had hidden the boy's body and told a string of lies. He
had done this to give himself *a little more time* with his wife before
he was taken away. He had killed the boy's innocent sister for the
same reason, because she was a witness whose testimony would
have precipitated his arrest and prevented him from spending *a
little more time* with his wife. If Maigret had not arrested him he
had intended to kill his wife in her turn and then to commit
suicide, exactly in the manner of Dr Alavoine in *Lettre à mon juge.*
'Romantic idea, isn't it,' the doctor says bitterly to Maigret.
Nonetheless, even the most intelligent of men has been tempted
to do 'just that at least once in his life'.

Simenon's continued preoccupation with this same theme –
jealousy justifying murder, even the murder of an innocent witness, jealousy taken to the point where it is necessary for both
principal parties to die – was interrupted when he received a
telegram from Henriette in Liège. His brother Christian, on active
service with the Foreign Legion in Vietnam, had been killed when
his unit was ambushed by Viet-Minh forces near the Chinese
border. Simenon never talked about his brother's death but he felt

guilty about it for the rest of his life. At first his work was unaffected. In the following month, December 1947, Simenon wrote another 'Maigret', *Maigret et son mort* (*Maigret's Special Murder*), unconcerned with either sexual jealousy or guilt over fraternal death. But by the following March the effect had been achieved. Still living in the house where he had heard the fatal news, Simenon started work on one of his finest novels and one of his most successful titles, *La neige était sale*.

La neige était sale is not usually listed among Simenon's war novels, but it deserves to be, since it is set in a country occupied by a foreign army and mentions a small resistance movement which is hunted by a Gestapo. No novel better expresses Simenon's feelings towards war. They are exemplified by the fact that he makes his hero not a member of the Resistance but a collaborator of the worst sort, a callous murderer, a rapist by proxy, and a man without scruples or normal human feelings. Simenon sets himself the challenge of finding this character redemption, and he succeeds triumphantly. Frank Friedmaier is not a portrait of Christian, but his activities bear some similarities to those of Christian in Belgium during the occupation. Simenon had always known his brother to be '*un homme de la droite*', whose political views would have been regarded as sound in clericalist, colonialist, petit-bourgeois circles. But there is a big distance between the local equivalent of the Rotarians and the pro-fascist 'Rexist' movement. Simenon had sent Christian into exile for his own safety and he wanted to know when it was safe for his brother to come out of hiding, and what crimes he might be charged with if he were caught. Christian had claimed to have done nothing except drive a car for some 'Rexist' gunmen who were assisting the Germans in hunting down resisters. Nonetheless, in his absence he had been condemned to death by a Belgian court. Simenon told Denise that there had been several collaborators in the Brüll family, and that the major influence over Christian had been his wife, Blanche, the real collaborator of the two of them. But if he considered Blanche responsible for Christian's behaviour during the occupation, Simenon blamed himself for his brother's death.

It was of course a wretched way to die. Christian had proved himself in the Legion, reaching the rank of sergeant. But he died on the other side of the world, fighting in the armed forces of a foreign country, in a colonial war that was of no personal concern to him, leaving behind a 15-year-old son whom he had not seen for two years, in disgrace, without the chance to clear his name or redeem his conduct. It is this last point which links Christian to the fictional character of Frank.

Frank Friedmaier is the sort of man Christian might have met in the 'Rexist' movement. He kills people for fun. He kills a drunken soldier in the occupying army, then he kills an old lady who had always been kind to him. Then an innocent girl falls in love with Frank and he arranges for his gross friend, Kromer, to enter her bedroom when she is expecting Frank and rape her. Everyone in the unnamed town is afraid. It is a town like Liège during the First World War; there are still some pâtisseries and music halls open, and there are still places to take girls who would never have been allowed out by their parents in peace-time. The 'General' of the occupying army is a member of 'the Party'; he used to work as a labourer in a lamp factory, he is interested in loot. The easiest way to kill someone is to denounce them. Frank's mother runs a brothel patronised by occupying soldiers. Frank sometimes watches the girls at work through the fanlight.

Frank is not an attractive character, but finally he too is arrested by one of the occupying police forces. He is locked up for weeks, interrogated and beaten. He refuses to answer questions, not because he is a patriot but out of some ultimate feeling of self-respect. He suffers, he shows fortitude, he is purified by courage; and when eventually he is executed he is redeemed. The comfort in the story for its author would have been that if Frank could be redeemed anyone could. The book is memorable for its technical achievement in making a loathsome character worthwhile, a feat dear to Simenon's heart. Anything could be forgiven, he believed, if it could be understood. In *Lettre à mon juge*, Dr Alavoine says, 'It's terrifying to think that we are all men, all more or less crushed under an alien sky, and yet we still refuse to make the little effort necessary to understand one another.'

But *La neige était sale* is also memorable for its picture of a European country in winter, in war-time, occupied, in fear; the bread queues, the casual violence, the absence of certainty, the absence of trust, the presence everywhere of death, hunger and denunciation. It is a world which could hardly have been further removed from the sunny, relaxed, welcoming, self-confident life of Snob Hollow where the book was written, but it was the world which still haunted Simenon and which was brought back to life so vividly by the news of his brother's violent death. When Holst, father of Sissy – the girl who loved Frank, whom he mistreated and who forgave him just before his execution – meets Frank, he says, '*Le métier d'homme est difficile*'.

Simenon did not quite rid himself of his fraternal guilt with *La neige était sale*. There is a brother on the run and an appeal for fraternal help in the novel he wrote five months later, *Le fond de la bouteille* (*The Bottom of the Bottle*); and a year after that, in *Les quatre jours du pauvre homme* (*Four Days in a Lifetime*), a brother returns from the colonies and stirs up numerous childhood demons. As with the sequence of *Lettre à mon juge* and *Les vacances de Maigret*, a phantom sometimes needed more than one airing before it was sufficiently quelled to make room for the next one. But by the end of 1948 Simenon had a new problem in his own life to resolve. With Denise's pregnancy the possibility of divorcing Tigy was raised for the first time.

Years later, shortly before her death, when she was still living in 'the grandmother's house' at Nieul, Tigy summed up her time in America:

> After the war we set off for America. We needed a change of air. Simenon had suffered in the Vendée from the gloomy life we had been forced to lead . . . We had been completely cut off from 'abroad' during the war and he wanted to travel to the countries where he was translated . . . He wanted to see what was going on over there. And then, unfortunately, we settled there, and our lives split up . . . He met a woman whom he subsequently married, '*et voilà*'. We parted on good enough terms. But it was a denial of an important part of his life all the same. However, we have remained very good friends.

Simenon recalled years later that when he told Tigy that he had after all decided on divorce she said to him, in just as simple and dignified a way, 'One day, Georges, you will come to me and ask me to console you.' 'I blamed her for that remark at the time,' Simenon wrote in *Mémoires intimes*. 'But I have often thought of it since.'

Simenon had always promised Tigy that he would never divorce her to marry Denise. His reasons for changing his mind were many and ingenious, although they never included the relatively simple fact that Denise was pregnant and he wanted to raise a family with her. At various times Simenon argued that he and Tigy had never wanted to marry in the first place, that he had been in love with her sister Tita at the time of his marriage, that Tigy had never wanted to live with him, that he himself had always been opposed to marriage in principle, that, due to cellular changes, two total strangers were bound together twenty years after a marriage had taken place, that Tigy had refused to give him a child until she was 39, and that she had always obliged him to wear a contraceptive; but his last reason was perhaps the most exotic of all.

Ever since his arrival in the United States, Simenon had been fascinated by the law that made it an offence 'to cross state lines for an immoral purpose'. This law was in philosophical relationship with another law which forbade hotel-keepers to let rooms to unmarried couples lest they be prosecuted for aiding and abetting immoral acts. Now Simenon discovered a third cousin of this same extraordinary law. After consulting a New York lawyer he told Tigy that Denise's pregnancy made it essential for them to divorce, or risk being deported as 'immoral aliens'. The extreme convenience of this law seems to have prevented him from noting that it was a rather serious breach of personal freedom, a quality which he generally appreciated in the United States.

The decision to divorce was the end of the *ménage à quatre*. Boule was shocked and hurt by the fact that Denise was allowed a pregnancy whereas she was not, and Tigy decided that she, Marc and Boule would leave Simenon in Arizona and set up their own household in California. When it came to the divorce settlement Tigy drove an unexpectedly tough bargain. She hired a Californian specialist who arranged that she should be set up in comfort for the rest of her life, at one point advising her to have Simenon jailed for immorality, just for the hell of it. Tigy declined this suggestion but let Simenon know that it had been made so that he should be under no illusions about the strength of his negotiating position. Tigy took the house at Nieul, all his shares, the furniture in store, the collection of paintings, by Utrillo, Vlaminck, Kisling, and an alimony payment that was the equiva-

lent of a senior Californian executive's annual salary. In return
Tigy had to agree to only two conditions. The first was that she
should reside in Reno, Nevada, for six weeks before the divorce.
The second, Simenon's only important victory, was that she
should agree to live within six miles of Simenon's house wherever
that might be or she would exchange her custody of Marc for
Simenon's weekly visiting rights. This extraordinary clause
shows that, for the duration of Marc's childhood at least,
Simenon was still trying to keep the *ménage à quatre* on the road.
The reading of the final version of the settlement took place in
Arizona and was punctuated by explosive protests from Denise.
Simenon left her and his lawyer together to fight it out and went
off to tend to Johnny, the baby who had been born to Denise in
September 1949, in Tucson. He liked looking after the little boy
and was also pleased that he no longer had to feel jealous of the
gynaecologist.

In the months between the birth of Johnny and the divorce
Simenon and Denise had left Arizona, where they had lived for
over two years, and moved to Carmel-by-the-Sea in California
where he could visit Marc. His eight-month stay in California
was the nearest he came to living in Hollywood, a place which
might have seemed to be his natural base in the United States. In
1948 he had been sufficiently interested in Hollywood to drive
1400 miles there and back from his home in Arizona in order to
attend a dinner which took place in Romanoff's restaurant.
Charlie Chaplin was present, who was later to become a friend
and neighbour in Switzerland, and Charles Boyer, who had set up
a foundation to serve French interests in Hollywood. More important, there was Georges Kessel – brother of Jef – who had
been Simenon's editor on the magazine *Détective* even before
Maigret had been created, and Jean Renoir, who had made the
first film based on a Simenon book shortly after the launch of the
'Maigret' series. Renoir's version of *La nuit du carrefour* had been
acclaimed but had left audiences rather puzzled, and it later turned
out that one of the reels had been permanently mislaid. Renoir
had been having problems at the time with a divorce and had been
drinking. Simenon was interested to learn that Renoir was now
having new marital problems. His former wife had sued him in
France for bigamy, on his remarriage. From the haven of
Hollywood, Renoir thought this was quite funny.

Shortly after the meal at Romanoff's, which Simenon had to leave early when Denise perceived an insult from a fellow guest and threw a scene, he sold his first Hollywood film rights, once more in *La tête d'un homme*, filmed this time as *The Man on the Eiffel Tower* in 1948, with Charles Laughton as Maigret. This was a good start, and Simenon must have thought that the doors to another hall of fame were opening rather easily, but they opened no further. An early setback occurred when Jean Renoir suggested filming *Trois chambres à Manhattan* to Charles Boyer, and Boyer replied that the Hayes Office (of censorship) would raise so many objections that there would be nothing left of the book. Renoir was unconvinced by this argument but the project was abandoned and Simenon must have been slightly shaken to learn that a novel based on an important episode in his own life in New York could be considered too 'immoral' to present on the nation's cinema screens. Renoir, an old acquaintance, was now becoming one of his closest friends, one of the few he called '*tu*', and the person who paid him one of the highest compliments he ever received when he wrote towards the end of his life, 'God made you to write like he made my father to paint, which is why you both do it so well.' Despite Renoir's enthusiasm only three more Hollywood films were made of Simenon's work, the most famous being *The Man Who Watched the Trains Go By* in 1951, starring Claude Rains and Anouk Aimée and with a screenplay by Patricia Highsmith.

It is almost a relief to find a failure in the professional life of Georges Simenon, but for whatever reason, perhaps because he did not use an agent, Hollywood was his failure. In his disappointment he may have recalled a similar setback he suffered with the French cinema in the years before Continental. In 1934, two years after his fiasco as a film producer, the newspaper *Le Jour* published a diatribe in which Simenon cursed '*cinéma-papier, cinéma-traître, cinéma-bancaire, cinéma-spéculation*'. Although he never admitted as much, one of his original motives in crossing the Atlantic must have been the possibilities of Hollywood. He would never have wanted to be another Scott Fitzgerald or Raymond Chandler, and he had too much self-confidence ever to have suffered at the hands of the studios as they did, but he saw Maigret as a naturally 'filmic' character and was keenly interested in the possibility of selling the film rights. His progress around

North America can be seen as an oblique approach to his target. Even in America in the 1940s Simenon was quite well known. He had been greeted by the press on his arrival in Manhattan; when his brother Christian was killed the New York papers telephoned Arizona in the belief that it was he who was dead; and on his remarriage in Reno he and Denise were besieged outside their hotel bedroom. The steady trickle of publicity would have done his Hollywood hopes no harm.

However disappointed he may have been in Hollywood, Simenon was intrigued by Carmel-by-the-Sea, which was at that time being run as an artists' colony. He noted little details such as the fact that although the town could easily afford to employ several postmen the citizens preferred to pick up their own mail at the post office, so ensuring that they met each other more frequently. Many of the inhabitants were writers, the food shops were stocked with delicacies from Europe and the town library was full of books in French. In Carmel, Simenon was not surrounded as he had been until then by 'average Americans', which may have been one reason why he did not settle there. The local golf club had an annual subscription of $20,000 and a long waiting list. Marc went to school with the children of Bing Crosby, which was amusing, and the town was close to Monterey which Simenon considered to be a place of pilgrimage because he associated it with John Steinbeck and because Robert Louis Stevenson, one of his favourite authors since childhood, had stayed there before embarking for the South Seas where he was to die.

It was while he was in Carmel that Simenon wrote *Les volets verts*, one of his finest novels, inspired by the death of the great French actor Raimu, which he had learnt about from a newspaper headline shortly after reading a letter written to him by Raimu in person. The story is set in Paris and Antibes and it is interesting that in a book written directly after his separation from Tigy, Simenon should have included references to the boulevard des Batignolles, the rue du Mont-Cenis and Fouquet's, where they had spent so much time together, and to the place Constantin-Pecqueur, where Tigy had sold her first two pictures.

Six months later he and Denise flew to Reno, Nevada. Looking back on his wedding at the end of his life Simenon saw the whole event as a nightmare. For a man who specialised in describing spiritual emptiness and desolation Reno provided a special horror. He advanced towards the rendezvous like a sleep-walker unable to arrest his progress. The divorce took place in the courthouse on 21 June 1950, and Simenon married Denise the following day and in the same building. While waiting for the trap to shut, and hoping to avoid any sentimental conversations with Denise, Simenon hit the fruit machines. He did this for two days, trying to lose but generally winning. The more he won, the more depressed he became, seeing the torrent of small coins as an omen of the last good luck he was going to enjoy. The ceremony provided everything that could be hoped for from a Reno court-house wedding: a lawyer who was too busy to wait for the judge and who handed over the papers in the waiting room and asked to be paid on the spot; a tall white-haired judge in a freshly-ironed Stetson who expected $5 to be slipped into his hand after the service; and two elderly cowboys standing by to act as witnesses. After the ceremony Denise led him down the street to a fountain into which, she suggested, he should throw his old wedding ring. And so, of course, he did.

TWELVE

Shadow Rock Farm

'What are you reading, Benny?' His fingers around the glass were yellow with nicotine and the fingernails ridged and thick. 'Did you look up that Simenon book I was telling you about? He's the deep one. And everybody thinks he's just a detective story writer. Did you know that Gide was writing about him at the time of his death? That's a fact. Have you read any Gide at all?'

'I'm still working my way through the Russians. Slowly.'

'Gogol,' he said, rolling his eyes with meaning that didn't need elucidation, except to me.

From Howard Engel, *The Suicide Murders*

On arriving in New York after his wedding Simenon's first idea was to take the boat to Europe. His new wife had never been there and he kept a mild nostalgia for his old haunts. He had made sure that Johnny's birth had been registered at the Belgian consulate and recorded on the family's page at the town hall in Liège. In the heat of Arizona he had sometimes missed the comfort of warm clothing in cold weather. But the outbreak of the Korean War in 1950 had caused a flood of visa applications from Europeans wanting to come to the United States and fearful of another war in Europe. Simenon learnt of this from the Belgian consul in New York and credited the rumours without question because he well understood the feelings of the would-be refugees. Accordingly he did what he had done in 1938, when the last rumours of war had

Simenon with Professor Lucien Pautrier, obstetrician and godfather, and Vlaminck at his son Marc's christening party in the Vendée in May 1939.

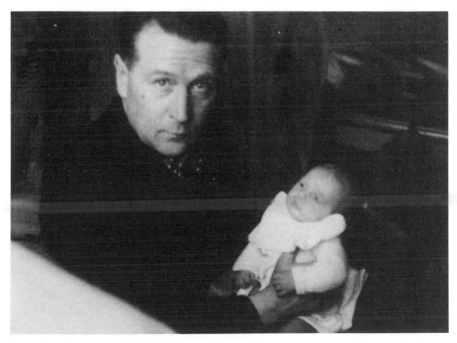

'Le métier d'homme est difficile'; Simenon with Marc.

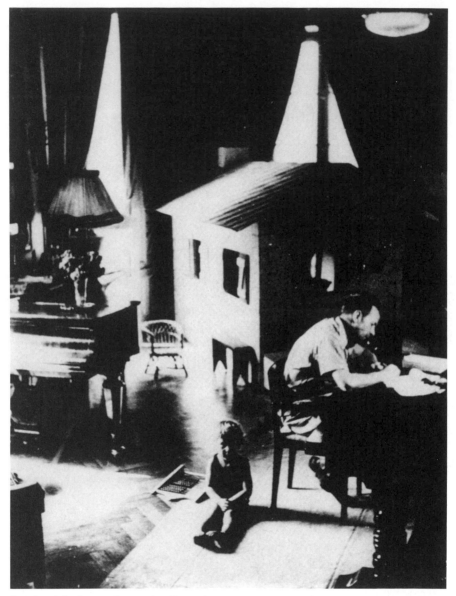

Convinced that he was about to die of heart disease Simenon wrote a family memoir, *Je me souviens*, in the Château de Terre-Neuve at Fontenay-le-Comte in 1941. Marc was normally the only person allowed to enter the room when he was writing.

In 1944, after the liberation of France, Simenon decided to emigrate to the United States with his family. Tigy (right) insisted that Boule (left) should stay behind.

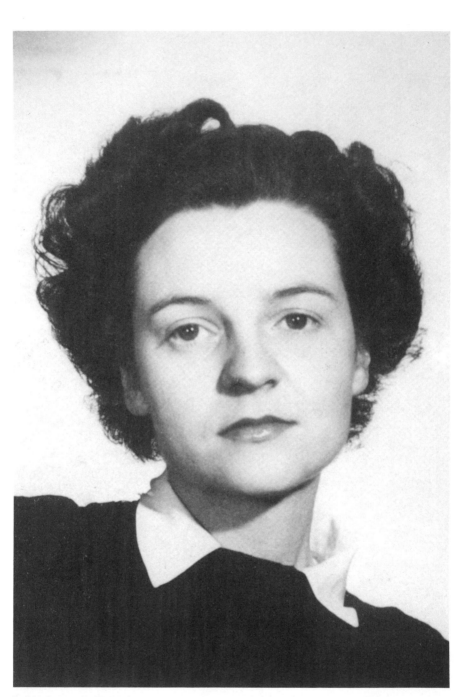

In Manhattan, in November 1945, Simenon met and fell in love with Denyse Ouimet, a young French–Canadian who he hired as his secretary. Rechristened 'Denise', she would later become his second wife.

In 1950 Simenon and Denise settled in New England purchasing Shadow Rock Farm, Lakeville, Connecticut. 'At last I have settled down . . . I am taking root,' he told *The New Yorker*.

Simenon with Fernandel during his triumphant European tour of 1952. Huge crowds chanting 'Si-me-non, Si-me-non' greeted his arrival at the Gare St Lazare.

Seated on the floor of his study at Shadow Rock Farm in 1953. His new titles were selling over half a million copies each in France alone. His world sales were running at 3 million a year.

The return to Europe in May 1955. Simenon's happiness was from now on to be overshadowed by marital problems.

An opportunity to try the new spectacles. Simenon encounters Brigitte Bardot at the Venice Film Festival in 1958. Bardot had just played the lead in the film of *En cas de malheur* opposite Jean Gabin.

By 1961 Simenon and Denise with their three children, Johnny, Pierre and Marie-Jo, had been living for four years in the Château d'Echandens, near Lausanne in the Swiss canton of Vaud.

Marie-Jo aged 7, 'coquette' and adoring. At the age of 8 she asked her father to buy her a wedding ring and she wore it for the rest of her life.

enise Simenon signing the visitors' book in October 1961 at the newly opened Bibliothèque Georges
menon in Liège. Between husband and wife stands mother, awaiting her turn.

In 1967, outside Epalinges, the mansion overlooking Lake Geneva which Simenon and Denise designed together but which only he lived in.

The last photograph of Simenon with Henriette. 'We never loved each other, Mother, while you lived . . . but we made it look as though we did.'

In 1978, Marie-Jo Simenon, aged 25, committed suicide in her apartment on the Champs-Elysées. 'One never recovers from the loss of a daughter one has cherished,' Simenon wrote in his last book. 'It leaves a void that nothing can fill.'

Simenon, aged 76, walking in Lausanne with Teresa Sburelin, originally Denise Simenon's maid, then for twenty-three years Georges Simenon's mistress and official companion.

Beneath the cedar tree in his garden at Lausanne, where his ashes and those of Marie-Jo were eventually to be scattered.

broken out. He set out to look for a house in a peaceful part of the countryside far from the big cities. He and Denise, on the advice of the consul, drove north into Connecticut and eventually arrived in a district by a beautiful lake where they decided to settle even before they had found a house. The principal street in the village was three or four hundred yards long and was called Main Street, and they eventually found a two-storey house constructed from wood and painted white, with green shutters. It had been built in 1748, had double-glazing and was surrounded by fifty acres of its own pine woods. The green shutters may have clinched it for Simenon. The previous January in *Les volets verts* one of the characters had said, 'Haven't you ever dreamed of a house with green shutters? . . . it's the house I have always dreamed of, that I was dreaming of even when I was only a little girl'. The settlement was called Lakeville, the house was called Shadow Rock Farm; it belonged to the journalist and publisher Ralph Ingersoll, it was for sale, and Simenon bought it with the help of a mortgage, the only time in his life he had to do such a thing; after the divorce settlement he was temporarily broke. Four miles away at Salmon Creek there was a second house which could be rented for Tigy, Marc and Boule. Lakeville was to become their home for the next five years, the last period in Simenon's life in which he was undoubtedly happy.

The years in Connecticut were among the most stable and productive he lived. In his memoirs for that period he makes more references to his work and the new friends he made than he does to Denise, in itself a sign that things were going relatively well. It was here that he wrote *La mort de Belle* (*Belle*), *Les frères Rico* (*The Brothers Rico*), *L'escalier de fer* (*The Iron Staircase*), *Feux rouges* (*Red Lights*), *Crime impuni* (*The Fugitive*), *L'horloger d'Everton* (*The Watchmaker of Everton*) and *Le grand Bob* (*Big Bob*), as well as *Les mémoires de Maigret* (*Maigret's Memoirs*), *Le revolver de Maigret* (*Maigret's Revolver*) and *Maigret chez le ministre* (*Maigret and the Minister*). In the five years he spent at Shadow Rock Farm he produced fourteen *romans* and thirteen 'Maigrets', an average of over five books a year at a regular pace. Here he assembled a large reference library which included most of the telephone directories of France and the United States as well as all the encyclopedias, atlases and works of history he could find. He also had files and files of names. Some of the names were English, some Jewish,

some French. Sometimes they were in alphabetical order, sometimes they included first names. One list read 'MALENK, MALEK,
MALENKI, MALESKE, MAKNI, MAJKA, MUNNO, ZARECK, ZAWILA,
ZBENK, ZBILSKI, ZAPIL, ZAPLIRIO, ZAPKA, ZAPOS'. It reads like a
Central European prose poem. Eventually two names are under-
lined: 'ZIPNICK' and 'ZOGRAFFI'. Zipnick, Joseph, night watch-
man in a London bank, appeared in a short story, 'Les nolepitois',
written in 1963. The Zograffi family appeared in *Crime impuni*,
written in Lakeville in 1953. The same lists were used over and
over again over many years.

At Shadow Rock Farm where the telephone number was
'Hemlock 5', Johnny could watch the beavers playing in the
stream, just as Marc had watched the bears at Ste Marguerite five
years earlier. It was here too that Simenon's beloved daughter
Marie-Georges Simenon ('Marie-Jo') was born, in February 1953.
All his dreams of a life built around children seemed to be realised
and he remained fascinated by the foreignness of America and
impressed by the democratic appearance of a society in which the
children of millionaires were sent out to earn their pocket-money
by working as waitresses or in supermarkets.

Simenon loved to feel that he was becoming American, that he
was now George Simenon, American writer of Belgian origin,
rather than Georges Simenon, the Belgian writer resident in
Connecticut. He loved sitting in front of his television set on
Friday evenings and watching the boxing programme which was
sponsored by 'Pabst Blue Ribbon' and waiting for the ad which
said, 'Ladies and Gentlemen, this is the moment to open your
fridge and quench your thirst with a big glass of Pabst Blue
Ribbon!' And then to get up, go to the fridge, open the bottle and
drink the beer – in time with millions of other Americans. He
noted that it would be unthinkable in France to step into a lift and
hear the company chairman greet a junior employee with 'Hi,
Fred!' But he also thought that these relaxed manners marked a
real difference in the boss–employee relationship. He was so
struck with America that he was even diverted when an indepen-
dent film producer in New York offered to pay for some film
rights by buying Denise a mink coat. They got the coat from a
furrier who was a friend of the producer. But when the producer
later returned the rights, saying that he could not find the appropriate actors, there was no question of Denise returning the coat

since it was a magnificent wild mink and she had fallen for it. So Simenon cheerfully paid up and was amused to think that the whole deal may have been a swindle from the start and that he had stumbled on an ancient Lower East Side custom.

In 1973, looking back on his early achievement, Simenon recalled that the first 'Maigrets' had been an immediate international success. This was true, but although the books were widely translated in the 1930s the sales momentum in England and America flagged in the 1940s. Simenon, in exuberant response to the 1951 Signet paperback edition of *La neige était sale*, which eventually sold 2 million copies, now decided to do something about his English-language contracts. He controlled his own translation rights. He had never ceded these to Gallimard, and he had bought back the subsidiary rights in the first nineteen 'Maigrets' originally sold to Fayard. He paid 1 million francs, in cash, out of a suitcase, on a Sunday morning, without an appointment, believing correctly that the sight of so much money would prove irresistible to the inexperienced banker who had succeeded Arthème Fayard as the head of the firm. He described this escapade as 'the best single day's business I ever did in my life'.

Simenon now sacked Routledge & Kegan Paul in London and both Harcourt and Prentice Hall in New York, and replaced them with Hamish Hamilton and Doubleday. In England only the first nineteen 'Maigrets' had been published by 1950 and only fourteen of the seventy *romans durs*. In America only twelve 'Maigrets' had been published between 1932 and 1953, and only thirteen *romans durs*. Under the contracts Simenon now drew up in Lakeville his books started appearing in both countries at the rate of about four titles a year. He also signed a deal with Penguin Books in London in 1952 which resulted in ten titles appearing in one year in an edition of 1 million copies that had to be reprinted three times in the first six months. Brendan Gill reported that his world sales were running at about 3 million a year, his total sales were estimated at 30 million copies. The arrangement with Doubleday lasted ten years, after which Harcourt Brace took over again, but the arrangement with Hamish Hamilton lasted for the rest of Simenon's career. 'Jamie' Hamish Hamilton, who had a gift for friendship, became a regular guest. Simenon was pleased to be joining a list which already included Raymond Chandler, a writer who like him had a double reputation as both popular and literary, and he used to look forward to Hamish Hamilton's visits and to the sight of his *'longue silhouette élégante'* striding down the drive.

The change of publishers started to pay off at once. Simenon was elected president of the Mystery Writers of America in 1952, an honour Raymond Chandler did not receive until 1959, and this was followed by election to the American Academy of Arts and Letters. He was invited to lecture at Yale and his work found its way on to the standard French literature texts for universities. Denise installed a regular secretariat in her part of Shadow Rock Farm, and although Simenon always considered that she made mountains out of every administrative molehill she in fact relieved him of an enormous amount of work and it was she who presided over the extraordinary boom in his world sales. When they met Simenon, in her view, had been neither rich nor famous (in America, at least). She proved herself to be an outstanding literary agent. She was also a stern critic of some of his English translations and together they ensured that the standard of these improved. In due course Simenon was approached by the Book-of-the-Month Club and was visited in Lakeville by a British member of the editorial board who was wearing a bowler hat and carrying a furled umbrella. Simenon became so angry when this character told him that the contract required him to write, and rewrite, under the direction of a committee that he threw the Englishman out of his house. A gentlemanly English business crook, of rather similar description, appeared some years later in *Maigret voyage* (*Maigret and the Millionaires*).

Among his neighbours in the Lakeville region were Thornton Wilder and James Thurber, and Wilder soon went out of his way to make Simenon's acquaintance. In a letter dated 30 June 1953, following one of their early meetings, Wilder wrote to the Simenons sending two of his own French 'Simenons' for signature and saying, 'The gift of narration is the rarest of all gifts in the twentieth century. We're offered in novel form everything else except the God-given gift of narration. Georges Simenon has that to the tips of his fingertips. Everybody can learn from him.' Wilder was such a fan that he would order Simenon's books from Paris, without waiting for the English translation. It was he who proposed that Simenon should lecture at Harvard and he spent some time mulling over Simenon's comment that he often worked at the same theme (or 'problem') first in a 'Maigret' and then in a *roman*. From the other side of the continent, Big Sur, Henry Miller wrote: 'Dear Monsieur Simenon, Please add my name to the incalculable list of your admirers the world over! I have just read *Lettre à mon juge* and *The Heart of a Man* [*Les volets verts*]. The first two books of yours to fall into my hands.' Miller added bluntly, 'Resisted reading you for years. Couldn't believe it possible that such a popular and prolific writer could be so good. You are really greater than people think you are. My heartfelt thanks (to the Creator) that you are in our midst.' That was in March. By August, Miller, still buried in his 'Simenons', was writing to tell the story of how he had pulled off the road to read *Four Days in a Lifetime* (*Les quatre jours du pauvre homme*): 'Six people pulled up to see if I was in trouble.' When he explained that he was reading a Simenon, one of them asked if he had read *Maigret et son mort*, 'the best of the series'. Miller thought that he discerned a 'tenderness' in Simenon's writing that was unusual in French authors, and which he ascribed to Simenon's Flemish connections – '*le côté Belge Hollandais, Nord, brume, mélancolie douce et tristesse voilée . . .*' Miller found the evocation of New England in *La mort de Belle* very accurate, and added, 'New England gives me the shudders.' He also offered to give Simenon an introduction to a friend who would act as his guide through the sleazier parts of Brooklyn. They exchanged copies of their works and Miller wrote that he was supporting himself in Big Sur as a bookseller since he could not live on his royalties. 'Walt Whitman sold *Leaves of Grass* from his house . . . What a picture of America!' he added. Simenon, who did not suffer from this problem, did not seem too upset by Miller's predicament and replied that he imagined that Miller must gain a certain 'craftsmanlike' satisfaction from his publishing and bookselling activities.

In another letter Miller informed Simenon that 'John Cowper Powys reads you every night.' No doubt Simenon was gratified by this news, but there is a humorous side to his correspondence with fellow writers who contacted him out of the blue to praise his work because he was very rarely able to enjoy theirs in return. 'I wish I liked the work of my friends who write,' he lamented in *Quand j'étais vieux*. 'I try to make myself, I try to pretend, for it's rarely true . . . I like them as men, while regretting that I cannot admire them professionally.' It started with Gide, whose books he always found unreadable, and he was clearly appalled when parcels of Henry Miller's work arrived by post with notes from the author asking for his reactions. He would have been still more nonplussed by the work of John Cowper Powys, who once said that Simenon was his favourite 'of all modern authors, English, American or French – the great, the human, the wise, the noble, Balzacian, Dostoyevskyan, Dickensian, Rabelaisian, and Gorkyan creator of the French Sherlock Holmes (but greatly superior to the original)'. Fortunately perhaps for Simenon's peace of mind Powys kept his praise to himself and his correspondence with friends.

Simenon received the usual flow of readers' letters and was meticulous about replying to them, unless they asked him for money. One which he received at about this time was from a former member of Colonel Maurice Buckmaster's Resistance network, a man named Barde, who showed a determination to finish his Simenons which was even more striking than Henry Miller's. Barde wrote to say that while in the concentration camp of Buchenwald he had been reading *Félicie est là* (*Maigret and the Toy Village*) when he was interrupted by the order to evacuate the camp, which was about to be liberated by the Americans. So he hid himself in the latrine ('*La merde ou la mort. Je n'ai pas hésité*'). While in the latrine he had distracted himself by inventing three possible endings to the book. Since he thought it would be too stupid to die without discovering the real one could Simenon send him a copy? When the book arrived M. Barde found that none of his possible endings had been the correct one. It was sensible to take M. Barde at his word, although Simenon may have wondered how a copy of a book that was published by Gallimard in 1944 could have reached Buchenwald by April 1945.

With another reader Simenon entered into a lengthy and uninhibited correspondence that was to continue for nearly four years, until the reader's death. The person in question, who will be called Valentine – not his real name – was living in South America with his wife and children. Before that he had lived in France for thirty-one years. His wife was French and he was an ardent Simenon follower. In his first letter, written in 1952, he explained one of the reasons why he read Simenon: 'The reader finds himself involved in a book which he feels he could have written himself, if only he had the talent.' Simenon liked this compliment so much he subsequently used it in a magazine interview, as though it were his own. He struck up an immediate rapport with Valentine, discerning in him what Valentine discerned in himself, that he was a Simenon character brought to life, an *aboulique* lost in the tropics. Valentine was an exile in his own country, having returned from Europe to run the family goldmine. But he felt so isolated that he took to drink, and he was convinced that he was on the point of spiritual and material death when he began to reread his Simenons and found the impossible miracle was taking place, he was beginning to feel better. Simenon replied he too had been an alcoholic, and that he was one of those who are incapable of drinking a glass or two without wanting to drink more. He had gone on drinking for years because he had thought that he would be incapable of working without the stimulus, but he now found that ginger ale or Coca-Cola were adequate fuel. (This was not always to be the case in the future.) Later in their correspondence Simenon invited Valentine to come and stay with him in Connecticut and they swapped reminiscences about a brothel they had both patronised, Mme Hélène's in the rue Brey in the 1920s; '*Moi aussi, un client assidu*', wrote Simenon, referring to his visits in 1925 or 1926. Despite the enormous encouragement he drew from his correspondence with his hero, life eventually became too much for Valentine. He fell back on the bottle in spectacular fashion and died before he could accept Simenon's invitation. After his death his widow wrote to thank Simenon for all the help he had given and told him that he had been the great hope of her husband's last years. Simenon's telegram of sympathy read, '*Apprends la mort mon grand ami jamais vu . . .*'

While he was living in Lakeville Simenon twice visited Europe. In October 1954 he made a publicity tour of Britain at the request of Hamish Hamilton. But his first trip, in March 1952, after a seven-year absence, had been a triumphant progress. Then they had sailed from New York on the *Ile de France*. One evening he had picked up 'a little countess' on the dance floor and she had come to his state-room, joining him and Denise in bed. The first reporters had come aboard at Plymouth. At Le Havre he had been mobbed by reporters and photographers, and when the boat train reached the Gare St Lazare he was received like a film-star. A crowd of

enthusiastic readers had gathered to greet him, including all three
of his publishers, Jean Fayard, Gaston Gallimard and Sven
Nielsen (who was paying for the trip). Seven of his titles published since his departure in 1945 had each sold between 470,000
and 610,000 copies. Simenon and Denise were taken to the Hôtel
Claridge, where they had a balcony overlooking the Champs-
Elysées, and that evening Nielsen threw a big party which was
attended by as many of his old friends as possible, among them
Pagnol, Pierre Lazareff, Marcel Achard, Cocteau, Fernandel,
Michel Simon and Jean Gabin. Gide had died a year earlier but no
doubt his ghost was hovering fastidiously overhead. Nielsen had
taken a large suite for Simenon which included an office for the
secretary who would be at his disposal throughout his visit. No
expense was spared to flatter Simenon and make him comfortable. Nielsen had built much of the success of his publishing firm
on the thirty-four titles his most popular author had supplied in
the previous eight years. He arranged for Simenon to sit on the
jury of a literary prize, and there were various other receptions
including one given by the *préfet de police* where Simenon was
presented with a silver police badge in the name of Commissaire
Maigret, to the applause of the massed ranks of the detective-
inspectors of the Quai des Orfèvres.

One night, to give more pleasure to Simenon, Nielsen organised a reconstruction of the famous *bal anthropométrique*. In place
of the original 500 lunatics there was a sedate gathering of forty,
although it did not remain sedate for very long since Simenon,
overcome by an urgent need, penetrated the changing room set
aside for the Martiniquaise dancers and took advantage of two of
them while the others gathered round to urge him on. 'This
incident,' he wrote later, 'greatly amused Denise.' When he met
the *préfet de police* Simenon learnt that since his arrival he and his
family had been under constant police surveillance since he was
thought to be rich enough and famous enough to be the target of
kidnappers. This was perhaps the highest tribute Simenon was
ever paid by the country of his adoption and marked the real
distance he had travelled between the Gare du Nord and the Gare
St Lazare. When he had originally arrived at the former the police
would have been more likely to look on him as a potential
criminal than the victim of one.

Until their visit to Europe in 1952 Denise had never quite

grasped how famous her husband was or the adulation which he was capable of inspiring. An example of the adulation was given by Mme Doringe, his editor at the Presses de la Cité, who wrote and signed the jacket copy for his hardback editions. Valentine, who like many fans was a connoisseur of Doringe's leaf copy, once said, 'one only had to read the jacket to understand the profound jealousy and sincere friendship and admiration that Madame Doringe has for you'. And Simenon replied, 'A former mistress could not be more jealous than Doringe . . . For years she corrected my proofs and she dealt ferociously with Ph.D. students who made a slip.' During the 1952 visit Doringe was given a room opposite Simenon's at the Claridge and she spied on him constantly. One day Denise said to her, 'I scarcely see more of him than you do nowadays, Doringe,' and far from being embarrassed Doringe replied, 'Yes, but you . . . *you* sleep in his bed.' Doringe was 72 at the time.

After Paris Simenon and Denise had gone to Rome where they stayed with Marcel Pagnol in his villa in Monte Carlo and then to Antibes where they stayed with Alexander Korda on his yacht, which was moored in the harbour. And then they went to Belgium. The official excuse for the whole visit was Simenon's election to the Académie Royale in Brussels, and the enthusiasm in Liège was even greater than it had been in Paris. Simenon's return made front-page news in all the local papers. He wanted to introduce Denise to Henriette, but this was a delicate task and he thought it best to make a preliminary reconnaissance. Daniel Fillipachi, then a *Paris-Match* photographer, who had been carrying out a *paparazzi* operation on the sombre pavements of Outremeuse (even though Simenon had taken care to arrive twenty-four hours early), was persuaded to desist, and the novelist made his way alone to 5 rue de l'Enseignement, the terrace house where his mother now lived and which was in sight of the house where he himself had grown up. It was almost thirty years to the day of his departure. His mother had remarried and been rewidowed, she had lost her beloved younger son; he himself had been divorced and remarried, but had not brought either of Henriette's grandchildren to see her. He had not seen her for fourteen years. When he reached the doorstep Simenon did not ring the bell, uncertain at the last moment whether he had the right address; instead he faced the door which was so similar to

the door of his own childhood and gave the signal which the
wrong occupant might not respond to, but which would certainly
bring his mother, even though he was a day early. He did what he
had always done as a child, he rattled the letter-box. The door
opened and his mother stood there. 'Georges, it's you!' They
embraced and Simenon said that he felt on the verge of tears.

> She looked at me with that timid, self-effacing smile which I
> had always remembered as hers. She still had the same way of
> apologising for being there, of apologising for her existence,
> perhaps because she was the thirteenth child of a German father
> and a Dutch mother.

They went inside and talked for a while. There was a portrait of
him on the wall, made by Tigy when he was 19 years old. One of
his mother's first remarks was, 'Why don't you settle down in
Liège? You would be very well placed here.' Thirty years on
Henriette was taking up her farewell remarks made to Georges on
the eve of his original departure. Eventually Georges refused her
invitation to stay to supper and went back to the Hôtel de Suede
where he had once interviewed Poincaré and the Crown Prince
Hirohito. The hotel was run down now, but he felt more comfortable there than he would have felt staying with Denise in his
mother's spare room. For the first half-hour of the visit, he noted
in *Mémoires intimes*, he and his mother avoided each other's eyes.

The fête that followed during the next few days in Liège was
memorable enough. It was further enlivened by a libel action over
Pedigree that came to court on the first day of his visit and which
Simenon lost. One of his mother's former lodgers had sued him
for making fun of his activities as a medical student. The case
increased Simenon's stature as Liège's most famous son, but it
resulted in several lengthy passages being removed from *Pedigree*.
He was very angry about the judgment which the plaintiffs had
obtained despite all the eloquence of Maître Maurice Garçon, who
had travelled from Paris to represent his old friend. Maître Garçon
asked Dr Marcel Chaumont, by now an oculist, if he had lost a
single patient because it was said in *Pedigree* that he had once
hidden a skeleton in a girl's bed. But the court was unmoved, and
Simenon had to pay damages and costs.

Simenon in Liège was now a personality of the sort he himself mocked as a young reporter, and it was his turn to be interviewed by the disrespectful members of his former trade, his turn to be guest of honour at the pompous official receptions which he had once been thrown out of. When he glanced at the reporters' table, did he see the shade of an irreverent boy columnist staggering to his feet and hear the accompanying cry, 'You bunch of old fools . . . God this is boring!'? His turn even came to lay a wreath on the Outremeuse war memorial in the place d'Yser; in view of his own memories of the first occupation and his brother's activities during the second, this event provided perhaps the most bizarre moment of the visit.

There was also a meeting with Joseph Demarteau III, who had survived deportation to a Nazi concentration camp and who was still editor of the *Gazette de Liège*, and still wearing his 'strawberry nose' with pride. Simenon was very moved by the meeting with his former employer and told him, 'You could have fired me five times a week or more, and you never did. It was thanks to your understanding that I didn't go to the bad . . .' And there was another memorable occasion, a lunch in his honour which went wrong. Simenon did not always recognise the members of his very large family; he met several for the first time at a public signing session, and he had failed to recognise two of his nieces in the streets of Outremeuse on the day of his arrival. But he had certainly not forgotten his family legends. One evening at a dinner at Embourg his hostess, and neighbour at the table, eventually identified herself as the granddaughter of the sewage haulier who had ruined his grandfather Brüll and thereby condemned his mother to a poverty-stricken childhood. Her amused manner at the memory of this made Simenon so angry that he walked out of the banquet. He got his revenge though, since the son of his hostess, a fanatical Simenon reader, pocketed a pipe with a gold band which had just been presented to him, and which he left behind by mistake. The boy was eventually made to return the pipe in front of his mother and Simenon was able to say that her family had tried to rob his twice.

On the day after their arrival in Liège, Denise and Henriette were introduced. It was not destined to be an easy relationship, Denise says even today that Henriette was 'obnoxious', and hostilities opened almost immediately when Denise, finding Henriette placed at a banquet in the seat of honour at Georges's right hand,

exchanged place cards before the meal. Simenon did nothing to
rectify this although he said that at the time he felt so ashamed of
his inaction that he subsequently remembered nothing of the
banquet.

Henriette did not accompany her son to Brussels on 30 May to
see him installed as a member of the Royal Belgian Academy.
Those present included Marcel Pagnol, Maurice Garçon, Pierre
Benoît and André Maurois, all members of the fraternal
Académie Française. Denise, who had bought a magnificent evening gown from Lanvin for the occasion, was in Brussels but she
was not admitted to the ceremony; nor were she and Simenon
introduced to King Léopold, as Simenon was a divorcé.
Simenon's feelings on accepting this honour were ambivalent. On
the one hand he had crossed the Atlantic to receive it, on the other
he felt uneasy about it. He was secretly delighted when several of
the French academicians, who unlike the Belgians wore heavily
embroidered Napoleonic uniforms and carried swords and tricorn
hats, became stuck in a hotel lift for an hour and, due to their age
and their tight-fitting collars, had to be sustained by oxygen fed to
them by the firemen, the whole scene being photographed by an
ecstatic *paparazzo*. Simenon read the eulogy of his deceased predecessor, Edmond Glesener, also born in Liège, and later confided
to Valentine that his speech had been deliberately ironical and that
he had gone as far as he dared in mocking the occasion. 'I thought
that a number of those present would notice and be furious,' he
wrote; 'in fact nobody noticed anything.' In his speech Simenon
had indeed mocked Glesener for spending his life as a *fonctionnaire*
in the ministry of agriculture, and had quoted Glesener's own
remark that he was 'a writer whom people were beginning to
forget'. The evening ended in a nightclub with the French academicians, still kitted out in their tricorn hats and swords, and
Simenon seems never to have set foot in the Académie Royale
again.

On the voyage home, undistracted by little countesses, Denise
and Simenon had conceived their daughter Marie-Jo. That
autumn Henriette agreed to cross the Atlantic and visit them in
Lakeville. The visit was a disaster. Henriette, on arrival, had
emerged from the steerage class, having traded down the first-
class ticket which Georges had sent her, and she was wearing
several of her oldest clothes. Denise took her on a shopping

expedition to Fifth Avenue and bought her, among other garments, a new corset. Henriette persisted in wearing her old one, so Denise stole into her bedroom one night, removed the old corset and threw it into the dustbin. Henriette recovered it later, and this struggle was carried on over several nights until Denise had the last word by placing the battered garment in the village incinerator. Denise remembers that she was shocked during the visit by Henriette's attitude to her son. She had a way of pronouncing his name – 'Geeeorrrges' – that was hateful and seemed full of contempt. She mentioned in front of Marc, then aged 14, that Désiré had been practically infertile, 'with sperm like water', and worst of all she once murmured in front of both Georges and Denise, 'What a pity it was Christian who died, he had such genius!' After ten days Henriette cut her visit short and flew home, her departure being a relief to all concerned. There is a photograph taken in the dining-room of Shadow Rock Farm some months after Henriette's visit. It shows Denise seated at the table facing her husband, appearing rather thick-set and plain, her baby safely delivered, wearing no make-up, her thick, dark hair twisted up around her head, looking in obedience to her husband's wishes as unattractive as possible to other men.

Shortly after the birth of Marie-Jo, Simenon sat down to write perhaps his best *roman dur* with an American setting, *Feux rouges*. His little daughter was four months old and he dedicated this horrifying tale to her. Thornton Wilder wrote to him about it:

> *Feux rouges* is a powerful book. And secondarily a most brilliant one . . . No American author would have dared admit to 'understanding' that problem of the woman *'violée'* . . . Bravo! Bravo! Again, out of suffering, and out of suffering in the realms of the homely facts of everyday life, he has revealed beauty and moral radiance . . . Georges *nous fait souffrir mais jamais inutilement. Il n'est pas le moins du monde sadique. Les souffrances que nous subissons – sont élargissantes! Voilà la définition de la Tragédie.*

Feux rouges is set in New England on the Labor Day holiday. It concerns a couple who are driving from New York to the camp where their children have been on vacation. The background to this journey is the heavy toll of holiday road accidents announced over the car radio. During the journey the husband, Steve, keeps stopping to have a drink. His wife, Nancy, decides to leave the car and to continue the journey by bus. When Steve walks out of one of the bars he finds that he has been joined in the car by an escaped convict from Sing-Sing, a person with whom he identifies as another 'real man' and whom he helps through a police road block. Shortly afterwards Steve passes out, and when he comes to he finds that his new friend has robbed him and disappeared. Then he discovers that his wife was attacked and raped before she could reach the safety of the bus. Then he discovers that the rapist was the convict whom he had been helping to escape. The final effect of this disaster on the lives of Steve and Nancy is to bring them closer together and to provide Steve with the courage to stop drinking.

By the time he wrote *Feux rouges* Simenon had been living in the United States for nearly eight years and he had mastered the atmosphere and the background. The bars of *Feux rouges* are New York bars, the public holiday is utterly American, the language and manners of Sid, fresh out of Sing-Sing, seem authentic, even the domestic dispute which precedes Nancy's departure is characteristically American. With extreme simplicity Simenon turns the car into a lifeboat and the highways of New England on a public holiday into a dangerous sea. When Steve learns that, as a result of the rape, Sid will be executed he feels a painful hatred and anger rise in him because he will not be able to carry out the execution personally with his bare hands. But once he has been confronted with the harm he himself has done to Nancy and her courage after her ordeal, the storm blows out and he is a normal man again, working in a travel bureau, with hopes of a routine happiness if he has the patience and generosity to win it. The horror has passed.

Simenon replied to Thornton Wilder's letter about *Feux rouges* as follows:

It's probably the novel which has cost me the greatest effort yet, by that I mean the greatest nervous tension. Once I wanted to start on it but I was frightened of the tension it would need. I wrote another novel instead [*L'escalier de fer*, or *Antoine et Julie* (*The Magician*)] and only six months later did I feel strong enough for this one. What I had to do was to live for ten days at the rhythm of the highway without losing it for a moment. By the end I felt as exhausted as if I had been driving that same highway amid the Labor Day traffic for ten days.

It was at Lakeville that Simenon first began to look forward to Christmas as a major family celebration. Lakeville had a big summer colony and Simenon was warmly welcomed by the locals because he too was 'year-round'. At Christmas they had the traditional right to take Christmas trees from his woods, as they filled up with snow, a custom which pleased him. The arrival of Marie-Jo in February 1953 had added a new intensity to his paternal feelings. Having had no sisters he found the presence of a baby girl in the house a precious novelty. His attention was heavily engaged by his daughter from the moment of her arrival. He decided that she was rather like him, a hypersensitive child with a deep need for affection. His theory was confirmed when he once failed to greet her in her pram: she was a few months old, and she fell into a trance from which she only emerged when he eventually spoke to her. Their relationship was built on Simenon's theory that his daughter had an overpowering need for his company, a theory that was finally to have lethal consequences. His protective feelings may have partly derived from a subconscious wish to shelter Marie-Jo from the fate of one day meeting a man with the same governing impulses as himself.

It was also in Lakeville that Boule forgave him for his behaviour. In Carmel he had comforted her in his conventional way, and decided that she found this reassuring. But within three months of moving to Connecticut, Boule said that she preferred to live with her '*petit monsieur joli*'. The main draw was Simenon but there was also the closer involvement with Johnny, then aged 1 year. Marc was by now 10 and showing signs of independence. He had learnt to shrug off the fact that his father 'did not have a "real" job'. When his friends asked him, Marc would say that his father was a writer, and he could tell from their reaction that this was not a good thing to be. (It was to be some time before his class were given one of his father's books to study.) Marc was glad that at Lakeville they had come to rest at last. He had grown tired of changing schools and changing friends. In Tumacacori he had joined the Cub Scout Pack, only to be removed from it a few months later when Denise became pregnant. In Lakeville he attended the Indian Mountain School, where he did well. He then went to Hotchkiss School but left after only one year. It was at this time that Tigy said that she could remember the little boy standing for hours at the kitchen window, waiting to see his father come up the drive. All too often Simenon never turned up, dissuaded by Denise's opposition.

Tigy protested about Boule's departure, but Boule was not part of the divorce settlement and could live where she chose. At Shadow Rock Farm Simenon and Boule resumed their old relationship, and in 1952, when Denise was pregnant with Marie-Jo, Simenon hired another maid from Normandy and consoled himself for the loss of his wife's company by spending many evenings in bed with her as well. He was encouraged to take this step when he found the new girl naked and writing letters one evening in the kitchen. After a while she left them abruptly to take a job in a New York nightclub, and the manner of her departure, and apparent lack of passion during their coupling, led Simenon to suspect rather bitterly that she might have taken the job and gone to bed with him with the sole purpose of getting a work permit. He considered this an underhand procedure on her part.

Simenon's happiness at Lakeville led him at one point to consider applying for US citizenship. It was at about this time, at the end of 1952, that he gave an interview to Brendan Gill for *The New Yorker*. Gill wrote a fine piece describing

a wiry man with brown hair, a gentle, gravelly voice and powerful hands. Neither tall nor short, neither ugly nor handsome, he would pass unnoticed in any crowd save for the extraordinary mobility of his square, clean-shaven face. It is the face of a superb clown, with small, lively eyes under slanting lids, a sharp, straight nose, and a wide mouth, and it seems capable of portraying every nuance of joy, incredulity and despair. It is a face so filled and alert with curiosity that even the pipe rocking constantly in a corner of his mouth is, one would swear, peering about and sizing things up . . . 'Look! I am happy,' he says, rolling his eyes in wonder about the living-room of his farmhouse. 'After thirty years of travel, travel, travel, I have settled down, I am taking root.' He attempts to lift one foot from the pine floor. Impossible – it has taken root.

The New Yorker interview records a time of growing fame, booming sales, a high reputation and great happiness. It was this interview which ended with the triumphant words 'I am one of the lucky ones. What is there to say about the lucky ones except that they got away?' In Connecticut it seemed that he finally had it made.

Just as Simenon was in the course of applying for his US naturalisation papers an engrossing new television series was mounted which captured his attention every night for weeks. Senator Joe McCarthy had started to conduct his notorious hearings. A fellow member of the Mystery Writers of America, Dashiell Hammett, was imprisoned for refusing to appear and Simenon was struck by the rather sinister silence which had fallen over the most self-confident and well-established members of his own profession, and how none of his friends would give their frank opinion of the McCarthy hearings for fear of being denounced in their turn. The experience was one of those exceptional episodes which, quite suddenly, enable a foreigner to see below the surface of a new country. Simenon could no longer perceive the United States through the sonorous phrases of the Gettysburg Address, as the land of freedom, and he abandoned his application for naturalisation.

It was also at about this time, shortly after the birth of Marie-Jo, that Simenon first noticed a disquieting change in Denise's behaviour. He later described the changes as 'signs'. There was her habit of fantasising about her past. Her father's coffin had been equipped with a little window which one could open and look into. Not true, said her mother. There had been a fly-screen fitted into the opening. Not true again. Then there was her behaviour on arriving at a hotel. Even if it was the Plaza in New York, Denise would take off all her clothes and proceed to disinfect the bathroom and the telephone. She would then take all the lining-paper out of the drawers and cupboards, produce from her suitcase a miniature Hoover and set to work. Only after she had relined the surfaces with her own paper would Simenon be authorised to take a bath. This procedure followed a single occasion when they had been forced to stay in a cheap hotel and Denise had been bitten by lice. She became obsessed with her weight. She thought that pregnancy had ruined her figure, but she was also convinced that Simenon was plotting to make her plumper. She

dreaded growing to resemble her mother, a 'majestic', or 'imposing', or 'massive' personality, whom Simenon eventually grew to
like. 'I began to suspect,' he wrote, 'that her vast and leathery hide
concealed a timid woman who had learnt during childhood how
to conceal her sensitivity.' On studying her profile he thought that
Mrs Ouimet Senior bore some resemblance to an Iroquois Indian,
but decided that this was not a subject to raise in conversation.

As time passed Simenon's affection for Denise did not lessen,
but he needed all his patience when she told him that she was
going to burn his diaries and records which dated back to the
years he had spent in Paris with Tigy in the 1920s. He had
possibly forgotten that in 1946 it was he who had forced Denise to
burn all the affectionate letters she had received from her father. In
those days his jealousy had been the problem. Now Denise, who
never showed any sexual jealousy, had became intensely jealous
of the time he had lived before he met her. Nor did she seem as
happy at Shadow Rock Farm as he was. It was perhaps too much
like the life she had always known. Everything that was exotic or
absorbing for him was banal for her. She stopped talking to him
and began to drink, frequently in bars. His doctor advised him to
take Denise on regular visits to New York to amuse her, but
when the effect of these wore off he decided that a longer journey
might be necessary. One day Hamish Hamilton came to visit and
happened to ask him why he lived in America. Simenon gave
several reasons, but sensed a lack of conviction about his own
reply, and the following day he decided to leave. Denise's happiness played some part in the decision. She had been dreaming of
settling in Europe since the visit of 1952.

Simenon had set out for America in 1945 in search of a new
experience and in need of a new life, and in disgust and disappointment with Europe. He returned to Europe in 1955 partly on
impulse but partly to restore the happiness of his French-
Canadian wife. Impulse had played a powerful role in his life. He
had left school on impulse aged 15; he had set out on his travels
across the world with Tigy frequently on impulse; he left Paris in
1938 on impulse, and had fallen in love with Denise in a moment
of passionate impulse which was to alter the rest of his life. One
day he was perfectly happy in his house in Lakeville, the next he
felt a stranger in it. In 1953 he had been convinced that he had
found his permanent home at last. 'I am one of the lucky ones,' he

said of Lakeville; one of those who got away. But he had not got away. The flight to America had failed, just as it had failed for Léon, the fugitive vagabond in one of the first 'Maigrets', *Le chien jaune*. Simenon, still pursued, was changing his ground again.

THIRTEEN

The act of hate

I shall never achieve the perfection you have arrived at in life.
You (both) inspire me, give me the courage to believe that all
is still possible.
Letter, Henry Miller to Denise and Georges Simenon
(November 1960)

When he left Shadow Rock Farm on 19 March 1955 Simenon had
no clear idea where he would settle next. In *Mémoires intimes* he
described his decision to depart as a permanent one and wrote that
as he drove away from the house which he had loved and which
he would never see again he had not the heart to look back. But
Marc's headmaster at Darrow School, New Lebanon, was expecting Marc to return in the fall and Simenon and Denise did not
pack up the furniture in Shadow Rock Farm. The house was left
ready for immediate reoccupation. So, uncertain about the future,
Simenon took the heavily loaded Dodge estate into the New York
dockyards and boarded the *Liberté*. Denise, who had been 25
when he had met her in this city, was now 35. Johnny was 6,
Marie-Jo was 2 and Marc 16. Tigy at least was delighted to be
returning to France. She had been increasingly isolated and
unhappy in Connecticut. Boule was happy to be with the children
wherever that was.

They went briefly to Paris but by April had moved into a house
called La Gatounière, in Mougins, between Cannes and Grasse. It
was here, during the course of the summer, that they decided not

to return to America, although two of the children, Johnny and Marie-Jo, always hoped that one day they would go back to the happiness of Shadow Rock Farm. They stayed at La Gatounière for six months (with Tigy and Marc nearby) while Simenon wrote two *romans* – one set in Connecticut, one in the Midi – and two 'Maigrets'. 'Why did I choose Cannes?' Simenon asked himself later, and decided that it must have been because he did not like living in a big city such as Nice or Marseille, but still wanted a place where Denise would have a certain amount of life around her. He also wanted a place where there was a full range of medical facilities, explaining to Denise that this was essential for the children, although he was just as anxious about her and, not least, about himself. In June, while they were still at La Gatounière, Denise suffered a miscarriage. When she had recovered they set off on a *'tour de France'* looking for a place where they might settle. They went to Marseille, Bergerac, La Rochelle and Les Sables d'Olonne. They drove past Tigy's house at Nieul and ended up back in the Midi at Porquerolles. All this time Tigy and Marc were living in a hotel near Cannes and Marc, who was not ready to enter a French *lycée*, was receiving private tuition. The tour provided no solutions and so in the autumn Simenon and Denise moved to a magnificent villa above Cannes itself called 'Golden Gate', which they rented for the next ten months, the last months that Simenon was to live in France.

In 1950 Thomas Narcejac had published one of the first full-length critical studies of Simenon's work, entitled *Le cas Simenon*. He was concerned with the 'paradox' that such a popular and prolific writer could be worth serious critical attention. Simenon's election to the Académie Royale had done him no harm among critics, but it had not compensated for the damage done by his departure from Gallimard, and his persistence with Commissaire Maigret. By moving from Gallimard to Nielsen, and flouting the advice of Gide, Simenon was saying that if he was to have literary success it would be on his own terms. Now a francophone writer of Belgian origin who had returned from ten years of American exile, he was out of the intellectual mainstream. In 1947, the year when Simenon had predicted that he would win the Nobel Prize, it went to a francophone novelist, but he was called André Gide. In Simenon's lifetime five other French writers were to be selected for the Nobel: Mauriac, Camus, St John Perse, Sartre and Claude

Simon. Simenon was not pleased about this. In 1961 he wrote in his diary that he probably wouldn't accept the Nobel, even it were offered. It was too late. 'Let them f—— off and leave me in peace.' But in 1964 he was abusing the Nobel jury as 'the cretins who still haven't awarded me their prize'. While he still had hopes of winning the Nobel he could not always hide his bitterness about the lack of critical acclaim. The critics remained uncertain what to write about Simenon, tending to seize on his supposed deficiencies, but his fellow writers were more and more generous in their praise. And as time passed Simenon no longer wanted literary success, even on his own terms, and grew to despise the 'literary' world which continued to withhold its adulation. His son Johnny remembers that Simenon's contempt for the world of honours and medals was genuine, but says that his father also felt disappointed that he had not had more recognition for what he considered he was good at, not 'literature' but the art of novel-making. Two more serious studies of his work were published during this period, one by Claude Mauriac entitled *L'alittérature contemporaine* (1958), and Bernard de Fallois's *Simenon* (1961). Mauriac's criticism was to some extent in sympathy with Narcejac, arguing that Simenon's work was of literary value *even though* it was in a new category of *'alittérature'*, or anti-literature. Simenon was much better pleased with de Fallois's argument, which took exactly the opposite line, insisting that the merit of a good writer lay not *in spite of* the pleasure he gave but because of it. De Fallois noted that the contemporary novel was too often a work of philosophy, a work in which the critical devoured the imaginative, where the power of analysis put a brake on the imagination. Simenon, he wrote, stood in solitary defiance of this trend.

Simenon also took some comfort from the continuing stream of unsolicited tributes he received from fellow writers, some of them critics of the first rank. In March 1955 T.S. Eliot wrote to thank him for sending a copy of *L'horloger d'Everton*:

> I had already read [it] . . . I am proud and happy to possess this copy with your *dédicace* . . . I am always particularly fascinated when I find you returning to one of your fundamental themes . . . [*L'horloger*] treats the problem of father and son from the point of view of the father seeking the son, the opposite

approach to that of either *Le destin des Malou* or *La neige était sale*.

Eliot twice adds in ink, beside his typed text, a rather anxious 'is it not?' Sacha Guitry wrote in the same year of how he and his wife were tearing Simenon's books out of each other's hands. '"No, that one's mine this evening." "I forbid you to tell me the plot." "It's two o'clock, for goodness' sake put out the light."' The image of the Simenon reader continuing throughout the night until he or she had finished was a common one. De Fallois had quoted Stendhal in its support: 'What use is a novel if it doesn't pass the night?'

Henry Miller continued his running commentary of appreciation:

> Few writers are able to express this everyday, intimate, universal realm of thought and sensation. It makes me envious . . . It's *what you leave out* that makes your books so full of reverberations. You create a real and honest collaboration with your readers. I would like nothing better than to some day write a book like this [*Antoine et Julie*] . . . It makes me realise how much I have omitted from my huge books!

Somerset Maugham was sufficiently intrigued by Simenon to travel from the Villa Mauresque for lunch. They had a number of interests in common, apart from the creation of popular fiction: money, tax and how to avoid it, health and begging letters. Also the dismissive views of the higher criticism. In his autobiography Maugham gives an account of this lunch and adds what, from his pen, was the ungrudging praise of a contemporary and rival: 'For my part I know of no better way to pass the time on a plane from Nice to Athens or, say, from Rangoon to Singapore, than to read one of Simenon's novels.' Simenon remembered Maugham's visit with mixed feelings, not because he considered his praise grudging but because Maugham had coached Denise in how to screw more money out of film companies when negotiating contracts, and Simenon considered that the advice was disastrous and led to the loss of several potentially valuable deals.

Simenon retained the instinctive respect for Gide that Maigret had for 'Madame la Comtesse', the *châtelaine* of Saint-Fiacre.

Maigret, who had been brought up on the estate, the son of the steward, never escaped from 'the shadow of the château', and Simenon, who had left school at 15, never considered that he could be the intellectual equal of Gide. Gide's letters continued until shortly before his death. The last that survives is dated 29 November 1950:

> How many people still don't know about you! When they come to me to ask, 'What should I read of his?' I reply, 'Everything.' What Narcejac, despite his well-motivated praise, fails to emphasise sufficiently is that kind of intoxication which overcomes the reader as soon as he opens one of your books; and which I have experienced again on rereading you. Without any possibility of being surprised, my delight is as strong, stronger even, than on first reading. What better guarantee of immortality! Dear Simenon, I am very fond of you and send you all my love.

When Simenon was in America, Gide had written suggesting the possibility of visiting him, 'provided that he was able to travel *incognito*', as Simenon recalled later. This comment summons up a wonderful picture of Gide struggling to preserve his *incognito* among the ranchers, sheriff's deputies, whores and wetbacks who were Simenon's neighbours in Arizona. Oddly enough the surviving letters in which Gide proposed such a trip (dated 12 and 16 February 1948) do not mention travelling *incognito*, and ill-health swiftly prevented the Nobel laureate's fame from being put to the test. Gide was getting slightly vague at this point in his life, with his 'heart flagging' as he wrote in his last letter, and in 1948 he 'discovered' *Le testament Donadieu*, forgetting that he had first praised it in 1939. To the end he talked of putting the finishing touches to his study of Simenon, which was never published (and what he had already written seems to have disappeared). However he confessed that he and his friends were all '*atteints d'une simenonite aiguë*' to the last, and he too drew a picture of a household absorbed in *Lettre à mon juge, Il pleut, bergère . . ., Le haut mal (The Woman of the Grey House), Le bourgmestre de Furnes, Le cheval blanc (The White Horse Inn)* and *Les fiançailles de M. Hire.*

   Simenon addressed the question of whether or not he was a literary figure in 1960, in his radio talk on Balzac. It is an unexpected fact that this 7000-word biographical essay took him one month to write, a period of time in which he was capable of writing three novels. Although he was always irritated with comparisons between his work and Balzac's the essay is notable for the number of similarities he traces between his destiny and that of his subject. Recalling that *Le père Goriot* was written in three days Simenon asked whether 'the need to create other men, to draw out of oneself a crowd of different characters' was 'found in a happy man, a man merged into a little world made to his own measure':

> Why struggle to live the life of others if one is self-assured and if one has no need to rebel against oneself . . . Isn't peace of mind given to a child by its mother's love and its love for its mother?

Balzac, wrote Simenon, was haunted by the conviction of his own mediocrity; the only solution was to achieve something marvellous. He was attracted to older women and he married one – 'Motherly women, sweet, forgiving, capable, who would not only love him but admire him.' He too was spurned by his peers, in his case the Académie Française. In order to succeed at his work Balzac had been obliged to wreck his life. On only one point did Simenon find no echo in the life of Balzac. Balzac apparently thought that, in order to develop a superior intelligence, it was necessary to be chaste:

> One saw him in neither the theatres nor the cafés. He did not take a mistress, he had no sexual relations and he never seems to have had recourse to the *filles faciles* who teemed in the arcades and gardens of the Palais-Royal.

There seems to be a note of genuine puzzlement rather than admiration in Simenon's text at this point. But the most important similarity concerned Balzac's unloving mother. 'A novelist,' Simenon wrote, '*is a man who does not like his mother, or who never received mother-love.*' And he concluded that Balzac's need for glory had been provoked by his need for revenge, and that his achievements were based on his shame at his own mediocrity. Balzac felt inferior because he had not been loved. The similarity to the boy from Liège who had once told his mother that *he* would never be one of the world's *fessées* is clear.

Perhaps the most important change that came over the public personality of Simenon on his return from America was that he no longer felt he had anything to lose, and with Gide dead he no longer had anyone to please. He was a 'made' man by now, he would not change. For better or worse the lines of his achievement were fixed, and he took on a somewhat truculent air. While living in Cannes he resumed his friendship with Georges Clouzot, who lived in St Paul-de-Vence and whom Simenon regarded as the 'real' director of *Les inconnus dans la maison* (he had in fact adapted the book for the film). Simenon now went out of his way to draw attention to this film, which was no longer blacklisted and which had been among his principal reasons for leaving France in 1945. In 1956 he read an introduction to a gramophone recording of Raimu's big speech in the film, the final speech for the defence made by the drunken barrister Loursat, and he described it as 'this good and sturdy film of Henri Decoin's'.

Clouzot and Simenon used to make regular visits to the strip-tease clubs in Cannes, usually in the company of Denise, and Simenon became friends with the girls. (In *Mémoires intimes* he recalled how he used to accompany one of them to the changing rooms above the stage while the other was performing and take her amid the frocks.) It was by his own account a carefree relationship; after the show he would accompany his friend home, dandle her baby on his knees and listen to the story of her life while she cooked supper. The anecdote suggests, wrongly, that one of the reasons why Simenon kept in touch with prostitutes, and girls on the verge of prostitution, was to gather material for his novels. But it was from the friendship with the girl in Cannes that he based one of his *romans* of the period, *Strip-tease* (*Strip-tease*). In the novel the relations between the dancers and their audience are not always so friendly, and one of the girls, the heroine, having narrowly failed to commit first murder and then suicide, takes to the streets and is bumped off by her Arab pimp.

Clouzot wanted to make *Strip-tease* into a film and together he and Simenon wrote a scenario, but once again the project failed. However Simenon received some compensation for his lifelong difficulties with the cinema when he was asked to become president first of the Brussels and then of the Cannes film festivals. His appearance at Cannes in 1960 was one of the great publicity triumphs of his career and a spiritual victory for the truculent people of the world. Simenon gave a hint of what was to follow when he told the organisers that, contrary to tradition, he would not be accepting any hospitality during the festival and would pay his own expenses. At the first meeting of the jury he was officially appointed president by M. Fabre-Lebret, the secretary of the organising committee. Simenon had carefully studied the rules and silently noted that this was a breach of them because the jury was supposed to elect its own president. At the next meeting Fabre-Lebret was once more present and Simenon politely asked him to leave as he was not a member of the jury. He did so, for that meeting at least, although no president had ever expelled him before. Simenon had also noted that among the jurors was his friend Henry Miller, who seldom watched the films, preferring to play ping-pong, which was his latest passion. Miller's vote was therefore in his pocket. He also had his own vote and his casting vote, and he quickly formed an alliance with a female juror.

During the festival Simenon fell under the spell of Giulietta, the beautiful wife of Fellini, whose film *La dolce vita* was among the contenders. He also met and immediately liked her husband. He claimed later to have practised alcoholic abstinence during the festival, which was probably true, and in the final judging he needed all his wits about him to impose his choice, *La dolce vita*, on a lobby led by the juror from French government television, which favoured a film by Antonioni which was judged more 'artistic' and which was certainly less scandalous. When the judging was over Simenon emerged with the results to find Fabre-Lebret waiting for him, together with an official from the Quai d'Orsay, the French foreign ministry. Fabre-Lebret had already let him know that it was essential, for diplomatic reasons, to give one of the major prizes to an American film, a practice which has become a tradition. The two *fonctionnaires* were not at all pleased with Simenon's list, but in those days it was still the president of the jury who announced the prizes and there was nothing they could do. Just before parting the curtains Simenon was able to whisper the good news to the adorable Giulietta, and so it was that he stepped out in front of the cameras and lights of the world's press to make his solemn announcement with an enormous lipstick mark on his cheek. A government-inspired claque

was waiting for him and the victory of *La dolce vita* was greeted
with boos, rattles and whistles while Giulietta sobbed on
Simenon's shoulder. Fellini himself enjoyed the fuss immensely
and the occasion was the beginning of one of the great friendships
of Simenon's later life. But he was never again asked to preside
over Cannes or any other jury by the French government. This
did not bother him at all. Simenon had a genuine and deep
loathing of President de Gaulle which grew with the great man's
return to power in 1958. He was opposed to the whole concept of
'the hero'. In *Quand j'étais vieux* he compared de Gaulle to
Napoleon and said that he should be locked up. Some comments
he subsequently made about Mme de Gaulle were removed from
one of his *Dictées* by his publisher.

One of the reasons why Simenon had agreed to go to Cannes
was that he thought it would amuse Denise, and he was right.
They had a suite with a balcony in the Hôtel Carlton, what
Simenon called his 'usual second-floor suite', overlooking La
Croisette and the *plage*. Every night they had to be escorted the
few hundred metres to the Palais des Festivals through excited
crowds hoping to catch a glimpse of the stars, and Denise showed
no signs of her usual tension and fragility. But in general the
move to Europe had not effected the change in Denise's health
that her husband had hoped for, and behind the façade which he
had erected of happy family man and immensely successful
writer, a domestic catastrophe was building up. It was while they
were living at Golden Gate, outside Cannes, that their son John,
aged 5, became aware that his parents were not getting on. 'That
was when I first saw the spaghetti hitting the wall,' he says.

The events that turned Simenon's passionate love for Denise into
an equally passionate hatred took place over the years from 1956
to 1965. After two years of indecision following their arrival on
the Côte d'Azur Simenon and Denise finally decided to settle –
this time it was to be for the rest of their lives – in Switzerland.
There were several reasons for this decision. One was because of
the children. They wanted them to be given a good education in
two languages, and to have the best medical facilities close at
hand. Another was that they both liked Lausanne, with its striking position on the shore of Lake Geneva, directly opposite the
French Alps. A third reason, which Simenon never mentioned,

was tax. Simenon was wary of the French tax authorities and Switzerland offered advantages to people who were wealthy enough to qualify for them.

In July 1957 they took the Château d'Echandens, outside Lausanne, on a six-year renewable lease, not having found anywhere suitable that was for sale. The château was both a fortified castle and a large country house. It stands on a hillside, dominating a valley which is full of vineyards, in a position which gives a splendid view of the lake and the French Alps; there is a little village at its gates. They had found Echandens after making numerous tours around the countryside in a taxi. Simenon was careful to choose a very slow taxi-driver, which in a city where the traffic moves with sedate predictability suggests how much he had aged mentally since Arizona, only seven years before. Marc was by now 17, and about to take his *baccalauréat* at the *lycée* in Nice; Johnny was 6; Marie-Jo was 3. By the time they left the house seven years later the marriage of Simenon and Denise was virtually over. The most remarkable thing about this period, one of the most stressful in his life, was that throughout it his work continued at its normal rate, and the quality if anything improved. It may be significant that although Simenon's characters sometimes visit Switzerland (*Maigret voyage, Le train de Venise* [*The Venice Train*], *La disparition d'Odile* [*The Disappearance of Odile*]) he never set one of his books in his last country of residence. Among the finest books he managed to write at Cannes and Echandens were *En cas de malheur* (*In Case of Emergency*), *Le fils* (*The Son*), *Le président* (*The Premier*), *Le passage de la ligne* and *Les anneaux de Bicêtre*. His usual habit was to sign his books on the last page with the date and the place in which they had been written. In the case of the books written in Château d'Echandens he signed each of them 'Noland', a habit which mystified his readers for many years. He himself later stated that he had done this to avoid the possibility of casual visits from readers, but Denise said that he had actually been more concerned about Swiss tax laws, and had been misled by Charlie Chaplin into thinking that it was inadvisable for foreign residents to earn money while in the country.

Simenon was by now able to live in some style. Advised by the *préfet de police* in Nice to get rid of his vast Dodge from Connecticut because it was too big for the little streets of Cannes and because it attracted too much attention, Simenon had bought not one but three 4–horsepower Renaults, and studded Denise's model with every gadget in the showroom. Simenon also bought her a little house in Cagnes-sur-Mer which they were supposed to use as a refuge together. It was linked by a bell to the restaurant opposite. The only time they tried to use it the man who lit a fire to welcome them managed to set the chimney alight. They never tried to use it again. Later, in a day of madness at the Geneva motor show, Simenon bought first a Chrysler and then a Rolls-Royce, paying for each with a cheque. Denise shopped at Lanvin, Hermès and Cartier, and went to Weill for her furs. Their new house was guarded by a high iron gate. The château had a courtyard, a tower, a dungeon and a range of outbuildings and garages as well as a walled park with lawns and trees. Such a large house needed servants and they started with a staff of six which gradually increased to eleven. At this time too Denise took on a secretary, Joyce Aitken, and soon a second secretary, Blima Silberberg. Simenon called all his staff by their surnames but he did not feel he could shout out 'Silberberg' all day long so, as Joyce Aitken recalls it, 'since she had a very sweet face and her complexion reminded him of a bun he thought of the Russian blinis in which you pour caviare,' and Silberberg was called 'Blinis' from then on. In addition there was a nurse for Marie-Jo, a laundress, a gardener/chauffeur/*maître d'hôtel* and, of course, Boule, who continued to do the cooking. There were two maids, one or other of whom was generally 'honoured' by Simenon on a daily basis.

In December 1961 his Italian publisher, Arnoldo Mondadori, responding to a request from Simenon, recommended a young woman from Venice, Teresa Sburelin, for the post of housemaid. Mondadori and Simenon had known each other for fifty years; they got on extremely well and Mondadori knew what was required. Teresa was interviewed by Denise and Simenon in Mondadori's office and started work soon afterwards. Some time later Simenon came upon Teresa about her duties one morning, bending over a dressing table, and, as he wrote in *Mémoires intimes*, 'penetrated her from behind, while she did not move or protest'. Teresa later recounted the same incident as follows: 'I was in the *salon*, bending over a table, polishing. He came up behind me, lifted my skirt, *et crac! . . . c'était la joie!*' Thus started an intimate relationship that was to last for the rest of Simenon's life. Teresa was then aged 34. Denise was soon made aware of the situation and accepted it; it was entirely normal for Simenon to have regular sexual connections with the maids. Denise wrote later that one new maid, on learning of the situation, asked a colleague: '*On passe toutes à la casserole?*' (Do we all get laid?) She was told that it was not compulsory, but she would certainly be asked.

The distance between Simenon and Denise, which had first become apparent in Connecticut, only became greater in Switzerland instead of narrowing as he had hoped. To start with, he used to take her for drives in the afternoon, talking to her about everything that interested him, but invariably finding when he eventually turned towards her that she had gone to sleep. He continued however to make love to her, his favourite time being after lunch when he would come to find her in her office and invite her to leave for a while. 'What do you want?' she would ask. 'You.' 'Again?' Then she would sigh, tell Aitken to wait a few moments and accompany him to the nearest bedroom where she would pull down her pants, lie on her back and say '*Fais vite*' (be quick). Slowly the act of love turned into the act of hate. 'Nearly every afternoon, perhaps because we were both naked after our showers, I wanted to make love. Either Denise would submit with resignation, or she would say "Oh no, not again today . . ."'

Simenon, remembering months of alcoholic bliss at the beginning of their relationship, tried to renew the experience but had to admit that the experiment was not a success. Once he summoned a doctor in the middle of the night to calm Denise with an injection, only to find the doctor deciding to give him the shot instead. Sometimes it was Denise taking refuge in Boule's room to escape Simenon, sometimes it was the children running out of the house into the night to escape Denise. Denise's behaviour seems to have been wilder and more irrational, but Simenon, at the best of times, was a man of strong moods who could fill a house with sunshine or intimidate everyone present. Years later, in her novel *Le phallus d'or*, Denise described the force of his personality. 'His voice rang through the house from morning to night, and when he was out it was as though the silence was awaiting his return.' Simenon has given a long account of his problems with Denise in *Mémoires intimes* and she has given a shorter account of her side of the story in *Un oiseau pour le chat*. What is clear from his fictional work written after his departure from the United States is that he began to associate sex with despair – sex assumed frightening, sometimes lethal, proportions, whereas before it sometimes carried a message of hope.

In 1956 Simenon was approached by RTF, the French government radio station, to talk about one of the seven deadly sins. He could choose whichever he wished except Sloth, which had already been chosen by Cocteau. Simenon promptly chose Lust. In his talk, which was never broadcast, Simenon depicted Lust as the most innocent of sins and traced it to a nostalgia for childhood. He described

the need to plunge back into a state of natural innocence . . . an existence without duties or rules . . . Surely the wonderful and secret life of a child is not only found in a sunbeam, or in the brightly coloured images of a world which is still quite fresh, but is also to be found in the joys the child can find, *without remorse*, in its own body, in the sensations which are awakened by cold or heat, from eating or drinking, and from subtler excitements which the child never seeks to explain. The child like any young animal . . . is a lustful creature. So why, when he has become a man, should he not try to rediscover the swift satisfaction of his sexuality? . . . I do not believe that the Lust I have described is necessarily a form of depravity, so much as a form of escapism . . . In time of revolution or war, when the pressure of events is at its strongest, there is frequently an explosion of sexuality . . . So if I were to be accused of Lust I would happily reply: 'A man (or woman) to whom you have given tasks which are beyond his powers to accomplish does what he can to behave like an adult. But it sometimes happens that he closes his eyes and on closing his eyes he rediscovers the scent of a lost world and he tries to regain it.'

And Bernard de Fallois has written: 'It is as if eroticism is of capital importance to Simenon because he sees it not as an exercise of intelligence and will-power but as a desperate attempt to connect with life and the very sources of existence.'

This view is supported by Simenon's work during this period. Sixteen of the twenty-three *romans durs* written between 1955 and 1965, when his marriage was breaking up, are concerned with marital poisonings, female alcoholism, *crimes passionnels* or suicide. In six of the books written between 1955, when he was living in Cannes, and 1961, six months before his wife's first departure to a psychiatric clinic near Lausanne, Simenon wrote some of his darkest fictions on a sexual theme. The first, *Les complices* (1955), was the most explosive. A moment's inattention on the part of Joseph Lambert, preoccupied with caressing his secretary, Edmonde, while driving his car, leads to the death of forty-eight schoolchildren in a holiday bus. The action of the book is over in the first two pages, virtually in the first four paragraphs, and the remainder of the story concerns Joseph Lambert's state of mind and the life of a small town in the Midi, in summer, stirred up by the horror of the disaster and the efforts of the police to find the culprit. Lambert's only escape from his overpowering sense of remorse lies first in his relations with Edmonde, who never makes any comment on the horrifying event she witnessed, and then in his friendship with a prostitute *de passage* who senses that he is a troubled man. In due course, and before his guilt is suspected, Lambert decides to kill himself, but he is only driven to this decision when he is unable to please Edmonde while making love to her and he realises that the last escape route from his torment is blocked. He loses the reassurance that his private truth is the valid one and shoots himself in his office leaving a suicide note that reveals his innermost conviction: 'I am not guilty.'

In *Strip-tease* (1957), the heroine, Célita, has degenerated from being a professional dancer to working in a strip-club in Cannes. She is engaged in a merciless battle with the proprietor's wife for the proprietor's affections, being the only girl on the staff who is capable of troubling him when he sleeps with her. Célita sees Léon as 'a real man with the urge to dominate'. She therefore sets out to prevent him from feeling so sure of himself; he can never be absolutely certain that he has 'vanquished' her. Léon remains attracted to her but is also wary, and Célita conceives their relationship in these combative terms: 'they would have made . . . a fine couple, tearing away from each other only to come together more completely, shattering each other's pride, humbling each other'. Léon's wife dies, but instead of winning Léon, Célita loses him to an *ingénue* at the club and, unable to revenge herself on him, she destroys herself instead. *Strip-tease* is not one of Simenon's most successful books, because he failed to enter the personality of his principal character, Célita, as effectively as he usually did. When he describes her occasional desire to have sex for pleasure alone, it is with a surprising lack of conviction.

En cas de malheur (1955) is a much better book, this time about a middle-aged man's obsession with a younger woman. Lucien Gobillot is a barrister who is asked to take on a hopeless case defending a rootless young woman accused of robbing an elderly jeweller. Lucien secures the acquittal of his client, Yvette, but then becomes obsessed with her to the point of damaging his career and putting his perfectly contented marriage at risk. Together he and Yvette have sex with her maid. He also has a younger rival who is equally obsessed with Yvette and who eventually murders her. After her death Gobillot hands over his dossier on Yvette, which recounts their affair in all its sordidness, to the colleague who is defending the younger rival on the murder charge.*

In *Dimanche* (1958), a hotel-keeper, Emile, living on the Côte d'Azur is dominated by Berthe, an unattractive and mean-spirited wife. Eventually he takes refuge in a happy carnal relationship with Ada, an uneducated young Italian maid. One day his wife surprises them together during their siesta and demands that Ada be dismissed. Emile flatly refuses to do this, the first time he has successfully opposed the wishes of his wife, and he and Berthe thereupon agree to keep up appearances but privately to give each other their freedom. Emile decides that he would rather rid himself of his wife completely and be able to lead a contented life with Ada. With infinite care he arranges to poison Berthe over a period of eleven months. All goes well, and eventually he manages to serve her with the lethal risotto. On returning to the hotel dining-room he meets his wife's gaze, *'calme et dur'*; she has handed the risotto to Ada, who has almost finished eating it.

Betty, the principal character of *Betty* (1960), is a drunk, an habituée of bar-stools on the Champs-Elysées who drowns her

* The book was filmed by Claude Autant-Lara with Jean Gabin and Brigitte Bardot in 1958.

sorrows in a sea of cocktails and casual affairs. Eventually she is expelled from the family home and loses all rights in her children in exchange for a regular remittance.

Finally, in *La porte* (1961), a man with no hands is cuckolded by a man with no legs. Bernard Foy, who lost his hands in an explosion during the war, is tended and loved by his attractive wife, Nelly. Forced to live at home and do what he can of the housekeeping while earning pocket-money by decorating lamp-shades, he becomes tormented by his inability to caress his wife and possessed with curiosity and jealousy about her activities. Every day Nelly visits Pierre, a younger man confined to a wheelchair who lives in a flat below. Pierre's sister works in the same shop as Nelly and her visits are merely to carry messages. Bernard eventually comes to believe in his wife's love and true devotion and is reassured enough to face life and the possibility of their happiness together. He sets out to do the day's shopping unexpectedly early, but passing the open door of Pierre's apartment sees Nelly bending over the wheelchair kissing Pierre, *who holds her in his arms*. Bernard does the shopping and returns home to find Nelly has killed herself. He follows suit.

The autobiographical references in this succession of six books on a theme of sexual despair, written over a period of six years, make an impressive list. In *Les complices* the successive incidents in which Edmonde, alone or with the aid of her employer, is brought to the moment of climax, in his car, at her desk in the office or in a convenient field, were echoed in Simenon's life when he enjoyed over a number of days the same experience with a temporary secretary who was taking dictation. The real girl's silence and apparent indifference to any form of communication, other than a physical one, is also repeated in the fictional Edmonde's habitual indifference and calm. While the police hunt for the driver of the car which caused the school bus to swerve into a stone wall, Joseph Lambert continues his routine of going each evening to the Café Riche to play the usual game of bridge with the police commissioner, the owner of Prisunic, the *sous-préfet* and the town's insurance agent – Simenon's daily routine in La Rochelle and Fontenay-le-Comte. Reporters and photographers arrive from all over France to carry out the tasks with which Simenon was so familiar, and there is the character of Léa, the '*fille publique*', with whom Joseph Lambert consoles himself, and who tells him, as so many prostitutes had told Simenon, the story of her life.

In *En cas de malheur* there is the familiar situation of a marriage without sexual attraction interrupted by a relationship based on sexual obsession. There is also a sexual relationship with a house-maid and the introduction of a scene in which Lucien Gobillot, to his own surprise, finds himself in bed with two women at once, one of whom he has scarcely been introduced to. The biographi-cal references in *Strip-tease* are fewer, perhaps because it is one of the few books which Simenon wrote at someone else's sugges-tion. The two main biographical elements are the state of mind of someone, in this case Célita, who has staked everything on the success of a sexual passion, and a secondary character, an amateur stripper who brings herself to the point of climax through excite-ment at her own performance, and who was based on a real dancer at the local club. There is also a male character, a customer at the club, who is more interested in talking to the girls than watching them perform and who 'studied people with a curiosity that seemed too compassionate'.

In *Dimanche* there is the marriage which is a living death succeeded by a relationship based on sexual passion, this time with an Italian maid (an interesting case of 'anticipated memory' in Simenon); then there is the discovery of the hero and his mistress by the wife during the afternoon siesta in a room outside the house, and the decision to keep the appearance of marriage going for reasons of convenience. In *Betty* there is another antici-pated memory with the 'lost soul', traumatised by experiences in her childhood and driven to alcohol and promiscuity, who is expelled from her own house and deprived of the company of her children. This, with the exception of the promiscuity, was to be the fate of Denise (although she was not the original of the character). But the autobiographical references in *La porte*, the last book in this series and the one written closest to the final crisis in Simenon's own marriage, are perhaps the most striking of all.

In August 1960 Simenon invited Bernard de Fallois, then a young academic and specialist in Proust, to stay for a period of time at Echandens. De Fallois had abandoned his original idea of developing his thesis on Proust into a book and had decided instead that it would be a more challenging and interesting task to make good the deficiency left by Gide and to produce a serious study of the most popular living author in world literature. The correspondence preceding the visit shows that Simenon was convinced that at last a serious critic had surfaced who might be able to give an intelligent and sympathetic interpretation of what he was trying to do. In the course of time Bernard de Fallois was to become both Simenon's publisher and one of his closest friends, but at the time of his first visit Simenon was confined to bed following an appendix operation. In consequence de Fallois was installed in a ground-floor room with a desk, while Simenon was confined to bed in the room above him. Denise would relay de Fallois's questions and requests to Simenon, and would return with the answers and with the appropriate papers from the writer's archives. This went on for several days, for the greater part of de Fallois's visit. At the time Simenon was completely obsessed with and jealous of Denise, and after de Fallois's departure he said, while at lunch with Denise and the children, partly laughing at himself but partly reflecting what he felt, '*Enfin on est ensemble, l'amoureux*★ *de Maman est parti*'. De Fallois, who had little idea at that time of the intensity of Simenon's feelings towards his wife, was therefore somewhat startled when in 1962 he received his copy of *La porte*, written in May 1961, which tells the story of a man who is confined for most of the time to his room and who is unable to express his physical need for his wife, while in the room beneath a younger man, also confined to his room and constantly visited by the wife, is able to do for her the one thing the husband cannot do, which is to caress her.

The interest of these six novels is not so much in the direct biographical references they contain as in the light they shed on the author's state of mind and methods of work. 'Pierre Mazeron' in *La porte* is not Bernard de Fallois, any more than 'Bernard Foy' is Georges Simenon. What the book does is explore the feelings and anguish of a man obsessed with an apparently groundless jealousy over frequent visits made by his wife to a younger man confined in a neighbouring room. In 1960 Simenon remained sufficiently possessive of Denise to be jealous of any attention she paid to a younger man visiting Echandens. The story behind *La porte* is illuminating because it shows both the extent to which Simenon relied on lived experience for many of his fictions, and

★ I.e., 'the person in love with'.

the limits of that lived experience, the point at which fact was abandoned and the novel took on its own life.

Throughout these years of increasing unhappiness Simenon fought hard to save his marriage. In May 1959 Denise gave birth to their youngest child, Pierre, and the couple were brought closer together when the baby, at 4 months, became ill and had to be taken to Lyon for treatment. There, despite getting the best attention available, Pierre very nearly died. 'For the first time in my life I knew real fear,' Simenon recalled of the time when he was told that Pierre had a 'fifty per cent chance with a lot of prayers'. For the first time he knew 'the sort of fear that freezes you, and leaves you speechless and incapable of reacting'. The effect on Simenon was to bring on such serious attacks of giddiness that he was unable, when in Lyon, to cross the road, unless he was surrounded by a crowd of people; writing of the memory of the event twenty-five years later he found himself immobile once again in his chair, with tears running down his cheeks, sobbing and unable to breathe. The original ordeal for Denise and Simenon lasted for nearly two months before the baby's life was declared out of danger.

But when unsupported by such moments of crisis the marriage steadily deteriorated. Both were given to moments of violence, though his were considerably more threatening; both drank heroic quantities, in her case whisky, in his wine; and both continued to work extremely hard. Simenon continued to make regular visits to '*les filles*' and Denise kept several pages of her telephone book for addresses and numbers in Cannes, Paris, Milan and Brussels, under the heading 'FILLES'. Simenon said that this word showed a lack of respect and so she changed the heading to 'FRIVOLITÉS'. Denise spent much of her life in her suite of offices with her team of secretaries. Simenon maintained his usual routine of short periods of intensive and utterly exhausting work followed by lengthy intervals of inactivity when he began to feel himself more and more of a stranger in his own house, superfluous to the administration of his own business affairs, superfluous to his wife's emotional requirements, and not even able to count on any sustained interest on her part in his conversation. In 1959 and 1960 he even suffered, and on several occasions, from 'writer's block'. His main emotional refuge in this situation was the children. Marc had left the house to make his own life and

Pierre was too young to provide company, but that left Johnny and Marie-Jo, and although he loved them equally, as he should, he undoubtedly received more emotional support from the company of his daughter. Simenon kept hoping that normal life would return. In February 1962 he went to London to attend the banquet given for 'the pipe-man of the year'. He was accompanied by Denise, her secretary, Aitken, and her new Italian maid, Teresa, and he set himself up in the Savoy Hotel, surrounded by women like a pasha with his harem. But Julian Symons, who met him on this visit, remembers that he was withdrawn and watchful, leaving most of the talking to Denise, who seemed to overshadow him. (It was during this visit that he heard from Marc, now married, that he had become a grandfather.)

At home Simenon was still capable of high spirits. A wild dinner party with medical friends ended with Simenon doing a striptease and wondering next day if he had gone too far. Bernard de Fallois remembers that meeting him one had the impression of 'a warm, talkative story-teller with an extraordinary strength in his regard'. But the situation between Simenon and Denise had deteriorated to such an extent four months later, in June, that on the advice of a psychiatrist Denise agreed to leave Echandens and to spend a period of time as a residential patient in a nearby clinic. In her opinion she was tricked into this move, which put her 'in the wrong' – and in a poor negotiating position – for the remainder of her marriage, but in the opinion of others, including her son Johnny and her secretary, one of them had to leave the house, and of the two Simenon was the less disturbed and the stronger character. De Fallois remembers that while she was away Simenon was very unhappy, and that he waited by the telephone all day hoping for news from the clinic.

In 1961 Simenon and Denise had learnt that a new motorway was to pass in front of the Château d'Echandens, and had decided that the best solution would be to build their own house on the heights above Lausanne. They purchased a large plot, at 'Epalinges', in a meadow with a magnificent view of the mountains, and hired an architect to draw up plans for the first house they had owned since Shadow Rock Farm, and only the third house Simenon had owned of the twenty-five he had lived in since coming to Paris. The structure which eventually emerged looks like a Texan ranch house – white, surrounded by timber fencing, with two wings and grouped round its own courtyard. Simenon wanted it to be big enough to house all his children and all their children, but by the time the house was ready for occupation in Christmas 1963 his marriage was at its last gasp, and Denise only lived at Epalinges for four months before returning to the clinic. She tried once to come back again, but Simenon, in tears on the doorstep, refused to admit her and told her she had to go back. He had taken his marriage and his passion *'jusqu'au bout'*. Bernard de Fallois says, 'He tried to give Denise confidence by involving her in his work. When this did not give her confidence, but complicated things, he decided to abandon the whole project.'

Looking back now Denise blames Dr Durand, the director of the clinic where she was treated, for driving her and her husband apart. She says that Durand told Simenon that if she came back to Epalinges she would remain a sick woman, and that he told her that Simenon was allergic to her. 'The last rows we had were staged,' she says:

> He was a man driving out his love. He was much older than me and I think he was afraid, although that is speculation. The day I went back there were tears running down his cheeks. He was a marvellous man, but what a difficult man he was. He was difficult because he was unhappy. For twenty years I was the kind of person he wanted to be with and I was violent enough to understand his violent way of loving. At the end I certainly didn't give Simenon all the loving attention I should have done. There were the children, and all the contracts. It was too much. So when we made love, I didn't enjoy it any more and I made believe. He was too demanding and I was too demanding because I wanted to be quiet. He didn't understand that I was exhausted. I couldn't stand him telling people at Epalinges how well I made love. 'Better than a 17-year-old prostitute,' he said, so I slapped him. And I told him I no longer enjoyed making love to him. And that I think was the end for him. He went downstairs and drank a bottle of whisky.

Simenon's memories are different:

> One day, trying to unfreeze her, I took her in my arms and pulled her on to a sofa. She let me take her without flinching,

without a word, without a single quiver, and faced with that reaction I swore never to do it again.

When Simenon gave up trying to save his marriage with Denise he did not begin to feel indifference for her. The passion that had been born in Manhattan in 1945 was not over, it had simply changed its form, and was now to be expressed in a hatred that was every bit as absorbing as the love had been. 'I never really understood the hate that my husband vowed towards me,' she says today. 'He hated me in the same way that he loved me. He hated me as *possessively* as he loved me.' It was a feeling that was to dominate the last twenty-five years of Simenon's life.

Simenon had sought in Denise the ideal companion. When things were going well between them he said that Denise was five people in one: she was his wife, his mistress, the mother of his children, the keeper of his house, and his agent. He also wanted a sixth person, the tender companion, the person who would, for the first time in his life, supply him with the affection and security which his mother had denied him and which his close friendship with Tigy had failed to supply. But Denise was a perfectionist, which sometimes made her over conscientious, exasperatingly inefficient and fatally inattentive to her husband. She began to feel overwhelmed by his demands and to stand up for herself in a very American way. 'One of the reasons why he began to hate me was that I was very frank,' she says. 'I wanted Simenon to understand *who* I was. I suppose I was too American to submit to him.' She was given far too much to do – being one woman is quite difficult, being five is more difficult. And as she withdrew into her daily tasks he began to feel deserted, 'a stranger in his own house'. Simenon could be a violent man, but Denise says that his violence was not the reason for their separation. Once when Marie-Jo saw her father hitting her mother Denise comforted the little girl by saying that he had been hitting her because he was angry and that he would get rid of his anger in his next novel. Simenon himself admits that he once hit Denise without intending to, because he was still *en roman*, acting out one of his characters. She noticed after they returned to Europe that he began to drink more when he had finished a novel, while he was getting rid of his *personnages*.

And frequently his violence occurred '*quand il était pris avec ses fantômes*', her words for his obsessive jealousy.

Simenon's jealousy was a consequence of the complete physical and romantic passion he had for Denise, the only time he experienced passion in his life. His love for his mother had been rejected, his love for Tigy had been limited; when his passion for Denise also failed, he became frightened. The characters who entered his imagination reflected this fear; and as his own unhappiness increased he found them increasingly hard to get rid of, and he found their preoccupations more difficult to get rid of. Just as his mother had a lifelong fear of poverty, so he had a lifelong fear of not being loved. They were both dominated by the fear that their childhood phantoms might return.

FOURTEEN

The man in the glass cage

'Why did you come, son?'
Remark made to Simenon by his mother as he reached her
death-bed.

(1970)

In September 1966 Simenon, aged 63 and the best-selling author in the world, took part in a public tribute to his most famous character, Commissaire Maigret. Leaving his newly built thirty-room mansion above Lausanne he flew to Amsterdam, where he was met by forty of his publishers, including four from Bulgaria, and was escorted to the Hotel Amstel which had been block-booked for the occasion.* Simenon was installed in a new suite which had been specially constructed for the state visit of Elizabeth II. A banquet followed; there were speeches, dancing, a press conference, interviews. On the day following the cele-brations a private train carried the entire party northwards to the little town of Delfzijl where a municipal reception had been arranged. Four of the actors who had played the part of Maigret on television or in the cinema were present for the unveiling of a statue of the *commissaire*. A further banquet was provided in the

---

* It is a measure of his success at this period that he had abandoned the usual basis of an author's earnings, which is payment by a 10 per cent royalty on sales, and substituted a high, one-off, advance payment. He was exasperated by the amount of time and money involved in supervising the royalty payment system and preferred to have the money immediately and forget about the subsequent sales. The new policy was instituted in 1965, shortly after the final departure of Denise.

Pavillon restaurant where Simenon said he had first imagined the character of the massive policeman. Then another private train, equipped with a mobile television studio, a band and a dancing car, carried the revellers back to a railway station outside Amsterdam which had been closed so that dancing could continue on the platform far into the night. The celebrations lasted three days; then Simenon flew home and wrote *Le chat*. This book was partly inspired by the second marriage of Henriette, who was by then aged 87, and Simenon described it as the cruellest book he had ever written. It told of how a widow and a widower who have remarried grow to hate each other. They start to keep their separate food supplies locked up in separate cupboards, for fear of being poisoned. Marcel Achard wrote to Simenon in April 1967 saying that *Le chat* was 'one of your most frightening books' and noted the difference in atmosphere between Simenon's most recent work and the books he had written before the war. 'The characters become harder and harder, culminating in the brutal savagery of *Le chat*,' Achard complained. Simenon's mother was plainly identifiable as the original of the widow who remarried a widower to gain the security of his pension. The separately locked cupboards of food were actually installed at 5 rue de l'Enseignement during the marriage of Henriette and Joseph André. Simenon made matters worse by writing *Le chat* from the point of view of the widower, who comes across as the more sympathetic character of the two. Given that he wrote this novel quite soon after the departure of Denise, it may be that he was subconsciously blaming his mother for the failure of his own second marriage. But there is one lighter element in the story. In striking contrast to the sequence of novels described earlier, sex in *Le chat*, between the widower and the barmaid, Nelly, is a cheerful experience. This had also been the case in *Le petit saint*, written only six months after Denise's final departure from Epalinges.

By the time of the celebrations in Delfzijl Simenon's final separation from Denise had lasted for over two years, yet the picture he gave both to the world at large and to many of his closest friends was that of a happy man, the centre of a large family, living in a household which was presided over by Mme Simenon. Earlier, in 1960, when the crisis between Simenon and Denise had already reached an advanced state, Henry Miller, who had known them for several years, who had been staying with them and who felt so close to Simenon that he said he was 'almost a brother', wrote to say that he would 'never achieve the perfection' Simenon had arrived at in his marriage. In September 1965, more than a year after Denise had left the house for ever, Pagnol, one of only eight correspondents who called Simenon '*tu*', sent Denise love and kisses. And Renoir, who was just as close a friend, was writing cheerfully to 'Georges and Denise' from 1966 to 1969. The fact that Simenon hid the truth about his marriage for so long suggests that he may have had hopes of saving it after Denise's departure.

Some friends of Simenon who visited Epalinges regularly, such as Bernard de Fallois, think that the peculiar atmosphere of the house commented on by many visitors has been exaggerated. And it is true that Charlie Chaplin, for example, wrote in June 1965 thanking Simenon for a 'superb lunch, superb wine [in] your beautiful house and swimming pool . . . The overcast weather had left me depressed and pessimistic until I had that charming visit with you . . .' But more casual visitors were otherwise impressed. There were several curious features about the arrangements. A chute led down from each bedroom to a central laundry room where six washing machines were in continuous operation under the supervision of a fulltime laundress. Ever the optimist, Simenon had installed a bed in his own room which was big enough for four. Many of the other rooms were wired for sound, on the excuse that the children must be heard in case they cried or hurt themselves when they were unsupervised. The result was that by flicking a switch Simenon could listen in to almost any room in the house. There was a complicated system of corridors, and at the end of two of them were identical portraits of Simenon by Bernard Buffet. Some said that Simenon had had the portrait duplicated to make it more difficult for thieves to steal the original, and that only he knew which was which. But the effect was to confuse guests as to exactly which part of the house they were in. The myth grew that in a house wired for sound the guests wandered, lost, repeatedly finding themselves confronted by the same impassive picture of their host. Miron Grindea, who visited Simenon in January 1966, twenty months after Denise's last exit, was told that she was resting in a nearby nursing home. Grindea was driven to Epalinges by 'Gino', the impeccably gloved Italian chauffeur who had met him with the Rolls. 'A hygienic silence reigned over the house,' recalled Grindea, although Simenon was *hors roman*. But the following week he would be *en roman*. He had just finished *Maigret et l'affaire Nahour* (*Maigret and the Nahour Case*) and was about to begin *La mort d'Auguste* (*The Old Man Dies*). He was supposed to be resting but 'he behaved like a slave to a ferocious routine', wrote Grindea:

> up at dawn, checking every aspect of the household, ovens, refrigerators, laundry-chutes . . . out for long walks through the woods, then to bed at 10 sharp. At least one kilometre round the stronghold was Simenon territory so that no new building would disturb his peace . . . [This was an exaggeration.] From early morning until dusk nothing unusual disturbed the routine except a few transatlantic calls or the arrival of several more 'Simenons' from countries as far apart as Argentina, Bulgaria, Japan, Israel. In the adjacent room I sized up the various sets of translations, some 18,000 volumes . . . At lunch Simenon sat at one end of the table, Marie-Jo [then 12] at the other . . . Caviare and wine in abundance, but the host drank only water and ate little. (Gino told me later that the master never went to his room without his bottle of whisky.)

For some reason Miron Grindea, who had been told that he could not make his visit when Simenon was writing a novel, described his host's need for total peace as 'maniacal'. Another obituarist, searching for an example of Simenon's extreme social attitudes, said that his children were not allowed to interrupt their parents when they were talking.

With the departure of Denise from Epalinges on 21 April 1964 all the duties of parenthood were assumed by Simenon, without regrets. He was a devoted father but he could be a frightening one. When the children called him 'The Godfather' it was an appropriate joke. At that time Johnny was 14, Marie-Jo was 11 and Pierre was only 4. If he was *en roman* the children were kept out of his way. When he took a break from his typewriter they could watch him from an upper-floor window as he walked alone in the garden, and from the way in which he walked they would guess what sort of character he was writing about. The children were frightened of his anger, according to both Denise and his friends; he was an impatient man and he had a confusing way of being generous and indulgent one moment and unexpectedly strict and tight-fisted the next. He sometimes withheld money from his children because he did not want them to grow up spoiled, but he did not understand that it was impossible to re-create his own impoverished childhood artificially. Epalinges had twenty-two principal rooms and an additional servants' wing. Each of the children had their own bathroom, 'to avoid disputes'. The swimming pool had a domed glass roof, the servants' dining room seated twelve, and there was a massage room for the master, which journalists soon transformed into an operating theatre. Simenon himself said later of his life alone in Epalinges that he felt ill at ease in the great house with its Adam or Louis XV furniture and that he began once again to drink. In November 1964 he dismissed Boule, after thirty-nine years; in tears she left her '*petit monsieur joli*' and went to live with Marc, who by then had children of his own.

Among those who came to visit Simenon was his mother. Henriette arrived in May 1967, three months after the publication of *Le chat*, a book which she had read as she read everything her son wrote when it came out, sometimes reproving him for writing about such immoral characters. (Simenon is said to have replied that if he wrote about himself it would be worse.) Simenon was aware that if he was ever to repair relations with his mother he had not much time left but the visit was not a great success from his point of view. Henriette was astonished by the size of Epalinges and questioned the servants closely to find out whether or not her son had paid for the house. She was offered one of the main guest rooms but asked to be moved to the children's television room, which was smaller. Having received no satisfaction from the rest of the staff, Henriette then asked Boule, who had returned for her visit and whom she had known for years, whether her son 'had many debts'. One day, when Henriette did not appear for breakfast, she was discovered lying on the floor of her room, pinned under a wardrobe which had fallen on top of her as she tried to hide some packages on top of it. The packages contained gold coins which represented all the money she had saved and which she was keeping for her grand-children. Later on the same day she handed Simenon an envelope containing all the money he had sent her over the years, a gesture which he admired, but which also hurt him deeply. It was Henriette's response to *Le chat*.

Simenon reproached himself after his mother's death for not having written to her more frequently. Henriette kept a number of his letters, which show a son who was an irregular correspondent but, from a distance at least, attentive and affectionate. On 24 September 1959 he wrote to her from Echandens about the death of his first cousin Lucien Brüll, a distinguished surgeon who had died in Liège at a comparatively young age. 'I hardly knew him,' Simenon wrote.

> I only saw him once, that day when as a young student with a beard he came to see you in the rue de l'Enseignement and took your photograph while you stood on the doorstep . . . I would have liked to have met him. On my last trip to Liège [probably in 1956] I asked him to a reception given by my colleagues, but he let them know that he would not be coming. Perhaps he did not want to meet me?

The letter seems to have been the first he had sent her since December 1958. In it he gives the ages of his children and adds, 'Denise is in top form. We are working hard, as you can see from the newspapers. We live all the same in the calm atmosphere of our village and travel very little. We think of you a lot.' Simenon added that he wished his mother would agree to take a maid to live in the house with her.

In November 1959 Simenon wrote to Henriette to tell her that Pierre had recovered from his dangerous illness, and sent further short letters in the following April and August. In November 1961 he paid one of his rare visits to Liège. If he was going to appear on the television he would write to his mother to alert her beforehand; otherwise his letters, addressed to '*Chère petite maman*' if written by hand, or '*Ma chère maman*' if typed, are rather stiff in style and concentrate on news about the children.

Henriette was quite a celebrity in Liège by this time, mainly as a result of *Pedigree*. The rue Pasteur had been renamed after her son, and in 1968 Belgian television interviewed her 'on the occasion of her 90th birthday'. (She was in fact aged 88.) When the writer and literary critic John Raymond called on her in 1966 Henriette, aged

86, was already claiming to be 92. 'She received me with great kindness,' wrote Raymond.

> A frail old lady with piercing blue eyes and a dramatic whisper. 'Have you read Georges's latest book?' she said, tapping *La mort d'Auguste* on a table near her armchair, her voice sinking a shade lower. 'It is about a missing will, monsieur . . .'

Henriette told John Raymond that '*Georges aimait toujours les petites gens*' and that he was '*très fier . . . mais, voyez-vous, monsieur, c'était une fierté très mal placée*'. Georges was actually writing *Le chat* while this maternal tribute and rebuke were being spoken.

As Henriette's strength began to fail she moved in 1969 from her house on Outremeuse to the old people's home run by the same Ursuline community of which Georges's aunt, Sister Marie-Madeleine, had been a lifelong member. Georges went to visit her in April and August that year, but put off another visit at the end of the year firstly because of work and then because he himself fell ill. The Reverend Mother Superior Marie-Germaine wrote to him in December 1969 saying that his mother was not well, and he replied on 6 January 1970 noting that he could see from her letters that Henriette was losing her memory. He was not able to visit her, however, and he added, rather unconvincingly, 'If only one could take the plane to Liège as one can to Brussels.' In the summer Henriette recovered some of her health. Simenon wrote again to Reverend Mother Marie-Germaine on 9 July saying that he could not visit, this time because his daughter was in a psychiatric clinic suffering from serious depression. On 20 October Simenon wrote his last letter to Henriette referring to a visit he had recently been able to make and telling her that he had just finished a novel (*La disparition d'Odile*, based on Marie-Jo's illness). He signed it '*Toute ma tendresse, chère petite maman.*' On 16 November he wrote to Reverend Mother Marie-Germaine asking for news, and it was shortly afterwards that he was summoned to Liège because Henriette had undergone an operation and was expected to die. He spent a week with her before her death on 8 December. She had been moved from the old people's home back on to Outremeuse, to the Hôpital de Bavière, the same hospital where he had served the 6 a.m. Mass sixty years before. When he walked into her room she looked at him and said, 'Why did you come, son?' In *Lettre à ma mère* he wrote later, 'We never loved each other while you lived, as you know well. But we made it look as though we did.' And in *Un homme comme un autre* he wrote that he had known more tenderness with prostitutes than he ever had with his mother.

Simenon described his feelings about his mother's death in *Lettre à ma mère*, which he dictated, as though he were reading a letter, in April 1974, more than three years after the event. Suddenly, for one week, he had found himself back on Outremeuse, making a daily visit to the Hôpital de Bavière, just as he had done when he was the little boy who carried the Sanctus bell before the priest on his way to visit the dying. His mother's funeral service had been held at her request in the hospital chapel, the chapel she had sent him to every day before he first began to suspect the truth about her indifference towards him. When Henriette died his imaginary world died too. He, who had written four to five novels a year every year for forty years, stopped writing novels twelve months after her death. It was as though he had no one left to write them for. With her death the major emotional battle in his life was over. She had had the last word but he had not yet suffered his final wound.

In the years following Denise's departure from Epalinges, Simenon's production of *romans* and 'Maigrets' continued at a steady pace. From 1965 to 1971 he wrote between three and four books a year. After *La porte* he wrote *Les anneaux de Bicêtre*, which received high praise, and the *romans* written at Epalinges include several of his best, such as *Le petit saint*, *La mort d'Auguste*, *Le chat* and *Il y a encore des noisetiers* (1968). He was not, needless to say, leading a celibate life, but had come to rely on Teresa Sburelin. Teresa was affectionate and the soul of tact, and for years she insisted on addressing Simenon as 'monsieur'. In the crisis that lay ahead Simenon turned to her more and more. In December 1965, after Denise's departure, he fell one night in the bathroom at Epalinges after drinking too much and succeeded in breaking several ribs. It was Teresa who eventually heard his cries for help and who rescued him from his predicament. She accompanied him to the hospital, slept in a cot beside his bed, nursed him, and from then on scarcely left his side until the moment when she scattered his ashes under the cedar tree. Like Denise, Teresa had been introduced by a publisher. Like Denise, Teresa's relationship with Simenon was ratified when she began to nurse him. She accompanied him everywhere, including to Delfzijl, but she kept in the background and it was years before the true nature of their relationship was made generally known. Since Simenon did not speak Italian they conversed in French. Teresa's French was 'usable', one friend recalls, and she used it without inhibition; 'she was very *bavarde*' (talkative).

In public Simenon continued to present the road show which he had started to devise in 1925 when he was interviewed by *Paris-Soir*. In 1963 he gave a virtuoso performance in a long television interview with Roger Stephane, the best and the most revealing published conversation he ever had about his work with anyone and the intellectual sequel to his essay on Balzac. He approached the interview like a world tennis finals, watching his interviewer in a quizzical, hostile way that made the conversation even more interesting for his audience. A worldly-wise observer might have thought that the hostility was assumed – Roger Stephane had after all commissioned Simenon's talk on Balzac – but Stephane has since made it clear that Simenon's intimidating manner was not assumed. It was in this interview that Simenon, goaded by Stephane's reference to the celebrated paradox that he was both a 'good' novelist and a highly popular and prolific one ('*un cas*'), finally lost his temper. When asked yet again about this curious dual achievement he referred to Lope de Vega, Dickens, Balzac, Dostoevsky and Victor Hugo, insisting that there was nothing peculiar about his status at all. 'Too many people today who are writing novels are not novelists,' he said.

> The novelist has always worked like an artisan, nobody marvels at the number of canvases painted by Matisse or Vlaminck . . . The art which is practised in two months or two years by sitting in Menton or Florence, dreaming or thinking, is not the art of the novel . . . A novelist enters the flesh of his characters, and has a need to live with other characters inside himself . . . A novelist is a person who writes because he needs to write, who does not ask himself whether a sentence should cover one line, one and a half lines or ten lines, but who quite simply works to perfect his craft from one day to the next. There is no such thing as '*le cas Simenon*'. I am not a case, I would be

appalled to be 'a case'. I am simply a novelist, that is all . . . Why am I considered 'a case'? Because people today no longer write, except occasionally at St Tropez. Say that some generations suffer from anaemia, but don't say that I am 'a case'. I . . . am . . . Normal.

The interview took place at Echandens in October 1963, when Denise's behaviour, on the eve of the move to Epalinges, had reached a peak of oddity. This was the period when according to her husband she had taken to chasing the children round the house at night. In the circumstances Simenon's behaviour was surprisingly normal – almost abnormally so.

In June 1968 Simenon gave another bravura performance, this time in front of an invited panel of five doctors who spent a day at Epalinges questioning him for seven hours. The encounter was subsequently published in the twenty-fifth anniversary issue of the Swiss magazine *Médecine et Hygiène*, and was once again a rich source of information about Simenon's unusual working methods. Simenon explained that before he could start to write he had to empty himself of his own personality so that he could attain 'the state of grace' which allowed him to enter that purely receptive frame of mind where he could be taken over by his principal character. The detail which he sought, which allowed him to start his story, was often a *fait divers* – it could be a road accident, a heart attack or an inheritance; what was essential was that it should 'quite suddenly alter the course of the character's life'. Simenon also mentioned the importance of smell in his memory, and said that he still had the habit occasionally of going to the linen cupboard in Epalinges and opening it so that he could smell the piles of freshly laundered and ironed sheets – 'they represent for me the ideal of the peaceful life'. (The doctors pointed out that Epalinges had nonetheless a curiously aseptic and odourless atmosphere.) Simenon also gave the doctors an apologia for his life's work, and in particular in relation to Maigret, the '*redresseur des destins*' (the mender of destinies):

The only way in which a writer can help a reader is by demonstrating that every human being has a dark side as well as a light side to him, of which he is more or less ashamed . . . When the reader meets a fictional character who has the same symptoms as he has, he says, 'So I'm not alone after all, I am not a monster.' And that can help. I want to show my readers that the personal dramas which they are struggling with, and of which they are ashamed, are not theirs alone, and that many other human beings suffer from the same torments, even people who one can love and who can occupy an enviable position in the world.

Earlier de Fallois had written, 'When the reader leaves one of [Simenon's] nightmares, while he still has the bitter taste of that weakness, fear and solitude in his mouth, he finds, without quite knowing why, that he himself feels a little less solitary and a little stronger.'

The interview with the five doctors did not go to the limits of Simenon's creative experience; it did not, for instance, mention something that Denise had realised – that Simenon himself did not understand exactly how he wrote. His writing depended on a mechanism that he could not start; he had to wait for it to start of its own accord; it was something he could not control. He could never be sure when or whether it would happen again, and that sometimes frightened him. 'He had always wanted to write,' says Denise, 'but he never understood *how* he was able to write. He considered it a kind of miracle.' The other aspect that he never fully understood or explored was the relationship between his writing and his subconscious, as manifested in his sleepwalking. Simenon, like many children, walked in his sleep. But in his case the habit continued into old age. Denise says that when they were together he sleepwalked only once, in Tucson, Arizona, when she woke one night to find him trying to climb up the bedroom wall. But after they broke up the habit revived, and in one of his autobiographical *Dictées*, *Un banc au soleil*, written in 1975, he ascribed two nights of insomnia to the full moon; he had recorded sleepwalking on another occasion two years earlier. He sometimes compared the trance he entered when he wrote a *roman dur* to a kind of sleepwalking. In any event, the last time 'the miracle' occurred was in October 1971, when Simenon completed his final novel, *Les innocents* (*The Innocents*). The last 'Maigret', *Maigret et M. Charles* (*Maigret and Monsieur Charles*), was finished in February 1972. When Simenon sat down to begin a new novel, 'Victor', or 'Oscar', on 18 September he found he had nothing to write. Two days later he abandoned the book and in February 1973 he summoned a reporter from a local paper and announced that he would write no more. In the memoirs which he dictated following his retirement he said, 'I no longer needed to put myself in the skin of everyone I met . . . I exulted, I was free at last.' The phantoms of his imagination had finally been laid to rest.

Simenon's last publicity coup occurred in 1977, and in some ways it was his greatest coup of all, for it produced the best-known remark he ever made. To publicise Fellini's new film *Casanova*, an agent in Rome thought it would be a good idea to arrange for Fellini to be interviewed by Simenon, who remained one of his leading admirers and a regular correspondent. The admiration was mutual. In August 1976, while he was still shooting the film, Fellini had written to Simenon saying that *Casanova* had been going very badly until he had had a curious dream. He had dreamed that he was asleep and that he was awakened by the noise of a typewriter. He had been sleeping in a garden and the noise came from a tower. Then the noise stopped. Fellini tiptoed to a circular window and peeped through. Inside was a room, white-washed like a cell. A monk facing the other way was busy doing something Fellini could not see. A dozen children seated at his feet were playing, touching his sandals and his cord. The monk turned. It was Simenon. He had a little white beard, obviously false. Then a voice whispered, '"It's false." "What is he doing?" I asked. "He's painting his new novel, it's about Neptune."' The next morning Fellini found that he had recovered from his depression and could continue work on his film. 'So, my *très cher ami*, Simenon – *maître de vie et de créativité* – intervenes like a magician to work miracles,' Fellini's letter concluded.

The interview with Fellini took place in Lausanne and was the cover-story in *L'Express* on 21 February 1977, a week after Simenon's 74th birthday. Fellini was 57. The two friends, much to Simenon's pleasure, spent the day together. The interview ran a more or less interesting course, with Simenon playing his role of interviewer almost without interruption, until towards the end when, following a remark from Fellini about the fact that he himself always made love wearing a bra, Simenon suddenly said, *à propos* of nothing that had gone before:

'You know, Fellini, I think that in my life I have been even
more of a Casanova than you. I did the sum a year or two ago
and since the age of 13 and a half I have had 10,000 women. It
was not at all a vice, I suffer from no sexual vice, but I have a
need to communicate. And even the 8000 prostitutes who must
be included in this total of 10,000 women were human beings,
female human beings . . . but one does not necessarily find
human contact merely by searching for it. One generally finds a
void, don't you think?

The curious result of this interjection was that it made Simenon
more famous than ever, and provided far more publicity for him
than it did for Fellini's *Casanova*. John Simenon, who was present
throughout this meeting, is certain that there was nothing calculated about it: his father simply mentioned something that came
into his head at that moment; so if it was a publicity coup it was a
subconscious one.

In the years following his retirement as a novelist Simenon set
to work on the *Dictées*, twenty-one volumes of memoirs dictated
into a tape-recorder. They emphasised the fact that his account of
his own life is not always reliable. In *Quand j'étais vieux*, written
between 1960 and 1963, he had already described *Je me souviens*
(1940) as 'often inaccurate', and *Pedigree* (1940–43) as 'not really
accurate'. And in the first of the *Dictées*, *Un homme comme un autre*
(1973), he described *Quand j'étais vieux* as 'contradictory'. He later
explained that this was because Denise had been reading it and
that he had had to falsify many passages.

It was after the death of Henriette that Simenon started to attack
Denise (who was by now once more spelling her name 'Denyse')
in his writings. With Denyse at least he did not follow his own
motto of *'comprendre et ne pas juger'*. The first serious assault was
mounted in *Lettre à ma mère*, when he associated his blind passion
for Denyse, whom *he* now referred to as 'D', with his guilt about
his mother: 'It was during the journey to Liège in 1952. My
second wife, "D", accompanied me and strove to occupy as
prominent a place as possible,' he wrote. Later in the same book,
referring to the war of the corsets, he said, 'D, who always had a
mania for poking around in the drawers and the private business
of other people . . .' and later still, 'On the one hand D, proud,

aggressive, pitiless, and on the other this little woman from Liège, dressed in her oldest clothes . . .'

By the time *Lettre à ma mère* was published Marie-Jo was 21. Simenon had made her into his favourite child and his privileged companion, and she offered him a level of adoration which at least equalled that which he had offered his own father. But Marie-Jo was not, unfortunately, nearly as robust a character as either of her parents. She was confused and distracted by the merciless battle that broke out between them, particularly when Simenon told her, apparently on the advice of Dr Durand, that he did not want her to go on seeing her mother. Johnny, who was older, generally took his father's side in the conflict, and was anyway able to escape from the house and pursue his studies before too much time had passed. He is also adamant that his father never prevented him from seeing his mother. Pierre was young enough to be sheltered from many of the worst aspects of the battle. But Marie-Jo was both the most fragile and the most exposed of the children, and much as she adored her father, she also loved her mother, and she was torn by her loyalty to both of them.

Simenon recounted the course of his relationship with Marie-Jo in *Mémoires intimes*. When she was young he would take her to a children's shop in Lausanne and choose her clothes with her. This innocent activity was taken much more seriously by his daughter than he realised and one day when they were passing a jeweller's window Marie-Jo asked him to buy her a gold wedding ring. She was 8. As she grew she had the ring enlarged, and she wore it for the rest of her life. When she died she asked that she be cremated wearing the ring and that her ashes be scattered beneath the cedar tree in her father's garden.

When they went on holiday together Marie-Jo insisted that her father dance with her. Her favourite tune was 'Tennessee Waltz', and the musicians became accustomed to playing this early each evening when the little girl sat down with her father at the table nearest the bandstand. When Marie-Jo was 9 her mother told her about her father's new relationship with Teresa. A psychiatrist was first summoned to examine her in 1964, when she was 11, shortly before she went on a skiing holiday to Villars, alone with her mother. When she became a teenager she wrote love songs and poems to her father, aware by now that she had '*un complexe de père*' and even able to joke about it with her mother. When her mother and father quarrelled she told the servants at Epalinges that she was frightened her mother would kill her father one day. Simenon tried to hide his physical relations with Teresa from the children but, according to Denyse, he was not always successful as far as Marie-Jo was concerned. When Marie-Jo completed her studies and went to Paris and started to lead her own life her relationship with her father remained unusually close. Twice she chose lovers of an older generation. In Paris she regularly ran out of money and regularly had to borrow from friends. She gave a lot of money to a waiter who exploited her. But she had various lifelines of her own. She had her hopes of making a career, as a singer, or a writer, or an actress. Marc, who was fifteen years older than her, did what he could to support her and protect her from the storm. She also received treatment from a number of psychiatrists. According to the harsh verdict of one of her doctors in Paris she was bound to commit suicide one day because psychologically she was like a snail removed from its shell, she had no spine. She made six unsuccessful suicide bids; then, in 1978, when she was 25, the situation once more became too much for her, and on 20 May, in her apartment on the Champs-Elysées, after making a last telephone call to her father, she shot herself through the heart with a rifle.

It was about this period that Simenon wrote in *Mémoires intimes*, 'One never recovers from the loss of a daughter one has cherished. It leaves a void that nothing can fill.' Simenon had many thoughtless actions to reproach himself with concerning his daughter. One of them was the publication in 1971, when she was 17 and had just suffered her first nervous breakdown, of *La disparition d'Odile*, a novel that described the mental breakdown, flight from Lausanne to Paris and attempted suicide of a young girl who strongly resembled his daughter. Marie-Jo was the only one of his children who devotedly read everything he wrote; and indeed in one of her earlier suicide notes, addressed to her father, she had quoted a phrase from one of his novels, *Les autres* (*The Others*).

But the biggest single blow Marie-Jo suffered was from her father's relationship with Teresa. Marie-Jo accepted that another woman should be the first person in his life, so long as that woman was her mother, but she was unable to accept that her mother could be replaced by Teresa. After her death her father tried to blame the tragedy on Denyse, convinced that it stemmed from the mental trauma inflicted by an incestuous gesture made by her mother during the holiday they had taken together in Villars, in February 1964. He also wrote that Marie-Jo's *'complexe de père'* was so serious that she had wanted to replace Teresa in his bed. Denyse denies the story about Villars, but also denies that her daughter would ever have suggested incest to Simenon. 'That was the devilish side of Simenon,' she says. Bernard de Fallois, who knew all three people involved extremely well, says that what really hurt Marie-Jo was her father's decision to reorganise the house he shared with Teresa in the avenue des Figuiers, so that when she came to see him in Lausanne she could no longer stay there.

It seems that at a certain point in the battle between her father and her mother Marie-Jo began to feel sorry for her mother. Contrary to what Simenon wrote in *Mémoires intimes*, she continued to have quite a good relationship with her mother before she died. They went together to see the young actor Roger Mirmont in *Hair*, and on the way Marie-Jo said, 'You are the only mother one could take to see one's boyfriend for the first time when he is completely nude.' She always hoped that her parents would one day come together again, but she was sufficiently aware of the problems to ask her mother not to come to Paris, 'because he would turn against me'. After her suicide Simenon felt responsible for it, and tried to pass his responsibility to Denyse in *Mémoires intimes*. But the problem was more intractable than he realised. Marie-Jo could never accept that the days in Burgenstock, when she had been 8 and had worn her father's ring and waltzed with him, would never come back. 'Remember me as the little girl of the *Tennessee Waltz*,' she wrote to him in one of her suicide notes.

The death of Marie-Jo was preceded by a major public offensive between her parents. After years of embittered correspondence on the subject of a divorce, which Simenon always refused to give Denyse, Denyse Simenon published in April 1978 her account of the marriage, *Un oiseau pour le chat*, which was billed as *'le mariage de Mme Maigret'*. Simenon watched a French television broadcast, intended to publicise the book, which consisted of a long attack on himself. So did Marie-Jo, who also bought the book and annotated her copy heavily in the margin. Her suicide one month after its publication was followed by a brief period of grief-stricken silence which was shortly afterwards broken by the renewed recriminations of her parents, this time disputing responsibility for her death.

In September 1978, four months after the death of Marie-Jo, Georges Simenon received a visitor from Liège. His way of life by this time was very different from the syle of Epalinges. In 1972, having tried and failed to write a successor to *Les innocents* and having declared his career over, he had put the great mansion on the market, dismissed ten of the eleven servants and moved to an eighth-floor flat in a tower block in central Lausanne. A year later, feeling uneasy up in his tower block, he had made his last move, to a little house with a garden which he could see from his apartment windows, a house dominated by a cedar tree, reputed to be the oldest tree in Lausanne. 'I'm happy at Lausanne,' Simenon said in 1973. 'I have never had anyone ringing my doorbell without an invitation.'

It was to this house, by invitation, that Mathieu Rutten, a retired professor of philology from the University of Liège, came on 19 September 1978. The year before Rutten had published in the Flemish language the book which was the culmination of his lifetime hobby – not philology, but the genealogy of Georges Simenon. He called his book *Simenon: ses origines, sa vie, son oeuvre* and the basis of it was a manhunt going back over 200 years from the writer's birth in 1903 and covering both his mother's and his father's sides of the family.

Simenon referred to Rutten's visit in an unpublished essay entitled 'Les cinq sens' (*The Five Senses*) written in the summer of 1980:

A professor from the University of Liège, of Flemish origin, had the curiosity to trace the Simenons back as far as possible, and he travelled patiently through the villages of the Belgian Limbourg, then of the Dutch Limburg and finally to that part of Germany which borders those two provinces. By means of consulting the community and parish registers which still exist he was able to go back as far as the seventeenth century where, in Vlijtingen, he found a Simenon who followed the most humble of occupations, that of casual agricultural labourer, a man who hired himself out by the day or the season . . . There were also one or two priests, a miller, and finally a first cousin of my grandfather who was an auxiliary bishop who bore the same name as me and whom I vaguely knew.

As a summary of Rutten's monumental work this is somewhat inadequate. Simenon mentions the fictional 'Bishop Simenon', but ignores the life and death of an ancestor who had far more influence over his fate. The man Simenon overlooked was called Gabriel Brüll. In 1743 a band of twelve robbers or highwaymen who had been roaming for seventeen years through the Limbourg in Belgium, Holland and Germany were arrested and tried. They were known as 'Les Verts-Boucs' (the Green Rams), on account of their clothing and their practice of rustling cattle and goats. Found guilty of numerous acts of brigandage, murder and burglary from farms, churches, presbyteries and dwelling-houses, the twelve, who included Gabriel Brüll, were sentenced to be hanged from the public gibbet in Ubach-over-Worms in the Dutch Limburg. Before Brüll was hanged he was burnt at the stake, and afterwards his body was cut down from the gallows and disembowelled. The body could not be buried in consecrated ground and a funeral service was forbidden. His family had to reimburse the costs of his trial and execution. Gabriel Brüll was the great-grandfather of Georges Simenon's great-grandfather, the novelist's direct ancestor six generations back.

Following the execution of Gabriel Brüll a fugitive tendency entered the Brüll family story. The Brülls moved to Prussia and the links with their notorious Dutch cousins were deliberately obscured. It was Rutten's work which established that the Brülls were scarcely German at all; they were Flemish. Simenon had one Prussian great-great-grandmother. His grandfather, Wilhelm Brüll, born in Prussia, had returned to the Dutch Limburg to marry, but he had not settled there. He and his bride moved to the Belgian Limbourg, to 'the house by the canal'. The Brülls' fugitive tendency continued with the effects on their daughter Henriette that we have seen. She spent her life apologising for her existence, burying her family history and withholding her love.

On the Simenon side of the family there were further surprises. In the first place Rutten established that there was no family connection with Brittany or any other part of France. The

Simenons, down to his grandfather Chrétien (Christiaan), had been born and grown up in Flemish villages, speaking Flemish. Simenon once told Fellini, in a letter dated 3 January 1977, 'Unlike you, dear Fellini, my life has been a succession of departures, probably for lack of an anchor, because I come from no country, whereas you are and will probably always be, above all, a Roman.' Rutten, although much too late to be of use, provided Simenon with an anchor. Simenon was not of mixed Walloon, Breton, Flemish and Prussian descent. He was essentially Flemish, and his country was the Flemish Limbourg.

Rutten's visit confirmed a feeling which Simenon had acknowledged two years earlier. 'I was always certain,' he wrote in 1976,

> that I was influenced by my father's side of the family . . . I realise today, at my age, that I owe just as much to my mother's descent. I have the same inheritance as my mother, though less extreme and balanced by the heritage of my father. But for a long time I thought I was a real Simenon. I now realise that is not true and that subconsciously I am deeply sensitive, almost hyper-sensitive.

And in 1974 Simenon had written in Lettre à ma mère that his family story was a mystery to him. Writing of his grandfather Wilhelm, later Guillaume, Brüll he had wondered why a German, born on the Dutch frontier, had moved to the Limbourg and then left it. 'There are great gaps in our family story as you, Mother, have recounted it to me,' he wrote. Rutten's lifework filled in those gaps. But did Simenon ever really absorb the information with which Rutten presented him? His letters to Rutten at the time of the visit are grateful, but noncommittal, and he did not receive the French edition of the book until 1986. He reluctantly renounced all claims on Brittany, but he never seems to have fully acknowledged his Flemish descent. In 'Les cinq sens' he was already beginning to reweave the legend, with more talk of his 'cousin the bishop' also 'called Georges Simenon'; the habit of story-telling was simply too strong for him.

No one I have spoken to who met Simenon after Rutten's visit remembers him mentioning Gabriel Brüll. Bernard de Fallois says that if Simenon had known of his connection with a man hanged for numerous murders and armed robberies, 'he would have been delighted'. It would certainly have been a striking confirmation of one of the author's favourite sayings: 'Every family has a skeleton in the cupboard.' The strange thing about Georges Simenon's family skeleton was that it was dangling from a gallows. The hanged man, the figure which had haunted him since he had first reported the death of Kleine and which features in so many of his books, sprang out again, at the end of his life, from the ranks of his ancestors.

In 1927 the entrepreneur Eugène Merle nearly succeeded in shutting Georges Simenon up in a glass cage for seven days and seven nights while he wrote a novel before the public's astonished gaze. The legend grew that he had actually done so, and it was many years before Simenon convinced people that the event had never taken place. But Simenon eventually accomplished a similar feat all by himself. He wrote *Mémoires intimes*, which was far more revealing than any novel written in a glass cage. When it came out in 1981 the book caused a sensation, mainly because of the frankness with which Simenon described his sex-life. But the stated purpose of *Mémoires intimes* was to explain the course of events to Marie-Jo, who had died three years earlier. It was a fictional letter to his daughter's ghost and as such a sequel to *Lettre à ma mère.*

'My darling little girl,' the book opens, 'I know that you are dead and yet this is not the first time that I have written to you.' His grief and horror run through an account which he frequently seems to be reliving as much as writing. The book is a lengthy justification of Simenon's private life, and an explanation of why he was not responsible for his daughter's death. As such it reads like a refusal to acknowledge an overwhelming feeling of guilt. The last section of the book is a transcript of tape-recordings left for him by Marie-Jo, and these are presented as proof that Denyse's conduct had driven Marie-Jo to suicide. However the transcript was heavily edited by Simenon before being published and is of little value as evidence. *Mémoires intimes* is also the work of a man who has given up inventing a fictional world and has started instead to select a fictional version of his own life. Like *Je me souviens*, written forty years earlier, under the stress of a different shock, *Mémoires intimes* is to some extent a self-justifying fable. Even in this, his final testament, written at the age of 77 in longhand with a Parker pen, Simenon shows himself to be a compulsive story-teller. Denyse, putting it bluntly, says, 'He started to lie when he could no longer write novels. And who did he lie about – me! Me!' The truth is perhaps a little more complicated, appropriately enough for a man who always gave so many different versions of it. While it is true that of all his '10,000 women' there was only one who consumed him to the point of obsession, there is a more significant pattern in Simenon's life – one of rejection.

The sense of worthlessness which Simenon identified in Balzac, and which he shared, the shame which drove him to accomplish great things, stemmed from his mother's low opinion of him and her rejection of his love. Originally his love for his mother was rejected. He then tried to reject his unhappy childhood by leaving Liège, leaving Europe, divorcing his Liégeoise wife and remarrying. Then he rejected America. He decided to leave it from one day to the next and never returned there again. On his visit to Liège in 1952 he watched his new wife and his mother lay the foundations of an enmity that was to last for as long as they knew each other, and he did nothing. He rejected his mother's invitation and chose the side of his wife. He told his wife that he actually hated his mother and she still believes it. Later he rejected his wife and tried to mend his relationship with his mother, but it was too late, and at Epalinges he was rejected by his mother again. He filled the hole in his heart with the love offered by Marie-Jo, but when this became too intense he rejected that too, with terrible, but foreseeable, consequences. Finally, returning to the scene of his childhood for his mother's death, he was rejected by her for the last time. She asked him why he had come to see her, and she told him that she wanted to be buried with her second husband, whom they had both detested, rather than with the father whom Simenon had idolised. As a consequence of this final rejection he wrote a book, *Lettre à ma mère*, which reads like an apology to his mother for not having been lovable enough. Even after her death he was trying to win her love. Much of his driven sexuality can be explained by his need for reassurance and for love. When he said that he made love 'in order to communicate', that was exactly what he meant. But as he told Fellini, 'It is not necessarily by looking for a human contact that one finds it. One usually finds a void, don't you think?' Bernard de Fallois, asked whether Simenon had a sense of humour, replies, 'Yes, about some things. *Mais le fond était tragique.*'

Simenon stopped going into his garden, which he liked very much, after Marie-Jo's ashes were scattered under the cedar tree. He remained a slave to routine, although he did less and less. A happy evening with his family, ending with reminiscences and champagne, would lead to recriminations in the morning because his routine had been broken. 'We practically had to make an appointment to see him after he moved to the avenue des Figuiers,' says John. Once his son Marc, in a fit of absentminded-ness, wrote to him to ask for Henriette's address, as he had not contacted her for some time. Simenon replied saying, 'Your grandmother's address is Plot X, Alley Y, the Cemetery of Robermont, Liège,' which confirms that he retained some sense of humour. On another occasion he became exasperated with his daughter-in-law and said, 'You take me for *un vieux con*, don't you?' Mylène replied, 'Yes,' and after that they got on much better. He received visits in the avenue des Figuiers, at different times, from both Tigy and Boule. Tigy, who had followed him back to Cannes and, when Marc was old enough, returned to her house at Nieul-sur-Mer, never remarried. In later life Simenon told some of his friends that she was a lesbian, but the truth is that she was never sufficiently interested in sex to be a lesbian, and although she had lesbian friends she preferred their company chiefly out of disappointment and disillusion with her husband's conduct towards her and towards his son. She remained friends with him, and became a grandmother to all his children, but she never understood how he could have broken up their family and harmed Marc, and broken his promises to her. In 1985 she sold her 'grandmother's house' at Nieul and moved down to Porquerolles to live with Marc and Mylène, and with Boule. She died shortly afterwards in the house where she and Simenon had stayed on their second visit to Porquerolles in 1927, and she is buried in the island's cemetery. In a letter to a mutual friend after her death her daughter-in-law Mylène Demongeot wrote, 'She was a woman of infinite dignity and discretion. In eighteen years she almost never made a bitter or vengeful remark.'

Boule lived with Georges Simenon for nearly forty years. In November 1964 she left Epalinges and went to live with Marc, whose two children by his first wife, Francette, were then aged 4 years and one month respectively. In *Mémoires intimes* Simenon said that he had been forced to ask Boule to leave because Denyse had sent a message from the clinic saying that she could not bear to think of Boule presiding over the household. Considering Simenon's fierce loyalty to Boule, and the fact that Denyse had herself left Epalinges for the last time seven months earlier, this version of events is unconvincing. Denyse says that it is quite untrue and that it was Teresa who insisted that Boule be asked to leave. Boule says that she left of her own accord to spend more time with Marc and his children. The truth seems to be that the decision was taken by Simenon because Boule, always a strong character, did not get on with Teresa at all and was inclined to rupture the domestic harmony of Epalinges, the one thing Simenon wanted never to happen again. The last time Boule saw Simenon was when he was staying at the Lausanne Palace for Easter in 1988. Boule was amazed to see Teresa wearing an apron even though she was a guest in the hotel's most luxurious suite. She also disapproved of the way in which Teresa's hair was pulled back behind her ears and so she (who was the older woman by 20 years) asked Simenon what he was doing '*avec ce vieux machin*'. Simenon said nothing in reply; Teresa laughed and told Boule she had not changed.

In 1991 Boule was living quietly in Marc's house at Porquerolles, aged 85, in reasonable health, and as outspoken as ever. She said that she had kept all the letters she had received from Simenon (whom she invariably called '*le père de Marc*'), written mostly when he was in America and she was in France. She had placed them in the bank and left instructions that they should be destroyed when she died. She also said that she refused to discuss her private life at all. Later I asked her what she thought about when she lay awake at night, and she replied, 'Oh, I hear you coming in your great clogs.' But she told me in due course that after she left Epalinges Simenon frequently wrote to her, and the envelope always contained '*un bon petit chèque*'. She added, '*Il était infiniment gentil avec moi.*' I asked her if they had used '*vous*' or '*tu*' with each other (in *Mémoires intimes* Simenon said that they had always used '*vous*'). She replied, 'We called each other "*vous*" at first. Then "*tu*", *dans l'intimité*, and sometimes in public when we forgot.' She said that she had fallen in love with Simenon immediately, and that he had fallen in love with her 'later'.

Some time after arriving in Porquerolles Boule wrote a short story which she called 'Le vieux navire'. Unfortunately the manuscript has been mislaid but she could remember something of what was in it. The story is in the Simenonian manner, since it is drawn from some of the real events of Boule's life. The first words were, 'Merde, alors! . . .' spoken by 'le vieux navire' (the old sailor) himself, Simenon, as he entered a ship's chandlers to purchase a ball of waxed twine which he needed to mend a sail. The girl whose family ran the shop, who was based on Tigy, went to fetch him the string. A beautiful young girl then entered the shop and fell into a conversation with 'le vieux navire' about how life was not what it used to be. 'Le vieux navire' then left the beautiful young girl and returned to his boat, where 'Teresa', thinking he looked unwell, made him a herbal tea from a recipe which her grandmother had given her. Boule explained that the suggestion in the story was that Teresa was a sorceress and that this in turn suggested a certain jealousy of Teresa on her own part. Boule said that during Simenon's lifetime she had been careful to keep the manuscript to herself, as she never wanted 'le père de Marc' to be troubled by the thought that *she* was capable of writing something about *him*. Shortly before my visit one of Boule's friends, who knew nothing about her life story, asked her why she had never married and she replied, 'Because my man did not want to marry me. But he gave me all his love.'

After leaving Simenon in 1964, Denyse asked him many times to agree to a divorce. He always refused, saying that as long as they were married he would maintain her but he would make sure she got nothing if she divorced him. At first Denyse moved to Avignon, where she qualified and practised for some time as a psychoanalyst. Then she moved back to Switzerland, and she now lives in the little town of Nyon, on the shore of Lake Geneva and only a short distance from the clinic at Prangins where she was staying when her marriage ended. She says that for years after she separated from Simenon she read only his books. Her first attack on him, Un oiseau pour le chat, was preceded by four years of provocation on his part – public attacks in Lettre à ma mère and Un homme comme un autre followed by his claim to have mounted 10,000 women (a figure which she recalculated at 1200). After the death of Marie-Jo, for which she believes she and Simenon together bear much of the responsibility, she wrote a satirical novel anticipating his death entitled *Le phallus d'or*, which was widely ignored at the time but which can be read as a *roman à clef*. It is a very funny portrait of the household of a rich old man who gives his Italian maid, also his mistress, a life-size solid gold phallus to remember him by. When he dies his family and secretary fall out over his will.

Denyse describes the decision to scatter Marie-Jo's ashes in Simenon's garden as 'obnoxious', and it is true that it deprived her of a grave to visit. She regrets that she did not fight harder to keep in touch with her children after she left Epalinges, but says that she was frightened of Simenon at the time. 'In this country,' she remarked, 'a rich man can do practically anything.' She too said that she had many passionate letters from Simenon, mostly written when she was in the clinic at Prangins. They were in the bank and she would leave them to her children. She last saw her husband walking slowly in the street in Lausanne, leaning on the arm of the woman she had once employed as her own maid. 'If he was so happy with Teresa,' she asks, 'why did he feel such an overwhelming need to demolish me?' One answer is suggested by the married couple in Simenon's novel *Le chat*. Their hatred 'had become their life. It was as natural to them, and as necessary . . . as politeness or embracing are to others.'

The highest compliment Simenon could pay a woman, the symbol of his complete trust, was to let her look after him when he was sick. The hero in *La veuve Couderc*, written when Simenon was 37, already wanted to be nursed by a woman who would 'lift him in her arms like a child, put him to bed . . . undress him, poultice him'. In 1961, in *Quand j'étais vieux*, Simenon noted how frequently rich elderly men marry their nurses. Bernard de Fallois says that Simenon appreciated Teresa because she was kind, attentive, affectionate, and because – above all – she never made a scene. Her life with Simenon would not have suited everyone. When he was dictating she had to sit with him and was forbidden even to read a book of her own, lest the noise of the pages being turned should distract him. If she wanted to read a book she had to get up in the middle of the night when he was asleep, and read it in the bathroom. Whereas Tigy, Boule and Denyse all remained true to themselves, Teresa was prepared to become whatever Simenon wanted. She was there to please him. Since his death Teresa has refused to talk about Simenon, but during a brief

conversation she told me that 'during his life I was his companion. Now I am nothing. He has left me just our memories and
they belong to me.' Asked if it was possible to visit the house in
the avenue des Figuiers, she said, 'No, the house belongs to me. It
is *un lieu de mémoire* and I do not wish to disturb it.'

Marc Simenon thinks that if it had not been for Teresa his father
would have killed himself after the suicide of Marie-Jo. He would
have ended as so many of his characters ended, sharing the fate of
Bernard Foy, of old Krull, of Emmanuel Vernes, Charles
Alavoine and Joseph Lambert. Having failed to win the recognition which he knew his achievement deserved he would have
finished his life as a man in a *faits divers*. In outliving Marie-Jo,
Simenon repeated the experience of Henriette, who outlived his
brother Christian, of his grandfather Chrétien, who outlived
Désiré, and of his great-grandfather '*Vieux-Papa*', who outlived
his daughter Marie Catherine. It was the family curse which came
to him, balanced by the genius he had inherited from the Flemish
Brülls, the tormented race. But Simenon had his hatred of Denyse
as well as the tenderness of Teresa to keep him going. The writing
of fiction had always been a torment for him, and he was liberated
from it, he was free of his *fantômes* and his terrible jealousy and
from the physically exhausting act of creation. In these circumstances he achieved a certain serenity towards the end of his life.
Marc remembers that his father remained curious to the end,
about everything. He read many biographies and he followed a
growing interest in the paranormal. He believed that mankind
had lost more than just a sixth sense, he took a close interest in
hypnotism and premonitions, and he was convinced that the
future lay with the insects, which possessed powers undreamed of
even by God.

Simenon didn't have to follow in the footsteps of his suicidal
personnages because he was rid of them. Instead he could recall
Désiré's words and look for pleasure in '*les petites joies*'. He
underwent a brain operation in 1984, from which he made a good
recovery. The last twelve months of his life were spent in a
wheelchair, but he even put up with that despite his earlier talk of
euthanasia. Eventually he died at 4.15 in the morning of 4
September 1989, following a fall from his bed, perhaps making a
final attempt to sleepwalk, and his last words, spoken to Teresa,
were 'I think at last I will be able to sleep.'

Simenon once wrote a novel, *La mort d'Auguste*, about a family quarrel over a will. After his death his own will revealed that he had left his estate to be divided equally between his widow, Denyse, and his three surviving children, Marc, John and Pierre. He left the house in the avenue des Figuiers and a substantial sum of money to Teresa. None of the other beneficiaries chose to challenge this provision. According to Denyse the only complication was that Simenon had stipulated that the widow's portion of the estate should not be drawn from his royalties but from his four properties in Lausanne and from his collection of pictures by Vlaminck, Buffet, Cocteau, Picasso and Matisse. The sheer size of the literary estate (10 per cent of 500 million world sales is quite a lot of money) made this provision virtually impossible to carry out.

His family do not think that Simenon was happy at the end of his life, despite his serenity. Denyse does not believe that he could ever have been happy with Teresa. Tigy said that she could not imagine him being happy, withdrawn and enclosed as he was in Switzerland. Boule says that the real Simenon was the one only she can now remember, as a young man, '*bouillonnant*', seething with energy, and that he changed and was never really happy after he went to America. Even his son John, his father's fiercest champion, says that he does not believe his father was happy at the end of his life. 'He died unhappy,' he says. John has also asked himself whether his father was a good man or a bad one, and decided that he was a good man because he brought more to life than he took from it. 'Did he make people richer or poorer? He made people richer. He made two people poorer, and for one of them that was unfortunate.'

The last book Simenon wrote was the 1047-page *Mémoires intimes*, which he completed eight years before his death. After that he had little to do but sit all day in the same room, in the house situated in a cul-de-sac, surrounded by three tower blocks and overlooked by a supermarket car-park and an oriental carpet warehouse. He frequently walked in the gardens of the nearby crematorium where he himself had chosen to be incinerated. When he returned home he could listen to the desolate music of the avenue des Figuiers, the music of the modern city that plays night and day above the wind and the birdsong, the ceaseless noise of passing traffic. He lived there for fifteen years, the longest period he spent in any single house throughout his life. Had he wanted to comment on the way in which he played the hand fate dealt him he might have used a phrase from his first novel, *La maison du canal*, spoken by Jef after he has killed the person he loved best: 'What would you have done?'

APPENDIX

A Flemish skeleton in the Walloon family cupboard

The Brüll family's connection with violent crime (outlined in Chapter Fourteen) may have continued into a subsequent generation. The original band of 'Verts-Boucs' were led by Niclaes Peters, who was executed with Gabriel Brüll (Georges Simenon's direct ancestor six generations back) in 1743. But the 'Verts-Boucs' were revived under the leadership of a retired Austrian army surgeon named Joseph Kirchoff between 1762 and 1772, and Kirchoff, until his own exeution in 1772, was based in Herzogenrath in a house subsequently inherited by Simenon's great-grandfather, Johannes Josephus Brüll.

Rutten has established that in 1822, eighty years after the public execution of Gabriel, by which time any family connections with brigandage had been severed but not forgotten, Gabriel Brüll's great-grandson, Johannes Josephus, left Ubach-over-Worms and the house he had acquired from the 'Verts-Boucs' clan, and left Holland, to start a new life across the border in Germany. When Johannes Josephus Brüll left Ubach he was described as a 'baker'. By the time his son Wilhelm was born at Herzogenrath in Prussia, Johannes Josephus had become a 'butcher'. And when Johannes Josephus eventually died in Herzogenrath his sons identified him as 'a Catholic who had been born in Ubach of unknown parents'. This was how the Brülls cut their links with the skeleton in the family cupboard. Johannes Josephus's son Wilhelm, born in Prussia of a father born in Holland, left Prussia in his turn and married a Dutch girl, an heiress in the rural hierarchy. His bride was called Maria Loijens, the daughter of a wealthy farmer, who lived in the Dutch Limburg district of Maastricht. But Wilhelm Brüll did not settle in his bride's territory either. Instead the young German-Dutch couple moved to a third country, the Belgian Limbourg. Wilhelm and Maria Brüll had thirteen children, and the youngest, Henriette, was Georges Simenon's mother.

In the French edition of his book Rutten denied that he was concerned to emphasise Simenon's 'Germanic' – that is, Dutch or Prussian – origins, but it is a theme which surfaces in every chapter of his work. Going back six generations from Henriette, two Brülls were born in Prussia, one of Dutch parents and one of Dutch-German parents, and four were born in the Dutch Limburg. Two of the six married German girls, the other four Dutch Limburg girls. The last German blood came into the Brüll family with the marriage of Henricus Brüll (Simenon's great-great-grandfather) to Maria Catharina Hansen in 1799. Since the Simenons had settled in the Belgian Limbourg in the seventeenth century they had married into Flemish families of Riemst or Vlijtingen. The Simenons were indeed, as their name suggested, of Walloon descent, but it was a Walloon identify heavily diluted by Flemish blood.

Bibliography

Notes on sources

In addition to the works listed in the bibliography my principal written sources have been the papers collected at the Centre d'Etudes Georges Simenon at the University of Liège. These include the collection of letters written between 1932 and 1980 to thirty-eight correspondents, among them Gide, Cocteau, Vlaminck, Colette, Mauriac, Pagnol, Jean Renoir, Sacha Guitry, Fellini, T.S. Eliot, Thornton Wilder, Somerset Maugham and Henry Miller. The Centre d'Etudes also holds an extensive collection of Simenon's manuscripts and typescripts and other material used in his writing such as his *'enveloppes jaunes'*, working calendars, files of proper names, and the other research material – maps, railway timetables and medical reports – he gathered before starting work on a novel. The Centre d'Etudes also holds the original editions or typescripts of works such as *Pedigree* and *Mémoires intimes* which were subsequently abridged by order of the Belgian or French courts. It also holds a collection of thousands of newspaper articles and reviews of Simenon's work from all over the world and an extensive picture archive.

I have been able to read a collection of Simenon's letters to his mother, Henriette Brüll, written between 1958 and her death in 1970, and not previously available for study. Marc Simenon allowed me to consult a collection of his mother's letters, diaries and other records and personal papers which after the death of Régine Renchon were stored in a trunk in the attic. Much of this material related to the war years and the subsequent period spent in the United States. Marc Simenon also gave me extracts from his mother and father's previously unpublished correspondence which covers the period between their marriage and Georges Simenon's arrival in Paris in 1922.

This is the first English–language biography of Simenon which has drawn on the work of the late Mathieu Rutten, *Simenon: ses origines, sa vie, son oeuvre*, which was originally published in Flemish in 1977 and subsequently translated into French. This is a remarkable book, despite its eccentric organisation, the product of a lifetime's obsession by a Flemish professor of philology. It reconstructs Simenon's family tree for ten generations on both his mother's and his father's side and is based on a detailed examination of communal records in Germany, Holland and Belgium over the last 450 years. I have also been able to consult, again for the first time by an English biographer, two other works by Belgian writers, Michel Lemoine's *Liège dans l'oeuvre de Simenon* and Jean-Christophe Camus's *Simenon avant Simenon: 1919–22*, which is based on research in the archives of the *Gazette de Liège* and on an interesting correspondence with Simenon himself. The learned controversy on the origins of Maigret, referred to in Chapter Seven, was published in *Traces* No. 1 by the Centre d'Etudes Georges Simenon.

For the period of the war-time occupation and subsequent *épuration* the series of *Les Lettres Françaises*, *L'Ecran Français* and *Ce Soir* published between September 1942 and January 1945 and held at the Bibliothèque Nationale in Paris were consulted.

SELECTED WORKS OF GEORGES SIMENON

The Maigret series (76 titles)

published 1931
M. Gallet, décédé (*The Death of Monsieur Gallet*)
Le pendu de St Pholien (*Maigret and the Hundred Gibbets*)
Le charretier de 'La Providence' (*The Crime at Lock 14*)
Le chien jaune (*A Face for a Clue*)
Pietr-le-Letton (*The Case of Peter the Lett*)
La nuit du carrefour (*The Crossroad Murders*)
Un crime en Hollande (*A Crime in Holland*)
Au rendez-vous des Terre-Neuvas (*The Sailors' Rendez-vous*)
La tête d'un homme (*A Battle of Nerves*)
La danseuse du Gai-Moulin (*At the Gai-Moulin*)
La guinguette à deux sous (*The Guinguette by the Seine*)
1932
L'ombre chinoise (*The Shadow in the Courtyard*)

L'affaire Saint-Fiacre (The Saint-Fiacre Affair)
Chez les Flamands (The Flemish Shop)
Le fou de Bergerac (The Madman of Bergerac)
Le port des brumes (Death of a Harbour Master)
'Liberty Bar' (Liberty Bar)
1933
L'écluse no. 1 (The Lock at Charenton)
1934
Maigret (Maigret Returns)
1942
Cécile est morte (Maigret and the Spinster)
Les caves du Majestic (Maigret and the Hotel Majestic)
La maison du juge (Maigret in Exile)
1944
Signé Picpus (To Any Lengths)
L'inspecteur cadavre (Maigret's Rival)
Félicie est là (Maigret and the Toy Village)
Maigret se fâche (Maigret in Retirement)
1947
Maigret à New-York (Inspector Maigret in New York's Underworld)
1948
Maigret et son mort (Maigret's Special Murder)
Les vacances de Maigret (A Summer Holiday)
1949
La première enquête de Maigret (Maigret's First Case)
Mon ami Maigret (My Friend Maigret)
Maigret chez le coroner (Maigret and the Coroner)
1950
Maigret et la vieille dame (Maigret and the Old Lady)
L'amie de Mme Maigret (Madame Maigret's Own Case)
1951
Les mémoires de Maigret (Maigret's Memoirs)
Un noël de Maigret (Maigret's Christmas)
Maigret au 'Picratt's' (Maigret in Montmartre)
Maigret en meublé (Maigret Takes a Room)
Maigret et la grande perche (Maigret and the Burglar's Wife)
1952
Maigret, Lognon et les gangsters (Maigret and the Gangsters)
Le revolver de Maigret (Maigret's Revolver)
1953
Maigret et l'homme du banc (Maigret and the Man on the Boulevard)

Maigret a peur (*Maigret Afraid*)
Maigret se trompe (*Maigret's Mistake*)
1954
Maigret à l'école (*Maigret Goes to School*)
Maigret et la jeune morte (*Maigret and the Young Girl*)
1955
Maigret chez le ministre (*Maigret and the Minister*)
Maigret et le corps sans tête (*Maigret and the Headless Corpse*)
Maigret tend un piège (*Maigret Sets a Trap*)
1956
Un échec de Maigret (*Maigret's Failure*)
1957
Maigret s'amuse (*Maigret's Little Joke*)
Maigret voyage (*Maigret and the Millionaires*)
1958
Les scrupules de Maigret (*Maigret Has Scruples*)
1959
Maigret et les témoins récalcitrants (*Maigret and the Reluctant Witnesses*)
Une confidence de Maigret (*Maigret Has Doubts*)
1960
Maigret aux Assises (*Maigret in Court*)
Maigret et les vieillards (*Maigret in Society*)
1961
Maigret et le voleur paresseux (*Maigret and the Lazy Burglar*)
1962
Maigret et les braves gens (*Maigret and the Black Sheep*)
Maigret et le client du Samedi (*Maigret and the Saturday Caller*)
1963
Maigret et le clochard (*Maigret and the Dosser*)
La colère de Maigret (*Maigret Loses his Temper*)
1964
Maigret et le fantôme (*Maigret and the Ghost*)
Maigret se défend (*Maigret on the Defensive*)
1965
La patience de Maigret (*The Patience of Maigret*)
1966
Maigret et l'affaire Nahour (*Maigret and the Nahour Case*)
1967
Le voleur de Maigret (*Maigret's Pickpocket*)
1968
Maigret à Vichy (*Maigret Takes the Waters*)

Maigret hésite (*Maigret Hesitates*)
L'ami d'enfance de Maigret (*Maigret's Boyhood Friend*)
1969
Maigret et le tueur (*Maigret and the Killer*)
1970
Maigret et le marchand de vin (*Maigret and the Wine Merchant*)
La folle de Maigret (*Maigret and the Madwoman*)
1971
Maigret et l'homme tout seul (*Maigret and the Loner*)
Maigret et l'indicateur (*Maigret and the Flea*)
1972
Maigret et M. Charles (*Maigret and Monsieur Charles*)

The novels (117 titles)

published 1931
Le relais d'Alsace (*The Man from Everywhere*)
1932
Le passager du 'Polarlys' (*The Mystery of the 'Polarlys'*)
1933
Les fiançailles de M. Hire (*Mr Hire's Engagement*)
Le coup de lune (*Tropic Moon*)
La maison du canal (*The House by the Canal*)
L'Ane-Rouge (*The Night Club*)
Les gens d'en face (*The Window over the Way*)
Le haut mal (*The Woman of the Grey House*)
L'homme de Londres (*Newhaven–Dieppe*)
1934
Le locataire (*The Lodger*)
Les suicidés (*One Way Out*)
1935
Les Pitard (*A Wife at Sea*)
Les clients d'Avrenos
Quartier nègre
1936
L'évadé (*The Disintegration of J.P.G.*)
Long cours (*The Long Exile*)
Les demoiselles de Concarneau (*The Breton Sisters*)
45° à l'ombre (*Aboard the Aquitaine*)
1937
Le testament Donadieu (*The Shadow Falls*)

L'assassin (*The Murderer*)
Le blanc à lunettes (*Talatala*)
Faubourg (*Home Town*)
1938
Ceux de la soif
Chemin sans issue (*Blind Path*)
Les rescapés du Télémaque (*The Survivors*)
Les trois crimes de mes amis
Le suspect (*The Green Thermos*)
Les soeurs Lacroix (*Poisoned Relations*)
Touriste de bananes (*Banana Tourist*)
M. La Souris (*Monsieur La Souris*)
La Marie du Port (*Chit of a Girl*)
L'homme qui regardait passer les trains (*The Man Who Watched the Trains Go
    By*)
Le cheval blanc (*The White Horse Inn*)
1939
Le coup de vague
Chez Krull (*Chez Krull*)
Le bourgmestre de Furnes (*The Burgomaster of Furnes*)
1940
Malempin (*The Family Lie*)
Les inconnus dans la maison (*The Strangers in the House*)
1941
Cour d'assises (*Justice*)
Bergelon (*The Country Doctor*)
L'outlaw (*The Outlaw*)
Il pleut, bergère . . . (*Black Rain*)
Le voyageur de la Toussaint (*Strange Inheritance*)
La maison de sept jeunes filles
1942
Oncle Charles s'est enfermé
La veuve Couderc (*Ticket of Leave*)
Le fils Cardinaud (*Young Cardinaud*)
La vérité sur Bébé Donge (*The Trial of Bébé Donge*)
1944
Le rapport du gendarme (*The Gendarme's Report*)
1945
La fuite de M. Monde (*Monsieur Monde Vanishes*)
La fenêtre des Rouet (*Across the Street*)
L'aîné des Ferchaux (*The First-born*)

1946
Les noces de Poitiers (*The Couple from Poitiers*)
Le cercle de Mahé
1947
Trois chambres à Manhattan (*Three Beds in Manhattan*)
Au bout du rouleau
Lettre à mon juge (*Act of Passion*)
Le destin des Malou (*The Fate of the Malous*)
Le clan des Ostendais (*The Ostenders*)
Le passager clandestin (*The Stowaway*)
1948
Le bilan Malétras (*The Reckoning*)
La jument perdue
La neige était sale (*The Stain on the Snow*)
Pedigree (*Pedigree*)
1949
Le fond de la bouteille (*The Bottom of the Bottle*)
Les fantômes du chapelier (*The Hatter's Ghosts*)
Les quatre jours du pauvre homme (*Four Days in a Lifetime*)
1950
Un nouveau dans la ville
L'enterrement de M. Bouvet (*The Burial of Monsieur Bouvet*)
Les volets verts (*The Heart of a Man*)
1951
Tante Jeanne (*Aunt Jeanne*)
Le temps d'Anaïs (*The Girl in his Past*)
Une vie comme neuve (*A New Lease of Life*)
1952
Marie qui louche (*The Girl with a Squint*)
La mort de Belle (*Belle*)
Les frères Rico (*The Brothers Rico*)
1953
Antoine et Julie (*The Magician*)
L'escalier de fer (*The Iron Staircase*)
Feux rouges (*Red Lights*)
1954
Crime impuni (*The Fugitive*)
L'horloger d'Everton (*The Watchmaker of Everton*)
Le grand Bob (*Big Bob*)
1955
Les témoins (*The Witnesses*)

La boule noire
1956
Les complices (The Accomplices)
En cas de malheur (In Case of Emergency)
Le petit homme d'Arkhangelsk (The Little Man from Archangel)
1957
Le fils (The Son)
Le nègre (The Negro)
1958
Strip-tease (Striptease)
Le président (The Premier)
Le passage de la ligne
Dimanche (Sunday)
1959
La vieille (The Grandmother)
Le veuf (The Widower)
1960
L'ours en peluche (Teddy Bear)
1961
Betty (Betty)
Le train (The Train)
1962
La porte (The Door)
Les autres (The Others)
1963
Les anneaux de Bicêtre (The Patient)
1964
La chambre bleue (The Blue Room)
L'homme au petit chien (The Man with the Little Dog)
1965
Le petit saint (The Little Saint)
Le train de Venise (The Venice Train)
1966
Le confessionnal (The Confessional)
La mort d'Auguste (The Old Man Dies)
1967
Le chat (The Cat)
Le déménagement (The Neighbours)
1968
La prison (The Prison)

La main (*The Man on the Bench in the Barn*)
1969
Il y a encore des noisetiers
Novembre (*November*)
1970
Le riche homme (*The Rich Man*)
1971
La disparition d'Odile (*The Disappearance of Odile*)
La cage de verre (*The Glass Cage*)
1972
Les innocents (*The Innocents*)

Autobiographical writings

Je me souviens (1945)
Quand j'étais vieux (*When I Was Old*; 1970)
Lettre à ma mère (*Letter to My Mother*; 1974)
Dictées:
Un homme comme un autre (1975)
Des traces de pas (1975)
Les petits hommes (1976)
Vent du nord, vent du sud (1976)
Un banc au soleil (1977)
De la cave au grenier (1977)
A l'abri de notre arbre (1977)
Tant que je suis vivant (1978)
Vacances obligatoires (1978)
La main dans la main (1978)
Au-delà de ma porte-fenêtre (1978)
Je suis resté un enfant de choeur (1979)
A quoi bon jurer? (1979)
Point-virgule (1979)
Le prix d'un homme (1980)
On dit que j'ai soixante-quinze ans (1980)
Quand vient le froid (1980)
Les libertés qu'il nous reste (1980)
La femme endormie (1981)
Jour et nuit (1981)
Destinées (1981)
Mémoires intimes (*Intimate Memoirs*; 1981)

Additional fiction and non-fiction sources

Juvenilia
Au Pont des Arches (1921)
Jehan Pinaguet (unpublished; 1921)
Les ridicules (unpublished; 1921)

by Georges Sim or Christian Brulls
La maison de l'inquiétude (1930)
Train de nuit (1930)
La femme rousse (1933)

Short stories
'Les 13 mystères' (1932)
'La chanteuse de Pigalle' (1952)
'L'invalide à la tête de bois' (1952)
'Le gros lot' (1953)

Various
Mes apprentissages (collected journalism 1931–58,
    ed. F. Lacassin and G. Sigaux)
    Vol 1: *A la découverte de la France*
    Vol 2: *A la recherche de l'homme nu*
    Vol 3: *A la rencontre des autres*
Compte-Rendu de Mission, La Rochelle (unpublished official
    report, 1940)
Address to the Académie Royale, Brussels (1952)
Les demis de Maigret (unpublished lecture, 1953)
Eloge de la luxure (unused radio broadcast, 1956)
Honoré de Balzac; portrait by Georges Simenon (text of radio
    broadcast of 1960)
La naissance de Maigret (essay 1966)
'*Dear Hamish*' (unpublished tribute for fiftieth anniversary of
    Hamish Hamilton's publishing house, 1978)
'Les cinq sens' (unpublished essay, 1980)

Selected secondary sources

Adam International Review (ed. Miron Grindea) No. 34 (Autumn 1969)
Amouroux, Henri *Les règlements de comptes* (Paris 1944–5)
Assouline, Pierre *Gaston Gallimard* (Paris 1984)
——*Simenon – Biographie* (Paris 1992)
Bertrand, Alain *Georges Simenon* (Lyon 1988)
Bourdrel, Philippe *L'épuration sauvage 1944–45*, 2 vols (Paris 1988, 1991)
Boutry, M.P. *Les 300 vies de Simenon* (Paris 1990)

Brassaï *The Secret Paris* (London 1976)

Bresler, Fenton *The Mystery of Georges Simenon* (London 1983)

'Cahiers du Nord', nos. 2–3 (Paris 1939)

'Cahiers Simenon' *Les amis de Georges Simenon*, no. 4 (Brussels 1990)

Camus, J.-C. *Simenon avant Simenon 1919–22* (Brussels 1989)

— *Simenon avant Simenon 1923–31* (Brussels 1990)

Chastenet, P. et Ph. *Simenon: Album de famille* (Paris 1989)

Cobb, Richard *French and Germans, Germans and French* (USA 1983)

— *People and Places* (Oxford 1985)

Cocteau, Jean *Journals* (Paris 1956)

Crespelle, J.P. *La vie quotidienne à Montparnasse à la grande époque 1905–30* (Paris 1976)

Debray-Ritzen, P. *Georges Simenon* (Lausanne 1989)

Dessane, Odile *Le phallus d'or* (Paris 1981) [see Simenon, Denyse]

Elsdorf, M. *Petits métiers et cris des rues* (Liège 1989)

Eskin, Stanley *Simenon: A Critical Biography* (USA 1987)

Fabre, Jean *Enquête sur un enquêteur* (Montpelier 1981)

Fallois, Bernard de *Simenon* (Lausanne 1971)

Gaillandre, A. *Aspects du titre chez Simenon* (unpublished MA thesis, Dept of Linguistics, Montreal University 1987)

Gauteur, Claude *Simenon au cinéma* (Brussels 1984)

Gill, Brendan 'Out of the Dark', *The New Yorker* (26 January 1953)

—— *A New York Life* (USA 1990)

Highsmith, Patricia 'Filatures', *Libération* (Paris, 3 March 1988)

Jacob, Max *Lettres à Jean Cocteau 1919–44* (Paris 1949)

Jadoux, Henri *Sacha Guitry: Le théâtre et l'amour* (Paris 1985)

Junger, Ernst *Journal Parisien* (Paris 1980)

Kaspi, A. et Mares, A. *Le Paris des étrangers* (Paris 1989)

Lacassin, F. *Conversations avec Simenon* (Geneva 1990)

Lacassin et Sigaux, eds. *Simenon* (Paris 1973)

Lemoine, Michel *Index des personnages de Georges Simenon* (Brussels 1985)

— *Liège dans l'oeuvre de Simenon* (Liège 1989)

Lottman, Herbert *Colette* (Paris 1990)

MacShane, Frank *The Life of Raymond Chandler* (London 1976)

Mauriac, Claude *L'alittérature contemporaine* (Paris 1958)

Narcejac, T. *Le cas Simenon* (Paris 1950)

Novick, Peter *L'épuration française 1944–49* (Paris 1985)

Ory, Pascal *Les collaborateurs 1940–45* (Paris 1976)

Piron, Maurice *L'univers de Simenon* (Paris 1983)

Pivot, Bernard 'Carnets', *Lire* (October 1989)

Ragache, G. et J.-P. *La vie quotidienne des écrivains et des artistes sous l'occupation 1940–44* (Paris 1988)

Raymond, John *Simenon in Court* (London 1968)
Rioux, J.-P., ed. *La vie culturelle sous Vichy* (Paris 1990)
Rutten, Mathieu *Simenon: ses origines, sa vie, son oeuvre* (Bruges 1977)
Sauvage, Marcel *Les mémoires de Josephine Baker* (Paris 1949)
Siclier, Jacques *La France de Pétain et son cinéma* (Paris 1981)
Simenon, Denyse *Un oiseau pour le chat* (Paris 1978)
— *Le phallus d'or* [see Dessane, Odile]
'Simenon sur le gril', interview with five doctors published in *Médecine et Hygiène*, Geneva (5 June 1968)
Stephane, Roger *Portrait souvenir de Georges Simenon* (Paris 1989)
Symons, Julian *Bloody Murder* (London 1972)
Tillinac, Denis *Le mystère Simenon* (Paris 1980)
'Traces', *Travaux du Centre d'Etudes Georges Simenon*, nos 1, 2 (Liège 1989, 1990)
Vilar, J.-F. 'Le cadavre sans tête d'une ombre rouge', *J'Accuse* (July 1990)
Williams, R., ed. *G. Simenon: A Bibliography* (Dragonby Press 1988)
Young, T. *G. Simenon: A Checklist* (USA 1976)

Index